LIBRARY OF SECOND TEMPLE STUDIES

65

Formerly the Journal for the Study of the Pseudepigrapha Supplement Series

Editor
Lester L. Grabbe

A TIME OF CHANGE

Judah and its Neighbours in the Persian and Early Hellenistic
Periods

EDITED BY YIGAL LEVIN

t&t clark

Yigal Levin has asserted his right under the Copyright, Designs and Patents Act, 1988, to be identified as Author of this work.

Published by T&T Clark
The Tower Building, 11 York Road, London SE1 7NX
80 Maiden Lane, Suite 704, New York, NY 10038

www.tandtclark.com

British Library Cataloguing-in-Publication Data
A catalogue record for this book is available from the British Library

ISBN-10: 0567045528 (hardback)
ISBN-13: 9780567045522 (hardback)

Typeset by Data Standards Ltd, Frome, Somerset, UK.
Printed on acid-free paper in Great Britain by Cromwell Press Ltd, Trowbridge, Wiltshire.

TABLE OF CONTENTS

LIST OF FIGURES

FOREWORD

The seeds of this book were planted in January of 2005, when I attended a conference on 'New Discoveries in the Study of *Yehud* Seals', held at Tel Aviv University. At that conference, I happened to meet my former teacher Amos Kloner, long-time director of the excavations at Mareshah. During our conversation, Professor Kloner mentioned that two of his doctoral students who had submitted papers to the Fourteenth World Congress of Jewish Studies which was to be held the following summer in Jerusalem had been turned down, because the Congress had not planned to hold an open section dealing with the Persian period. However, he continued, if someone was to organize such a section, the Congress secretariat would be willing to consider accepting it. Professor Kloner himself, however, would be attending a Josephus seminar in New Zealand . . .

Several weeks, many emails and even more personal conversations later, we had a first-rate section – nine papers in two sessions, one in English and one in Hebrew. The title given to the section was 'Changes in Settlement and Culture in the Persian Period', the sessions were very well attended and the papers sparked off some excellent discussions.

It was Hanan Eshel who, at some point during the organizing process, suggested that we use the papers as the basis for a future volume. An initial survey of the participants showed that most were willing to submit papers for review, and so this volume was conceived. Professor Eshel also made initial contact with Lester L. Grabbe, editor of T&T Clark's Second Temple Studies series, for which I am grateful.

In its final form, this volume is far removed from being a collection of conference proceedings. For various reasons, a few of the papers that were given at the original conference were not included in this volume. On the other hand, several additional papers were submitted and found to be appropriate, greatly enhancing the book. As the chronological scope of some of the papers extended into the years following the conquests of Alexander, the title was changed accordingly.

As this project nears its completion, I wish to thank all of those who made it possible. First of all, the presenters at the World Congress, the session chairs and the Congress secretariat. Next, all of those whose papers are included in this volume, for their patience and their willingness to revise their articles again and again, until all were satisfied. To

Professor Grabbe for his encouragement and help, and to all those at T&T Clark and Continuum International Publishing, for their help with the technical aspects of bringing the book to print. To the Vice President for Academic Affairs and the Research Authority of the College of Judea and Sartania at Ariel for their support. To all those who helped me through this project in so many ways. And, of course, to my wife Sharon and our children, who have suffered through these many months of my late nights and endless days at the computer.

Yigal Levin

LIST OF BIBLIOGRAPHICAL ABBREVIATIONS

AASOR	Annual of the American Schools of Oriental Research
AB	Anchor Bible
ADAJ	*Annual of the Department of Antiquities of Jordan*
AJA	*American Journal of Archaeology*
AOAT	Alter Orient und Altes Testament
BA	*Biblical Archaeologist*
BAIAS	*Bulletin of the Anglo-Israel Archaeological Society*
BARev	*Biblical Archaeology Review*
BASOR	*Bulletin of the American Schools of Oriental Research*
BEATAJ	Beiträge zur Erforschung des Alten Testaments und des antiken Judentums
BWANT	Beiträge zur Wissenschaft vom Alten und Neuen Testament
BZAW	Beihefte zur *ZAW*
CBQ	*Catholic Biblical Quarterly*
DJD	Discoveries in the Judaean Desert
ESI	*Excavations and Surveys in Israel*
FAT·	Forschungen zum Alten Testament
FRLANT	Forschungen zur Religion und Literatur des Alten und Neuen Testaments
HKAT	Handkommentar zum Alten Testament
HTR	*Harvard Theological Review*
ICC	International Critical Commentary
IEJ	*Israel Exploration Journal*
INJ	*Israel Numismatic Journal*
JANES	*Journal of the Ancient Near Eastern Society*
JAOS	*Journal of the American Oriental Society*
JBL	*Journal of Biblical Literature*
JNES	*Journal of Near Eastern Studies*
JNSL	*Journal of Northwest Semitic Languages*
JSOT	*Journal for the Study of the Old Testament*
JSOTSup	*Journal for the Study of the Old Testament*, Supplement Series
JTS	*Journal of Theological Studies*
KAI H.	Donner and W. Röllig, *Kanaanäische und aramäische Inschriften* (3 vols; Wiesbaden: Harrassowitz, 2nd ed. 1966–69)
LCL	Loeb Classical Library
NCB ᴸ	New Century Bible

NEA	*Near Eastern Archaeology*
NEAEHL	E. Stern (ed.), *The New Encyclopedia of Archaeological Excavations in the Holy Land* (4 vols; Jerusalem: Israel Exploration Society & Carta, 1993)
OBO	Orbis biblicus et orientalis
OrAnt	*Oriens antiquus*
OTL	Old Testament Library
PEFQS	*Palestine Exploration Fund, Quarterly Statement*
PEQ	*Palestine Exploration Quarterly*
QDAP	*Quarterly of the Department of Antiquities in Palestine*
RB	*Revue biblique*
SBLSBS	SBL Sources for Biblical Study
SBS	Stuttgarter Bibelstudien
UF	*Ugarit-Forschungen*
VT	*Vetus Testamentum*
VTSup	*Vetus Testamentum*, Supplements
WBC	Word Biblical Commentary
ZDPV	*Zeitschrift des deutschen Palästina-Vereins*

LIST OF CONTRIBUTORS

Einat Ambar-Armon
    Martin (Szusz) Department of Land of Israel Studies and
    Archaeology, Bar-Ilan University
Rona S. Avissar
    Martin (Szusz) Department of Land of Israel Studies and
    Archaeology, Bar-Ilan University; The Tell eṣ-Ṣâfi/Gath
    Archaeological Project
Diana Edelman
    Department of Biblical Studies, Sheffield University
Esther Eshel
    Department of Bible, Bar-Ilan University
Hanan Eshel
    Martin (Szusz) Department of Land of Israel Studies and
    Archaeology, Bar-Ilan University
Avraham Faust
    Martin (Szusz) Department of Land of Israel Studies and
    Archaeology, Bar-Ilan University
Lisbeth S. Fried
    Frankel Center for Judaic Studies and the Department of Near
    Eastern Studies, University of Michigan
Amos Kloner
    Martin (Szusz) Department of Land of Israel Studies and
    Archaeology, Bar-Ilan University
Yigal Levin
    The College of Judea and Samaria, Ariel; The Department of Jewish
    History and the Martin (Szusz) Department of Land of Israel
    Studies and Archaeology, Bar-Ilan University
Aren M. Maeir
    Martin (Szusz) Department of Land of Israel Studies and
    Archaeology, Bar-Ilan University; The Tell eṣ-Ṣâfi/Gath
    Archaeological Project
Bezalel Porten
    Department of Jewish History, The Hebrew University in Jerusalem
Ian Stern
    Archaeological Seminars, Jerusalem

Joe Uziel
> Martin (Szusz) Department of Land of Israel Studies and
> Archaeology, Bar-Ilan University; The Tell eṣ-Ṣâfi/Gath
> Archaeological Project

Ada Yardeni
> The Hebrew University in Jerusalem

INTRODUCTION

Yigal Levin

One of the most common clichés in the study of the history and archaeology of the Holy Land over recent decades is that the Persian period, long-time 'Cinderella of biblical studies', has finally 'come of age'. To quote Kent H. Richards, '[the Persian period] has gone from being described as the dark ages to being acclaimed as *the* most generative time for the formation of the library of books that we call the Hebrew Bible'.[1] Renewed scholarly interest in the period seems to have begun in the late 1960s, with the publication of several monographs by scholars such as Peter R. Ackroyd and Morton Smith.[2] At about the same time Ephraim Stern published his definitive study of the archaeology of the Persian period, giving later scholars an archaeological base with which to work.[3] Following these studies, scholars such as Sarah Japhet and H. G. M. Williamson revolutionized our understanding of the biblical books of the post-exilic period.[4] Since the 1980s a plethora of new studies on the

---

1.   K. H. Richards, 'Introduction: The Persian Period: Coming of Age', in T. C. Eskenazi and K. H. Richards (eds), *Second Temple Studies 2. Temple Community in the Persian Period* (Sheffield: Sheffield Academic Press, 1994), p. 13.

2.   To name a few: P. R. Ackroyd, *Exile and Restoration: A Study of Hebrew Thought of the Sixth Century B.C.* (OTL; London: SCM Press, 1968); idem, *Israel Under Babylon and Persia* (London: Oxford University Press, 1970); idem, *I & II Chronicles, Ezra, Nehemiah* (Torch Bible Commentaries; London: SCM. Press, 1973); idem, *The Chronicler in his Age* (JSOTSup 101; Sheffield: JSOT Press, 1991); M. Smith, *Palestinian Parties and Politics that Shaped the Old Testament* (New York: Columbia University Press, 1971).

3.   Originally presented in 1969 as a doctoral dissertation, then published in Hebrew in 1973 and later updated and published in English as E. Stern, *Material Culture of the Land of the Bible in the Persian Period, 538–332 B.C.* (Warminster: Aris & Phillips, 1982).

4.   S. Japhet, *I & II Chronicles: A Commentary* (OTL; Louisville: Westminster/John Knox Press, 1993); idem, *The Ideology of the Book of Chronicles and its Place in Biblical Thought* (2nd revised edition, trans. by Anna Barber; BEATAJ 9; Frankfurt am Main : Lang, 1997); H. G. M. Williamson, *Israel in the Books of Chronicles* (Cambridge: Cambridge University Press, 1977); idem, *1 and 2 Chronicles* (New Century Bible; Grand Rapids: Eerdmans, 1982); idem, *Ezra, Nehemiah* (WBC; Waco: Word Books, 1985); idem, *Ezra and Nehemiah* (Old Testament Guides; Sheffield: JSOT Press, 1987); idem, *Studies in Persian Period History and Historiography* (FAT 38;Tübingen: Mohr Siebeck, 2004).

archaeology, history and biblical books of the period, many written by a new generation of scholars, has filled the library shelves. This even includes a journal, *Transeuphratène*, dedicated to the study of the Levant in the Persian period. Just the first half of the present decade has seen Pierre Briant's 1996 *Histoire de l'Empire perse* translated into English,[5] several new major commentaries on Chronicles,[6] and a long list of new monographs and collections of articles on the period.[7]

Reviewing even this partial list, one may easily discern that, as opposed to the situation of just a couple of decades ago, the main problem that now faces the interested scholar, student and lay person is one of *too much information*. So many new archaeological excavations have been reporting discoveries from the Persian period, so many new epigraphic finds have been published, so many new ideas about the existing material and so many theories about the biblical books of the period have been expounded, that the reader finds him- or herself in danger of drowning in the flood of new data.

The purpose of this book is to present the reader with a lifeboat, or at least to extend a paddle. It is *not*, however, a systematic summary of the period.[8] It is, rather, a collection of ten original papers, each of which presents the reader with a new study in one of the areas in which the research of the Holy Land during the Persian period has been rapidly progressing. Each of these papers has been assigned to one of three sections: archaeological, epigraphic and historical studies. This categorization is of course somewhat artificial: one of the qualities of modern research is its drawing from varied scholarly disciplines: 'field archae-

---

5. P. Briant, *From Cyrus to Alexander: A History of the Persian Empire* (trans. P. T. Daniels; Winona Lake: Eisenbrauns, 2002).

6. G. N. Knoppers, *I Chronicles 1–9: A New Translation with Introduction and Commentary* (AB; New York: Doubleday, 2003); idem, *I Chronicles 10–29: A New Translation with Introduction and Commentary* (AB; New York: Doubleday, 2004); K. Hognesius, *The Text of 2 Chronicles 1–16: A Critical Edition with Textual Commentary* (Stockholm: Almqvist & Wiksell, 2003); P. K. Hooker, *First and Second Chronicles* (Westminster Bible Companion; Louisville: Westminster John Knox Press, 2001); S. L. McKenzie, *1–2 Chronicles* (Abingdon Old Testament Commentaries; Nashville: Abingdon Press, 2004); R. W. Klein, *1 Chronicles: A Commentary* (Hermeneia; Minneapolis: Fortress Press, 2006).

7. Two of those monographs were written by contributors to this volume: L. S. Fried, *The Priest and the Great King: Temple-Palace Relations in the Persian Empire* (Winona Lake: Eisenbrauns, 2004) and D. Edelman, *The Origins of the 'Second' Temple: Persian Imperial Policy and the Rebuilding of Jerusalem* (London: Equinox, 2005). For one of the recent collections of articles see O. Lipschits and M. Oeming (eds), *Judah and Judeans in the Persian Period* (Winona Lake: Eisenbrauns, 2005).

8. For which see L. L. Grabbe, *A History of the Jews and Judaism in the Second Temple Period: Vol.1. Yehud – A History of the Persian Province of Judah* (London: T&T Clark, 2004); J. W. Betlyon, 'A People Transformed: Palestine in the Persian Period', *NEA* 68 (2005), pp. 4–58.

ology', history, biblical study, linguistics and philology, epigraphy and the social sciences, to name but a few. Most of the studies in this volume make use of a wide variety of methodologies and source material. Reading through the volume will familiarize the reader with many of the issues with which scholars of the period have recently dealt and are dealing with still.

The first of the issues dealt with in this volume is the measure to which Greek culture penetrated the southern Levant during the two centuries prior to Alexander's conquest of the region. The paper authored by Einat Ambar-Armon and Amos Kloner investigates the archaeological evidence of such influence, in the fields of economy (as shown by coins and pottery, both sure signs of trade), technology (adoption of western methods of producing lamps, figurines and oil presses, as well as metallurgic techniques) and religion (finds from temples, *favissae* and tombs). They then go on to discuss the wider issue of cultural influences, especially as evidenced in Greek epigraphic finds, concluding with a view of regional variations and a look into the years after the Macedonian conquest.

The contribution by Hanan Eshel deals with a similar theme, but with an unusual twist: Eshel examines the extent of Greek influence through a study of Greek words in *Semitic* (Aramaic and Hebrew) inscriptions, also emphasizing the difference between different parts of the country.

Eshel's paper is also the first in the book that introduces us to the huge corpus of inscriptions, originating in such southern sites as Mareshah and Khirbet el-Kôm, identified as the town of Makkedah. These ostraca, many of which have been published in recent years and more of which await publication, give us a new look at the southern regions of the country, the area often referred to as 'Idumea'. Bezalel Porten and Ada Yardeni present us with a detailed analysis of the known ostraca from Makkedah, in which there seems to have been a '*maskanta*' or storehouse for agricultural goods. These ostraca offer us a look into the economy and administration of the area during the fourth century BCE: the types of produce stored there, the weights and measures used, the ways in which the transactions were recorded, and of course the names of the people involved. Esther Eshel's contribution is the publication of two ostraca found at Mareshah, which include a list of names and their origin. Eshel sees these ostraca as providing evidence of the Transjordanian origin of at least some of the population of what became known as 'Idumea'.

Ian Stern's study of the 'Makkedah' material takes us into the realm of sociology. Stern analyses the personal names, patronyms and clan names that appear in the ostraca, tracing the development of those clans through several generations and tracking the use of theophoric elements such as *yahu*, *ba'al*, and *qos* as a sign of ethnic self-identity – especially the developing self-identity of the people whom we call 'Idumeans'.

The question of the origin of the Idumeans and the formation of

Idumea as a distinct political unit is also addressed in my own article, mostly through the historical and geographical analysis of more 'traditional' sources, such as the Bible and the classical authors, although the epigraphic evidence is also utilized. My main conclusion is that although the population of the southern regions was mixed, political control of the area and its lucrative trade routes was awarded by Cambyses to his Qedarite Arab allies after they had aided him in his march to Egypt in 525 BCE. The Qedarites continued to control the area until their power was broken by Alexander. Sometime after, when the new regime reorganized the provincial administration, the new 'province' of Idumea was formed, named for the people who had by then become the dominant group.

The theme of ethnicity and distinctiveness is taken inside the Judean province by Lisbeth Fried, who traces the attitude of the biblical sources towards the *gēr* or 'resident alien' from the exilic through the post-exilic period. Fried observes this attitude changing from one of acceptance and openness to one of rejection as the *Yehud* community consolidated its own self-identity. Since such an attitude is not typical of Mesopotamian or Persian culture, Fried seeks its origins in contemporary Athenian citizenship laws – yet another example of pre-conquest Greek influence.

The remaining three archaeological studies give three different approaches to the use of archaeology as a primary source of information about the social and settlement processes that occurred during the Persian period. The paper by Avissar, Uziel and Maeir, the last of whom is the director of the ongoing Tell es-Sâfi/Gath archaeological project, brings together Persian-period material excavated at Tell es-Sâfi over a century ago and now 'rediscovered' in the archives of the Palestine Exploration Fund, a more recent surface survey of the site and an actual Persian-period stratum, albeit small, first identified and excavated as recently as the summer of 2006.

Avraham Faust and Diana Edelman both take the 'larger' view, each in his or her unique way. Faust uses the data collected from both excavations and surveys to show the considerable decline in settlement throughout Judah as a result of the Babylonian conquest and its very gradual revival through the Persian and the Hellenistic periods. The decline at the end of the Iron Age is in fact so sudden and massive, that Persian-period Judean society can only be characterized as a 'post-collapse society'. This, of course, has major repercussions on our understanding of this society, especially in light of recent theories about the historical reality of the biblical accounts of exile and return.

Edelman looks at the relationship between the forts or administrative centres that seem to have been built throughout the province of *Yehud* and the small settlements, or farmsteads, which were founded during the same period. In her opinion, these sites, often built on virgin soil, represent the settling of foreigners, perhaps as a type of royal land-grant system. If she is correct, her conclusions should perhaps be read in conjunction with Fried's paper in order to give a fuller picture of inter-ethnic relationships within the *Yehud* province.

There remain, of course, many issues which have not been treated in this volume and which must await further study. It is my hope that we will be able to address them at some time in the future.

Chapter 1

ARCHAEOLOGICAL EVIDENCE OF LINKS BETWEEN THE AEGEAN
WORLD AND THE LAND OF ISRAEL IN THE PERSIAN PERIOD

Einat Ambar-Armon and Amos Kloner[*]

The Hellenistic period, beginning with Alexander's conquest of the Persian Empire, was the first time in which Western influences made a significant penetration into the East. The ties between the Greek world and the Land of Israel reach their zenith during this period, ties that included various degrees of Hellenization of the East, a concept that reflects the influences between the various regions of the Hellenized world. These influences were evident in many spheres of life, including language, culture, religion, sports and art. Hellenization persisted to varying degrees throughout the Roman, Byzantine and even the Muslim periods. The profound implications of the long years of Hellenistic domination left their imprint on the development of the Land of Israel, the Near East and on Europe as well; nothing seems to have exerted greater influence on Western culture than did classical Greece.

It is conventionally assumed that the intensive relations between Greece and the Land of Israel began in the wake of the Macedonian conquest of 332 BCE. Scholars have attributed major importance to this date.[1] Despite this date's importance, however, the network of relations between the regions had actually emerged many years before the Hellenistic conquest and existed through almost the entire Ancient

* The authors wish to thank the following people for their invaluable help in the preparation of this article: Yigal Levin, Avraham Faust, Adi Erlich and Sherri Whetstone. All mistakes, of course, are ours alone.
    1. Tcherikover posited that the conquest by Alexander the Great set off an extremely rapid process in which Oriental cities turned into Greek *poleis*. See A. Tcherikover, *Jews and Greeks in the Hellenistic Age*, (Tel Aviv: Dvir, 1963), especially p. 71 (Hebrew); M. Stern, too, holds that 'the Macedonian conquest was definitely a decisive turning point in the history of the country and led to the serious Hellenization of Eretz Israel'; M. Stern, 'Judaism and Hellenism in Eretz Israel in the Third and Second Centuries BCE', in Y. Kaplan and M. Stern, (eds), *Assimilation: Continuity and Change among the Nations and Israel* (Jerusalem: Zalman Shazar Center, 1989), p. 42 (Hebrew).

period[2] as well as during the Persian era.[3] Thus the Persian period is crucial for our understanding of the network of relations between the regions. The purpose of this article is to examine the contacts between Greece and its neighbours on the one hand and the Land of Israel on the other.[4] We will focus on the changes in material culture that took place in the Land of Israel as a result of those relations in order to investigate the beginning of Hellenistic influence in the Land of Israel.

Evidence for Ties between Greece and the Land of Israel

The two foci of the relations between the regions in the Persian period were war and economics.[5] War was inevitable in an age replete with power struggles. For centuries various powers attempted to conquer the Land of Israel or to use it as a jumping-off point because of its strategic position. The economies of Phoenicia and Greece, both mountainous lands bordered by the sea, were heavily influenced by the scarcity of agricultural land. These two points were intimately related. The shortage of land and the problems created by the incessant warfare generated repeated waves of migrants, merchants and mercenaries, constantly changing the relations

2.   For example see T. Dothan, 'The Arrival of the Sea Peoples: Cultural Diversity in Early Iron Age Canaan', in S. Gitin and W. G. Dever (eds), *Recent Excavations in Israel: Studies in Iron Age Archaeology* (AASOR 49; Winona Lake: American Schools of Oriental Research and Eisenbrauns, 1989), pp. 1–14.

3.   A number of scholars have addressed various aspects of this topic: D. Auscher, 'Les Relations entre la Grèce et la Palestine avant la Conquète d' Alexandre' *VT* 17 (1967), pp. 8–30; M. Smith, *Palestinian Parties and Politics that Shaped the Old Testament* (London: Columbia University Press, 1971), pp. 351–60; J. Elayi, *Pénétration grecque en Phénicie sous l'empire perse* (Nancy: Sheffield Academic, 1988); M. Colledge, 'Greek and Non-Greek Interaction in the Art and Architecture of the Hellenistic East', in A. Kuhrt and S. Sherwin-White (eds), *Hellenism in the East* (London: University of California, 1987), pp. 134–9; M. Hengel, 'Judaism and Hellenism Revisited', in J. J. Collins and G. E. Sterling (eds), *Hellenism in the Land of Israel* (Notre Dame: University of Notre Dame, 2001), pp. 10–14; S. Hornblower, *The Greek World 479–323 BC* (Oxford: Clarendon Pr., 1991); M. J. W. Leith, *Wadi Daliyeh I: The Wadi Daliyeh Seal Impressions* (DJD 24; Oxford: Clarendon Press, 1997).

4.   Dealing with specific ties between Greece and the Land of Israel is appropriate only toward the end of the Persian period, when a pan-Hellenic identity coalesced. Future research may make it possible to distinguish between different parts of the Aegean world over the course of the Persian period. For the moment such distinctions tend to be extremely general and rarely more focused. We do not intend to present all the material finds but only to distinguish different types of relations, and will consequently use selected examples only. For further details see E. Ambar-Armon, 'The Greek World and the Coastal Plain of Eretz Israel prior to the Macedonian Conquest', *Cathedra* 116 (2005), pp. 5–30 (Hebrew).

5.   This is also true to varying degrees in earlier periods. See for example, W. D. Niemeier, 'Archaic Greeks in the Orient: Textual and Archaeological Evidence', *BASOR* 322 (2001), pp. 11–32.

between the cultures.[6] With this in mind, we wish to ask what bonds evolved beneath the surface, beyond the wars and the economic links.

I. *Economic Influences*

Numismatic and ceramic finds, as well as those of other imported products, are crucial sources of information about the economic ties between the Land of Israel and Greece, especially Attica.

1. *Numismatic Finds*

The Persian period saw an economic revolution in the entire Levant, involving the transition from payment in metal to payment in coins. The source of this revolution was in the West. Coinage seems to have first appeared in Lydia in Asia Minor in the seventh century BCE. The invention made its way to the Greek world, from where it was disseminated throughout the Mediterranean basin and beyond.[7] So while it is true that coinage was invented outside Greece and some even argue that it was based on a more ancient source, related to bullae, which originated in the East,[8] we would contend that not only is the place of an invention's origin important; so is its diffusion. Colin Renfrew has made the distinction between *invention,* the discovery of something new by human beings, and *innovation,* the process of disseminating the novelty and its widespread adoption. That is, the real change occurs when an invention is adopted widely.[9] In this case, the spread of coinage was due to its use by the Greek cities, and had a decisive effect on the economy of the ancient world. The Persian Empire also adopted a monetary system, but coinage spread to the heart of the empire slowly, where it was adopted apparently because of the need to pay Greek mercenaries.[10] The numismatic finds from the Persian period in the Land of Israel include

---

6.   One can learn about this movement from historical sources as well. See for example, E. Ambar-Armon, 'Hellenization of the Northern Coastal Plain of Israel During the Persian Period' (unpublished MA thesis, Bar Ilan University, 2002), pp. 32–42.

7.   C. M. Kraay, *Archaic and Classical Greek Coins* (London: Methuen, 1976), p. 291; C. Howgego, *Ancient History from Coins* (London: Routledge, 1997), pp. 1–2.

8.   See for example, C. Thompson, 'Sealed Silver in Iron Age Cisjordan and the "Invention" of Coinage', *Oxford Journal of Archaeology* 22 (2003), pp. 67–107. We would like to thank Dr Oren Tal who called this point to our attention. However this does not affect the general argument, because the invention soon became widespread throughout Greece.

9.   C. Renfrew, *Approaches to Social Archaeology* (Edinburgh: University Press, 1984), pp. 390–2.

10.   This was also proposed by Dan Barag in his lecture, 'Judaean Coins in the Fourth Century BCE and the Early Hellenistic Age', delivered at a conference entitled 'New Discoveries in the Study of Yehud Seals', Tel Aviv University, January 12, 2005.

dozens of Greek coins[11] but only one Persian coin, reinforcing the idea that Greece had a decisive influence on the ancient economy of the Land of Israel.

The coins found in various excavations in the Land of Israel reflect that network of economic ties whose visible result is the use of Greek coins as early as the second half of the fifth century BCE, not long after they appeared in Greece itself. Archaic coins appeared first, followed by Attic coins.[12] Archaic coins are rarer than Attic coins in excavations in the Land of Israel and to date have been found at only a few sites. But whereas the archaic coins found are original, most of the Attic-standard coins are local imitations of the originals.[13] It is interesting that the four oldest coins unearthed in the Land of Israel (from the sixth century BCE) were discovered in Jerusalem and Nablus.[14]

The systematic use of coinage became commonplace only during the course of the fifth century BCE. Around this time Greek coins also began to appear alongside non-Greek ones. Even though the evidence is limited, it is plausible that the imitations of the Athenian tetradrachma circulated extensively in the Land of Israel,[15] reflecting the economic penetration

11. H. A. Cahn, 'Stagira in Tel Aviv', in A. Houghton, S. Hurter, P. E. Mottahedeh and J. A. Scott (eds), *Studies in Honor of Leo Mildenberg: Numismatics, Art History, Archaeology* (Wetteren: Editions NR, 1984), pp. 43–50.

12. The Attic coin with the highest nominal value is the silver tetradrachma, which weighs about 17 grams. It features the head of the goddess Athena on the obverse side, with her emblematic owl on the reverse. The coin is in the archaic style and bears the inscription AΘE. Coins of lesser value, didrachmas and drachmas, had similar designs. The Attic coinage was extremely important, because it changed only slightly over the course of more than 300 years, from the early sixth century BCE until the end of the fourth century BCE, and also because beginning in the sixth century BCE it served as an international currency that was used by non-Greeks as well.

13. About the imitation process and about the hoard coin from Tel Michal, see D. T. Ariel, 'Coins from Tel Mikhal (Tel Michal)', *Atiqot* 52 (2006), pp.71–88 (73–8).

14. The oldest coin, from the island of Cos, was found in burial cave No. 25 on the slope of the Hinnom Valley in Jerusalem. It has been dated to the middle of the sixth-century BCE. Two other sixth-century BCE coins found in Jerusalem are Athenian: one, from the middle to late sixth century BCE, was found at Givat Ram; the other, from the end of the sixth century BCE, was found on Mount Zion. See Y. Meshorer, 'An Attic Archaic Coin from Jerusalem', *Atiqot* 3 (1961), p. 185; R. Barkay, 'An Archaic Greek Coin from the "Shoulder of Hinnom" Excavations in Jerusalem', *INJ* 8 (1984–85), pp. 1–5. Another sixth-century BCE coin was unearthed in Nablus; see M. Thompson, O. Mørkholm, and C. M. Kraay, *An Inventory of Greek Coin Hoards* (New York: The American Numismatic Society, for the International Numismatic Commission, 1973), p. 205, No. 1504.

15. This can be inferred from a comparison of regions neighbouring the Land of Israel, such as the hoards of coins found in the Hauran district and in the Nile Delta. The coins found in excavations do not reflect the situation that existed in the Persian period. E. Stern notes that several hundred coins of this type held in private collections are to be attributed to the Land of Israel. E. Stern, *Archeology of the Land of the Bible, Vol. II: The Assyrian, Babylonian and Persian Periods 732–332* (New York: Doubleday, 2001), p. 559.

that began as early as the start of the Persian period and continued through its end.

The local coins also reflect the phenomenon of the adoption and imitation of Greek models and their recasting in local forms.[16] This process emerged because Attic coinage dominated the financial markets of the ancient world and was imitated all over that world – in Asia Minor, Egypt, Phoenicia, Mesopotamia and southern Arabia, as well as in the mints of the Land of Israel, such as those at Ashdod, Ashkelon, Gaza, Samaria and Jerusalem.[17] The head of the goddess Athena and her owl served as the archetype for all the mints established in the Land of Israel; this model was generally copied to ensure that the coins would be accepted.

The use of Greek models by the *Yehud* mint is testimony to the strength of the economic ties between the regions. The Greek models were supplemented to varying degrees by others more in keeping with local tradition. For example, the full frontal owl became a falcon or hawk in profile. The goddess Athena, always shown in profile, usually turned into a frontal image of a woman. The olive leaf became a rose and the inscription ΑΘΕ was replaced by *yhd*. In addition, sometimes the images were mixed up or discarded and new images, such as an ear or a ram's horn, were added.[18]

Samarian coins reflect a greater penetration by Greek influences than do the products of other mints in the country. These coins depict various figures from Greek mythology and Greek inscriptions, including several that mention Zeus and Heracles.[19] Many Greek-style seals were also found in Samaria.[20] E. Stern noted a correspondence and even identity between some of the images on the coins and those on the seals found in the same region.[21] Cross had also noted, on the basis of these finds, the prominence of Athenian influence in pre-Hellenistic Samaria.[22]

16. C. M. Kraay, *Archaic and Classical Greek Coins* (London: Methuen, 1976), pp. 73–5; J. G. Milne, 'The Origin of Certain Copies of Athenian Tetradrachms', *Iraq* 4 (1937), pp. 54–8; H. Nicolet–Pierre, 'Tetradrachmes Athéniens en Transeuphratène', *Transeuphratène* 20 (2000), pp.107–19.

17. Y. Meshorer, *A Treasury of Jewish Coins from the Persian Period to Bar-Kochba* (Jerusalem: Yad Yitzhak Ben-Zvi, 1997), p. 16 (Hebrew); L. Mildenberg, 'On the Imagery of the Philisto-Arabian Coinage – A Preview', *Transeuphratène* 13 (1997), pp. 9–16.

18. Y. Meshorer, *A Treasury of Jewish Coins from the Persian Period to Bar-Kochba* (Jerusalem: Yad Yitzhak Ben-Zvi, 1997), pls. 1–4 (Hebrew).

19. Y. Meshorer and S. Qedar, *Samarian Coinage* (Jerusalem: The Israel Numismatic Society, 1999), pp. 18, 28–9, 40–2, 66.

20. Leith, *Wadi Daliyeh I: The Wadi Daliyeh Seal Impressions*, 30–2.

21. On the similarity to seals see: E. Stern, 'A Hoard of Persian Period Bullae from the Vicinity of Samaria', *Michmanim* 6 (1992), pp. 6–30 (Hebrew); Meshorer and Qedar, *Samarian Coinage*, p. 81.

22. F. M. Cross, 'The Discovery of the Samaria Papyri', *BA* 26 (1963), pp. 110–21 (115) and H. Eshel's contribution to this volume.

The images produced by the mints that imitated Athenian coins were of lesser quality than those in the originals, possibly because the monetary value of the coin was more important than its aesthetic aspect. In any case, the variety of types reflects the varying degrees of influence on the different population groups in the Land of Israel, which stemmed from diverse social and political factors. The very decision to imitate an Athenian coin rather than a Persian or some other coin, or even designing a new coin, demonstrates that the need was purely economic. This argument is reinforced by several coin hoards found at such places as Tell Abu Hawam, Acre and Wadi Daliyeh,[23] which indicate that the Attic coinage standard was known and used in the Land of Israel before the Macedonian conquest.[24]

2. *Ceramics*

Ceramic finds are another source of material evidence of the varying intensity of the links between Greece and the Levant through different periods.[25] In the late seventh and early sixth centuries BCE most of the imported pottery found in the Land of Israel was of the type known as 'East Greek Ware'. From the fifth century BCE onwards, most Greek imports were from the Athenian sphere of influence. Ceramics from eastern Greece became negligible and Attic ware, like Attic coins, predominated. Huge quantities of Attic vessels began to arrive in the country – first black-figure vessels and later red-figure and black-polished vessels.[26] The pottery found in excavations in the Land of Israel includes a broad variety of types such as amphorae, kraters, skyphoi, kantharoi,

---

23.   C. Lambert, 'A Hoard of Phoenician Coins', *QDAP* 1 (1932), pp. 10–19; A. Kindler, 'The Mint of Tyre – The Major Source of Silver Coins in Ancient Palestine', *Eretz-Israel* 8 (1967), pp. 318–24 (Hebrew); Cross, 'The Discovery of the Samaria Papyri', 110–21.

24.   In the early stages of numismatic research it was assumed that the Attic-standard coins from Tell Abu Hawam and Acre post-dated the Macedonian conquest; scholars found it difficult to accept the idea that coins were minted according to the Greek standard before this time. However, as early as 1939, Narkiss suggested that the coins from the Tell Abu Hawam hoard should be dated earlier, to the very end of the Persian period (350–334 BCE), in part because he thought it implausible that Alexander would have allowed continued use of a Tyrian-style owl after his arduous siege of the city. See M. Narkiss, *Coins of Eretz Israel: Non-Jewish Coins* (Jerusalem: Bialik Institute, 1939), p. 48. The discovery of a hoard of Attic-standard coins in Wadi Daliyeh alongside documents dated to the end of the Persian period (375–335 BCE) made it possible to date other coins. Today there is no longer any doubt that the coins in these hoards antedate Alexander the Great.

25.   For such evidence from the early Iron Age see Dothan, 'The Arrival of the Sea Peoples: Cultural Diversity in Early Iron Age Canaan', 1–14.

26.   B. A. Sparkes, *The Red and the Black: Studies in Greek Pottery* (London: Routledge, 1996); R. M. Cook, *Greek Painted Pottery* (London: Methuen, 1997); B. B. Shefton, 'Reflections on the Presence of Attic Pottery at the Eastern End of the Mediterranean during the Persian Period', *Transeuphratène* 19 (2000), pp. 75–82.

lekythoi, kylikes, bolsal and salt cellars, some of which were not previously known in the country.[27] It is important to note that Attic ceramics can be found in every part of the country, both along the coast and inland.[28]

In the past, most scholars assumed that it was inconceivable for locals to have used such large quantities of Attic vessels, and thus inferred that the ceramic finds indicated the presence of Greeks in the country.[29] The consensus today however, is that these vessels are not evidence of a Greek population but of strong economic links between the regions. These ties could produce significant influences on consumer products, a topic that merits further study.[30] The ceramic finds thus become crucial evidence of the network of commercial relations between the regions.

The numismatic and ceramic evidence, as well as that of other imports, indicates that during the period under discussion there were abundant trade relations between the population of the Land of Israel, especially in the coastal plain, and the population of Greece, especially Attica. These trade relations engendered a significant Hellenic economic influence throughout the Land of Israel. However, while material remains such as coins and pottery are easy to identify and to trace, it is more difficult to ascertain the depth of the cultural influence that they indicate. For example, does the acceptance of new products indicate a change in fashion? This question cannot be answered with confidence at present, but we may certainly hypothesize that the substantial economic influence produced other and more profound influences as well.

II. *Technological Influences*

The Peloponnesian War of the late fifth century BCE caused many Greek artisans to emigrate west to Sicily and east to the shores of Asia Minor

---

27.   H. J. Franken, *History of Potters and Pottery in Ancient Jerusalem. Excavations by K. M. Kenyon in Jerusalem 1961–1967* (London: Oakville, 2005), p. 93.

28.   R. Wenning, 'Periods of "Hellenism' in Palestine', in *Praktika of the International Meeting of History and Archaeology Hellenism in the Near East* (Proceedings of Conference at Delphi 6–9 November 1986; Athens: European Cultural Centre of Delphi, 1991), pp. 145–59 (150); S. Klinger 'Attic Black and Red Figure Pottery in Israel' *Ancient West and East* 2 (2003), pp. 135–45; A. Stewart and S. R. Martin, 'Attic Import Pottery at Tel Dor, Israel', *BASOR* 337 (2005), pp. 33–47.

29.   For example see C. Clairmont, 'Greek Pottery from the Near East', *Berytus: Archeological Studies* 11 (1954), pp. 85–141 (87); M. Dothan, 'An Attic Red-Figured Bell-Krater from Tel Akko', *IEJ* 29 (1979), pp. 148–51 (151).

30.   We should note that certain types of vessels, such as the cooking pots found in a number of sites in the coastal plain (albeit in small quantities) should perhaps be seen as evidence of a Greek population. J. C. Waldbaum, 'Greek in the East or Greek and the East? Problem in the Definition and Recognition of Presence', *BASOR* 305 (1997), pp. 1–17 (5–6).

and Phoenicia. The emigrants included sculptors, potters, architects and builders. These artisans also found their way to the Levantine shore, where they left their imprint on the region.[31] Phoenician artisans, known for their eclectic tastes, investigated the novelties and inventions and expanded their familiar crafts by adopting inventions they had learned about through their ties with the West. Local imitations and mixed styles found expression *inter alia* in coinage (as noted above), pottery (chiefly in the types and less in the decorative style),[32] figurines[33] and seals.[34] They provide evidence for the models that the local populations willingly chose to incorporate into their own culture, consciously or unconsciously.[35] There is a difference between purchasing an imported item and creating something similar locally. The imitations attest to the influence of Greek wares on the local market and the indigenous population's interest in using items that were originally Greek. A study of local objects such as

31.   There is unequivocal evidence of Greek artistic influence on Persia and of the presence of Greek artists in Persia, and perhaps also of a Greek influence on local artists. This process progressed more quickly in those regions closer to Greece that had been conquered by the Persians; but it also took place in the heart of the Persian Empire, far from Greece. See S. Hornblower, *The Greek World 479–323 BC* (London: Routledge, 1991), p. 171; M. Colledge, 'Greek and Non-Greek Interaction in the Art and Architecture of the Hellenistic East', in A. Kuhrt and S. Sherwin–White (eds), *Hellenism in the East* (London: Duckworth, 1987), pp. 134–9; J. P. Guepin, 'On The Position of Greek Artists under Achaemenid Rule', *Persica* I (1963–4), pp. 34–43. According to Diodorus, when Alexander conquered Persia he liberated the Greeks who had been brought there by the Persian rulers. He reported on some 800 people working there, most of whom were missing limbs; the Persians allowed amputees to work if the limb needed for their job was unimpaired (Diodorus Siculus, XVII, 69. 3 [Loeb Classical Library, Trans. C. Bradford Welles; London: Harvard University Press, 1963], pp. 316–17).

32.   'Athenian vessels had a direct impact on the local ceramic industry and definitely fostered imitations. These however were in shape only, since the black glazing technique was beyond the abilities of the local potters.' So R. T. Marchese, 'Aegean and Cypriote Imports in the Persian Period (Strata XI-VI)', in Z. Herzog, G. Rapp and O. Negbi, *Excavations at Tel Michal, Israel* (Minneapolis: University of Minnesota, 1989), pp. 145–52 (150). See also G. Lehmann, 'Trends in the Local Pottery Development of the Late Iron Age and Persian Period in Syria and Lebanon, ca. 700 to 300 B.C.' *BASOR* 311 (1988), pp. 7–31. For Iron Age sites with local imitations of Greek vessels see E. Oren, 'Migdol: A New Fortress on the Edge of the Eastern Nile Delta', *BASOR* 256 (1984), pp. 7–44 (27).

33.   Most of the Greek-style figurines from Tel Sippor are made of the local clay, from both the coastal region and the Tel Sippor area. See O. Negbi, 'Terracottas and Statuettes from Tel Sippor', *Atiqot* 6 (1966), pp. 1–10 (7).

34.   Although no tests have been conducted, the very mixture of styles is evidence of local manufacturing, or at least of manufacturing outside Greece. See for example the seals from Tell Abu Hawam (R. W. Hamilton, 'Excavations at Tell Abu Hawam', *QDAP* 4 [1934], pp. 1–69 [18]) and Atlit (N. Johns, 'Excavations at Atlit [1930–1931]: The South-Eastern Cemetery', *QDAP* 2 [1933], pp. 41–104 [71–6]).

35.   D. Miller, 'Structures and Strategies: an Aspect of the Relationship Between Social Hierarchy and Cultural Change', in I. Hodder, (ed.), *Symbolic and Structural Archaeology* (Cambridge: Cambridge University Press, 1982), pp. 89–98.

clay lamps and figurines reveals that technologies imported from Greece were incorporated into the manufacturing process.

1. *Lamps*

The open-body lamp that was common throughout the Persian era is among the last of the traditional types of open lamps that can be traced back to the third millennium BCE.[36] During the Persian period, and especially during the second half of that period, a new type of lamp – the closed-body lamp – supplanted it. This technological and typological advance made by Greek potters in the seventh century BCE was related to two changes: changing the pinched spout into a bridge and turning the rim inward, making it possible to create a closed-body lamp.[37] To produce closed lamps Greek potters exploited their knowledge of ceramics, technique and the use of rich clay and a high-quality compound.[38] The capacity of the 'new' closed lamp and especially of its local imitations was smaller than that of open lamps, but it was much more convenient to carry closed lamps from place to place.[39] The technological innovation was evidently stimulated by the instability of the open lamp; even when it was fashioned with a flat base and its centre of gravity shifted, the reservoir still tended to allow the oil to spill out. The closed-body lamp solved this problem.

It took about a century for the closed lamp to become common in the Land of Israel.[40] We shall not expand on this, given that an analysis of the cultural implications of such a transformation is largely speculative, but we shall note that there was a change in the manufacturing process, even during the Persian period, setting off a phenomenon of imitation. Because of the 'new' lamps' obvious advantages, the Greek lamp industry influenced local production, and over time open lamps disappeared and closed lamps were used almost exclusively. This process was part of the

36.   R. Rosenthal and R. Sivan, *Ancient Lamps in the Schloessinger Collection* (Qedem 8; Jerusalem: The Institute of Archeology, The Hebrew University, 1978), p. 75.

37.   F. W. Robins, *The Story of the Lamp and the Candle* (London: Oxford University Press, 1939), p. 51.

38.   O. Broneer, *Corinth Vol. IV, Part II, Terracotta Lamps* (Cambridge, Mass.: Harvard University Press, 1930), p. 6.

39.   R. H. Smith, 'The Household Lamps of Palestine in Intertestamental Times', *BA* 27/1 (1964), pp. 1–31 (27–8).

40.   Imports of closed lamps from Greece to the Land of Israel in the seventh, sixth and fifth centuries BCE were relatively marginal; hence such lamps can be found only at sites where there was close contact with Greece (such as Dor) or at sites inhabited by Greek mercenaries (such as Mezad Hashavyahu). This type of the lamp began to penetrate the country in much larger quantities at the end of the fifth century BCE and especially during the fourth and third centuries, when it became the most common type of lamp in the country. For a partial list see E. Stern, *Material Culture of the Land of the Bible in the Persian Period 538–332 B.C.* (Warminster: Aris & Phillips, 1982), p. 129.

Greek technological influence on the Land of Israel in particular and on the ancient world in general.

2. *Figurines*

More sophisticated methods were also introduced in the figurine industry during this period. The change is particularly noticeable in the differences between Iron Age figurines and those of the Hellenistic period. During the Iron Age most figurines were solid and shaped by hand; if a mould was employed it was generally used only for the face.[41] In the Hellenistic period most figurines were hollow and the entire front was cast in a mould.[42] We can generalize and say that the technique of solid handmade figurines is typical of ancient varieties while hollow figurines cast in moulds are typical of later varieties. The change in technology began during the Persian period and was expressed in the shift from solid to hollow figurines and the abandonment of shaping by hand in favour of casting in moulds.

The technique of hollow moulded figurines first became widespread in the West and the use of moulds spread from there. This process was typical of Greece in the Archaic and especially in the Classical periods.[43] Some scholars believe that the adoption of moulds for hollow figurines was influenced by the metal-casting industry; in Athens, a workshop producing bronze sculptures has been found near one for clay figurines.[44] It seems plausible that the technological change in the Land of Israel derived from the close economic ties between West and East. Beginning in the Persian period the mould technique became widespread throughout the East as well, as indicated by excavations at various sites.[45] This

---

41. It is important to emphasize that moulds were known and occasionally used much earlier, at least from the Bronze Age. See for example M. Tadmor, 'Female Cult Figurines in Late Canaan and Early Israel: Archaeological Evidence', in T. Ishida (ed.), *The Period of David and Solomon* (Tokyo: Yamakawa-Shuppansha, 1982), pp. 139–73. But they were chiefly meant for one-time use; see R. Kletter, 'Between Archaeology and Theology: The Pillar Figurines from Judah and the Asherah', in A. Mazar (ed.), *Studies in the Archaeology of the Iron Age in Israel and Jordan* (Sheffield: Sheffield Academic Press, 2001), pp.179–216 (189).

42. For example at Mareshah, which is the source of the largest collection of Hellenistic figurines ever found in the Land of Israel. See A. Erlich, 'Hellenistic Terracotta Figurines of Maresha', (unpublished MA thesis; Bar Ilan University, 1996), p. 37 (Hebrew).

43. R. A. Higgins, *Catalogue of the Terracottas in the Department of Greek and Roman Antiquities* (London: Trustees of the British Museum, 1969), p. 11; J. P. Uhlenbrock, 'The Coroplast and his Craft', in J. P. Uhlenbrock (ed.), *The Coroplast Art: Greek Terracottas of the Hellenistic World* (College Art Gallery; The College at New Paltz, State University of New York: New Rochelle, N. Y., 1990), pp. 15–21 (16).

44. Uhlenbrock, 'The Coroplast and his Craft', 15.

45. For example at Shavey Zion; see E. Linder, 'The Figurines from Shavey Zion: A Re-examination', in M. Yeda'aya (ed.), *The Western Galilee Antiquities* (Haifa: Ministry of

suggestion is reinforced by the fact that most of the hollow-cast figurines of the Persian period are Western-style images, while figurines in the Oriental style continued to be shaped by hand, thrown on the wheel or cast in partial moulds.[46] Although handmade figurines never totally disappeared (not even in the West),[47] the use of moulds became increasingly common from the Persian period onward and became the typical technique of figurine manufacture in the Land of Israel.

The shift from shaping figurines by hand to making them in moulds influenced the local industry in other ways as well, since the use of moulds shortened the process and made mass production possible.[48] Many workshops adopted the technology because of the greater mobility of hollow figurines. The technological change influenced, among other factors, the place of production, the materials, the duration of manufacture and the costs. Two new professions also emerged: that of the skilled artist who created the archetype, and the less sophisticated craft of the coroplast, who cast the figurines in moulds. The mould technique reduced the prestige of making figurines, in part because they were no longer individual items but objects of mass production.[49] In any case the process of using moulds involved a different chain of steps than those in production by hand or on a wheel and can thus be seen as a technological change. To summarize, the process of manufacturing hollow figurines in

---

Defense, 1986), pp. 409–15 (Hebrew). A mould for the manufacture of figurines was discovered at Acre; see N. Messika, 'Terracotta Figurine from Acco in the Persian and the Hellenistic Period (sixth-first century BCE)', (unpublished MA thesis, Hebrew University, 1996), pp. 38–9, 53 (Hebrew) as well as at Tel Sippor; see Negbi, 'Terracottas and Statuettes from Tel Sippor', 1–10, and at Mareshah, where most of the figurines were made in moulds (although the Greek-style figurines are in the minority). Erlich notes 'The figurines are all mould-made, except for the riders, which combine hand-made and mould-made techniques.' A. Erlich, 'The Persian Terracotta Figurines from Maresha in Idumea: Local and Regional Aspects', *Transeuphratène* 32 (forthcoming).

46. E. Lipinski, 'Coroplastie', in E. Lipinski (ed.), *Dictionnaire de la Civilisation Phénicienne et Punique* (Turnhout: Brepols, 1992), pp. 119–20. Messika, too, notes that one can distinguish figurines from the northern part of the tell, most of which were made by hand, from figurines from the western sector, most of which were made in moulds. See N. Messika, 'Terracotta Figurines from Acco in the Persian and the Hellenistic Period', 18. This is interesting in light of the fact that many Greek artifacts were found in Area F on the western side of the tell; M. Dothan suggested that this neighbourhood was settled by Greek immigrants. See M. Dothan, 'An Attic Red-Figured Bell-Krater from Tel Akko', *IEJ* 29 (1979), pp. 148–51 (151).

47. Higgins, *Catalogue of the Terracottas in the Department of Greek and Roman Antiquities*, 3.

48. On the manufacture of figurines in moulds see for example R. A. Higgins, *Tangra and the Figurines* (London: Trefoil Books, 1986), p. 66; see also G. M. A. Richter, *A Handbook of Greek Art* (London: Phaidon Press, 1974), p. 229.

49. For example, A. Erlich, 'Hellenistic Terracottas from Maresha: Between Art and Craft', *Assaph, Studies in Art History* 7 (2002), pp. 1–15 (2).

moulds, which originated in the West, became widespread in the Land of Israel beginning in the Persian period.[50]

During most historical periods, the relations between the Greek world and the Levant were bilateral; technological influences operated in both directions. It is interesting to note that in antiquity both the oil lamps[51] and the mould method of manufacturing figurines[52] were originally transmitted from the East to the West.[53] In the West they underwent modifications that made them more efficient before returning to the East in their new form during the Persian period.

Persian-period figurines hint at another process indirectly associated with technology and more directly associated with artistic, religious and cultural developments. This period saw a shift between two radically different tendencies: conservatism on one side and openness to innovation on the other. This change, too, may have had its source in the West. The difference is evident in a comparison of figurines from earlier and later periods. The Iron Age figurines were marked by a clear conservatism both in the number of types and their appearance, whereas in the Hellenistic period there was more diversity of types and designs. This contrast is clearly brought out in collections of figurines from Iron Age sites such as Ashdod[54] when compared with Hellenistic sites such as Acre[55] and

50.   It is important to note that there was another major change in the Hellenistic period, when several moulds were used to create a single figurine. We learn of this, for example, from a study of the figurines found at Naucratis: 'Most are made in double moulds, a technique developed in Greece that does not appear in the near east before the Greek Conquest' (S. B. Downey, *Terracotta Figurines and Plaques from Dura-Europos* [Ann Arbor: University of Michigan Press, 2003], pp. 8–9). One result of this change was that the product was closer to being completed when it was removed from the moulds. Three moulds have been found in Acre; one of them, from the Persian period, is designed in schematic fashion without facial details or hair. This means that the artist had to complete the figurine after it was removed from the mould. By contrast, the other two moulds are from the Hellenistic period, and the figurines made in them would have been removed in a more finished state. See N. Messika, 'Terracotta Figurine from Acco in the Persian and the Hellenistic Period', 97.

51.   Broneer, *Corinth Vol. IV, Part II, Terracotta Lamps*, 5; V. Sussman, *Ornamented Jewish Oil Lamps from the Destruction of the Second Temple Through the Bar-Kokhba Revolt*, (Warminster: Aris and Phillips, 1982), p. 6.

52.   Higgins, *Catalogue of the Terracottas in the Department of Greek and Roman Antiquities*, 10; Additional influences, such as alphabetic writing, travelled from east to west at the end of the eighth century BCE.

53.   These changes were part of the colonization movement. On various aspects of this process see J. Boardman, 'Aspects of "Colonization"', *BASOR* 322 (2001), pp. 33–42.

54.   M. Dothan, and D. N. Freedman, 'Ashdod I: The First Season of Excavations 1962', *Atiqot* 7 (1967), p. 137.

55.   Messika, 'Terracotta Figurines from Acco in the Persian and the Hellenistic Period (sixth-first century BCE)', 98.

Mareshah.[56] A relatively small number of types are known from the Iron Age while in the Hellenistic period there is broad diversity and many types were meant for daily use. It is possible that this earlier conservatism and later openness can be traced to the change between the religious and cultic character of Iron Age figurines and the religious, cultic and day-to-day character of their use in the Hellenistic period. The Persian period was an intermediate stage between conservatism and openness. There were still fixed types, such as the horse and rider, but there were also new models and the repertoire included figurines based on Greek models. Facial expressions also changed, with the familiar frozen expression of the Iron Age sometimes replaced by the hint of a smile (archaic), chiefly in figurines in the Western style but also in some local figurines. These changes, too, may have been a result of the contacts between the regions.

3. *Metallurgy*

Other types of ties are manifested in additional finds that have been linked to the metalworking industry. R. Reich has suggested that the blocks of haematite (the chief raw material for iron production) found in several late Iron Age sites, such as Mezad Hashavyahu, are evidence of early Greek settlement. He proposed that metalworking in general and ironwork in particular were characteristic of most of the Greek settlements on the southeastern shores of the Mediterranean during the last quarter of the seventh century BCE, notably at Daphne, Naucratis (where piles of haematite were found) and Migdol (where traces of the metalworking industry were found).[57] Persian period sites such as Jaffa and Nahariya also offer substantial evidence of a metalworking industry.[58] It should be noted that the forge at Jaffa is not far from the warehouse structure, which strongly resembles the warehouse structure excavated in al-Mina and attributed to Greek merchants. The iron dross in Nahariya was found in the storage building. The hypothetical connection between metalworking and a Greek population is interesting and worthy of further study, since it may be another instance of Greek technological influence on local technology. As noted, the technique of minting coins was also of Western origin.

4. *Olive Presses*

The Hellenistic period also saw a technological revolution in olive presses, with the appearance of a new type of crushing stone. Crushing stones with

---

56. A. Erlich, 'Hellenistic Terracotta Figurines of Maresha', 89–91.

57. R. Reich, 'A Third Season of Excavations at Mesad Hashavyahu', *Eretz-Israel* 20 (1989), pp. 228–32 (Hebrew).

58. O. Yogev, 'Nahariya', *NEAEHL* 3, p. 1089; J. Kaplan and H. R. Kaplan, 'Jaffa', *NEAEHL* 2, pp. 657–8.

a lenticular cross-section, made of the local limestone known as 'nari', have been found in Subterranean Complex 44 at Mareshah and at other underground complexes dated to the third–second centuries BCE. To date 22 olive presses have been reported from this site; most of them have crushing stones of this type. Such installations have also been found elsewhere in the Judean Shephelah. A. Kloner and N. Sagiv have suggested that these facilities are evidence of contact with classical Greece.[59] Other technological innovations associated with the production of flour, including hopper-rubber (Olynthian) millstones found in the Land of Israel as early as the Persian period, may also indicate contacts with Greece.[60]

Based on the material finds unearthed at various sites in the Land of Israel, we may conjecture that the first signs of Western influence on technology, local industry and art began to appear during the Persian period at the latest. These artifacts are evidence both of the manufacture of products in the Greek style and of technological influences on local industry. The local population opted to accept techniques developed in Greece, evidently because they were more efficient and economical; otherwise they would have made do with local products and technologies.

The implications of the innovations and inventions described above should not be dismissed lightly. Like modern-day innovations in such areas as transportation and communications, these changes were more than just superficial. Changes such as these could often spark cultural development. Anthropological research has found that there is sometimes a link between technological innovation and cultural change. Various scholars have argued that there is a connection between the development of a culture and the adoption of new technologies. The link between technology and culture is two-way, since technological development leads to cultural change, while inventions are often the result of a cultural need for innovation.[61]

---

59. A. Kloner and N. Sagiv, 'Subterranean Complexes 44 and 45' in A. Kloner (ed.), *Maresha Excavation Final Report I, Subterranean Complexes 21, 44, 77* (Jerusalem: Israel Antiquities Authority, 2003), pp. 52–72 (71); L. Foxhall, 'Oil Extraction and Processing Equipment in Classical Greece', in M. C. Amouretti and J. P Brun (eds), *Le production du vin et de l'huile en Méditerranée* (BCH suppl. XXVI; Paris: De Boccard, 1993), pp.183–200.

60. R. Frankel, 'The Olynthus Mill: Its Origin and Diffusion, Typology and Distribution', *AJA* 107 (2003), pp. 1–21. Recently published results of a chemical study of basaltic hopper-rubber (Olynthus) mills from Nahal Tut (a late fourth-century BCE storage depot) show that the mills from Nahal Tut were manufactured in the area of Nisyros in the Aegean region. See I. Segal, 'Chemical Study of Basaltic Hopper-Rubber (Olynthus) Mills from Nahal Tut and 'En Hofez', *Atiqot* 52 (2006), pp.197–200.

61. For which see B. Pfaffenberg, 'Social Anthropology of Technology', *Annual Review of Anthropology* 21 (1992), pp. 491–516.

III. *Religious Influences*

When we turn to the question of a possible Greek religious influence on the Land of Israel in the Persian period, we should remember that the influence of Greek religious practice on the area in the Hellenistic period was not all that substantial either. For example G. Fuks recently summarized his discussion of gods and cults in Hellenistic-period Ashkelon as follows: 'The conclusion to be drawn is that even though Ashkelon was a Greek polis in every respect (and in some periods was even home to Greek intellectuals), when it comes to religion the dominance of the Oriental cults is evident, even if it is dressed up in a Greek chlamys'.[62] All the more so, then, during the Persian period; we should not be looking for evidence of the domination of Western cults but only for evidence of their first tentative diffusion into the East.

1. *Temples and* Favissae

The most important archaeological finds that can inform us about cultic practices during the Persian period are from temples and temple repositories (*favissae*). These pits were especially dug inside or near temples in order to serve as repositories for cultic articles or related items. Ritual objects were placed in these pits when they were removed from service and accordingly provide a treasure-house of information about religious and cultic life in the ancient world. Many Persian-period *favissae* (or grouped artifacts that were probably used in cultic activity or may be the remains of such pits) have been found in Israel. They have been found chiefly in the coastal region: at Acre, Tell Abu Hawam, Dor, Apollonia, Tel Michal, Makmish, Ashkelon and Gaza, as well as at inland sites such as Dan, Beth Shean, Lachish, Tel Erani, Tell eṣ-Ṣâfi, Tel Sippor, Tel Halif and Beer Sheba.[63] Interestingly enough, while most of these sites are situated along the coast and some in the Judean Shephelah and the inland valleys, none are within the central hill country of Judea and Samaria.

In all, these repositories have yielded a diverse range of articles that attest to influences from many regions, including some that indicate

62. G. Fuks, *A City of Many Seas, Ashkelon during the Hellenistic and Roman Periods* (Jerusalem: Yad Ben-Zvi, 2001), p. 121 (Hebrew).

63. Negbi, 'Terracottas and Statuettes from Tel Sippor', 1; Stern, *Material Culture of the Land of the Bible in the Persian Period 538–332 B.C*, 158–60; O. Tal, 'The Persian Period', in I. Roll and O. Tal (eds), *Apollonia-Arsuf, Final Report of the Excavation, Volume 1: The Persian and the Hellenistic Periods*, (Tel Aviv: Tel Aviv University Press, 1999), pp. 83–222 (91); M. Dothan, 'An Attic Red-Figured Bell-Krater from Tel Akko', 148–51. On the figurines from Tel Halif see: Paul F. Jacobs: 'Ancient World, Digital World: Excavation at Halif', *Adriane* 27 (2001) (http://www.ariadne.ac.uk/issue27/jacobs/). See also the paper on Tell eṣ-Ṣâfi by Avissar, Uziel and Maeir in this volume.

contacts with Greece, such as Ionian and Attic ceramics, epigraphic finds (about which see below), Cypriot figurines and stone statuettes[64] and even fragments of a Gorgon's head at Dor.[65] The Greek-style figurines found in these repositories are important as well.[66]

Are these Greek artifacts evidence of commercial relations only or may we infer something about religious ties as well? To answer this question we must first distinguish between two types of pits: those in which Greek artifacts are dominant and those in which they are part of a more diverse assortment. In fact, there are only two of the first type, both from Dor. Perhaps we should conclude that these pits were associated with Greek temples that served a Greek population.[67] Greek colonists in the area, though few in number, exerted a cultural influence on the indigenous population because of the attractive, different and special nature of their culture.

The contents of the second type of pit are heterogeneous and can be attributed to many cultures. The finds include Phoenician and Egyptian-style figurines along with some Greek ones. This diversity is generally read as evidence of the eclectic taste of Phoenician mariners, who served as middlemen between the various cultures while at the same time cultivating their own unique style.[68] These finds seem to constitute evidence of strong commercial ties between the regions and may indicate other sorts of ties as well. Because of the interactions between trade and religion, the introduction of foreign goods was accompanied by foreign religious influences, particularly in an era when religion occupied such an important place in daily life. Goods were traded, and so was their content, at least in part. The presence of Greek-style figurines in the pits is evidence of the use of Greek cultic articles. The initial penetration by Greek cults stands out in light of the fact that most of the Greek-style figurines were found in pits and only a few in other urban contexts, whereas most Eastern-style figurines are found in urban contexts and very

---

64.   Negbi, 'Terracottas and Statuettes from Tel Sippor', 1–10; Stern, *Archeology of the Land of the Bible,* 500–4.

65.   E. Stern, 'Gorgon Excavated at Dor', *BARev* 28, 6 (2002), pp. 50–7.

66.   Bisi argued that the figurines found on the Phoenician and southern Levantine coasts are evidence of Greek influence. She also believes that this influence is more prominent there than in northern Phoenicia and Syria. See A. M. Bisi, 'Quelques Remarques Sur la Coroplastie Palestinienne à l'époque perse: tradition Locale et emprunts étrangers', *Transeuphratène* 3 (1990), pp.75–84 (78–9).

67.   E. Stern, 'Gorgon Excavated at Dor'. New finds reinforce this suggestion, such as the tombstone from Apollonia (see below).

68.   N. Avigad, 'Excavations at Makmish 1958, Preliminary Report', *IEJ* 10 (1960), pp. 90–6 (96).

few, relatively speaking, in the pits.[69] In any case, the finds in the pits are evidence of the initial penetration of the local cults by Greek religion, or of at least some kind of relationship between the two.

Another change that occurred during the Persian period was the very burial of figurines in such *favissae*.[70] The use of pits is an ancient and well-known custom, but the phenomenon of burying figurines in them became more common in the Persian period. The source for this practice may derive from contacts with Greece. If so, this would constitute a substantial change in religious behaviour, even if we do not understand its specific meaning.

2. *Burial Practices*

Another manifestation of contacts between the regions is seen in burial practices. While some finds can be seen as evidence of burials of Greek immigrants, others suggest that Greek burial practices may have inspired or influenced changes in local customs. For example, a relief featuring a Doric scene with distinctly Greek characteristics, dated to the fourth century BCE, was found at Apollonia.[71] Another example is known from Atlit, where burial sites have yielded many Greek finds. Jones, who excavated there, believed that these graves were of Greek mercenaries who fought in the wars between Persia and Egypt.[72] In addition there is the evidence of the burial in Greece of Phoenicians who adopted Greek ways while living abroad, such as the tombstone of the Ashkelonite in Athens.[73]

Various other finds indicate that the local population adopted Greek or Greek-style burial customs. Near both Sidon and Omrit, Greek-style anthropoid coffins have been found in large numbers; a similar coffin has

---

69. As may be understood from the distribution tables of the figurines both in Stern, *Material Culture of the Land of the Bible in the Persian Period 538–332 B.C.*, 178, and Messika, 'Terracotta Figurine from Acco in the Persian and the Hellenistic Period (sixth-first century BCE)', 31–2.

70. Kletter, 'Between Archaeology and Theology: The Pillar Figurines from Judah and the Asherah', 184.

71. M. Fisher and O. Tal, 'A Fourth-Century BCE Attic Marble "Totenmahlrelief" at Apollonia-Arsuf', *IEJ* 53 (2003), pp. 49–60.

72. N. Johns, 'Excavations at Atlit (1930–1931): The South-Eastern Cemetery', *QDAP* 2 (1933), pp. 41–104 (58).

73. A grave in Athens bears evidence of the burial, in the fourth century BCE, of a Phoenician who had kept up his ties with his homeland. The bilingual inscription, in Phoenician and Greek, was inscribed by a Sidonian for his friend, referred to in the inscriptions as an Ashkelonite. In the Greek portion of the inscription he is referred to by typical Greek names (Αντιπατρος Αφροδισιυ Ασκας[λωνιτης]. The extent to which the two men had assimilated into Greek culture is reflected by the mythological scene and Greek epigram engraved on the stele. See *KAI* 2, pp. 70–1, no. 45. For discussion see G. Fuks, *A City of Many Seas*, 17.

also been found in Gaza.[74] Other finds suggest the coexistence of Greek practices with local customs, such as the use of Greek-style masks in the northeastern Nile Delta, where mercenaries of various nationalities, including Greeks and Judaeans, lived side by side.[75] Another Greek practice, the use of protective tiles, has been found at Tell Sukas.[76] While these last cases are from outside Israel, they do suggest that such influences might well be found there as well. Many other graves reflect foreign customs, such as the burial of utensils in drinking vessels. Further research is needed to determine whether these derive from a Greek source.[77] Finally, a grave at Tel Far'ah (South) that contains many Persian artifacts also contains typically Greek items.[78] The gravestone from Apollonia bears a relief of furniture that recalls the proposed reconstruction of the furniture in the grave at Tel Far'ah.

Evidence of Greek influence on burials of the local population in the Land of Israel during the Persian period is extremely limited. It should be remembered, however, that burial practices change much more slowly than customs in other spheres and are seen chiefly in artifacts and external procedures rather than in the basic system of interment. The finds discussed above are evidence of relations, contacts and influences between the regions, manifested in the economic, technological, religious and cultural domains. It is true that the evidence for such influences is not abundant for the period in question, but the finds do allow us to define the beginning of the process and its complexity.

---

74. It is important to note that anthropoid coffins originated in Egypt, where they were used to bury mummies. Phoenician artists began imitating the Egyptian coffins in the fifth century BCE. The Greek influence on the Phoenicians increased in the late fifth century BCE and in the fourth century; see E. Stern, 'Phoenician Anthropoid coffins from Eretz-Israel', *Qadmoniot* 4 (1971), pp. 27–8 (Hebrew). From his study of Greek-style coffins, Contenau concluded that the ruling caste of Sidon was influenced by Greece as early as the mid-fifth century BCE. See D. G. Contenau, *La Civilisation Phenicienne* (Paris: Payot, 1949), pp. 186–220).

75. E. Oren, 'Northern Sinai', *NEAEHL* 4, pp. 1386–96.

76. P. J. Riis, *Sukas VI: The Graeco-Phoenician Cemetery and Sanctuary at the Southern Harbour* (Kobenhavn: Kommissionaer, Munksgaard, 1979), pp. 31–2.

77. Burying utensils for the dead in drinking vessels was a common custom in the Greek-Hellenistic world; see P. R. S. Moorey, 'Metal Wine-Sets in the Ancient Near East', *Iranica Antica* 15 (1980), pp. 181–97. Similar vessels can be found in the Land of Israel in Persian period graves; see for example: N. Johns, 'Excavations at Atlit (1930–1931): The South-Eastern Cemetery', *QDAP* 2 (1933), pp. 41–104 (56–7). There may be other evidence of the custom in the burial caves in Jaffa. Here the dead were laid on their backs with their hands open and lying symmetrically on their thighs. Another widespread custom there involves placing one or two vials next to the head of the corpse, see R. Avner and E. Eshel, 'A Juglet with Phoenician Inscription from a Recent Excavation in Jaffa, Israel', *Transeuphratène* 12 (1996), pp. 59–63.

78. J. H. Iliffe, 'Tell Far'ah Tomb Group Reconsidered: Silver Vessels of the Persian Period', *QDAP* 4 (1935), pp. 182–6.

IV. *Cultural Influences*

Various finds from the Persian period in the Land of Israel are evidence of contacts that were manifested in economic, technological, and (to a far lesser extent) religious influences. All three types of influence would seem to suggest the existence of cultural influences as well. The material culture in the country and the changes it underwent during the Persian period suggest that Greek cultural influences, albeit small, began to be felt at this time. Greek wares and local products manufactured under Greek influence could and did modify local consumption patterns.[79] Technological advances were instrumental in changing methods of production and professional specializations, and consequently had an impact on culture; the religious ties between the two regions could also produce cultural influences. The use of the Greek language, albeit limited, is another sign of Greek cultural influence.

V. *Epigraphic Finds*

Although the Greek and Greek-related epigraphic finds are not many, they do point to various kinds of cultural relations. A Phoenician inscription from Acre that contains Greek words is evidence of the influence of the Greek language on the local dialect.[80] An inscription found in Jaffa is evidence for the use of the Greek name Hermes in the Phoenician onomasticon.[81] An inscription from Tell el-Hesi includes a Phoenician name written in the Greek alphabet.[82] The shoulder bone of a cow, found at Dor, bears a dedicatory inscription in Greek, in the Cypriot syllabic script.[83] There are other examples of less direct influence, such as Greek inscriptions on ostraca (for example from Dor and Yavne Yam),[84] which may indicate that the Greek language was used in the Land of Israel during the Persian period. However, since we do not know who wrote

---

79.   G. Lehmann, 'Trends in the Local Pottery Development of the Late Iron Age and Persian Period in Syria and Lebanon', *BASOR* 311 (1998), pp. 7–37 (32). Nevertheless, as Fantalkin showed, merchants sometimes adapted their wares to the needs of the local community; see A. Fantalkin, 'Mezad Hashavyahu: its Material Culture and Historical Background', *Tel Aviv* 28, (2001), pp. 128–47 (138).

80.   M. Dothan, 'Phoenician Inscription from Akko', *IEJ* 35 (1985), pp. 81–96 (87–8).

81.   R. Avner and E. Eshel, 'A Juglet with Phoenician Inscription'.

82.   F. J. Bliss, *A Mound of Many Cities – Tell el Hesy Excavations* (London: Palestine Exploration Fund, 1894), p. 104.

83.   E. Stern, 'Cypriot Votive Scapula from Tel Dor, A Maritime Scene', *IEJ* 44 (1994), pp.1–12; O. Masson, 'Pelerins Chypriotes en Phénicie (Sarpta et Sidon)', *Semitica* 32 (1982), pp. 45–8.

84.   E. Stern, 'Dor', *NEAEHL* 1, pp. 357–68; M. Fisher, 'Yavne-Yam 1992–1999 – Interim Report', *Qadmoniot* 123 (2002), pp. 2–11 (Hebrew).

these inscriptions, we cannot know whether the authors belonged to the indigenous population or were Greek travellers or immigrants.[85]

Regional Distinctions

The intensity of the ties between the Levant and the Greek world varied from region to region. An examination of the finds suggests that these ties were strongest along the coast, which was naturally exposed to overseas influences as the venue of physical contact between West and East. The many and diverse finds there attest to the strength of those initial influences. A similar process took place in the Shephelah, especially the lower Shephelah, though to some extent also at Tel Halif in the southern upper Shephelah. In Samaria, unlike the coastal plain, there is no evidence of influences other than economic throughout the first half of the Persian period. The picture starts to become more complex towards the end of the period. During the second quarter of the fourth century, artifacts, seals and coins from Samaria show more significant Greek influence, which, while still chiefly economic, could also reflect a certain Greek presence in the region.[86] Material finds from Judah also indicate economic penetration and the absence of other kinds of influences. The very fact that almost no Greek-style artifacts have been uncovered there indicates that the economic inroads did not lead to substantial cultural influence.

The simplest explanation for these differences is that physical conditions and especially topography made it natural for the population of the coastal plain and Shephelah to have closer ties with Greece and Greeks than did the inhabitants of the hill country. The hill country's relative isolation from the main trade routes delayed contacts with Greece to some extent.

Another possible explanation would lie in the character of the different populations of the regions, as known from the historical sources. The finds discussed here suggest a distinction between polytheistic and monotheistic populations. The progress of Greek influences seems to have stopped at the boundary of the monotheists' territories, that of Jews and Samarians. These monotheists allowed goods to pass, but did not allow those goods and their influence to penetrate too deeply. This may be an example of how material finds reflect processes of influence and assimilation in the different regions. When the local population was open

---

85.   The bulk of the Greek inscriptions are graffiti on Attic vessels. As was customary in this period, one may assume that the inscriptions date from the manufacture of the vessel; for example, the graffiti from Apollonia – see Tal, 'The Persian Period', 195–6 – hence their contribution to the study of cultural influences is not very great.

86.   For which see: F. M. Cross, 'The Discovery of the Samaria Papyri', *BA* 26 (1963), pp. 110–21; Leith, *Wadi Daliyeh I: The Wadi Daliyeh Seal Impressions*, 33–5.

to accepting these influences it absorbed them; but it could also resist them. Ceramics and coins penetrated *Yehud* and Samaria, but not figurines. This indicates differential receptivity to Greek influences and shows that the coastal plain and Shephelah, inhabited chiefly by Phoenicians, 'Philistines', Idumeans and Arabs, were subject to more diverse influences than was the hill country, where only economic influences were admitted.

The Meaning of These Influences in Light of Relations with Greece during the Hellenistic Period

It is conventionally assumed that the ties between the Greek world and the Levant, including the process that we term 'Hellenization' reached their acme during the Hellenistic period. Many scholars consider this concept to refer chiefly to the process of fusion (synthesis, hybridization, and integration) between Greek and Oriental cultures. Other scholars expand the definition and maintain that it refers to various kinds of penetration and that instances of cultural reception are rarer than those of other kinds of influences.[87]

Some of the historians who have studied the process as it took place during the Hellenistic period have noted that there is evidence that the process began even earlier. For example, A. Kasher noted that 'it seems that before the Hellenistic conquest the idea of fusion was a novelty for which there is little evidence. After the conquest the idea of the process of Hellenization was accepted.'[88] Some archaeologists, led by E. Stern, especially in the wake of his excavations at Tel Dor, have weighed the evidence for this process.[89] The archaeological finds discussed here indicate that Greek influences antedated the Macedonian conquest and were manifested, in differing degrees, in various economic, technological and religious spheres.

To the extent that one's definition of Hellenization emphasizes cultural influences, the process began relatively late, after the third century BCE: the first stages of cultural fusion involved only a few cities and the process reached its zenith only later. R. H. Smith concluded that there was no great difference between the culture of the Persian period and that of the

---

87. On the various definitions see L. I. Levine, *Judaism and Hellenism in Antiquity, Conflict or Confluence?*, (Seattle: University of Washington Press, 1998), pp. 6–32.

88. A. Kasher, *Canaan, Philistia, Greece and Israel: Relations of the Jews in Eretz Israel with the Hellenistic Cities (332 BCE-70 CE)*, (Jerusalem: Yad Ben-Zvi, 1989), p. 25 (Hebrew).

89. E. Stern, 'The Beginning of the Greek Settlement in Palestine in Light of the Excavations at Tel Dor,' in S. Gitin and W. G. Dever (eds), *Recent Excavations in Israel: Studies in Iron Age Archaeology* (AASOR 49; Winona Lake: American Schools of Oriental Research and Eisenbrauns, 1989), pp. 107–24.

third century BCE.[90] Since, however, in our view the term refers to the overall process and includes a variety of influences, there is evidence for such ties even within the Persian period. An analysis of the finds allows us to argue that Greek ties, contacts and influences began many years before the Macedonian conquest and increased over time. Hellenization was a complex process; if plotted on a graph it might begin with a slowly rising curve with several abrupt jumps along the way. This curve would begin before the Hellenistic period and would continue after it.

The conventional explanation for the origin of these ties is that Phoenician sailors brought many of these influences to the Land of Israel from the Greek world.[91] Nevertheless, it is important to note the role played by Greek sailors, immigrants and mercenaries,[92] as well as various intermediaries along the sea route between Greece and the Land of Israel, especially in Cyprus.

Focusing on the Macedonian conquest and considering it to be the turning point is imprecise because contacts began long before Alexander, and at least a century passed after his death until there were substantial links between the regions, which influenced many spheres of life and were manifested in a broad range of finds.

Our own time is frequently referred to as the 'Age of Globalization', evidence of the significant role of international economics in our lives. In the ancient world, too, economics were an extremely important motive for contacts between regions, at least between the Aegean world and the Levantine coast. As in our own time, goods, technologies, land, mercenaries and manpower in general were traded between the regions, allowing various influences to penetrate to varying degrees. It took time, however, for Greek influences to be more fully assimilated by the local population and to be expressed in its material culture. The finds described here allow us to argue that although the relations between the regions were chiefly economic, other influences did affect the indigenous population throughout the entire Persian period, well before the Macedonian conquest.

90. R. H. Smith, 'The Southern Levant in the Hellenistic Period', *Levant* 22 (1990), pp. 123–30.

91. Stern, 'The Beginning of the Greek Settlement in Palestine in Light of the Excavations at Tel Dor', 108.

92. As proposed by W. F. Albright, *The Archaeology of Palestine* (Harmondsworth: Penguin Books, 1954), p. 124.

Chapter 2

SETTLEMENT DYNAMICS AND DEMOGRAPHIC FLUCTUATIONS IN
JUDAH FROM THE LATE IRON AGE TO THE HELLENISTIC PERIOD AND
THE ARCHAEOLOGY OF PERSIAN-PERIOD *YEHUD*

Avraham Faust

Introduction

The 500 years that spanned the late Iron Age, the Persian and the Hellenistic periods in the southern Levant were troubled ones. This period began with Assyrian domination during the seventh century BCE, accompanied by economic prosperity in the semi-independent regions of Philistia and Judah. This domination was followed, after an interlude of Egyptian hegemony, with Babylonian rule during the late seventh century and most of the sixth century. Then came the Persians, whose rule lasted for 200 years. The conquests of Alexander the Great put an end to the Persian domination, and were followed by competing Hellenistic dynasties that fought each other for domination over the region. Finally, during the second century, came the Hasmonean revolt and the expansion of their state.

The present paper aims to study this period, with an emphasis on the *Yehud* province of the Persian period, not from a 'traditional' historical perspective, but with an emphasis on long-term settlement and demographic processes. The archaeological evidence from excavations and surveys will be at the forefront of the discussion, and historical information will be used only as complementary data.

Interestingly, there have been few attempts at such an endeavour in the past. Most studies of the biblical period have ended at the end of the Iron Age, and while several have discussed the Persian period, even these did not go into a detailed analysis of the data from the Hellenistic period.[1] The

---

1. C. E. Carter, *The Emergence of Yehud in the Persian Period: a Social and Demographic Study* (JSOTSup. 294; Sheffield: Sheffield Academic Press, 1999) is a notable exception. While not discussing all three periods at equal length, Carter did examine the settlement in all three (e.g. pp. 233–48). Note that even O. Lipschits' detailed studies ('Demographic Changes in Judah between the Seventh and the Fifth Centuries BCE', in O. Lipschits and J. Blenkinsopp [eds], *Judah and Judeans in the Neo-Babylonian Period*, [Winona Lake: Eisenbrauns, 2003] pp. 323–76; idem, *The Fall and Rise of Jerusalem: Judah under Babylonian Rule*, [Winona Lake: Eisenbrauns, 2005]), while stressing the importance of discussing the entire time-span until the Hellenistic period (an exercise which he mistakenly connected with 'the long duration'), did not really examine the settlement and demography of the latter.

Table 1

Settlement in Judah during the Iron Age, Persian and Hellenistic Periods according to the data from Surveys[2]

	Ramallah and el-Bireh (North) (Finkelstein)[3]	Ramallah and el-Bireh (South), Ein Karem (North) (Feldstein etal.)[4]	Wadi el-Makukh (Goldfus and Golani)[5]	Eastern Jerusalem (Dinur and Feig)[6]	Nes Harim (Weiss, Zissu and Sulimany)[7]	Jerusalem (Kloner)[8]	Hebron hill country (Ofer)[9]	Shephelah (Dagan)[10]	Tel Malhata and Nahal Yatir (Beit Arie; Govrin)[11]	Herodiom (Hirschfeld)[12] and Deir Mar Saba (Patrich)[13]	Summary
IA	14	64	21	68	24[18]	143[15]	113	87	27	23	586
PP	7	27	0	13	12	15	87	47	7	1	216
H	35	70	10	27	33	110[16]	98	110	7[17]	10	510

2. Notably, we did not include the results of the 'emergency survey' (M. Kochavi, 'The Land of Judah', in M. Kochavi [ed.], *Judea, Samaria and the Golan, Archaeological Survey 1967–1968*, [Jerusalem: Archaeological Survey of Israel, 1972], pp. 19–89 [Hebrew]), which, despite its great importance, is now generally outdated. Also, the table does not include the results of the Beit Sira map (published as part of the Benjamin survey), as it relates to an area which behaves completely differently. These data will be discussed below.

3. I. Finkelstein, 'Northern Part of the Maps of Beit Sira, Ramallah and el-Bireh', in I. Finkelstein and Y. Magen (eds), *Archaeological Survey of the Hill Country of Benjamin* (Jerusalem: Israel Antiquities Authority, 1993), pp. 15–95 (Hebrew), 13*–23* (English summaries). Note that Carter (*The Emergence of Yehud in the Persian Period*, 235) examined the number of settlements in this region of Benjamin and came up with the following results: Iron Age: 157; Persian period: 39; Hellenistic period: 163. The trends clearly follow these of the more general data supplied by the surveyors.

4. A. Feldstein, G. Kidron, N. Hanin, Y. Kamaisky and D. Eitam, 'Southern Part of the Maps of Ramallah and el-Bireh and Northern Part of the Maps of 'Ein Kerem', in I. Finkelstein and Y. Magen (eds), *Archaeological Survey of the Hill Country of Benjamin* (Jerusalem: Israel Antiquities Authority, 1993), pp. 133–264 (Hebrew), 28*–47* (English summaries).

5. H.Goldfus and A. Golani, 'Map of the Wadi el-Makukh', in I. Finkelstein and Y. Magen (eds), *Archaeological Survey of the Hill Country of Benjamin* (Jerusalem: Israel Antiquities Authority, 1993), pp. 265–338 (Hebrew), 47*-58* (English summaries).

6. U. Dinur and N. Feig, 'Eastern Part of the Map of Jerusalem', in I. Finkelstein and Y. Magen (eds), *Archaeological Survey of the Hill Country of Benjamin* (Jerusalem: Israel Antiquities Authority, 1993), pp. 339–427 (Hebrew), 58*-70* (English summaries).

7. D. Weiss, B. Zissu and G. Solimany, *Map of Nes Harim* (Archaeological Survey of Israel; Jerusalem: Israel Antiquities Authority, 2004).

8. A. Kloner, *Survey of Jerusalem: The Southern Sector* (Archaeological Survey of Israel; Jerusalem: Israel Antiquities Authority, 2000); idem, *Survey of Jerusalem: The Northeastern Sector* (Archaeological Survey of Israel; Jerusalem: Israel Antiquities Authority, 2001); idem, *Survey of Jerusalem: The Northwestern Sector, Introduction and Indices* (Archaeological Survey of Israel; Jerusalem: Israel Antiquities Authority, 2003).

9. A. Ofer, 'The Highlands of Judah during the Biblical Period' (unpublished Ph.D. dissertation, Tel-Aviv University, 1993) (Hebrew). Note that according to I. Finkelstein, 'The Archaeology of the Days of Manasseh', in M.D. Coogan, J.C. Exum and L.E. Stager (eds), *Scripture and Other Artifacts: Essays on the Bible and Archaeology in Honor of Philip J. King* (Louisville: Westminster John Knox Press, 1994), pp. 169–87 (174–5), Ofer underestimated the number of 7th century settlements due to methodological problems (see also below).

10. Y. Dagan, 'The Settlement in the Judean Shephela in the Second and First Millennium BCE: A Test-Case of Settlement Processes in a Geographic Region' (unpublished Ph.D. dissertation, Tel Aviv University, 2000). The figures relate only to settlements (or buildings) of various sorts. In his summaries, Dagan differentiated between sites and other find spots (cemeteries, agricultural activities etc.) and we followed suit. The Iron Age figure relates to the 7th century. Note that according to some, Dagan underestimated (due to methodological problems) the number of sites from this period (Ofer, 'The Highlands of Judah during the Biblical Period', 2: 153 and see more below). Should this criticism be true the late Iron Age figure should be even higher. It should be noted that the inclusion of 'find spots' might have changed the data from this region significantly.

11. I. Beit Arieh, *Map of Tell Malhata*, (Archaeological Survey of Israel; Jerusalem: Israel Antiquities Authority, 2003); Y. Govrin, *Map of Nahal Yatir* (Archaeological Survey of Israel; Jerusalem: Israel Antiquities Authority, 1992).

12. Y. Hirschfeld, *Map of Herodium* (Archaeological Survey of Israel; Jerusalem: Israel Antiquities Authority, 1985).

13. J. Patrich, *Map of Deir Mar Saba* (Archaeological Survey of Israel; Jerusalem: Israel Antiquities Authority, 1994).

14. Note that there were 16 sites that were identified only as 'Iron Age'. Since most identified Iron Age sites were dated to the Iron Age III, it is likely that most of these 16 should be added to the Iron III, hence increasing the number of settlements in this period even further.

15. Note that the figure relates also to groups of sites, and the real figure was much larger (Kloner, *Survey of Jerusalem: The Northeastern Sector*, 92).

16. Note that the figure 110 refers to the late Hellenistic/Hasmonean period, which seems to have been the peak in this region (Kloner, *Survey of Jerusalem: The Northwestern Sector, Introduction and Indices*, 26), as well as others (such as: Finkelstein, 'Northern Part of the Maps of Beit Sira, Ramallah and el-Bireh', 27). From the early Hellenistic period only 37 sites were reported. It should be noted that there were many additional remains that were reported as 'Second Temple' period only (49), and it is likely that a few of these belonged to the Hellenistic/Hasmonean period.

17. While in the summary it appears that at the Map of Tel Malhata there was only 1 site with Hellenistic finds, the text indicates the existence of another one (Beit Arieh, *Map of Tell Malhata*, 12*-13*).

same is true regarding studies of the Second Temple period. These have usually begun with the Hellenistic period, and even when the Persian period was examined, hardly any study compared it with the late Iron Age. We believe that the fact that the Persian period is usually not embedded within studies of long-term processes has seriously hampered the study of this period. Only when the study of the Persian period is embedded within a larger framework of archaeological data, will we truly be able to assess its nature and the demographic and settlement reality of the time.

In the following sections, therefore, we will examine settlement dynamics and demographic fluctuations from the late Iron Age through the Hellenistic period. This will be followed by an analysis of these changes and, later, by a discussion of the implications of this analysis on our understanding of the nature of the Persian period.

Settlement Dynamics

In the present section, we will examine the available information regarding settlement in the late Iron Age, the Persian and the Hellenistic periods (when possible, we will differentiate between the early Hellenistic and the Hasmonean periods).[18]

Our knowledge of settlement dynamics derives from several related sources of archaeological information. We will begin by analysing the vast database created by the gradual publication of the many surveys that have been conducted over the years.

Surveys

Notably, the regions discussed here were extensively surveyed. While the data from surveys is, in many respects, far from conclusive,[19] the patterns that are observed are, in the present case, quite straightforward (note that the patterns are confirmed by the use of 'stronger' types of data, see below).

Table 1 represents the results of the surveys of the area of Judah that have been published to date.[20] While some statistical differences can be observed

---

18. The 'contested' 6th century will not be discussed in the present section. It will, however, receive a short treatment below.

19. For a discussion of the use of survey data see A. Faust and Z. Safrai, 'Salvage Excavations as a Source for Reconstructing Settlement History in Ancient Israel', *PEQ* 132 (2005), pp. 139–58.

20. Note that we used the data, even rough data, presented by the surveyors, and did not re-analyse it. This means that in a few cases the figures include also tombs, etc. Admittedly, using all the reported 'sites' is a problematic procedure, but it resulted from the data available. It should be stressed that in most cases the **trends** would not be affected, therefore permitting the usage of the data. It is likely that the Hellenistic period is somewhat over-represented due to the large number of tombs from this period. Still, as we will see below, this

within the various sub-regions, the pattern of settlement dynamics is quite clear. The late Iron Age II, a settlement peak by all standards, is followed by a decline, in many cases even sharp decline, in the Persian period, followed by a significant recovery in the Hellenistic period.[21]

Despite some regional variations that need to be analysed, the trends are quite clear. A peak in the late Iron Age (586 sites) is followed by a decline in the Persian period (216 sites), and then by a recovery in the Hellenistic period (510 sites).[22]

Notably, the data from the regions of Judea which are closer to the coast shows a different pattern. A comparison with the area of Modiin-Shoham, which was outside the borders of Persian-period *Yehud*, is most revealing. Here, the surveys gave the following results:

Table 2
Settlement in the Modiin-Shoham Region during the Iron Age, Persian and Hellenistic Periods according to the surveys

	Beit Sira (Hizmi; Finkelstein)[23]	Lod (Kochavi and Beit-Arieh)[24]	Rosh Ha'ayin (Gophna and Beit Arieh)[25]	Summary
IA	5	46	34	85
PP	13	28	37	78
H	28	19	26	73
Summary of trend	Gradual increase	Gradual decline	Peak in the PP	Very modest gradual decline

period (just like the Iron Age) is under-represented due to other factors, so this should compensate for the former factor. The relative accuracy of the trends can be seen in the case of the Benjamin region, in which the 'rough data' was analysed by Carter (see note below). At any event, in most regions the surveyors made the distinction and offered listings of settlements only.

21. Most studies do not report finds from the Neo-Babylonian period; the few that do, identified very little activity at the time (see more below).

22. Our information on the marginal areas of the Negev and the desert are more partial than those of other regions. Since scholars from all schools seem to agree today that these areas suffered devastation in the early 6th century (see even Lipschits, 'Demographic Changes in Judah', 338–41; idem, *The Fall and Rise of Jerusalem*, 224–37), it appears that if data from these regions were more complete, the overall picture of the decline in the Persian period would have been even greater (though the importance of settlements in these regions was somewhat limited).

23. H. Hizmi, 'Southern Part of the Map of Beit Sira', in I. Finkelstein and Y. Magen (eds), *Archaeological Survey of the Hill Country of Benjamin* (Jerusalem: Israel Antiquities Authority, 1993), pp. 97–131 (Hebrew), 23*-28* (English summaries); Finkelstein, 'Northern Part of the Maps of Beit Sira, Ramallah and el-Bireh'.

24. M. Kochavi and I. Beit-Arieh, *Map of Rosh Ha-'Ayin* (Archaeological Survey of Israel; Jerusalem: Israel Antiquities Authority, 1994).

25. R. Gophna and I. Beit-Arieh, *Map of Lod* (Archaeological Survey of Israel; Jerusalem: Israel Antiquities Authority, 1997).

Clearly, the trends within this region are by no means identical, but none of these surveys resembles the picture from Judah, in which there is always a decline followed by recovery. Clearly, these regions behave differently and were influenced by different processes (notably, the more reliable data from the salvage excavations is more similar to that from the Beit Sira map, see more below).

A Note on Chronology: The Iron Age data presented above is representative mainly of the seventh century. While many surveys do not differentiate between the various sub-periods within Iron Age II and the data may be seen as representing the eighth century, which is usually regarded as the settlement peak in the Land of Israel,[26] this is NOT the case here: Dagan and Ofer, who were responsible for surveying the larger part of the region, did make the distinction (perhaps even underestimating the seventh century BCE),[27] and the same is true for the Nes Harim map.[28] As far as the Jerusalem area is concerned, the seventh century, and not the eighth, seems to have been the peak of settlement in the region,[29] and the same is true for the Negev and the Judean desert.[30] Regarding the Benjamin area, in some cases the surveyors explicitly claimed that the data represent the last phase of the Iron Age.[31] It is clear, therefore, that the overall picture is that of the end of the Iron Age.

A similar problem exists regarding the Persian and Hellenistic periods, since the finds are usually not subdivided into sub-periods. The 200-year-long Persian period will receive more attention below. Regarding the Hellenistic period, it should be noted that some surveyors have commented on the matter, and either stated that the peak was at its later stage,[32] or even did the sub-division themselves, with similar

26. See, for example, M. Broshi and I. Finkelstein, 'The Population of Palestine in the Iron Age II', *BASOR* 287 (1992), pp. 47–60.

27. Dagan, 'The Settlement in the Judean Shephela in the Second and First Millennium BCE'; Ofer, 'The Highlands of Judah during the Biblical Period'. Several scholars have even claimed that the 7th century settlement was underestimated in these surveys because it was identified on the basis of a few types of pottery which are easily overlooked; in the absence of these finds, the 8th–7th century assemblage was regarded as reflecting only the 8th century. Finkelstein ('The Archaeology of the Days of Manasseh', 174–5) had raised this claim regarding the survey of the Judean hill-country, and Ofer ('The Highlands of Judah during the Biblical Period', 3: 153) raised a similar claim regarding the survey in the Shephelah.

28. Weiss, Zissu and Solimany, *Map of Nes Harim*.

29. A. Faust, 'The Settlement on Jerusalem's Western Hill and the City's Status in the Iron Age II Revisited', *ZDPV* 121 (2005), pp. 97–118; idem, 'Jerusalem's Hinterland and the City's Status in the Bronze and Iron Ages', *Eretz Israel* 28 (Kolek volume – in press).

30. Finkelstein, 'The Archaeology of the Days of Manasseh'.

31. Finkelstein, 'Northern Part of the Maps of Beit Sira, Ramallah and el-Bireh', 27.

32. So Finkelstein, 'Northern Part of the Maps of Beit Sira, Ramallah and el-Bireh', 27.

results.[33] It appears that the peak of settlement in the Hellenistic period was indeed toward its end.

Before the data from the various surveys can be properly studied, it would be worthwhile to analyse the data from excavations.

Excavations

A methodical examination of excavation data should distinguish between the two main types of excavations: planned excavations, mainly of large sites; and salvage excavations, usually of smaller settlements.

Planned excavations: These were not examined statistically, but the dearth of Persian-period remains in Judah (with the exception of the Benjamin region[34]) is a well-known phenomenon that is recognized even today.[35] The lack of substantial finds from Judah in the Persian period had prevented scholars from discussing various archaeological details, such as town planning.[36] The dearth of finds has also given rise to various explanations, such as that the houses in this period were built outside existing settlements, that the Persian-period strata were destroyed by later activities and that the *tell*s housed only palaces.[37] These suggestions, however, even if they can account for part of the problem, are clearly insufficient to explain the phenomenon.[38] The fact is that the dramatic decrease in remains is much more significant in the highlands,[39] while the

33.   Such as Kloner, *Survey of Jerusalem: The Northwestern Sector, Introduction and Indices*, 26.

34.   See, for example E. Stern, 'The Material Culture and Economic Life in the Land of Israel in the Persian Period', in H. Tadmor (ed.), *The Restoration – the Persian Period* (World History of the Jewish People; Jerusalem: 'Am 'Oved, 1983), pp. 117–38 (120) (Hebrew) and see below.

35.   Carter, *The Emergence of Yehud in the Persian Period*; Stern, 'The Material Culture and Economic Life in the Land of Israel in the Persian Period', 119–20; idem, 'Cities: Cities of the Persian Period', in E. M. Meyers (ed.), *Oxford Encyclopedia of Archaeology in the Near East* 2 (New York: Oxford University Press, 1997), pp. 25–9 (25); idem, *Archaeology of the Land of the Bible, vol. 2: The Assyrian, Babylonian and Persian Periods*, (New York: Doubleday, 2001), pp. 461–2; O. Lipschits, 'The Policy of the Persian Empire and the Meager Architectonic Finds in the Province of Yehud', in A. Faust and E. Baruch (eds), *New Studies on Jerusalem, Proceedings of the 7th Conference* (Ramat Gan: Bar Ilan University, 2001), pp. 45–76 (Hebrew).

36.   Such as in Stern, 'Cities: Cities of the Persian Period', 25; idem, *Archaeology of the Land of the Bible*, 461–2.

37.   Such as Stern, 'The Material Culture and Economic Life in the Land of Israel in the Persian Period'; idem, *Archaeology of the Land of the Bible*, 461–2; Lipschits, 'The Policy of the Persian Empire'.

38.   As already observed by Stern, 'The Material Culture and Economic Life in the Land of Israel in the Persian Period', 120.

39.   Lipschits, 'The Policy of the Persian Empire', 46–7; Stern, *Archaeology of the Land of the Bible*, 462, 466.

finds from the very same period in the coastal plain are numerous. This seems to disprove the above-mentioned suggestions, since they should have accounted for both highland and lowland sites to the same degree. Clearly, the finds attest to a much higher degree of human activity in the coastal plain. In addition, much of our knowledge today is based on data from the many salvage excavations (below), and those were conducted mostly outside the main *tell*s.[40] Lipschits has recently suggested that the dearth of architectural finds should be attributed to Persian imperial policy which, in the highlands, allowed only settlement in villages.[41] Such a policy, however, is not attested anywhere, and only the scant remains in the highlands lead Lipschits to suggest it. Furthermore, even if the Persian Empire did have a policy that prevented the establishment of cities in Judah, there would have been remains of houses in rural settlements. The relative lack of building remains (even in villages, as discovered in salvage excavations, see below) cannot, therefore, be fully attributed to any of the above.

The simplest explanation for the phenomenon is that there was relatively little settlement in Judah, and the remains that we find attest to the reality of the time. It seems, therefore, that the dearth of finds simply reflects the dearth of settlements, and while some of the above explanations might 'increase' the 'statistical' significance of the Persian-period settlements that have been found, what we see is still a phenomenon which resulted from the fact that settlements, and especially large settlements which are best reflected in planned excavations, were sparse during the period under discussion.

In summary: despite the lack of statistical data, the decline in the Persian period is well attested in the planned excavations.

Salvage Excavations: Salvage excavations are usually carried out before construction, mainly at small sites. As of yet, well over 3000 such excavations have been carried out in Israel, but until recently no systematic attempt at using this large database has been conducted. Over the last couple of years Zeev Safrai and myself have been carrying out a systematic study of all **published** data from these excavations.[42] The data from salvage excavations is detailed enough to enable us to learn of settlement patterns and dynamics. When examining the number of salvage excavations from greater Judea, with the exception of the Modiin-Shoham region, we have 30 excavations in the database which reported finds from

---

40. Faust and Safrai, 'Salvage Excavations as a Source for Reconstructing Settlement History in Ancient Israel', and see below.

41. Lipschits, 'The Policy of the Persian Empire and the Meager Architectonic Finds'.

42. Faust and Safrai, 'Salvage Excavations as a Source for Reconstructing Settlement History in Ancient Israel'.

the Iron Age II (including what was defined as both architectural remains and pottery finds).[43] Only 17 excavations reported finds from the Persian period and 36 had relevant finds from the Hellenistic period.[44] The data from the salvage excavations' database, like that of the surveys, shows a significant decline after the Iron Age and recovery in the Hellenistic period.

Interestingly, the data from the Modiin-Shoham region is completely different. Here, the number of settled sites increases from the Iron Age (8), through the Persian period (14) to the Hellenistic period (29), showing a completely different pattern. Furthermore, when examining the relative importance of the region during the various periods (including all types of finds, from the whole of Judea), the following picture emerges: during the Iron Age the relative importance of the region of Judea was almost 27% (i.e., almost 27% of all the excavations in which finds from this period were uncovered, were conducted in the area that was defined as greater Judea), during the Persian period it was about 16%, and during the Hellenistic period it was about 25%. One should note that since all of Judea is included in these statistics, there is a certain bias toward the Persian period, as the statistics include the region of Modiin-Shoham. This even strengthened the importance of the statistics and the decline in the Persian period in comparison to both periods is highlighted.

The salvage excavations' data clearly shows a decline in the Persian period and recovery in the Hellenistic period, both in the number of sites and of relative importance of the region.

A Note on Regional Variation

As we have seen, all regions in Judea proper (not including the Modiin-Shoham region) reported a decline followed by a recovery. Still, differences between the regions can be observed. Ofer, for example, reported that in northern Judah (north of Beth-Zur) there were only minor changes in the transition to the Persian period (and even increase in settlement during this period).[45] We shall return to the significance of this data later, but this should not obliterate the importance of the general

43. Note that in reality there were probably more Iron Age sites II excavated; several sites were reported as IAIIc, and others were reported as Iron Age with no subdivision. We did not count these because we preferred to err on the side of caution.

44. Note that this has nothing to do with the question of settlement continuity, which should be examined on a site by site basis (see A. Faust, 'Abandonment, Urbanization, Resettlement and the Formation of the Israelite State', *NEA* 66 (2003), pp. 147–61; idem, 'Judah in the Sixth Century BCE: A Rural Perspective', *PEQ* 135 (2003), pp. 37–53; Faust and Safrai 'Salvage Excavations as a Source for Reconstructing Settlement History in Ancient Israel'. On this, see below.

45. Ofer, 'The Highlands of Judah during the Biblical Period', 2: 132.

pattern – even if not in all of Judah, settlement in the Persian period was much weaker than that of both the Iron Age and the Hellenistic period.

Another issue that requires clarification is the discrepancy between the survey results and the data gained from excavations in the Benjamin region. The survey, as we have seen, reported a great decline,[46] while excavations reported continuity for some time after the fall 'of Jerusalem.[47] Lipschits attempted to correct the surveys to match the data from the excavations,[48] but one should remember that it is possible that the major centres (i.e., the sites that were excavated in planned excavations) 'behaved' differently than the rural sites which are reported in the surveys. Notably, the data from salvage excavations in the region[49] is in accordance with the data from surveys, further supporting this suggestion. A discrepancy between the history of rural and urban sites should not be a surprise; rather, it is to be expected.[50] The issue will be developed below.

Settlement Dynamics: A Summary

The late Iron Age was a period of relative prosperity as far as settlement is concerned. Some 586 sites from this period were reported in the surveys. During the Persian period, the number of sites decreased dramatically. At the peak of the Persian period the number of sites was 216, about 35% of that of the late Iron Age. Furthermore, the settlements of the Persian period were relatively small and rural in nature. Large and dense settlements are hardly in existence in Persian-period Judea – Jerusalem being the only 'real' centre, and even it was quite small (see more below).[51] Later, settlement intensity rose once again, reaching 510 sites during the height of the Hellenistic period, and it appears as if settlement then was close to that of the Iron Age. As far as settlement dynamics are concerned, the Persian period was clearly overshadowed by the Iron Age and the Hellenistic period. Notably, the figures regarding the Persian period

---

46. See also Y. Magen, 'The Land of Benjamin in the Second Temple Period', in Y. Magen, D. T. Ariel, G. Bijovsky, Y. Tzionit and O. Sirkis (eds), *The Land of Benjamin* (Jerusalem: Staff Officer of Archaeology – Civil Administration of Judea and Samaria, Israel Antiquities Authority, 2004), p. 5.

47. See, for example, A. Malamat, 'The Last Wars of the Kingdom of Judah', *JNES* 9 (1950), pp. 218–27; Stern, 'The Material Culture and Economic Life in the Land of Israel in the Persian Period', 120; idem, *Archaeology of the Land of the Bible*, 321–3.

48. Lipschits, *The Fall and Rise of Jerusalem*, 245–8.

49. Such as the relevant sites in Faust, 'Judah in the Sixth Century BCE: A Rural Perspective', *PEQ* 135 (2003), pp. 37–53.

50. See for instance Faust, 'Abandonment, Urbanization, Resettlement and the Formation of the Israelite State', regarding the early Iron Age II.

51. In addition, it is doubtful that all of the Persian period sites coexisted even during the height of this period.

represent the peak of settlement, and during most of the period the number of settlements was significantly lower (see more below).

Before examining the significance of these trends, we would also like to discuss demographic trends during these periods.

Demographic Trends

Many studies have attempted to determine the population of ancient Israel in various periods.[52] Counting ancient populations, however, is a dangerous endeavour. Even calculating the number of inhabitants of a single site is a tricky business, which may give results with a margin of some 400%;[53] to study an entire region, where the unknown variables are numerous, is almost impossible. What can be learnt, and even this very carefully, is demographic trends – even if the actual figures are quite meaningless. In this light, while the following discussion will quote the figures given by the various scholars, we should concentrate on the trends (although even the trends are not accurate as far as exact percentage goes, this is the best tool we have).

There have been several demographic studies that have dealt with Judea in the Persian period. Carter, in his detailed study of Persian *Yehud*, concluded that the population of the province in the Persian I period was 13,350 people, and that it grew to some 20,650 in the Persian II period.[54] The Meyers' reached similar conclusions (10,850 people in the Persian I), estimating that this was about one-third of the population in the late Iron Age (based to a large extent on their interpretation of literary sources; note that their estimation of the Iron Age is also not founded on firm archaeological data).[55] Carter estimated the Iron Age population in the areas that later encompassed Persian *Yehud* as some 60,000–68,500 people (based on previous studies), concluding that the Persian-period II population at its peak was about one third of these figures (settlement in the Persian I period was, accordingly, about one-fifth of that of the Iron

52. Such as M. Broshi, 'The Population of Western Palestine in the Roman-Byzantine Period', *BASOR* 236 (1979), pp. 1–10; Broshi and Finkelstein, 'The Population of Palestine in the Iron Age II'; M. Broshi and R. Gophna, 'The Settlements and Population of Palestine During the Early Bronze Age II-III', *BASOR* 253 (1984), pp. 41–53; M. Broshi and R. Gophna, 'Middle Bronze Age II Palestine: Its Settlement and Population', *BASOR* 261 (1986), pp. 73–90.

53. N. Postgate, 'How Many Sumerians per Hectare? – Probing the Anatomy of an Early City', *Cambridge Archaeological Journal* 4 (1994), pp. 47–65; Faust, 'The Settlement on Jerusalem's Western Hill'.

54. Carter, *The Emergence of Yehud in the Persian Period*, 201–2.

55. C. L. and E. M. Meyers, 'Demography and Diatribes: Yehud's Population and the Prophecy of Second Zechariah', in M. D. Coogan, J. C. Exum and L. E. Stager (eds), *Scripture and Other Artifacts* (Louisville: Westminster John Knox, 1994), pp. 268–85 (282).

Age).[56] Notably, Carter examined only those areas that were part of the
Persian province of *Yehud*, therefore excluding the Shephelah, the desert
etc. from his calculations. Clearly, were these regions (that all scholars
agree were devastated at the end of the Iron Age) to be included, the
demographic decrease would be much larger! While comparing only the
limited area of the Persian province of *Yehud* is of course legitimate (this
was, after all, the focus of Carter's study), anyone who is interested in the
demographic processes that occurred in Judea from the Late Iron Age to
the Hellenistic period should examine the processes in the entire territory.
In the end, when examining demographic changes from the Iron Age
onward, the fate of the entire population of Judah is of importance, and
all of the territories that had been part of late Iron Age Judah should be
investigated. As such, Carter's figures only underestimate the Persian-
period decline.

The most detailed attempt to calculate the population of Iron Age and
Persian-period Judah was undertaken by Lipschits. His conclusion was
that the population of Judah in the seventh century BCE was 108,000, and
that of the Persian period was 30,125 (about 28% of the former).[57]

Before proceeding, it should be noted that Lipschits' demographic
study is fraught with problems which necessitate various corrections. For
example, he examined different areas for the two periods – his calculations
for the Iron Age were based on the area of the entire kingdom of Judah,
while his estimation for the Persian period included only the much smaller
area of the province of *Yehud*. Such a comparison is misleading, and the
population figures for the Persian period should be **increased** (see below
for corrections, based on his own data). His figures, on the other hand, err
in favour of the Persian period: 1) A number of Iron Age sites were not
taken into account, decreasing the relative importance of the period. For
example, Lipschits correctly regarded the city of Jerusalem as a large
metropolis of about 1000 dunams,[58] but failed to take into account its
significant hinterland, which included large towns and centres such as
Moza (over 100 dunams),[59] el-Burj (some 40 dunams)[60] and others, as

56. Carter, *The Emergence of Yehud in the Persian Period*, 246–7.

57. Lipschits, *The Fall and Rise of Jerusalem*, 270. See also Lipschits, 'Demographic
Changes in Judah'.

58. Lipschits, 'Demographic Changes in Judah', 361–2, 363, following G. Barkay,
'Jerusalem as a Primate City', in S. Bunimovitz, M. Kochavi and A. Kasher (eds), *Settlement,
Population and Economy in the Land of Israel* (Tel-Aviv: Tel Aviv University, 1989), pp. 124–
5 (Hebrew).

59. A. De Groot and Z. Greenhut, 'Iron Age II Settlements Around Jerusalem', in *The
Twentieth Archaeological Conference in Israel (abstracts)*, (Jerusalem: Yad Ben Zvi, 1994),
pp. 20–1; Note that Greenhut now estimates the size as only 15–20 dunams (personal
communication).

60. De Groot and Greenhut, 'Iron Age II Settlements Around Jerusalem'.

well as **hundreds** of farmsteads.[61] The demographic reality in the Iron Age was thus underestimated. 2) On the other hand, Lipschits' calculations for the Persian period are exaggerated, since he failed to take into account the fact that most of the sites of this period are very small and rural in nature, making it impossible to calculate their population density according to 'typical' coefficients (a fact that Lipschits acknowledges).[62] Farmsteads, or small hamlets, which apparently compose an important part of the Persian-period small sites, house a limited number of people (about 8–15 people for farmsteads, and a few dozens for hamlets), even if the remains are scattered across 3 dunams.[63] 3) Furthermore, the Persian period is much longer then the seventh century, to which Lipschits compares the data.[64] It is therefore likely that not all the sites existed contemporaneously, hence reducing the figure even further. The contrast between the treatment of the Iron Age, when many sites are not taken into account, to that of the Persian period, which exaggerates the population, exemplifies the problems with the figures presented by Lipschits. The actual demographic decrease in the Persian period in comparison with the Iron Age was therefore much larger than that shown by Lipschits' figures.

Iron Age and Persian-Period Demography

Carter estimated the population of *Yehud* during the height of the Persian-period as being one third that of the Iron Age. Lipschits' figures were less than 28%, but since he compared the small Persian *Yehud* to the larger Iron Age Judah, clearly the relative importance of the Persian period should be enlarged. Based on Lipschits' own figures[65] we should add 8,375 people, so the relative importance of the Persian period should be about 35%. While both estimations err toward the Persian period, we would still

---

61.   See A. Kloner, 'Jerusalem's Environs in the Persian Period', in A. Faust and E. Baruch (eds), *New Studies on Jerusalem: Proceedings of the Seventh Conference* (Ramat Gan: Bar-Ilan University, 2001), pp. 83–9 (Hebrew). Notably, Lipschits, 'Demographic Changes in Judah', 361–2, states that 90% of the settled area in Jerusalem environments was within the city-walls, making it clear that he did not calculate the many settlements in the city's vicinity.

62.   Such as in Lipschits, *The Fall and Rise of Jerusalem*, 261.

63.   See also Carter, *The Emergence of Yehud in the Persian Period*, 215, 249. While the majority of settlements during the Iron Age and the Hellenistic period were also rural in nature, during these periods there were also many large and more crowded settlements. The difference should have been taken into account.

64.   Notably, even the data from the area around Jerusalem mainly reflects the late Iron Age, not the entire Iron Age II (*contra* Lipschits, *The Fall and Rise of Jerusalem*, 215, n. 118). On this, see Kloner, *Survey of Jerusalem: The Northwestern Sector, Introduction and Indices*, 20; Finkelstein, 'The Archaeology of the Days of Manasseh', 174; Faust, 'The Settlement on Jerusalem's Western Hill'.

65.   Lipschits, 'Demographic Changes in Judah', 356–64, Tables 1–3.

use these figures, in order to err on the side of caution. In any case, the implications are significant.

Clearly, when some two-thirds of the population simply 'disappears', one must realize that this represents not only a major and almost unparalleled demographic collapse, but also a social and cultural one.[66]

Furthermore, viewing these figures as comprising a simple decrease to a third of the population is simply wrong! The decline was much more significant than can be seen at first glance. Which brings us to the next issue.[67]

Methodology: Analysing the Trends

The observation that the population of the Persian period was about one-third of that of the late Iron Age is somewhat misleading, with important implications for the study of the Persian period. Our aim is to show that the simple analysis of the data is wrong, and the decrease from the Iron Age to the Persian period was much larger than 66% (in the following we will use the 'one-third estimation' of Judah's Persian-period population in relation to the Iron Age as our point of departure, despite the reservations raised).[68]

A Note on Dates

The dates in the following discussion are also basically taken from Lipschits who referred to the seventh century BCE as representing the late Iron Age – this will be our point of departure. Lipschits also claimed that the peak of the Persian period was during the fifth century.[69] The date for the Hellenistic period was arbitrarily chosen, as it was not discussed by Lipschits. Notably, the dates are not necessarily accurate (as we will see below, they are not), and are given as a general guide only. More detailed

---

66. A. Faust, 'Social and Cultural Changes in Judah during the 6th Century BCE and their Implications for our Understanding of the Nature of the Neo-Babylonian Period', *UF* 36 (2004), pp. 157–76; *contra* H. M. Barstad, *The Myth of the Empty Land* (Oslo: Scandinavian University Press, 1996); Lipschits, 'Demographic Changes in Judah'.

67. The demographic reality of the Hellenistic period did not receive much attention by the above-cited scholars. The following discussion on settlement and demographic dynamics will be based on the trends observed in the number and size of settlements, and not on a new reconstruction of the period's demography. In order to err on the side of caution, we prefer to stick to existing figures, even though we have proved them to be biased. At any event, as already stated, we do not trust the figures – only the trends.

68. The following discussion will concentrate on demography, although from time to time we will refer also to settlement changes. The trends in both are similar, and this makes the interchange in terminology legitimate. Theoretically, of course, demography and settlement can behave in a different manner, but this does not seem to be the case here.

69. Lipschits, *The Fall and Rise of Jerusalem*, 166, 259.

chronology will be discussed later. Since the purpose of the present section is methodological, the exact dates are of no importance.

Discussion

We have seen that according to Lipschits and Carter the Persian period had a population of about 33–35% of that of the Iron Age. Assuming that the demography of the Hellenistic period was somewhat similar to that of the later Iron Age (based on the data from settlement dynamics, above, this seems to be the case; the demography of the Hellenistic period has not yet been studied), then their demographic trends are apparently represented in the following graph:

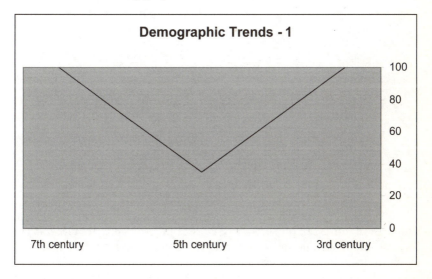

The graph represents a population decrease to 35% in the Persian period, a major decline by any standards.[70]

This graph, however, is false. We should be aware of the fact that each of the 3 'dots' on the graph represents the **peak** of the relevant periods. While important for all three periods (below), this has grave consequences especially for our understanding of the demography of the Persian period.

---

70.   That this line of thinking governed some past reconstructions is apparent in Lipschits' work. He explicitly claimed that the finds from the Persian period in Benjamin represent the nadir of settlement in the period, rather than its peak! In his own words: '. . . the finds of the Persian period discovered in the survey reflect this low point, rather than a peak in settlement activity or a stage of rebuilding' ('Demographic Changes in Judah', 349; see also: *The Fall and Rise of Jerusalem*, 246). This is of course impossible. The Persian-period finds represent the period's peak, whenever one proposes to date that peak (in fact, if not all of the sites were contemporaneous, then the peak was even lower than that).

In the above graph, the 35% represents the nadir of the Persian period while, in reality, it should represent the peak of that period. The vast majority of the Persian period should actually be **below** this point (the degree the figures go below this point is a mere estimation, and the figures used in the graphs might be far from accurate. See more below.).

Should the peak of the Persian period be during the fifth century (as argued by Lipschits), the following graph would more accurately represent the settlement trends of the periods discussed here:

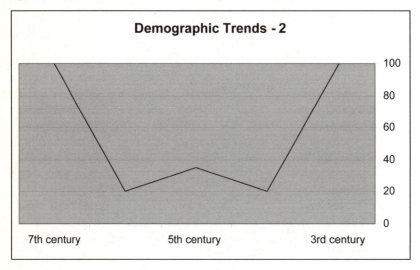

The exact nadir is of course, a mere guess, but the trends are clear. If the peak of the Persian period was during the fifth century, then the decrease after the Iron Age was much more significant than to 35% (of the Iron Age settlement) as this figure refers to the peak of the Persian period. This peak came only after a nadir, and it was followed by another nadir. Only then did the demographic growth toward the Hellenistic period begin.

There are, however, several problems with this reconstruction. We usually assume that demographic trends are relatively long-term processes (unless we have evidence for the contrary). While various events can have great impacts on demographic trends, we generally tend not to 'invent' such episodes. We shall return to this later, but we may assume that the trend was more gradual than the above graph, which has too many unexplained ups and downs, seems to exhibit.[71]

71. Naturally, it is clear that there were demographic/settlement fluctuations within the Persian period. These, however, were probably on a relatively small scale when compared to the processes discussed here, and do not negate the overall pattern of decline and recovery. It is therefore likely that the peak of the Persian period was part of such long-term processes, and not part of small-scale fluctuations.

In this case we are faced with two theoretical possibilities. The settlement peak could have been either at the beginning of the Persian period, or toward its end. A graph that follows the first possibility, locating the 35% peak at the first stage of the period, would look something like the following:

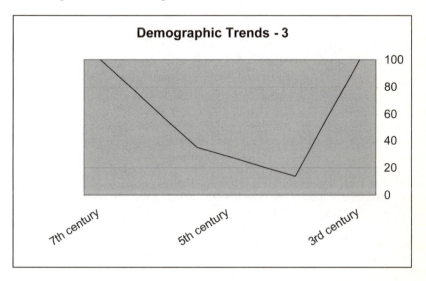

Indeed, the graph seems more logical than the previous one in terms of long-term processes. If this graph is correct, then we witness a major decline (to 35%) in the transition from the Iron Age to the Persian period. The decline continues through most of the Persian period, although the rate of the decline decreases (assuming the same rate of decline would leave the end of the Persian period with hardly any population at all). The increase in population starts at some point towards the end of the period, reaching its peak during the Hellenistic period.

A second possible graph is one which shows a demographic peak towards the end of the Persian period. Such a demographic reality is represented in the graph overleaf,

This graph represents a **relatively gradual** decline from the end of the Iron Age into the Persian period (and not a sharp decline in the early sixth century – the decline presented in the above graph is quite sharp of course, but as we will see below, in reality decline was even sharper). This decline was followed by a gradual increase in settlement until the end of the Persian period. Settlement/demography continued to intensify into the Hellenistic period.

As mentioned earlier, both graphs 3 and 4 seem to be more reasonable than graph no. 2, but is there a way to choose between them?

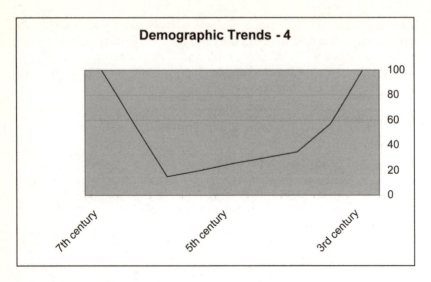

Demographic Trends - 4

When examined within the historical background of the period, it is obvious that there is a big advantage to the fourth graph. We don't know of any reason for a huge demographic decline throughout the Persian period, let alone toward the Hellenistic period. On the contrary: we do know of a crisis at the beginning of the period, in the sixth century BCE. The Babylonian conquests of the region brought about settlement instability and demographic decline that is acknowledged even by scholars such as Barstad and Lipschits. Although these scholars greatly under-estimate the importance of the demographic changes, they still acknow-ledge them. We have therefore both positive and negative evidence that support a decline in the beginning of the Persian period and a gradual recovery during this period (and not *vice-versa*). In this light, it is clear that it is the fourth graph that best represents the trends. Indeed, this was the view of such scholars as Carter, Stern, Kloner, Berlin, the Meyers' and others.[72]

In this case, however, there is a little adjustment that needs to be made.

---

72. Carter, *The Emergence of Yehud in the Persian Period*; Stern, *Archaeology of the Land of the Bible*, 581; Kloner, *Survey of Jerusalem: The Northwestern Sector, Introduction and Indices*, 25–6; A. Berlin, 'Between Large Forces: Palestine in the Hellenistic Period', *BA* 60 (1997), pp. 2–51; Meyers and Meyers, 'Demography and Diatribes: Yehud's Population and the Prophecy of Second Zechariah'. All these in contrast to Lipschits. The latter, moreover, presented contrasting estimations regarding the trends during the Persian period, in some places suggesting that the 5th century was the peak of the Persian period, but in others writing that the decrease from the Iron Age to the Persian period was gradual and hence (though he did not realize it) placing the peak at the period's first day. Clearly, both his (contrasting) estimations are wrong. See also B. Oded and A. Faust, 'The Land of Judah in the Neo-Babylonian Period – A Review Article', *Cathedra* 121 (2006), pp. 171–8 (Hebrew).

Since the Babylonian conquests were, directly or indirectly, the reason behind the decline, we need not make the decline gradual, covering the entire sixth and early fifth centuries. The following graph is therefore more suitable:

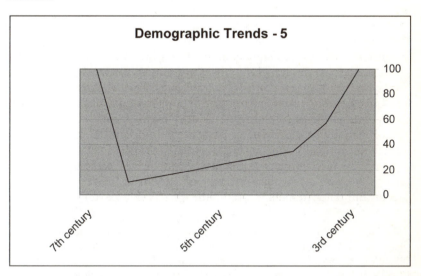

Demographic Trends - 5

Clearly, in light of the fact that previous studies have underestimated the Iron Age settlement and overestimated that of the Persian period, it is possible that the decline was even more severe, but since any reference to real figures is a mere estimation, we believe that the above graph is useful as it is. We should just bear in mind that it is possible that the decline toward the beginning of the Persian period (i.e., in the sixth century BCE) was even stronger.

Demographic Trends: A Summary

The demographic studies by Carter and Lipschits err in favour of the Persian period. Still, even they indicate that during the peak of this period, probably toward its end, the population was only about one-third of that of the late Iron Age. Regarding the earlier phases of the period it appears as if one has to accept Carter's estimation that the population was only about 20% of what it had been during the previous period. These estimations allow us to appreciate the crisis that occurred at the end of the Iron Age – after all, after a few generations of recovery the population reached some 20%, and after 250 years it reached only some 33–35%.

The significance of these figures will be discussed below, but in the meantime we should add a few words on the transition from the Iron Age to the Persian period, or in other words, on the Neo-Babylonian period.

A Note on the Debate over the Sixth Century BCE

The above analysis has clear implications for the debate on the demographic reality of the sixth century BCE. While the majority of scholars view it as a period of great decline,[73] a number of biblical scholars and theologians have come to believe that not much had changed following the Babylonian conquest and the destruction of Jerusalem, and that most of the population was unaffected. Life for most Judahites, according to this view, simply continued as usual.[74] The figures presented above, even those given by Lipschits, show that the decline had to be great – much more than (consciously) acknowledged by scholars like Barstad and Lipschits. They erred partially because they assumed that the peak of the Persian period is the nadir (that is, they followed our above graph no. 1) and partially because of their basic assumptions. After all, **even** graph no. 1 does not really support the 'continuity theory'.

That they were wrong is clearly attested by the archaeological evidence: their failure to find significant traces of settlement in the sixth century, despite our large database,[75] and the clear evidence for a social and

73.   Such as W. F. Albright, *The Archaeology of Palestine* (Harmondsworth: Penguin, 1960), pp. 140–2; K. Kenyon, *Archaeology in the Holy Land* (London: Methuen, 1965), p. 295–304, A. Mazar, *The Archaeology of the Land of the Bible, 10,000–586 BCE* (New York: Doubleday, 1990), pp. 458–60; Stern, *Archaeology of the Land of the Bible*, 301–50; idem, 'The Babylonian Gap: The Archaeological Reality', *JSOT* 28 (2004), pp. 273–7; B. Oded, 'Where is the "Myth of the Empty Land" To Be Found? History versus Myth', in O. Lipschits and J. Blenkinsopp (eds), *Judah and Judeans in the Neo-Babylonian Period* (Winona Lake: Eisenbrauns, 2003), pp. 55–74; D. Vanderhooft, 'Babylonian Strategies of Imperial Control in the West: Royal Practice and Rhetoric', in O. Lipschits and J. Blenkinsopp (eds), *Judah and Judeans in the Neo-Babylonian Period* (Winona Lake: Eisenbrauns, 2003), pp. 235–62.

74.   R. P. Caroll, 'The Myth of the Empty Land', *Semeia* 59 (1992), pp. 79–93; Barstad, *The Myth of the Empty Land*; Lipschits, 'Demographic Changes in Judah'; idem, *The Fall and Rise of Jerusalem*; J. Blenkinsopp, 'There was no Gap', *BARev* 28/3 (2002), pp. 37–8, 59; idem, 'The Bible, Archaeology and Politics; or The Empty Land Revisited', *JSOT* 27 (2002), pp. 169–87.

75.   Faust, 'Judah in the Sixth Century BCE: A Rural Perspective', and references therein. Notably, Lipschits ('Rural Settlement in Judah in the Sixth Century BCE: A Rejoinder', *PEQ* 136 [2004], pp. 99–107) has tried to counter some of the arguments I raised in my paper. His arguments are extremely problematic. While this is not the place for a detailed discussion of his claims, most of which are countered by the very data already presented in my original paper, I would like to briefly mention a few additional points. First of all, Lipschits simply **ignored** the main argument – that almost all of the Iron Age sites ceased to exist! No matter how he manipulates the data (or divides it into sub-regions), the results are the same – the rural sector was devastated. Moreover, many sites were excavated in the area between Bethlehem and Beth Zur, precisely where he speculates that there was continuity. The excavations, however, prove otherwise. His methodological arguments regarding the use of data from salvage excavations and surveys are simply wrong, and moreover, he uses them arbitrarily, preferring one set of data in the land of Benjamin (excavations) and another in northern Judah (surveys). In both cases the data is used uncritically (for more on

cultural break during this century (such as the disappearance of the four-room house and the Judahite tombs).[76]

Above, we have seen, that the very figures used by Barstad and Lipschits serve to prove them wrong, forcing us to realize that the demographic decline from the late Iron Age into the Persian period was great, even if one assumes that the exaggerated figures that they used were correct (and they are not!).

The processes observed above are quite straightforward. The figures themselves are of course less clear. It is technically possible that the nadir of the sixth century was not as low as presented in the graph (approximately 10%), and was as much as 20% of the Iron Age figures.[77] Still, this is a huge decline! When taking into account all the above considerations, including the bias in the 'demographic' data in favour of the Persian period, it is reasonable to estimate the population of Judah in the sixth century at around 10% or slightly more, at best approaching 15%, of that of the late Iron Age (and even the improbably high figure of 20% would completely disprove the minimalist position).

There are many known parallels to such sharp declines, in many different places and times. One outstanding example is that of the Intermediate Bronze Age in the southern Levant (more below). This brings us to the next issue.

Yehud *in the Persian Period as a 'Post-Collapse Society'*

What is the significance of the above for the study of the Persian period? The demographic trends observed in Judea indicate that the prosperity of the late Iron Age was brought to an end by a sudden and severe crisis. Then, during the Persian and Hellenistic periods, came a slow and gradual

---

methodology, see Faust and Safrai, 'Salvage Excavations as a Source for Reconstructing Settlement History in Ancient Israel'). It should be stressed that there seems to be an agreement among scholars regarding continuity in the land of Benjamin as far as the central sites are concerned (for which: Faust, 'Judah in the Sixth Century BCE: A Rural Perspective', 46, 50 n. 16), but the reality in the rural sector of this region seems to be more complex than he assumes. In addition, the demographic catastrophe did not occur only because of deportations, but also due to death in the wars, as well as by famine, epidemics and so on in their aftermath. And finally, the very data from surveys, when scrutinized, shows a pattern similar to the one observed by excavations (see more below).

76. See Stern, *Archaeology of the Land of the Bible*, 470–9; I. Yezerski, 'Burial Caves in the Land of Judah in the Iron Age – Archaeological and Architectural Aspects' (unpublished MA Thesis, Tel Aviv University, 1995), pp. 113–14 (Hebrew); S. R. Wolff, 'Mortuary Practices in the Persian Period of the Levant', *NEA* 65 (2002), pp. 131–7 (132, 133, 136); see also the detailed discussion in Faust, 'Social and Cultural Changes in Judah during the 6th Century BCE and their Implications for our Understanding of the Nature of the Neo-Babylonian Period'.

77. So Carter, *The Emergence of Yehud in the Persian Period*, 201–2.

recovery, which reached a peak only at some point in the Hellenistic period (probably only late within that period). It is clear that during the entire Persian period, the people of Judah lived in the shadow of the late Iron Age collapse.

Many studies conducted over the past couple of decades have been devoted to processes of collapse.[78] Less research was invested in the periods and processes that follow such a collapse. In one seminal study, Joseph Tainter has summarized various features that are common to many societies after their collapse, which he called 'post-collapse societies'.[79] I have dealt with his list of features elsewhere;[80] here I would like to refer to only a few of them.

The first feature of Tainter's synthesis is **population**, on which he writes: 'Whether as cause, consequence, or both, depopulation frequently accompanies collapse. Not only do urban populations decline, so also do the support populations of the countryside. Many settlements are concurrently abandoned. The levels of population and settlement may revert to those of centuries or even millennia before.'[81] Moreover, Tainter shows that, at times, the depopulation could have reached 75%–90% and even as high as 94%![82]

Tainter notes that from an architectural perspective, 'there is an end to monumental construction'.[83] In many cases, people reuse older structures.[84] Collapse is also accompanied by territorial and political fragmentation.[85]

And finally, perhaps the most important feature in Tainter's study for our purposes is the fact that recovery takes time – usually a couple of hundred years.[86] Clearly, all these points are easily reflected in the Persian-period archaeological record. The significant demographic decline, the dearth of impressive architectural finds, the lack of monumental buildings as well as the political fragmentation that accompanied the collapse of the kingdom of Judah (which was later divided among several polities), and

78. Such as N. Yoffee and G. L. Cowgill, *The Collapse of Ancient States and Civilizations* (Tucson: University of Arizona Press, 1991); J. A. Tainter, *The Collapse of Complex Societies* (Cambridge: CUP, 1988).

79. J. A. Tainter, 'Post-Collapse Societies', in G. Barker (ed.), *Companion Encyclopedia of Archaeology* II (London: Routledge, 1999), pp. 988–1039.

80. Faust, 'Social and Cultural Changes in Judah during the 6th Century BCE and their Implications for our Understanding of the Nature of the Neo-Babylonian Period'.

81. Tainter, 'Post-Collapse Societies', 1021.

82. Tainter, 'Post-Collapse Societies', 1010, 1016.

83. Tainter, 'Post-Collapse Societies', 1024.

84. Such as the finds at Kh. Abu et-Twein. See A. Mazar, 'Iron Age Fortresses in the Judean Hills', *PEQ* 114 (1982), pp. 87–109 (105); see also Lipschits, 'The Policy of the Persian Empire'.

85. Tainter, 'Post-Collapse Societies', 1026.

86. Tainter, 'Post-Collapse Societies', 1026–7.

the very slow and gradual recovery are, among other features, symptomatic of post-collapse societies.[87]

Furthermore, this grave situation is reflected in the period's sources.[88] This can be seen, for example, in Ezra 7.4: 'The city was wide and large, but the people within were few and no houses had been built.' The exact dating or historical reality behind the verse is not the important issue – what is important is the impression conveyed by the words; one of low density, especially when compared with the ruins which dominated the City of David as well as the Western Hill.[89] Moreover, various prophecies in Zechariah 9–14 (second Zechariah) give the very same impression. It appears that the lower demographic density of Judah had a strong impact on Zechariah, as noted by the Meyers': '... the eschatological setting of a divinely effected in-gathering in chapter 10 emerges from the sense that the population of Yehud is extraordinarily limited in size ... The sense that the prophet is speaking from the context of a weak and much reduced population is highlighted by the eschatological emphasis on population growth and of expansion ...'[90] They summarize: 'The eschaton, in military-political matters and also in demography, will be a dramatic reversal of the dismal situation of the first half of the postexilic period.'[91] From the above it is quite clear that the inhabitants of Judah felt that they were few and weak.[92]

Clearly, like in many other instances, the recovery of Judah took hundreds of years,[93] culminating only in the late Hellenistic period.[94]

Understanding the lengthy processes of recovery from collapse helps us put Persian-period Judah in its proper context and explains the dearth of architectural finds and other characteristics of this period. We shall return

87. See also Faust, 'Social and Cultural Changes in Judah during the 6th Century BCE and their Implications for our Understanding of the Nature of the Neo-Babylonian Period'.

88. Tainter, 'Post-Collapse Societies', 1022, 1028–9.

89. See also H. Eshel, 'Jerusalem Under Persian Rule: The City's Layout and the Historical Background', in S. Ahituv and A. Mazar (eds), *The History of Jerusalem, The Biblical Period* (Jerusalem: Yad Ben Zvi, 2000), pp. 327–43 (341) (Hebrew).

90. Meyers and Meyers, 'Demography and Diatribes: Yehud's Population and the Prophecy of Second Zechariah', 271.

91. Meyers and Meyers, 'Demography and Diatribes: Yehud's Population and the Prophecy of Second Zechariah', 273. See also their discussion of Zechariah 13 and 14 on pp. 273–8.

92. See also Tainter, 'Post-Collapse Societies', 1028, who shows that in most instances people in post-collapse societies treat their past as 'a paradise lost, a golden age of good government, wise rule, harmony and peace'.

93. Tainter, 'Post-Collapse Societies', 1026–7 and see above.

94. See also R. H. Smith, 'The Southern Levant in the Hellenistic Period', *Levant* XXII (1990), pp. 123–30; Berlin, 'Between Large Forces: Palestine in the Hellenistic Period'; Kloner, *Survey of Jerusalem: The Northwestern Sector, Introduction and Indices*, 26; Magen, 'The Land of Benjamin in the Second Temple Period', 5, 7.

to this issue later, but in the meantime I would like to examine, briefly, some regional aspects of the data discussed above.

Regional Aspects

Overall, although the area of the former kingdom of Judah was divided between different political units in the Persian period, demographically speaking the various regions behave quite uniformly; almost all show a decline that was followed by recovery. Still, every micro-region had its own history, and a few comments are in order.

Benjamin: This region has probably received more attention than any other, ever since it was first suggested that it was not destroyed by the Babylonians in the sixth century.[95] Indeed, it appears that the collapse was somewhat less rapid in the area of Benjamin, but after a short period (tens of years at most), the region's central sites (mainly *tell*s) followed suit.[96] Notably, in contrast to the 'planned' excavations (of *tell*s, where the collapse was apparently postponed), immediate decline in the Persian period is apparently evident in the surveys and in the salvage excavations which mainly represent the rural sector. Assuming that the interpretation of the 'planned' excavations did not result from biblical bias,[97] then the discrepancy shows that the decline in the rural sector was immediate, while that of the urban sector was more gradual. Such a dichotomy is to be expected, as insecurity could easily lead to immediate settlement decline in the rural sector. The specific history of the area of Benjamin, in which the remaining administration under Gedaliah survived during the early part of the Babylonian period, should serve to explain why some central sites did not collapse right away, but had a longer dying process than sites in other parts of Judah.[98]

Northern Judah: An in-depth analysis of the trends seems to indicate that the area of northern Judah, like other parts of the kingdom, suffered a major blow by the Babylonians. The excavated cities were destroyed or

95.   Malamat, 'The Last Wars of the Kingdom of Judah'; Stern, 'The Material Culture and Economic Life in the Land of Israel in the Persian Period', 120; idem, *Archaeology of the Land of the Bible*, 321–3; O. Lipschits, 'The History of the Benjamin Region under Babylonian Rule', *Tel Aviv* 26 (1999), pp. 155–190.

96.   For the decline of the central settlements, see even Lipschits, *The Fall and Rise of Jerusalem*, 237–45.

97.   Vanderhooft, 'Babylonian Strategies of Imperial Control in the West: Royal Practice and Rhetoric', 254, n. 18; see also the 'archaeological' criticism of A. De Groot, 'Jerusalem During the Persian Period', in A. Faust and E. Baruch (eds), *New Studies on Jerusalem, Proceedings of the 7th Conference* (Ramat-Gan: Bar Ilan University, 2001), pp. 77–81 (79–80) (Hebrew).

98.   Notably, the land of Benjamin deserves a more detailed discussion, which will be undertaken elsewhere.

abandoned,[99] and the same is true regarding the excavated rural sites, the vast majority of which did not exist in the Persian period.[100] The disastrous consequences of the Babylonian campaigns are attested everywhere. Gradually, this region became the centre of the *Yehud* province and its population grew. The relative importance of this region within the province of *Yehud* led to a faster recovery, which attracted more population, and this escalated the process of demographic growth. This was probably not only a result of natural growth, but was accompanied by migration from the devastated areas in the south, east and even west – areas whose recovery was much slower. It is also likely, of course, that some of the growth should be attributed to the returnees, but we cannot, archaeologically, estimate their demographic significance.

The demographic reality of this region has been widely discussed by Lipschits,[101] and a few words on his study are therefore in order, at least as a methodological cautionary tale. Lipschits, following Ofer,[102] realized that settlement in this region during the Persian period was significant, even denser than that of the Iron Age. Due to this similarity in settlement between the two periods he assumed that there was no break between them.[103] Methodologically, this is simply wrong. As an example, the demographic peaks of the Early Bronze Age and of the Middle Bronze

---

99.   Stern, *Archaeology of the Land of the Bible*, 324; see even Lipschits, *Jerusalem between Destruction and Restoration*, 283–5, who only claims that the agent of destruction is unknown. Interestingly, Lipschits claims that there is no real evidence for destruction (p. 283), but has to admit, when discussing the sites themselves, that they were probably abandoned and not resettled at least until the late Persian period. His attempt to use some pottery forms found in mixed loci at Beth-Zur to claim that this view is not substantiated (regarding this site), is misguided. Lipschits does not realize that pottery forms exist for long periods and that many 'Persian' forms began to appear during the Iron Age. Only well-stratified assemblages should be used for fine-tuned dating. For the long duration of pottery forms see J. Deetz, *Invitation to Archaeology* (New York: The Natural History Press, 1967), pp. 26–33; K. W. Wesler, 'Chronological Sequences in Nigerian Ceramics', *African Archaeological Review* 16 (1999), pp. 239–58; C. M. Sinopoli, *Approaches to Archaeological Ceramics* (New York: Plenum, 1991), pp. 74–5; C. Orton, P. Tyres and A. Vince, *Pottery in Archaeology* (Cambridge: Cambridge University Press, 1993), pp. 190–1 and many others.

100.   For a list of **excavated** sites, see Faust, 'Judah in the Sixth Century BCE: A Rural Perspective'; additional sites include, for example, a group of farmsteads near Ramot and one near Beit Hakerem; see, U. Davidovich, Y. Farhi, S. Kol-Ya'akov, M. Har-Peled, D. Weinblatt-Krauz, Y. Alon, 'Salvage Excavations at Ramot Forest and Ramat Bet-Hakerem: New Data Regarding Jerusalem's Periphery during the First and Second Temple Periods', in E. Baruch, Z. Greenhut and A. Faust (eds), *New Studies on Jerusalem* 11 (Ramat-Gan: Bar Ilan University, 2006), pp. 35–111.

101.   Lipschits, 'Demographic Changes in Judah between the Seventh and the Fifth Centuries BCE', 351–5; idem, *Jerusalem between Destruction and Restoration*, 283–90.

102.   Ofer, 'The Highlands of Judah during the Biblical Period', 2: 131–4.

103.   Lipschits, 'Demographic Changes in Judah', 353; idem, *Jerusalem between Destruction and Restoration*, 285–91.

Age were almost identical.[104] Can we conclude that there was no break between them? Of course not – the demographic decline in the end of the Early Bronze Age and during the Intermediate Bronze Age is well attested.[105] The same is true here – the similarity between the seventh and the fifth centuries BCE[106] does not say anything about the situation in the sixth century.

Furthermore, when the level of continuity between the two periods is examined at the site level – the best means to study continuity – a major break is evident.[107] This is evident, as we have seen, in both planned and salvage excavations, which represent all types of settlement. Lipschits, however, attempted to base his conclusions on survey data. Not only are surveys less reliable as a source of information for such studies in general, but they even tend to 'flatten' the data from such processes.[108] Still, when scrutinized, Ofer's survey clearly reveals the same trends. An examination of all the **small** seventh-century sites (sites whose overall size was smaller then 10 dunams)[109] shows that despite the similar numbers of such sites in both periods, almost half of the late-Iron Age sites did not continue to exist in the Persian period (14 small late Iron Age sites, all located north of Beth Zur, did not continue to exist in the Persian period; 17 sites did continue to exist), while half of the Persian-period sites were new (17 Persian-period sites were established *de novo*). This shows that continuity was limited. And if one would like to claim that 50% (or even slightly more) is still a high degree of continuity, then we must put that figure, derived from Ofer's survey, in its proper context. When examining the transition from the eighth century to the seventh, **following Sennacherib's campaign**, it appears that only 2 out of 22 of the small sites did not continue to exist – obviously, in reality, there were probably more changes, but as we have stated, surveys tend to 'flatten' trends. The change during the transition from the Iron Age into the Persian period is

104. Broshi and R. Gophna, 'The Settlements and Population of Palestine During the Early Bronze Age II-III'; idem, 'Middle Bronze Age II Palestine: Its Settlement and Population'.

105. R. Gophna, 1992, 'The Intermediate Bronze Age', in: A. Ben-Tor (ed.), *The Archaeology of Ancient Israel* (New Haven: Yale University Press, 1992), pp. 126–58.

106. Which is not complete – see even Lipschits, 'Demographic Changes in Judah', 354.

107. For which see Faust, 'Judah in the Sixth Century BCE: A Rural Perspective'; Faust and Safrai, 'Salvage Excavations as a Source for Reconstructing Settlement History in Ancient Israel', 145–7, 156 notes 12–15.

108. Faust and Safrai, 'Settlement Fluctuations and Surveys' in preparation.

109. The importance of rural sites for the debate is stressed by all scholars, as this is where the minimalists claim continuity on the one hand and where settlement continuity can be easily examined on the other. See Faust, 'Judah in the Sixth Century BCE: A Rural Perspective' and references there, and note that the method is accepted even by Lipschits, 'Rural Settlement in Judah in the Sixth Century BCE: A Rejoinder'.

therefore extremely significant, and this confirms the major break which is evident in this region by the more reliable analysis of the excavations.

Other Regions, Outside of Judah: Notably, such processes of collapse and recovery took place in other parts of the Land of Israel following the Assyrian and Babylonian conquests, but discussion of this is beyond the scope of the present paper. Both the extent of collapse and the rate of recovery should be examined within the specific context of each region. It should be stressed, however, that not all regions experienced the fate of Judah, and some even prospered during the Persian period. This is true, for example, for the coastal plain. Both urban and rural settlements in this region flourished, as is evident by both planned and salvage excavations.[110] This clearly supports Stern's claim that some past estimations regarding the extent of the decline were somewhat exaggerated and it did not cover the entire country.[111] Here, I would only like to point to this direction, and to note that 'collapse' and 'post-collapse' should be taken into consideration when discussing the Assyrian, Babylonian and Persian periods throughout the country.

Conclusions

An examination of the various data regarding demographic and settlement trends during the late Iron Age through the Hellenistic-period era shows that the relative prosperity of the seventh century was followed by a major decline, and then a gradual recovery. While there are several theoretical scenarios that can outline such demographic ups and downs, we have seen that the only plausible reconstruction is that of a sharp and abrupt decline immediately after the Iron Age, and then a gradual recovery that lasted during the Persian period and matured only during the (late) Hellenistic period.

The demographic and settlement **peak** of the Persian period was (at most) about one-third of those of the late Iron Age and Hellenistic periods. The nadir of the Persian period, however, was much lower. It seems as if the lowest demographic point (probably in the sixth century BCE) was probably around 10% of the late Iron Age (20% would be a highly exaggerated figure).

Admittedly, the figures we present are lower than those previously assumed. But they are not based on a new 'reading' of the data (although we hinted that this too is in order), but rather on putting the figures in

110.   See Stern, *Archaeology of the Land of the Bible*, 385–422, 462; Lipschits, 'The Policy of the Persian Empire'.

111.   Stern, 'The Material Culture and Economic Life in the Land of Israel in the Persian Period', 120.

their proper perspective. To reiterate, we have followed the figures presented by Lispschits and others, but even they necessitate a new estimation of the Persian period in Judea and **inevitably** lead to an evaluation that the period was one of great settlement decline. Realizing how low the nadir is on the one hand, and the overall processes described above on the other, is the first step in assessing the Persian period.

The collapse of Judahite society in the sixth century BCE had long-term results. The entire Persian period should be viewed as one of post-collapse. All of Judean/Jewish society of the Persian period existed in the shadow of this collapse

In the past, scholars like Watzinger claimed that urban life ceased to exist during this period.[112] Kenyon, for example, also wrote 'The low ebb of civilization in Palestine, which lasts for the next three centuries or so, makes it difficult for archaeology to recover any evidence. Town life suffered a severe setback, and such reduced settlements as there were, with little in the way of substantial buildings, were most likely obliterated by later building operations'.[113] To which she adds: 'The great cities of the Israelite period therefore play little part in the life of the country under the Babylonians and the succeeding Persian empire. The slight glimpses we get of the culture of Palestine come largely from unimportant sites. It is perhaps significant that most of them come from the coastal belt'.[114] Albright also claimed that 'To judge from the results of excavations, the resettlement of Judah was a slow process, and it was not until the third century B.C. that the country recovered anything like its old density of population'.[115] Admittedly, some of these evaluations were somewhat exaggerated. Urban life seems to have flourished in some regions, but mainly in the coastal plain.[116] While these gloomy estimations for the Persian period might not be an accurate reflection of the reality all over the country, they are surely accurate regarding some areas. As far as Judea is concerned, those estimations seem to represent the bleak reality in this region. A real recovery did not take place before the Hellenistic period.[117]

---

112.   C. Watzinger, *Denkmaler Palästinas* II (Leipzig: J. C. Hinrich, 1935); quoted by Stern, 'The Material Culture and Economic Life in the Land of Israel in the Persian Period', 119.

113.   Kenyon, *Archaeology in the Holy Land*, 296–8.

114.   Kenyon, *Archaeology in the Holy Land*, 302.

115.   Albright, *The Archaeology of Palestine*, 142. See also V. Fritz, 'Cities: Cities of the Bronze and Iron Ages', in E. M. Meyers (ed.), *Oxford Encyclopedia of Archaeology in the Near East* 2 (New York: Oxford University Press, 1997), pp. 19–25 (24).

116.   See also Berlin, 'Between Large Forces: Palestine in the Hellenistic Period', 4.

117.   This estimation that *Yehud* province was poor is accepted by many today. See, for example, Carter, *The Emergence of Yehud in the Persian Period*, 285; Berlin, 'Between Large Forces: Palestine in the Hellenistic Period'.

The importance of the Persian period for anthropology might lie exactly in studying it as a period of 'post-collapse'. We would like to close this paper with the words with which Tainter closed his innovative article: 'While it may be that social evolution tends in general toward greater complexity, periodic simplification is to be expected as well, and is worth our best efforts to understand'.[118]

118. Tainter, 'Post-Collapse Societies', 1030.

Chapter 3

SETTLEMENT PATTERNS IN PERSIAN-ERA *YEHUD*

Diana Edelman

The results of the many regional surveys that have been conducted throughout the land of Israel in the last three decades provide historians with invaluable information about settlement trends in various historical eras. Even taking into account the many inherent limitations in surveys and the problems in identifying clear diagnostics for the two centuries during which *Yehud* was part of the Persian empire, it is possible to establish from the available data a trend toward small farmsteads and possible hamlets located near administrative sites. There is no clear evidence for larger villages or towns. In addition, there was a surge in newly established sites during this time period, many on ground never before occupied. I will present the data and then propose a tentative explanation of these settlement trends.

The boundaries of *Yehud* in the first half of the Persian period, from 538–400 BCE, are disputed. After a thorough investigation of this thorny issue, I have concluded that the Persians left intact the provincial boundaries that had been established by the Neo-Babylonians. The southern boundary lay just north of the Beersheba Valley. The northern boundary was the northern limit of Benjamin, from Bethel southwards. The eastern boundary was probably the Dead Sea and the Jordan Rift, while the western one was the edge of the Shephelah before reaching the adjoining lowlands. In my opinion, these boundaries were changed only *ca.* 400 BCE when the province of Idumea was created.[1] In the ensuing discussion, I will present the settlement patterns that fell within the limits delineated, between Bethel and the southernmost extent of the Judean hills on the north side of the Beersheba Valley, and from the Shephelah to the Jordan Valley, during the Persian period.

Although very few Persian-era levels have been excavated to date within the regions of Benjamin, the southern Shephelah, and the central and southern Judean hill country north of the Beersheba Valley, survey results

---

1. For full arguments, see D. Edelman, *The Origins of the 'Second' Temple: Persian Imperial Policy and the Rebuilding of Jerusalem* (London: Equinox, 2005), pp. 209–80. For a different view see Y. Levin's article in this volume.

allow us to begin to examine general settlement trends within these areas in the Persian period.[2] The data about to be presented is meant to focus on the first half of the Persian period, from 538–400 BCE, but in many instances, the collected sherds can only be identified as Persian, which would reflect potential settlement anywhere within the period from 538 to 332 BCE. The statistics include sites labelled as Persian but have excluded those labelled Persian/Hellenistic in certain surveys, which would seem to represent the second half of the Persian period specifically. There is no way to determine how many of the sites would have been occupied simultaneously during this period, when they were founded, or their length of occupation. I have only included Persian-era sites with building remains as well as at least one sherd of pottery; since many sites were farmsteads, the presence of a single Persian sherd collected in survey is significant, especially in areas where previous survey work has taken place.[3] The statistics compiled from the available evidence will not reflect a complete picture of settlement patterns; the surveys were unable to provide 100% coverage of the regions examined. The figures about to be given are rough guides based on current knowledge and not definitive for Persian-era *Yehud*.

In general, there is a trend toward small settlements consisting of unwalled farmsteads or hamlets, with very few possible village and town sites. This is the case in the territory of Benjamin as well as the territory of the Judean hills and the Shephelah. Thus, it is logical to conclude that the mainstay of the economy was agricultural production, probably combined with the raising of sheep and goats, as had been traditional in the region for millennia. Many of the farmsteads have evidence of oil presses and

2. These include M. Kochavi, *Judea, Samaria, and the Golan: Archaeological Survey 1967–1968* (Jerusalem: The Archaeological Survey of Israel, 1972); Y. Hirschfeld, *Map of Herodium (108/2 17–11)* (Jerusalem: The Archaeological Survey of Israel, 1985); Y. Govrin, *Map of Nahal Yattir (139)* (Archaeological Survey of Israel; Jerusalem: Israel Antiquities Authority, 1991); Y. Dagan, *Map of Lakhish (98)* (Archaeological Survey of Israel; Jerusalem: Israel Antiquities Authority, 1992); I. Finkelstein and Y. Magen, *Archaeological Survey of the Hill-Country of Benjamin* (Jerusalem: Israel Antiquities Authority, 1993); A. Ofer, 'The Highland of Judah during the Biblical Period' (2 vols; unpublished Ph.D. thesis, Tel Aviv University, 1993); I. Milevski, 'Settlement Patterns in Northern Judah during the Achaemenid Period, According to the Hill Country of Benjamin and Jerusalem Surveys', *BAIAS* 15 (1996/97), pp. 7–29; Y. Dagan, 'The Settlement in the Judean Shephela in the Second and First Millenium B.C.: A Test Case of Settlement Processes in a Geographic Region', (unpublished Ph.D. thesis, Tel Aviv University, 2000); A. Kloner, *Archaeological Survey of Jerusalem. The Southern Sector* (Jerusalem: Israel Antiquities Authority, 2000); idem, *Archaeological Survey of Jerusalem. The Northeastern Sector* (Jerusalem: Israel Antiquities Authority, 2001); A. Kloner, *Archaeological Survey of Jerusalem. The Northwestern Sector. Introduction and Indices* (Jerusalem: Israel Antiquities Authority, 2003).

3. The Iron II sites that were not reoccupied include agricultural terraces as well as building remains, on the assumption that the terraces were used by families that lived nearby.

vats for processing grapes into wine, so it is likely that they produced primarily grains (wheat and barley), wine and olive oil. Without excavation, however, it cannot be determined if these installations relate to the Persian period, to the preceding Iron Age, or to the later Hellenistic, Roman and/or Byzantine periods. The settlement pattern overlaps in large part with what had been in place at the end of the monarchy, although there appear to have been almost double the number of settled sites occupied in the Iron II period, and they included walled settlements interspersed among the farmsteads and forts.

Let us begin with the settlement pattern in the Neo-Babylonian period. This is already a problem, since the late Iron Age pottery tradition in the delineated region did not end with the creation of the province of *Yehud* in 586 BCE. Thus, the presence of Iron IIC pottery at a site that has only been surveyed and not excavated could indicate occupation until 586 BCE, uninterrupted occupation through the Neo-Babylonian period and into the early Persian period, or a destruction in 586 and a subsequent re-occupation at some point either in the Neo-Babylonian or early Persian period. If we assume for the moment that sites with Iron IIC pottery but with no evidence of Persian occupation were destroyed in 586 BCE and remained unoccupied over time, while those that have both Iron IIC and Persian pottery were continuously occupied throughout the Neo-Babylonian period and into the early Persian period, we have the following results. There were 372 sites that contained Iron II pottery but no Persian pottery, which presumably were destroyed or abandoned in or before 586 BCE, and 154 sites that have both Iron IIC pottery and Persian pottery. The latter are our best candidates for reflecting settlement within the province of *Yehud* in the Neo-Babylonian period, whether with a temporary hiatus or with uninterrupted occupation.

These can then be set alongside the 108 sites that were newly settled in the Persian period. Of these, 48 were reoccupations of older facilities that had been abandoned since either the Iron IIB, probably after 701 BCE when Sennacherib ceded control over the Shephelah and perhaps some of the Judean highland areas to Philistia, or in the Iron IIC with the destruction of Jerusalem. The latter sites are either identified on the basis of excavation results or are found in the survey of A. Ofer,[4] who has designated Neo-Babylonian sites under the heading Iron IID, leaving Iron IIC to designate sites occupied prior to 586 BCE. By contrast, the remaining 60 sites culled from surveys (see note 2) were new foundations in the Persian period on virgin land that had never been occupied previously.

The Persian-era settlements tend to cluster in five regions: 1) west of Bethel, Mizpah and Geba, in the territory of Benjamin (#1–22); 2) in the

4.   Ofer, 'Highland of Judah during the Persian Period'.

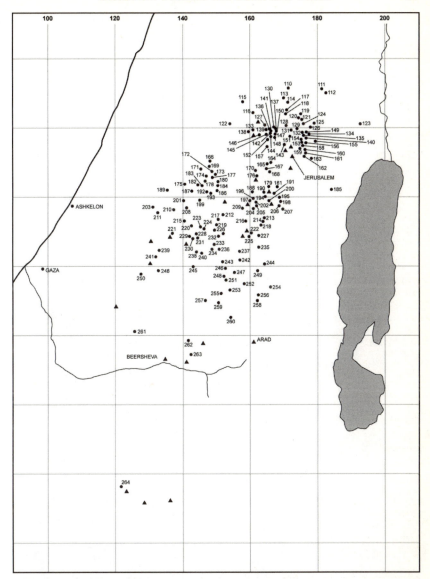

Map 1: Sites in *Yehud* with Iron IIc, and Persian Period Occupation

central Judean hill country between latitudes 1263 and 1042, around the string of fortresses at Khirbet Umm el-Qala, Khirbet Kabbar, Khirbet Abu Twain, Khirbet el-Qatt, Khirbet Zawiyye, and Beth-Zur (#28, 29, 31, 32, 34, 37–39, 41, 45–51, 53, 56, 58–60, 62–68, 73, 78–79, 81, 89, 90); 3) in the Shephelah west of the fort at Khirbet er-Rasm between latitudes 1240 and 1159 (#30, 33, 35, 36, 42–44, 52, 54, 55, 57, 61); 4) southeast of the

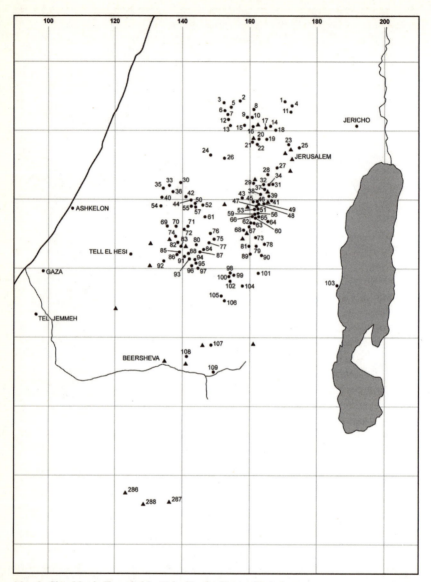

Map 2: Sites Newly Founded in *Yehud* in the Persian Period

facilities at Lachish and Khirbet Rasm Shuʻliya, with a few to the north (#69–72, 74–77, 80, 82–88, 91–97); and 5) south of cluster 3 and southeast of cluster 4 in the southern Judean highlands (#98–102, 104–106).[5]

5. For details of the sites included in the five regions and further references see Edelman, *Origins of the 'Second' Temple*, 292–310.

In the Benjamin region, settlement in the Neo-Babylonian period was already fairly dense, with 52 sites continuing to be occupied from the Iron IIC into the Persian period. Even so, there were 27 sites added during the course of the Persian period, 23 of which were foundations on virgin soil and only three of which were at sites that had been abandoned since Iron IIB or, in one instance, at some point in the Iron II period.

In the second grouping in the central Judean hill country between latitudes 1263 and 1042, around the string of fortresses at Khirbet Umm el-Qala, Khirbet Kabbar, Khirbet Abu Twain, Khirbet el-Qatt, Khirbet Zawiyye, and Beth-Zur, there were 36 sites that were occupied at the end of the monarchy that may have continued to be occupied through the Neo-Babylonian period and into the Persian period. To these were added 22 new settlements on virgin land in the Persian period and 14 that reused pre-existing facilities that had been abandoned for a period of time. Two had not been used since the Iron I period, three had not been settled since Iron IIB, presumably since Sennacherib's campaigns in 701 BCE, and the remaining nine were theoretically destroyed or abandoned in 586 BCE (#34, 38–40, 46–48, 56, 76). Thus, the number of sites in use doubled in the Persian period (36 new; 36 old).

Groupings 3 and 4 in the northern and southern Shephelah, respectively, saw a marked increase in the numbers of occupied sites. In the northern Shephelah, the pre-existing 23 sites with Iron IIC remains and Persian remains were augmented by 16 newly established Persian-era sites. Of these, only three were on virgin soil; the remaining 13 were reoccupations after abandonment in Iron IIB. This represents a 32% increase in settlements. The picture in the southern Shephelah is similar. There were 17 sites with both Iron IIC and Persian remains, which could suggest continuous occupation in the Neo-Babylonian period. In the Persian period, 22 new sites sprang up, of which nine were on virgin soil, including the fort and adjoining settlement at Khirbet Rasm Shu'liyeh, just east of Lachish. Of the remaining 13, 11 were reoccupied Iron IIB farmsteads and the other two were farmsteads that had been occupied previously at some point in the Iron II. This represents a 55% increase in occupied sites.

Finally, in the fifth grouping in the southern Judean hills, there were 16 settlements that were potentially settled continuously from the end of the monarchy, through the Neo-Babylonian period, and into the Persian period. To this base of farmsteads, hamlets, and possible villages, seven new farmsteads were established in the Persian period, four of which were pristine foundations. Of the remaining three reoccupied farmsteads, one had been abandoned since the Iron IIB period, probably after 701 BCE, and the other two had theoretically been abandoned after 586 BCE. This marked almost a 30% increase in the land use in the region in the Persian era.

REGION	IRON IIC/D + PERSIAN POTTERY	NEW FOUNDA- TION IN THE PERSIAN PERIOD
BENJAMIN	52	27 24 VIRGIN 　　3　REUSED
CENTRAL JUDEAN HILL COUNTRY	36	36 22 VIRGIN 　　14 REUSED
NORTHERN SHEPHELAH	23	16 3　VIRGIN 　　13 REUSED
SOUTHERN SHEPHELAH	17	22 9　VIRGIN 　　13 REUSED
SOUTHERN JUDEAN HILL COUNTRY	16	7 4　VIRGIN 　　3　REUSED
TOTAL	154	108

The size of the majority of these sites is small, even when there are multiple periods of occupation. This tends to indicate that a given site was used over and over as a farmstead. I use the term 'farmstead' to refer to a cluster of buildings that would include a main residence as well as outbuildings and facilities used for agricultural purposes, such as barns, storage shed, silos, and wine and olive presses, or terraces with such features. Remembering that there are approximately 4 dunams to an acre, there are 78 sites that have their total building remains from cumulative periods of occupation spread on 1.25 acres or less and 33 sites with cumulative buildings covering 1.5–2 acres or less, These would all represent single farmsteads or possibly a splitting of an original farmstead in half over time in the latter case. The sizes of 47 sites (17% of non-administrative settlements) are not given in the surveys; out of 262 Persian-era settlement sites (this excludes the administrative facilities), 108, or 41%, can be identified as farmsteads without further excavation.

0–5 dunams	6–10 dunams	11–20 dunams	20 + dunams	No size given
76	32	45	62	47

Non-administrative Sites in *Yehud* in the Persian Period

Of the 108 new foundations in the Persian period, whether on virgin soil or at previously existing sites, 49 are 5 dunams or less, 13 measure 6–10 dunams, and 15 have no size information given. Of the remaining 31 new sites, 13 encompass 11–20 dunams, while 18 are situated on sites measuring more than 20 dunams, many on large *tell*s. Over two-thirds of these new sites can safely be identified as farmsteads, and the remainder may have also contained farmsteads in this particular time period; only excavation will be able to determine the extent and nature of Persian-era settlement on *tell*s and former town sites.

0–5 dunams	6–10 dunams	11–20 dunams	20 + dunams	No size given
49	13	13	18	15

Sites Newly Established in the Persian Period (108 in total)

Of the 154 sites that have Iron IIC/IID occupation and Persian occupation, which in theory could represent continuous settlement, 32 lack size information. There are 27 that are 5 dunams or less; 19 cover 6–10 dunams; 32 cover 11–20 dunams, and 44 measure 21 dunams or more. From these figures, 30% can be identified as farmsteads; the status of the others is uncertain without excavation.

0–5 dunams	6–10 dunams	11–20 dunams	20 + dunams	No size given
27	19	32	44	32

Sites with Iron IIC/D Occupation and Persian Occupation

This review of figures has demonstrated a trend toward farmsteads in Persian-era *Yehud*, seen especially in the sites that were developed on previously unoccupied land. The extent of settlement on *tell*s and former town sites cannot be determined without excavation, but in cases where pottery percentages have been noted, Persian sherds usually represent a low percentage of the overall count, suggesting that only a portion of the site was reused in the Persian period.

In Persian-era *Yehud*, two strings of administrative facilities were established, one on a N–S axis and the other on an E–W axis. The former included seven sites that traced the main trunk road through the highlands, leaving the north side of the Beersheba Valley opposite the site of Tel Beersheba and proceeding to Jerusalem: it passed by Tel Shoqet (#262), then Khirbet Rabud (#255) via Khirbet Bism (#251), el-Hadab (#247) and Khirbet Kan'an (#242). It skirted Hebron and headed north, past Halhul (#222), the fort at Beth-Zur/Khirbet et-Tubeiqeh (#276), the one at Khirbet ez-Zawiyye (#275), the fort at Khirbet el-Qatt (#274), and onwards past Khirbet Umm et-Tala' (#60), Rujm es-Sabit (#53), Khirbet Zakandah/Khirbet Faghur (#48) Khirbet Umm el-Qita' (#194) and

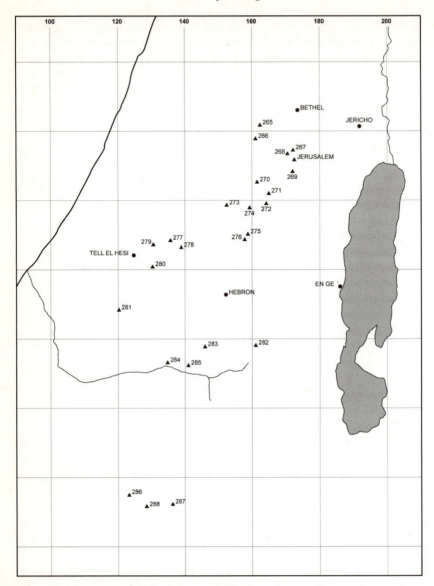

Map 3: Administrative Facilities in Persian Era *Yehud*

Khirbet el-Kwakh (#191). Then, after passing by the forts of Khirbet Kabbar (#271) and Ramat Rahel (#269), it arrived at Jerusalem.[6]

6. D. Dorsey, *The Roads and Highways of Ancient Israel* (London: Johns Hopkins University Press, 1991), pp. 119–23. It is likely that there was at least one additional

The E–W axis, by contrast, does not seem to follow any particular, established road from the coast to Jerusalem. Instead, it represents a roughly diagonal line from the provincial seat at Jerusalem that ran southwest through the Shephelah to the coastal plain. The forts at Khirbet Umm el-Qal'a (#270) and Khirbet er-Rasm (#273) marked this line, which passed through the Shephelah at Khirbet Rasm Shu'liya (#278), and went on past Tel Lachish, with its governor's residency (#277), exiting the foothills at Khirbet Umm el-Baqar (#279).[7]

The function of these structures needs consideration. Along the royal road systems in the empire, the Persians established postal relay stations a day's ride apart, where couriers could be relieved by a new rider and a fresh team of horses.[8] In addition, these roads had guard-posts spaced regularly, and stations that served as stopping places, with hostels.[9] But it is highly unlikely that either route identified in *Yehud* qualified as a royal road. The north–south royal routes would have run through the coastal plain and perhaps in the Jordan Rift, while east–west royal routes would logically have cut through the Jezreel Valley and the Beersheba Valley. Also, as noted, the E–W line of structures does not sit alongside an established internal road.

Nevertheless, there would have been designated routes by which couriers would have travelled to inland provincial capitals, like Jerusalem and Samaria. The N–S route outlined above seems to have functioned in this secondary capacity. Relay stations and hostels would not have been required on this route, however, since it would have been possible to reach Jerusalem within a day of travelling from the Beersheba Valley. Similarly, it would only have taken a day to travel to Jerusalem from the coastal plain or the Shephelah.

The proposal by E. Stern[10] that the forts protected trade routes within *Yehud* seems unlikely; caravans would have had their own armed escorts, and hostel and military facilities would not have been needed in the hill country for such caravans since travel to Jerusalem from either the coast or the Beersheba Valley took a single day. The proposal by K. Hoglund

---

administrative site along the segment of route between Harei Anim (#283) and Beth-Zur/ Khirbet et-Tubeiqeh (#276) that has not yet been identified. The distance between these two sites is about four times greater than between other identified sites, and it is logical to suspect that there was a site in the vicinity of Hebron.

7.   For the roads in the area, see Dorsey, *Roads and Highways of Ancient Israel*, 152.

8.   P. Briant, *From Cyrus to Alexander: A History of the Persian Empire* (trans. P. T. Daniels; Winona Lake, IN: Eisenbrauns, 2002), pp. 369–70.

9.   Briant, *From Cyrus to Alexander*, 357.

10.   E. Stern, 'The Persian Empire and the Political and Social History of Palestine in the Persian Period', in W. D. Davies and L. Finkelstein (eds), *The Cambridge History of Judaism in the Persian Period. I. Introduction: The Persian Period* (Cambridge: Cambridge University Press, 1984), pp. 70–87 (86).

that these forts were built to provide additional soldiers in case of invasion by Greece or Egypt after the rebellion of Inaros (*ca.* 465 BCE) holds more merit[11] but still does not seem to have been the primary motivation for their creation. Had such an aim been in mind, it would have been more logical to increase the troops assigned to the string of fortresses running down the coast from Gaza to the Nile Delta, or to have built more fortresses along the Mediterranean to prevent approach by sea.

The two strings of structures that are tightly spaced along the route from Beersheba to Jerusalem but not along a comparable W–E route need another explanation. It seems more plausible to associate them with the practice of using fires to send important news to the provincial seat at Jerusalem from the main royal roads to the west and south. Such a system had already been used within the kingdom of Judah, as evidenced by Lachish ostracon 4, which mentions that the guards at a certain fort have been looking for the fire signals from Azekah but have not seen them.[12] Thus, in this case, it would have been a continuation of an established local practice, but now in the service of the larger Persian empire.[13] Whatever their function, it should be noted that in the case of both strings, each facility has a cluster of Persian-era farmsteads in its immediate vicinity, many of which were created on previously unoccupied land (see maps 1 and 2).

Let us return to the overall settlement pattern and focus particularly on the newly established farmsteads in *Yehud* in the Persian period. Of the 108 new foundations, 48 were on abandoned Iron II sites, most probably farmsteads, which in most cases had not been occupied since 701 BCE, and 60 were on virgin ground. In the surveys of Benjamin, the Shephelah and the Judean hills within the boundaries I have proposed for *Yehud*, there were 372 sites with Iron II occupation that were not resettled in the Persian period. Of these, however, only 27 were never resettled again; 102 were resettled in the Hellenistic period, 137 in the Roman period, 96 in the Byzantine period, and 10 in subsequent eras. Of these 372 sites, 139 were 5 dunams or less; 69 were 6–10 dunams; 58 were 11–20 dunams, and 56 were on sites over 21 dunams. Another 49 had no size given but could be classified as farmsteads from their described remains, while three lie within

11.   K. Hoglund, *Achaemenid Imperial Administration in Syria-Palestine and the Missions of Ezra and Nehemiah* (SBLDS, 125; Atlanta: GA: Scholars Press, 1992), pp. 202–5. It has been adopted by e.g. J. Berquist, *Judaism in Persia's Shadow: A Social and Historical Approach* (Minneapolis: Fortress Press, 1995), p. 108 and C. Carter, *The Emergence of Yehud in the Persian Period: A Social and Demographic Study* (JSOTSup, 297; Sheffield: Sheffield Academic Press, 1999), p. 293.

12.   D. Pardee *et al.*, *Handbook of Ancient Hebrew Letters* (SBLSBS 15; Chico: Scholars Press, 1982), pp. 89–95.

13.   Briant cites several examples of this practice in the Persian empire (*From Cyrus to Alexander*, 371).

inhabited modern Arab villages with no size estimates given. This means that 69% can confidently be identified as farmsteads. Since there were so many other abandoned farmsteads available for occupation from the end of the monarchy, why were these not chosen for re-occupation by the 60 families/clans who instead, took on the onerous task of clearing ground, building from scratch, and digging cisterns? These farmsteads and/or hamlets represent 23% of the total number of currently identified Persian-era farmsteads and settlements.

I would suggest that this phenomenon arose not by chance and personal choice but rather as a result of Persian imperial policy. When the Persians decided to redevelop *Yehud* to incorporate it more fully into their provincial, postal and military systems, they repopulated the area to bolster its food production and eligible manpower. The Bible describes this event as the return from exile, and implies that all the returnees were descendants of former Judahites who were returning to their patrimonies (Ezra 1–6). However, the census lists found in Ezra 2 and Nehemiah 7, whenever they were taken, include sizeable numbers of non-Jews amongst those registered; specifically, the sons of Bigvai, a Persian name (2,056 in Ezra 2.14; 2,067 in Neh. 7.19), the sons of Elam, a territory in the Iranian plateau whose heart was in the present province of Fars that, like *Yehud*, became part of the Persian empire (1,254; Ezra 2.7; Neh. 7.12), and the sons of Azgad – another non-Semitic name (1,222 in Ezra 2.12; 2,322 in Neh. 7.17). The Xanthus inscription indicates that the Persian kings moved groups of ethnically related soldiers to new assignments throughout the empire.[14] Another example of this kind of movement is provided by the Saka, *Ḫatru* who had been settled in Babylonia on *Ḫatru*-estates after they had been conquered and their lands annexed to the Persian empire.[15]

Nehemiah 2.9 relates that amongst those who went to *Yehud* were army officers and cavalry. While many consider these to be the requisite escort for the settlers, I think that they are more than that. Cavalry are a specialist, elite corps in the army, and while a single officer might have been part of an escort contingent, multiple officers would not have been needed. I see little need to mention the presence of the escort party, which would have been standard, so I prefer to deduce that this information was given because it indicated that the cavalry and officers were integral members of those being moved to *Yehud* for resettlement.

The statistics on settlements in the Persian period represent trends over the entire 200 years in many cases, where no distinction was or could be made between the first 100 and second 100 years. We cannot know at any

14. J. Teixidor, 'The Aramaic Text in the Trilingual Stele from Xanthus', *JNES* 37 (1978), pp. 181–5.

15. Briant, *From Cyrus to Alexander*, 747.

given point which sites were settled simultaneously, and it usually is
assumed that sites in a given region will peak at some point due to the
natural increase in population, but be less in number before the peak and
decline after the peak. On an archaeological basis alone, the location of
new settlements in the vicinity of the two strings of Persian administrative
structures tends to favour a deliberate increase of new settlers by imperial
design rather than natural increase, without new settlers. When taken in
conjunction with textual evidence, however, the likelihood of a deliberate
movement of new settlers into the area as part of an imperial policy to
redevelop *Yehud* is greatly strengthened. I have argued elsewhere that this
policy was implemented during the reign of Artaxerxes I,[16] so I would see
a strong spike in settlement to have occurred already *ca.* 450 BCE, with
some further natural growth taking place subsequently. I have not
included sites founded in the second 100 years of the Persian period in my
statistics, though some have been identified in survey.

Bearing in mind the archaeological and textual evidence, I am
tentatively proposing that the sites established in *Yehud* on previously
unoccupied land were assigned to non-native military personnel as *Ḥatru*-
estates or something similar, in which land was granted to soldiers in
return for mandatory military service.[17] This would account for the
location of so many of these new settlements in the vicinity of the two
strings of administrative structures, which I have suggested were primarily
fire relay stations. This would have been a newly introduced administrative system within *Yehud*, which would have existed side by side with the
older, traditional *bêt 'ābôt* system. Settlers of Judahite background
returned to their ancestral lands when they could prove their genealogical
connections, or were perhaps allowed to settle on abandoned farmsteads
that were then regulated within the traditional system. It certainly is
possible that some of the 154 sites with Iron IIC and Persian occupation
(see map 1) were abandoned during the Neo-Babylonian period and
resettled by some of these settlers. Only with excavation can such a trend
be confirmed.

The settlement patterns that can be deduced in Persian *Yehud* from
currently available survey results and theories of pottery chronology have
no intrinsic meaning; we must supply the interpretive framework. I have
suggested one to account for the phenomenon of the creation of many
new farmsteads on virgin land that account for 23% of the total
settlements currently identified: a new system of *Ḥatru*-estates that was
administered side by side with the traditional *bêt 'ābôt* system. Others are
certainly possible.

16.   *Origins of the 'Second' Temple*, 332–51.
17.   For this type of land tenure system, see Briant, *Cyrus and Alexander*, 75–6, 363, 405,
417, 459, 461–2, 485–6, 506, 597–8, 633, 747, 795, 892.

Chapter 4

TELL EṢ-ṢÂFI/GATH DURING THE PERSIAN PERIOD

Rona S. Avissar, Joe Uziel and Aren M. Maeir

Introduction

As can be seen from various general surveys of the archaeology of the Land of Israel during the Persian period, the finds from the 1899 excavations at Tell eṣ-Ṣâfi/Gath by Frederick Jones Bliss and R. A. Stewart Macalister, are of importance for the study of this period.[1] Many years have passed since these excavations were conducted and published, and a reassessment of the finds is clearly needed.[2] The combination of the poor methods of excavation and publication of these finds, a need to review their relationship to current scholarship, and in particular, their correlation to the results of the current excavations and surveys of the site, on-going since 1996,[3] necessitate a re-evaluation of all the evidence relating to the Persian period from this site.

During the Persian period, the Land of Israel was included in the Persian satrapy of 'Ever Hanahar/Abar Nahara' (= 'beyond the river', which included Syria, Phoenicia, the Land of Israel and Cyprus). The satrapy in turn consisted of various '*medinta*' (= provinces) such as Megiddo, Ashdod, Samaria, *Yehud* etc.[4]

The southern Coastal Plain and the Shephelah were included in the

---

1. Such as E. Stern, *Material Culture of the Land of the Bible in the Persian Period* (Warminster: Aris and Philips, 1982), p. 20; idem, *Archaeology of the Land of the Bible, vol. II: The Assyrian, Babylonian, and Persian Periods (732–332 BCE)* (New York: Doubleday, 2001), pp. 407–8, 416–18.

2. See R. S. Avissar, 'Reanalysis of Bliss and Macalister's Excavations at Tell eṣ-Ṣâfi in 1899' (unpublished MA thesis, Bar-Ilan University, 2004), (Hebrew with English summary).

3. A. M. Maeir, 'Tell eṣ-Ṣâfi/Gath 1996–2002', *IEJ* 53 (2003), pp. 237–46; J. Uziel and A. M. Maeir, 'Scratching the Surface at Gath: Implications of the Tell eṣ-Ṣâfi/Gath Surface Survey', *Tel-Aviv* 32 (2005), pp. 50–75.

4. For a review of the political structure of the region during this period, see, among others, Stern, *Archaeology of the Land of the Bible*, 366–72; P. Briant, *From Cyrus to Alexander: A History of the Persian Empire* (trans. P. T. Daniels; Winona Lake: Eisenbrauns,

province of Ashdod. The borders of the region have been defined as
including the region between the Sorek valley in the north and the Gerar
valley in the south.[5] Sites within the province include Ashdod, Ashkelon,
Nebi Yunis, Tel Zippor, Tel Erani, Tell el-Hesi, Mareshah, Lachish,
Gezer, Beth Shemesh, Tel Azekah and Beit Lehiaya. Tell eṣ-Ṣâfi/Gath was
also part of this region. In the following discussion, the finds dating to the
Persian period from both the earlier, British excavations, and those from
the present project at the site will be assessed, both in relation to each
other, as well as in relation to relevant finds from other sites in the general
region, in order to further understand the role and function of Tell eṣ-Ṣâfi/
Gath during the Persian period.

The PEF Excavations at Tell eṣ-Ṣâfi/Gath

Background

On the basis of a rather grandiose plan for conducting the first major
regional archaeological project in Palestine, the Palestine Exploration
Fund (PEF) applied for a permit from the Ottoman authorities to
excavate several ancient sites in the Shephelah (Judean foothills) region.
Frederick Jones Bliss was appointed by the directors of the PEF as the
head of this delegation, while Robert Alexander Stewart Macalister was
sent from London to serve as his assistant.[6] During 1899–1900, the
expedition conducted excavations at several large sites in the Shephelah:
Tell eṣ-Ṣâfi (Gath), Tell Zakariya (Azekah), Tell el-Judeideh (Tel Goded)
and Tell Sandahannah (Mareshah), as well as five smaller sites: Khirbet el-
Judeideh, Khirbet es-Surah, Khirbet Okbur, Khirbet Nuweitif and
Khirbet Dhikerin (Figure 1). Although, as Bliss and Macalister explain,
the main objective of their excavation project in the Shephelah region was
to excavate Tell eṣ-Ṣâfi, in light of its suggested identification as Philistine
Gath, this was found to be rather difficult, since the immediate vicinity of
the site was stricken by malaria, most of the site was covered by a modern

---

2002), pp. 487–90; O. Lipschits, *Jerusalem Between Destruction and Revival: Jerusalem Under
Babylonian Rule* (Jerusalem: Yad Yizhak Ben Zvi, 2004), pp. 24–30 (Hebrew); J. W. Betlyon,
'A People Transformed: Palestine in the Persian Period', *NEA* 68 (2005), pp. 4–58 (9–35).

    5.   A. Stern , 'The Southern Shephelah – its Borders and Geographical Boundaries', in D.
Urman and A. Stern (eds), *Man and His Environment in the Southern Shephelah* (Tel Aviv:
Masada, 1998), pp.12–16 (Hebrew); idem, *Archaeology of the Land of the Bible*, 407–12;
Betlyon, 'A People Transformed', 11–16 (who does not mention Tell eṣ-Ṣâfi as a Persian-
period site). Note that Briant, *From Cyrus to Alexander*, 766, suggests that the Shephelah was
part of a province of Idumea, as it was in the Hellenistic period.

    6.   Replacing Archibald Dickie, who had served as Bliss' assistant in previous excavations
conducted for the PEF; see N. A. Silberman, *Digging for God and Country: Exploration,
Archeology, and the Secret Struggle for the Holy Land, 1799–1917* (New York: A. A. Knopf,
1982), pp. 163–4.

village (whose inhabitants were not very co-operative), and other parts of the site were covered by modern graveyards. For these reasons it was decided to begin the actual excavations at the other sites, starting with Tell Zakariya (Figure 1).

The excavation at Tell eṣ-Ṣâfi itself commenced when the Elah valley riverbed dried up in the spring of 1899 and the imminent danger of malaria subsided. The excavation lasted for three short seasons in 1899: the first in May-June, the second in September, and the third in October-November.

The extent and duration of the excavation of the *tell* was limited primarily by the lack of co-operation with the local villagers. Due to this, excavations could not be conducted in the area of the village or in the adjacent cemeteries, as well as in the immediate vicinity of the *maqam* that was located on the summit of the *tell* (in the area of the Crusader fort, *Blanche Garde*). Several areas of various sizes and types were excavated on the *tell* (Figure 2a). Some of these were large, expansive areas without any clear subdivision; other areas were sub-divided into squares of 10x10 feet; while in other areas, only sporadic pits were excavated. In addition, the

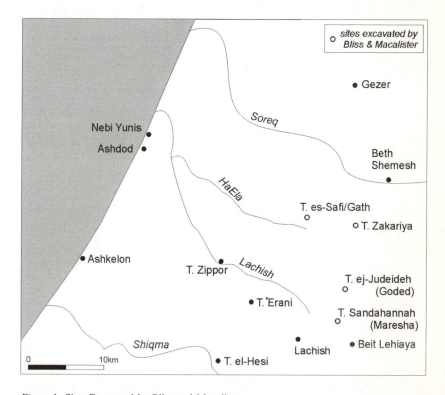

Figure 1: Sites Excavated by Bliss and Macalister

entire length of the (apparent) city wall was traced. Finally, the area of the Crusader fortress was surveyed but was not excavated.

Although far from sufficient according to modern standards, Bliss did make an attempt to both excavate and document the excavation in a somewhat consistent manner. All architectural features were dismantled only after the excavation had reached the same layer in all of its immediate vicinity; every architectural phase was drawn and photographed; all special finds were handed over to Bliss by the workers – in exchange for *baksheesh* (special payment). Special finds were defined as: metal, glass, stone, and bone objects – the pottery sherds and the ceramic vessels were not considered special finds. Decorated sherds or unique sherds that could be restored were saved, but all the rest, even if they were indicative (according to present-day standards), were not kept or documented. In addition, Bliss kept a daily journal, in which he reported where they had excavated and what finds they had gathered.

Bliss, as the director of the dig, wrote and published the preliminary reports, while Macalister was in charge of drawing the finds and the architectural features.

In those preliminary reports, the details of the excavation areas were described in a very cursory manner. Drawings of the main architectural features appeared in these reports, as well as plates of the special finds. They also attempted to date the different stratigraphic layers based on the pottery.

The final report was published in 1902 by Bliss and Macalister, in which

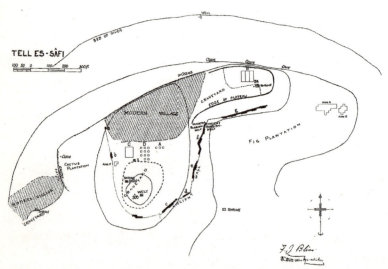

Figure 2a: Tell eṣ-Ṣâfi: Original map as drawn by Bliss and Macalister (with new excavation areas added)

they presented a general summary of all their excavations in the Shephelah region, including Tell eṣ-Ṣâfi/Gath.[7]

According to the permit received from the Turkish authorities, all finds from the excavations had to be sent to the Imperial Museum in Istanbul, while the excavators could only retain replicas of the original objects. The exact division of the objects between the museums in Istanbul and in Jerusalem is not clear. In any case, according to a summary composed by Gibson, at the beginning of the British Mandate over Palestine established after the end of the First World War, the state of the finds was as follows: some of the finds were located in the Rockefeller Museum in Jerusalem: some had been moved to the Istanbul Archeological Museum; some replicas were located in the Archives of the PEF in London; while a portion of the objects simply had disappeared.[8]

In addition, when Avissar recently attempted to locate all of the various finds in the various museums, it was discovered that some of the published objects had since disappeared and could not be located; on the other hand, some finds that had not been published were located in these museums and collections (see Table 1).

Methodology

It goes without saying that much has changed in the theoretical and methodological approaches to archaeological research since the times of Bliss and Macalister's excavations. For example, the very methods of excavation and recording are quite different today; even the typological sequence of the ancient pottery of the Land of Israel, such a basic tool for modern archaeological research, was not yet sufficiently known at the time. Clearly then, much of what was excavated and reported is quite obsolete, and in fact, often of little use. Nevertheless, as has been shown with the publication of other 'early digs', a meticulous re-analysis of the finds, along with a comparison to more modern research methods and conclusions (especially from the same site), can open up new vistas in understanding the archaeological and historical background of the site.[9] It is such a combination of the results of the earlier excavations on the one hand, along with newer methods, information, and understandings on the other, as well as archaeological data from the renewed excavations, that will be presented here.

7. F. J. Bliss and R. A. S. Macalister, *Excavations in Palestine during the Years 1898–1900* (London: Palestine Exploration Society, 1902).

8. S. Gibson, 'British Archaeological Institutions in Mandatory Palestine, 1917–1948', *PEQ* 131 (1999), pp. 115–43 (131–2, 136).

9. S. Gibson, 'The Tell El-Judeideh (Tel Goded) Excavations: a Re-Appraisal Based on Archival Records in the Palestine Exploration Fund', *Tel Aviv* 21 (1994), pp. 194–233; A. M. Maeir, 'Tell eṣ-Ṣâfi/Gath 1996–2002', *IEJ* 53 (2003), pp. 237–46.

As part of this research, an attempt was made to examine all of the existing objects from Bliss and Macalister's excavations at Tell es-Ṣâfi/ Gath. These objects are housed in the Rockefeller Museum in Jerusalem and in the Istanbul Archaeology Museum. In addition, copies of some of the finds are located in the archives of the PEF in London.

In addition, in order to enable an in-depth re-analysis of these excavations, the original excavation diaries and other documentation from the excavation that were deposited by Bliss and Macalister in the PEF in London, were checked. It should be noted that this included previously unpublished documentation.

There are many problems in our attempt to analyse and understand the finds from the excavations. One of the most basic problems is that the exact location of various of the excavation areas is not provided in the excavation reports and documentation. Although a very basic map of the excavations was provided in some of the publications (Fig. 2a), it is, in fact, extremely inaccurate, and does not allow for the accurate location of these areas. We attempted to locate these various points of excavation by comparing the different publications, their journals, and the tell-tale evidence seen today on the site itself. Some of the features and/or structures that appear on their maps and descriptions can still be identified today on the site. Based on this and other factors, we were able to identify the approximate location of the various excavation areas, and position them on a modern map of the site (Figure 2b).

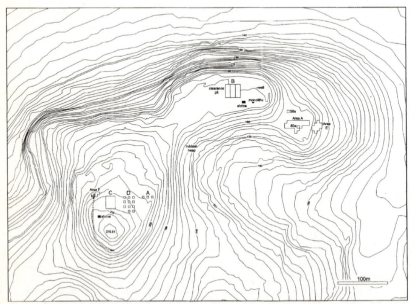

Figure 2b: Tell es-Ṣâfi: PEF excavation areas acording to reanalysis (including new excavation areas)

The Finds from the Excavations

In their reports, Bliss and Macalister did not note the existence of architectural features that they dated to the Persian period. In fact, the Persian-period finds from their excavations were only recognized as belonging to the so-called 'Jewish Stratum', which they dated to 800–300 BCE. Although Albright subsequently suggested dating this stratum to the Iron Age II-III (1000–586 BCE),[10] as Stern already pointed out, various objects from this stratum can in fact be dated to later than the Iron Age, and, more specifically, the Persian period.[11]

It seems that most of the Persian period finds were not found in a distinct stratum or phase in their excavations. Rather, they derive from what Bliss and Macalister described as the 'Rubbish Heap'.[12] This 'Rubbish Heap' was exposed during the tracing of the city wall, at the southern part of the central portion of the site. It was located just beneath a modern rubbish heap, next to and above, their 'Area F' of the city wall (Figure 2a-b; as opposed to the Area F of the current project). Approximately 35 feet of this feature were exposed. It was demarcated from the east by a wall and from the west by the inner part of the city wall. Bliss and Macalister assumed that all the finds from this location were discarded at the same time, once the city wall was no longer in use.[13] The actual location of the 'Rubbish Heap' is quite easy to locate on the *tell* based on Bliss and Macalister's map, since it is just southeast of the 'saddle' of the *tell*, in an area that today is completely covered with prickly-pear cacti plants (Figure 2a-b). Two unpublished drawings of the 'Rubbish Heap' and its relation to the city wall were discovered in the excavators' diaries (Figures 3, 4).

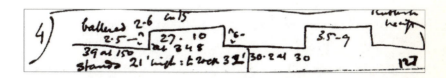

Figure 3: Sketch of rubbish pit from Bliss and Macalister's diaries; the diaries P.E.F p. 124

10.　W. F. Albright, 'Contributions to the Historical Geography of Palestine', *AASOR* II-III (1923), pp. 1–17 (15); idem, *The Archaeology of Palestine* (London: Penguin, 1960), pp. 30–1.

11.　Stern, *Material Culture of the Land of the Bible in the Persian Period*, 20.

12.　Bliss and Macalister, *Excavations in Palestine during the Years 1898–1900*, 26.

13.　F. J. Bliss, 'First Report on the Excavations at Tell Es-Safi', *PEFQS* 31 (1899), pp. 183–99 (194–7); idem, 'Third Report on the Excavations at Tell Es-Safi', *PEFQS* 32 (1900), pp. 16–29 (25–6).

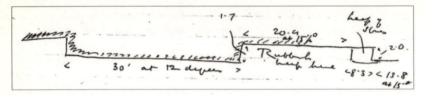

Figure 4: Sketch of rubbish pit from Bliss and Macalister's diaries; the diaries P.E.F p. 127

As part of the general study of the excavations, 221 objects from the various excavation areas were 're-discovered', re-checked and re-analysed. Of these 221 objects, 54 can be dated to the Persian period.[14]

As mentioned above, Bliss and Macalister did not date any items to the Persian period. They believed that seven objects should be dated to the sixth century BCE, three to the 'Seleucid' culture, one as 'Archaic', and three as 'Jewish'. Furthermore, many of the items were not chronologically assigned, some were only assigned stylistically (Assyrian-Babylonian style, Classic style, Greek Phoenician style), while others were not even mentioned. Despite this, after reanalysis of the finds, it is clear that the Persian period was quite well represented in the PEF excavations, as approximately 25% of the finds that were kept by the excavators date to this period.

A comparison between the Persian-period finds from Tell eṣ-Ṣâfi/Gath with those from other sites in the region (see Table 1), points to certain similarities, as well as differences. At Beth Shemesh, remains of a sixth-century BCE village were discovered, along with a Persian-period tomb (Tomb 14 in area Q20) in Stratum IIb-c. The tomb finds included a ring, bronze bowls and arrowheads, a bronze blade, a seal with Hebrew writing, and a seal with a winged creature and beads. The ceramic finds from the grave include various juglets with brown slip and red and white decoration, lamps with various bases and orange-brown slip and white decoration, a brown-slipped decanter, a vertically burnished decanter with brown slip and white decoration.[15] In comparing these finds from the tomb at Beth Shemesh with those from Tell eṣ-Ṣâfi/Gath, it would appear that the finds from Tell eṣ-Ṣâfi/Gath do not represent the finds from tombs, since they are so different from the finds in the tomb from Beth Shemesh.

At Gezer Stratum IV, Persian-period finds dating to the fifth and fourth centuries BCE were discovered in two areas. In addition, five graves that were originally defined as 'Philistine' by Macalister were dated to the

---

14. For a complete discussion and catalogue of these finds, see Avissar, 'Reanalysis of Bliss and Macalister's Excavations at Tell eṣ-Ṣâfi in 1899'.

15. E. Grant and G. E. Wright, *Ain Shems Excavations Vol. IV* (Haverford: Haverford College, 1938), Plate XLVIII.

Persian period according to the finds, including metal vessels, *yhd* seals, Persian-period pottery, and the plaster that seals the graves.[16] Alongside the buried individuals, various offerings were found, including animal bones, alabaster vessels, silver and bronze objects, an Assyrian cylinder seal, scarabs, fibulas, and a gold ring. Once again, the character of the finds from Gezer are quite different from the finds from Tell eṣ-Ṣâfi/Gath.

At Lachish, the Persian-and early Hellenistic-period remains were assigned to Stratum I. Starkey uncovered Building 106 – the so-called 'solar shrine', and claimed that it was built in the Persian period. In the temple's courtyard, a stone incense altar was found lying on its side, with an incised depiction of an individual with upraised hands. In addition, another 200 altars were found in three caves in the vicinity of the *tell*.[17]

After re-analysing the stratigraphy and finds, and after renewed excavations, Aharoni suggested that the 'solar shrine' was actually Hellenistic, as no actual connection was found between the altars and building. In his opinion, the *favissa* belonged to Building 15–16 (which he termed Building 10), which is located 40 metres southeast of the temple. Building 10 is similar in plan to Building 106, in that its basic structure is a room within a room, both surrounded by a courtyard. Aharoni maintained that Building 106 replaced Building 10, with the altars being transferred to the new temple.[18]

Stern agreed with Aharoni, designating Cave 534 as a *favissa*, where 150 limestone altars were found. The pottery in the cave can be dated to the fifth and fourth centuries BCE. Stern however does not make note whether the altar with the incised figure belongs to Temple 10 or the 'solar shrine'.[19]

In Ussishkin's excavations at Lachish additional remains from the Persian period were discovered. In the recent publication, most of these finds were dated to the end of the Persian period, to the late fifth and early

16.   R. A. S. Macalister, *The Excavation of Gezer, 1902–1905 & 1907–1909* (London: P. E. F, 1912), pp. 284–300; S. Gitin, *Gezer III: A Ceramic Typology of the Late Iron II, Persian and Hellenistic Periods at Tell Gezer* (Jerusalem: Hebrew Union College, 1990), pp. 229–38.

17.   O. Tufnell, *Lachish III* (Oxford: Oxford University Press, 1953), pp. 140–1.

18.   Y. Aharoni, *Investigations at Lachish - Lachish V* (Tel Aviv: Tel Aviv University, 1975), pp. 1–11.

19.   E. Stern, 'Note on a Decorated Limestone Altar from Lachish', *Atiqot* 11 (1976), pp.107–9. Note that Ussishkin prefers to date the 'solar shrine' to the Persian period, as originally suggested by Tufnell; see D. Ussishkin, 'Chapter 3: A Synopsis of the Stratigraphical, Chronological and Historical Issues', in D. Ussishkin (ed.), *The Renewed Archaeological Excavations at Lachish (1973–1994), Volume IV* (Tel Aviv: Tel Aviv University, 2004), pp. 50–119 (97).

fourth centuries BCE, and were related to Persian administrative, cultic and settlement activities at the site during this period.[20]

Once again, the finds at Lachish are not similar to those at Tell es-Ṣâfi/Gath, suggesting that there may possibly have been two different types of *favissa* in use at the time – the first for offerings, and the second for items that served in the temple.

Macalister and Bliss excavated at Mareshah as well, where they also found figurines from the Persian period. Although in their publication the excavators did not elaborate on this, it seems that many figurines were found, including a figurine of a woman with a child sitting on her shoulder,[21] and a seated pregnant fertility goddess, with bare breasts and stomach. Ciasca and Negbi compared the finds from Mareshah with the *favissa* at Tell es-Ṣâfi/Gath, Tel Zippor and Tel Erani.[22] In light of the recent excavations at Mareshah, it appears that the finds from Mareshah are not from a *favissa*.[23] Rather, these excavations have revealed a settlement on the northeast side of the *tell*, dating to the fifth century BCE. While the amount of Persian finds from Mareshah is quite small in comparison to those from Tell es-Ṣâfi/Gath, many of the figurines from both sites are quite similar.

At Tel Erani, two strata (II-III) from the Persian period were uncovered, dating to the end of the sixth-early fifth centuries BCE. On the south side of the *tell* (Area D), two *favissae* were found on the lower terrace.[24] Ciasca divided the finds into three groups: hollow figurines, including that of a woman holding a baby on her shoulder and a man with a crown; solid figurines, including one of a horseman with a pointed hat and hands stretched forward grabbing the horse's neck; and a group of partially-filled figurines, including a young, large-eyed man with curly hair, with a crown on his head made of bay leaves and another, partially nude man, with his arms against his body. The back of this latter figurine is not worked. According to Ciasca, the finds belong to a fifth- or fourth-century BCE *favissa* which served to 'store' figurines. She added that this may point to a local 'Israelite' cult, merging elements from the Persian and

20. A. Fantalkin and O. Tal, 'The Persian and Hellenistic Pottery of Level I', in D. Ussishkin (ed.), *The Renewed Archaeological Excavations at Lachish (1973–1994), Volume IV* (Tel Aviv: Tel Aviv University, 2004), pp. 2174–94; D. Ussishkin, 'Chapter 3: A Synopsis of the Stratigraphical, Chronological and Historical Issues', in Ussishkin, *The Renewed Archaeological Excavations at Lachish*, 96–7.

21. Bliss and Macalister (*Excavations in Palestine during the Years 1898–1900*, 138) dated this piece to the Seleucid period – about 300 BCE.

22. A. Ciasca, 'Un Deposito di Statuette da Tell Gat', *OrAnt* II (1963), pp. 5–63 (45–63); O. Negbi, *A Deposit of Terracotta's & Statuettes from Tel Sippor* (Atiqot VI; Jerusalem: Israel Department of Antiquities, 1966), pp. 1–5.

23. A. Kloner, personal communication.

24. S. Yevin, 'Tell Gath', *IEJ* 10 (1960), pp. 122–3.

Phoenician worlds.[25] The finds from the *favissae* at Tel Erani are very similar to those from Tell eṣ-Ṣâfi/Gath, strengthening the idea that the 'Rubbish Heap' at Tell eṣ-Ṣâfi/Gath is in fact a *favissa*.

The Persian-period finds from Tel Zippor were in fact not actually found on the site, but at a distance from the site, during the course of survey work. The finds include stone and pottery figurines. Subsequent to the survey, a salvage excavation was conducted to the north of the site, revealing a pit 80cm deep and 1m wide. The pit contained figurines and sculptures, linking the finds from the survey to the pit. It seems that this is a *favissa* that was connected to a temple, the remains of which did not survive.

The finds from this *favissa* include more than 200 figurines, although of them, only 107 pottery figurines and 11 stone figurines were published. Some of the items are hollow, others are solid, and others are partially hollow. Of the published examples, 53 figurines depict women, 54 men, 23 riders, and an additional eight are of various other types. They include 'Pillar Astarte' figurines, mother and baby figurines, figurines of the head of women, the head of Hermes, as well as figurines of horses – with and without riders. Biran and Negbi dated the assemblage to the Persian period based on typological and technical criteria. Nevertheless, they did note that some of the figurines could be dated to the Iron Age, possibly indicating the existence of an earlier temple, prior to that of the Persian period, and that items from this earlier temple were moved to the later one upon its construction. It seems that the temple existed for approximately 200 years, from 530–350 BCE, and the *favissa* was sealed no later that 350 BCE.[26] It is most significant to note that overall, the assemblage from Tel Zippor is very similar to that of Tell eṣ-Ṣâfi/Gath.

The Tell eṣ-Ṣâfi/Gath Surface Survey

Background

In the summer of 1996, a surface survey was conducted at the site of Tell eṣ-Ṣâfi/Gath, prior to the commencement of the excavations which are the central component of the ongoing Tell eṣ-Ṣâfi/Gath Archaeological Project. One of the primary motives behind the survey was to locate potential excavation areas, particularly areas in which the pre-Classical

25. Ciasca, 'Un Deposito di Statuette da Tell Gat', 45–63. This interpretation cannot be accepted today, since it is clear that in the Judean/Israelite cult of the Persian period there was little, if any, use of figurative elements, while in the cult of other cultures, in the non-Judean parts of the land, figurative objects were common in cultic contexts. See for example, E. Stern, 'What Happened to the Cult Figurines?', *BARev* 15/4 (1989), pp. 22–9, 53–4.

26. A. Biran and O. Negbi, 'A Stratigraphical Sequence at Tel Sippor', *IEJ* 16 (1966), pp. 1–7.

levels were accessible and/or not completely covered and destroyed by later cultural remains. The survey was subsequently completed in the summer and fall of 2001. All told, the survey enabled the definition of potential excavation areas, as well as defining the various periods of settlement represented on the site, determining the size of the site during the various periods, and mapping the estimated location and size of the settlement in the respective periods.[27]

Methodology

The primary focus of the study revolved around surface artifact collection. Prior to its commencement, the area that was to be surveyed was delineated, so as to include both the site and its immediate periphery. The boundaries used were the Elah valley riverbed to the north and northwest and the man-made trench that surrounds the site from the south, east and southwest. In order to assure coverage of the total area of the site (including all pre-modern periods), the survey extended beyond the above-mentioned boundaries in those areas in which finds were found adjacent to the border. These areas were found to be void of finds, reinforcing the

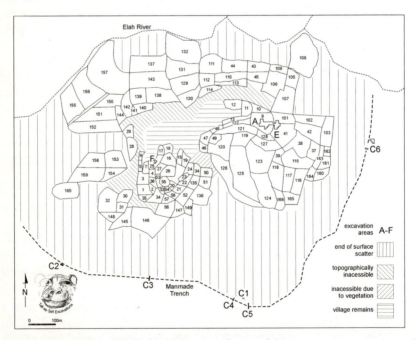

Figure 5: Map of Tell eṣ-Ṣâfi/Gath with location of survey fields

27.   Uziel and Maeir, 'Scratching the Surface at Gath: Implications of the Tell eṣ-Ṣâfi/ Gath Surface Survey'.

assumption that the survey had in fact covered the entire site. The site was divided into 'survey fields' based on topographic, geographic and architectural boundaries and features (Figure 5).

The finds collected from the surface were marked and analysed according to the separate fields, leading to the definition of the individual topographic units. Subsequently, the various fields with finds dating to a specific period were joined, enabling us to present maps in which the approximate size and location of the settlement of the various periods was presented.

During the fieldwork and the subsequent analysis of the finds, certain assumptions were made concerning the survey findings. First, it was believed that there should be a direct correlation between artifact dispersal and site size. At the same time, external factors (such as erosion) may cause a misrepresentation if not taken into account. In order to account for such factors, the analysis of the survey results was based on the notion that such factors would increase the interpreted site size. Therefore, two separate figures were calculated – *surface scatter* and *estimated site size* (Figure 6). The first figure presents the actual area in which finds from a certain period were discovered, while the second represents the interpretation that we suggest for the actual

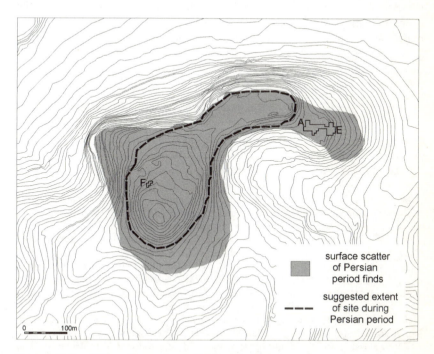

Figure 6: Tell eṣ-Ṣâfi: surface scatter and suggested site size

size of the site during the various periods (after having removed areas that seemed to be a misrepresentation due to external processes such as erosion). Regardless, the estimated site size should still be considered the maximum possible area of the settlement, as most external factors increase the surface scatter (and increase the interpreted site size).[28] We also believed that surface scatter was a more accurate method for calculating site size than a computation based on relative sherd quantities from the various periods.[29]

Finds from the Survey

The Persian period marks the revival of the settlement at Tell eṣ-Ṣâfi, following a substantial decline at the end of the Iron Age. All told, 2% (n = 246) of the diagnostic sherds collected on the site were dated to the Persian period. This is in contrast to only three sherds – a pair of rosette-stamped jar handles, and a jar handle with stamped concentric circles – that can be unequivocally dated to the Iron Age III; or, on the other hand, the 13 sherds that were dated to the Hellenistic period.[30] The Persian-period sherds were recovered primarily from the summit of the *tell* and its eastern slopes. While the total area yielding Persian finds tallied 12 hectares, it can be assumed that the settlement at the site was somewhat smaller. An approximate size of 8.5 hectares seems to be a reasonable estimate. Among the various finds from the survey that date to the Persian period, one can mention several examples of 'mortaria' bowls, as well as jars characteristic of the period. In addition, several Attic sherds that seem to date to the period were recovered (see Figure 7).

The Persian Period at Tell eṣ-Ṣâfi in Context

Tell eṣ-Ṣâfi during the Persian Period

As of the 2006 season, the current excavations of the Tell eṣ-Ṣâfi/Gath Archaeological Project have revealed only a small amount of stratified

28. This *contra* M. A. Miller, 'The Spatial Distribution of Ancient Human Occupation: Results of an Intensive Surface Survey and Test Excavations', in Y. Garfinkel and M. A. Miller (eds), *Shaar Hagolan* 1 (Oxford: Oxbow, 2002), pp. 35–46.

29. *Contra* A. Ofer, 'The Highland of Judah During the Biblical Period' (unpublished Ph.D. dissertation, Tel Aviv University, 1994), p. 97 (Hebrew); idem, 'The Monarchic Period in the Judaean Highland: A Spatial Overview', in A. Mazar (ed.) *Studies in the Archaeology of the Iron Age in Israel and Jordan*, (JSOTSup 331; Sheffield: Sheffield Academic Press, 2001), pp. 35–46. For additional comments, see Uziel and Maeir, 'Scratching the Surface at Gath: Implications of the Tell eṣ-Ṣâfi/Gath Surface Survey'.

30. For more extensive discussions on the survey and its results, see J. Uziel, 'The Tell eṣ-Ṣâfi Archaeological Survey' (unpublished MA thesis, Bar-Ilan University, Ramat-Gan, 2002); Uziel and Maeir, 'Scratching the Surface at Gath: Implications of the Tell eṣ-Ṣâfi/Gath Surface Survey'.

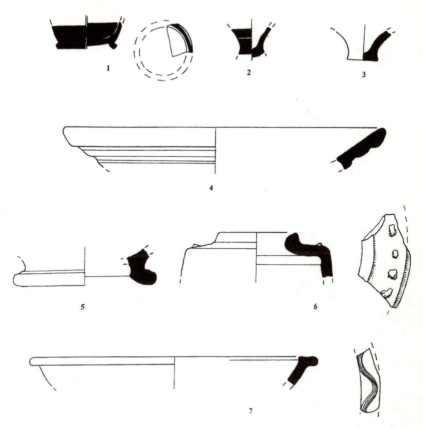

Figure 7. Tell eṣ-Ṣâfi/Gath survey: Pottery from the Persian Period

finds from the Persian period: an as-of-yet rather minimal Persian-period level was discovered in the 2006 season in Area F (northwest of the *tell* summit), along with occasional finds from the period in non-stratified deposits and in secondary/tertiary contexts in the excavations. Nevertheless, the evidence from the surface survey, in conjunction with the results of the PEF excavations, indicates that there was a rather substantial amount of activity at Tell eṣ-Ṣâfi/Gath during the Persian period. While the relatively high percentage of finds from this period that were recovered by Bliss and Macalister can be explained by the excavation of the 'Rubbish Heap' – as a *favissa* – the results of the surface survey indicate that this was not just a random feature. The Persian-period site was most likely quite extensive, even if it did not extend to the eastern slopes of the *tell* (where the current areas of excavation are located).

Tell eṣ-Ṣâfi/Gath, Before, During and After the Persian Period

Up until the late ninth or early eighth centuries BCE, Tell eṣ-Ṣâfi/Gath was a major site in the southern coastal plain/Shephelah, first as Canaanite Gath and subsequently as Philistine Gath.[31] After the destruction of the site at the end of the Iron Age IIA, most probably by Hazael of Aram Damascus,[32] the site rapidly declined, and although it was settled during the Iron Age IIB (apparently with a strong Judean influence), it was scarcely – if at all – settled during the Iron Age III, prior to the Persian period. As noted above, very few finds can be unequivocally dated to the Iron Age III. It seems therefore that the Persian period marks the revival of substantial activity at the site. Yet this revival seems to be short-lived, as the Hellenistic finds at the site are also minimal. This makes the activity at the site all the more interesting, as it stands alone, quite distinct from the overall continuity of settlement at the site, recognized in almost all other periods.

The gap in settlement (or at least of intensive and extensive activity) at the site during the final stages of the Iron Age and once again during the Hellenistic period, may be one of the reasons that the toponym 'Gath' did not survive into subsequent periods. As opposed to the four other major Philistine sites in which the Bronze and Iron Age names were clearly retained during later periods,[33] the name 'Gath' is not mirrored in the later names of the site: 'eṣ-Ṣâfi' and 'Blanche Garde'. It may very well be that these above-mentioned gaps in settlement and the apparent changes in the population in the region of Philistia, were the primary reasons for the loss of the original name of the site. Since the site does not seem to be mentioned in any known Persian-period literary sources or inscriptions, it is impossible to know whether the site was still called 'Gath', or, perchance, the name-transition, evidenced in later periods, had already occurred by this time.

---

31. The identification of Philistine Gath has been much debated over the years, but most scholars now agree with its identification at Tell eṣ-Ṣâfi. For more on this debate see: K. Elliger, 'Die Heimat des Propheten Micha', *ZDPV* 57 (1934), pp. 81–52 (148–152); A. F. Rainey, 'The Identification of Philistine Gath: A Problem in Source Analysis for Historical Geography', *Eretz-Israel* 12 (1975), pp. 63*-76*; W. M. Schniedewind, 'The Geopolitical History of Philistine Gath', *BASOR* 309 (1989), pp. 69–77. We feel that the results of the present archaeological project support this identification.

32. See A. M. Maeir, 'The Historical Background and Dating of Amos VI 2: An Archaeological Perspective from Tell eṣ-Ṣâfi/Gath', *VT* 54 (2004) 319–34.

33. In the case of Ekron, despite the fact that the site was abandoned at the end of the Iron Age, the Arabic toponym of the site (Kh. Muqaneh) quite closely retained the original name.

Conclusions

The first sign of stratified remains from the Persian period at Tell eṣ-Ṣâfi/ Gath were discovered during the 2006 excavation season. The character of the activities at the site during this time is still unclear, however. What can be said is that there was substantial activity at Tell eṣ-Ṣâfi/Gath during the period. On the one hand, what was once labelled a 'rubbish heap' and generally dated by Bliss and Macalister to 800–300 BCE can now be quite clearly recognized as a Persian-period *favissa*. This feature was most likely linked with a substantial cultic feature (such as a temple). This would explain the rather substantial dispersal of finds at Tell eṣ-Ṣâfi/Gath, which is similar to the situation at Tel Zippor, where, although the *favissa* was the only Persian period feature found, the dispersal of finds covered a much larger area. Finally, as mentioned above, the substantial amount of activity at Tell eṣ-Ṣâfi/Gath stands out in comparison to both the periods preceding (Iron Age IIB-III) and following (Hellenistic) the Persian period.

We have seen that the archaeological remains at Tell eṣ-Ṣâfi/Gath fit in well with both the archaeological and historical evidence from the Shephelah region. The material culture is quite similar to that of other sites in the region, and is distinctively different from that of sites in the area of *Yehud*. As such, it sheds interesting light on the population and settlement patterns in this part of the Shephelah during the Persian period.

Table 1: Persian-Period Finds from the PEF Excavations with Parallels
Finds Located and Photographed

Item	Dimensions	Material	Original Publication	Comments and Parallels
Scarab, (R, j321), worn out, no remains of original incisions, bronze wire inside.	0.7x1x1.2cm	White stone	In the second excavation report, it is stated that the scarab was found in a heap of rubbish, that it was made of bone and had a bronze bezel, and was made in Egyptian style.[1] In the final report, they add that it is possible to make out the writing '*nfr'nh*', meaning good life.[2]	Rowe claims that the scarab is inscribed '*nefer ib ra lives*', referring to *Ra nefer ib*, the name of King Psamatek, the second king of the 26th dynasty, who ruled between 589–595 BCE.[3] However, one can also read '*ra ankh nefer ib*', which would place the scarab between 280–265 BCE. According to its location in the rubbish heap, the latter is less feasible (since the rubbish heap dates at the latest, to the 4th century BCE).
Scarab (R, j879). A man standing with his legs apart, his left hand on his hip and his right arm straight.	1x1x1.2cm	Dark green stone with light brown patina	The scarab was found in the rubbish heap, carved in blue stone, with a depiction of a man on it. This is a Babylonian-Assyrian style scarab.[4]	No parallel was found for this scarab, however its location in the rubbish heap attests to its dating during the Persian period.

1. F. J. Bliss, 'Second Report on the Excavations at Tell Es-Safi', *PEFQS* 31 (1899), pp. 317–33 (330–1; pl. VI.8).
2. Bliss and Macalister, *Excavations in Palestine During the years 1898–1900*, 153, pl. 83.30.
3. A. Rowe, *A Catalogue of Egyptian Scarabs (Scaraboids, Seals and Amulets in the Palestine Archaeological Museum)* (Cairo: Institut Français d'Archéologie Orientale, 1936), p. 211.
4. Bliss, 'Second Report on the Excavations at Tell Es-Safi', 330–1; Pl. VI.7.

Item	Dimensions	Material	Original Publication	Comments and Parallels
Stamp seal (R, j849), pyramid-shaped. The seal has a hole in the centre, indicating that it was used as a pendant. It has a depiction of a man standing next to a tall table, and above him there is a poorly-incised solar symbol of the sun.	2x1.5cm	Brown-red stone	The scarab was found in the rubbish heap, carved of red stone. This is a Babylonian-Assyrian-style scarab depicting a priest performing a cultic ceremony on an altar.[5]	Keel and Kuchler state that this seal is of Assyrian style but date it to the Persian period.[6] At Ein Gedi, a similar seal was found, with a Babylonian priest before an altar, above him symbols of Marduk, with a spear and chisel in his hand, and the sun depicted above him. The seal was found in a 6th century BCE grave.[7] An additional seal with a similar depiction is located in the British Museum, and is dated to the 5th Century BCE. This seal is of pyramid shape, depicting a man bowing to Marduk and Nabu.

5. Bliss, 'Second Report on the Excavations at Tell Es-Safi', 332; Bliss and Macalister, *Excavations in Palestine During the years 1898–1900*, 41, 153; fig.16.1.

6. O. Keel and M. Kuchler, *Orte und Landschaften der bibel, Band 2* (Zurich: Benziger, 1982), p. 842: fig. 547.

7. Stern, *Archaeology of the Land of the Bible*, 535–7.

Item	Dimensions	Material	Original Publication	Comments and Parallels
Stamp seal (I, 1845), pyramid-shaped, the edge has a hole with part of the bronze attachment that was part of the pendant. The seal is incised with unorganized lines with circles at the ends.	2.1x1.3	Clear agate	The report of the second season states that the seal was found in the rubbish heap, made of stone, with unclear markings. In the final report, they add that the seal is made in a simple manner, with circles and lines, and should be dated to the Archaic period.[8]	Keel and Kuchler state that this is an Assyrian-style seal from the Persian period.[9]

8. Bliss, 'Second Report on the Excavations at Tell Es-Safi', 332; Bliss and Macalister, *Excavations in Palestine During the years 1898–1900*, 41, 332; fig.16.
9. Keel and Kuchler, *Orte und Landschaften der bibel*, 842; fig. 547.

Item	Dimensions	Material	Original Publication	Comments and Parallels
Mask (R, p103) of the face of a woman with a braid wrapped around her head. The features are well-proportioned and realistic, save for the ears, which are unusually large.	16.5 cm high	Brown pottery	The report describes this and other similar masks as Greek-Phoenician-style masks portraying women with styled hair, earrings and painted in red. Bliss agrees with Hanauer that the masks were used in Dionysiac celebrations in vineyards.[10] The report only presents mask 38, decorated in red and white, similar to Cypriot figurines.[11]	No complete examples of similar masks were found in Israel, although two fragments of such masks were found at Dor. Stern states that the masks were used in cultic ceremonies in the Persian period.[12] Elsewhere he mentions that pottery masks are characteristic of the Canaanite-Phoenician tradition, connected to the worship of Dionysius.[13] In the Fogg Museum at Cambridge there is a fragment of clay mask similar to these two, which according to the vendor was found at Thebes.[14]
Mask (I, 2014) depicting the face of a woman with a braid rapped around her head. The features are well-proportioned and realistic save for the ears, which are unusually large.	17.5 cm high	Light red pottery		

10. R. J. E. Hanauer, 'Notes', *PEFQSt* 26 (1894), pp. 209–10 (209); Bliss, 'Second Report on the Excavations at Tell Es-Safi', 328–9.
11. Bliss and Macalister, *Excavations in Palestine During the years 1898–1900*, 39, 140, Fig. 13.
12. E. Stern, 'Clay Figurines, Popular Cult Objects, and Sculpture', in E. Stern (ed.), *Excavations at Dor, Final Report* Vol. IB (Qedem Reports 2; Jerusalem: Institute of Archaeology, 1995), pp. 435–53 (447, Fig. 7.6.1, 2).
13. E. Stern, *The Material Culture of Israel during the Persian Period* (Jerusalem: Israel Exploration Society, 1973), pp. 173–4 (Hebrew); idem, *Archaeology of the Land of the Bible*, 508.
14. H. R. W. Smith, 'A Goddess from Lebadeia', *Hesperia Supplements* 8 (1949), pp. 353–60 (353–8, pl. 47: 6, 7).

Item	Dimensions	Material	Original Publication	Comments and Parallels
Part of a relief or statue (I, 2013), depicting the upper torso of a woman dressed in a folded garment, with her left hand extending out of the garment towards her neck.	14x12.2 cm	Red pottery with white slip	Not mentioned	This relief is similar to Persian masks. A similar piece was found at Tel Zippor.[15]
Relief fragment (R, p154), depicting a hand under a person's chest.	9x7 cm	Brownish-red pottery	Bliss and Macalister mention that it is a hand grasping a breast. This piece is made in a similar fashion as the masks, and there are three examples of this type.[16]	Similar to pl. 1.7

15. Negbi, *A Deposit of Terracotta's & Statuettes from Tel Sippor*, 14–15, Fig. 43.
16. Bliss and Macalister, *Excavations in Palestine During the years 1898–1900*, 138, 141, Pl. 70.8.

Item	Dimensions	Material	Original Publication	Comments and Parallels
Figurine of nude woman (R, p95). The right hand is broken, her left hand touches her stomach. The genitals are marked with holes. The figurine is hollow and is missing its head and the legs.	13 cm	Pottery	In the second interim report, it is mentioned that the figurines are female and hollow, in Greek-Phoenician style. No. 42 has a bent hand touching her stomach. No. 43 has both arms broken below the elbow; around the neck, a tall collar is marked. The excavators claim that the figurines depict Astarte.[17]	In the Tel Zippor *favissa* a similar, hollow figurine of a naked woman was found. This figurine's legs are held together, the arms are placed along the body, and the genitals and back side marked. This item is from the Persian period, dating from the end of the 6th to the middle of the 4th Century BCE.[18] A similar figurine was discovered in Byblos.[19] Stern claims that these are figurines of fertility goddesses, in eastern style, since the genitals are marked, and the hands supporting the breasts continue earlier traditions. Concerning these two examples, he notes that they are handmade pillar figurines, which he would date prior to the Persian period were it not for the stratigraphic placement.[20]
Figurine of nude woman (R, p54). The figurine is solid around the head and legs, the middle is hollow. She has an Egyptian headdress, with both arms broken from the elbow. The genitals are marked with incisions.	19.5 cm	Pottery		

17. Bliss, 'Second Report on the Excavations at Tell Es-Safi', 329; Bliss and Macalister, *Excavations in Palestine During the years 1898–1900*, 139, Pl. 70–11, 12.
18. Negbi, *A Deposit of Terracotta's & Statuettes from Tel Sippor*, 11, Pl. IV.8.
19. M. Dunand, *Fouilles de Byblos II* (Paris: Adrien Maisonneuve, 1958). p. 621.
20. *Material Culture of the Land of the Bible in the Persian Period*, 167–8.

Item	Dimensions	Material	Original Publication	Comments and Parallels
continued				
The legs are joined, and broken from the point where the figurine becomes solid. The posterior is also marked.				
Figurine of a rider (I, 2020), with the body of the horse and the rider squatting down on the horse. The features are not discernible.	11x6.2 cm	Pottery	Bliss and Macalister note that this is a very unique piece. Only two such figurines were found at Tell es-Ṣâfi, and until that time no others had been found anywhere. According to the production method, they determined it was of Greek origin. They noticed the horse's nose, hair and ears, as well as the rider's helmet.[21]	Similar figurines were found at Lachish and Tel Zippor, where the rider's body blends into the horse.[22] These figurines can be dated to the Persian period. Stern states that the rider is of eastern style, typical of the Persian period.[23] The rider usually has a moustache and is completely covered in a garment.

21. Bliss and Macalister, *Excavations in Palestine During the years 1898–1900*, 138, Pl. 70. 2.
22. Tufnell, *Lachish III*, 376, Pl. 33.1; Negbi, *A Deposit of Terracotta's & Statuettes from Tel Sippor*, 20, Pl. XIV.95.
23. Stern, *Archaeology of the Land of the Bible*, 493.

Item	Dimensions	Material	Original Publication	Comments and Parallels
Figurine of a pregnant woman (R, p94)	13.5 cm	Pottery	In the second interim report, the excavators report only one such figurine, which is hollow, with the back side flat and unworked. The figurine is broken from from the knees down, nude with a bump on the stomach, symbolizing pregnancy. The right hand is on the stomach, while the left hand is on the knee. The headdress is Egyptian, with the scarf falling onto the neck.[24]	A similar figurine of a nude pregnant woman was found at Byblos, with a pointy head and a square headdress.[26] Moscati claims that this type of figurine is Phoenician, dating to the 8th–6th centuries BCE. Stern notes that this type of figurine was common in the Persian period, and is of Phoenician style, despite the Egyptian headdress.[27]
Figurine of a pregnant woman (I, 2019). The lower body is broken. Both figurines are similar, depicting nude pregnant women that are sitting. The head is triangular, and the features are not discernable, other than the nose. A scarf is wrapped around the head. The right hand is on the stomach, while the left hand is on the knee.	9.2 cm	Pottery	In the final report, 12 such figurines are reported. The pregnant state links them to the Mother Goddess or the goddess of fertility. The figurines are sloppily made, making it difficult to discern features on the face and hands. A scarf covers the head and body until the knees. The figurine is dated to Seleucid times, as parallels from a secure stratigraphic context were found at Mareshah.[25]	

24. Bliss, 'Second Report on the Excavations at Tell Es-Safi', 328.
25. Bliss and Macalister, *Excavations in Palestine During the years 1898–1900*, 138, Pl. 70.10.
26. Dunand, *Fouilles de Byblos*, 241.
27. Muscati, S. (ed.), *The Phoenicians* (London: Tuaris, 1988), pp. 590, 38; Stern, *Archaeology of the Land of the Bible*, 494–5.

Item	Dimensions	Material	Original Publication	Comments and Parallels
Head of a figurine (R, p93)	4.2x2.5 cm	Pottery	Figurine of the head of a warrior with a helmet, belongs to the Classic style.[28]	A parallel dating to the Persian period was found at Dor, depicting a bearded man with a pointy hat. Stern adds that this is a Greek warrior wearing a helmet. The face was made using a mould, with additional features made by hand. It is of western-Greek style, dating to the second half of the 5th century BCE.[29]
Head of a figurine (copy of a possibly different item than that listed above). Both items are of the same type, depicting the head of a man wearing a tall hat that is bent towards the top, with a scarf dropping to his shoulders. The difference between the two is the beard, where the first is pointy, and the second is rounded.	4x2.5 cm	Pottery		

28. Bliss and Macalister, *Excavations in Palestine During the years 1898–1900*, 40, 141, Fig. 14d.
29. Stern, 'Clay Figurines, Popular Cult Objects, and Sculpture', 442–3, Fig. 7. 3: 4; idem, *Archaeology of the Land of the Bible*, 501–3.

Item	Dimensions	Material	Original Publication	Comments and Parallels
Figurine head (R, p80) depicting the face of a woman wearing a flat hat, with long curly hair. The head is hollow and seems to have belonged to a larger figurine.		Pottery	Bliss and Macalister state that this is a figurine of Silenus in Classic style.[30]	Stern claims that the figurine is in western-Greek style.[31] The woman is smiling, and has curly, shoulder-length hair. On her head is a round flat hat. This is a depiction of Aphrodite dating to the Persian Period.
Figurine of a couple hugging/wrestling (R, p1103). Two naked figures with their legs and hands hugging each other.	6.5x5.5x 5cm	Pottery	Bliss and Macalister state that this is a relief of two wrestlers.[32]	Stern notes that these are two adolescents wrestling. This is a typical Greek religious motif. These figurines are typical of the Persian period. He also notes that there are similar figurines where the two figures are hugging.[33]

30. Bliss and Macalister, *Excavations in Palestine During the years 1898–1900*, 40, 141, Fig. 14c.
31. Stern, *Archaeology of the Land of the Bible*, 503.
32. Bliss and Macalister, *Excavations in Palestine During the years 1898–1900*, 138, Pl. 70. 3.
33. Stern, *Archaeology of the Land of the Bible*, 500.

Item	Dimensions	Material	Original Publication	Comments and Parallels
Hollow figurine head (R, p99) depicting a worn-out face, although the eyes and nose are discernible. The hair is styled in an Egyptian headdress. The upper part of the body is decorated with red lines.	7x8cm	Pottery	It is noted that this is the head of a woman with an Egyptian headdress, with two red lines on the neck.[34]	Stern claims that this is from the Persian period and represents a mixed style, combining both eastern and western features.[35]

34. Bliss and Macalister, *Excavations in Palestine During the years 1898–1900*, 139, Pl. 70. 13.
35. Stern, *The Material Culture of Israel during the Persian Period*, 169.

Item	Dimensions	Material	Original Publication	Comments and Parallels
Male figurine (I, 2016) hollow, with the lower body broken off. The figurine is painted in dark red, with the back side not worked. The right hand holds the beard, and the head is adorned with a round flat hat.	12x5.7cm	Pottery	In various publications, the figurine is displayed with those shown in plates 2.10 and 2.11, stating that the three are the same style. The figure has a long beard, with his right hand holding its end. He wears a flat hat, with a scarf dropping from it to his shoulders. It is not clear if the figure is standing or sitting, as the lower part has not survived. It is in Semitic style.[36]	Almost identical figurines were found at Tel Zippor and Lachish – hollow figurines with an unworked posterior. The figurines depict a man with a long beard and moustache, a cylindrical hat, and his right hand holding the beard.[37] Stern states that this is a Persian-period eastern-style figurine, where the figure is sitting and wearing a cape. The beard and moustache are large, and are held. The figure represents the Phoenician god Baal.[38]

36. Bliss and Macalister, *Excavations in Palestine During the years 1898–1900*, 141, Fig. 53.2.
37. Tufnell, *Lachish III*, 378, Pl. 33.7; Negbi, *A Deposit of Terracotta's & Statuettes from Tel Sippor*, Pl. 17, Pl. XI.65.
38. Stern, *Material Culture of the Land of the Bible in the Persian Period*, 492–3.

Item	Dimensions	Material	Original Publication	Comments and Parallels
Male figurine (Replica P) with the right hand holding his beard, and wearing a pointy hat with a scarf dropping to his shoulders. The left hand rests on the knee. The figure is depicted wearing a long cape.	13x5cm	Pottery	A man sitting with his right hand holding his beard. He is wearing a pointy hat, with a scarf dropping from it (Bliss and Macalister 1902.141, Fig. 53).[39]	An almost identical figurine was found at Beth Shean. Stern states that this is a Persian-period eastern-style figurine, where the figure is sitting and wears a cape. The beard and moustache are large, and are held. According to Egyptian iconography, the pointy hat represents Osiris, although the figurine most probably represents the Semitic god Baal.[40]
Head of a male figurine (R, p74). The face is pinched and unclear. He is holding his beard in the right hand, and wearing a pointy hat.	8cm long	Reddish-brown pottery	Bliss and Macalister note that the figurine is sloppily made, with incorrect proportions. Due to the right hand holding the beard, they group it with the previous two figurines.[41]	Stern states that this is a Persian-period eastern-style figurine, where the figure is sitting and wearing a cape. The beard and moustache are large, and are held.[42]

39. Bliss and Macalister, *Excavations in Palestine During the years 1898–1900*, 141, Fig. 53.
40. Stern, *Material Culture of the Land of the Bible in the Persian Period*, 492–4.
41. Bliss and Macalister, *Excavations in Palestine During the years 1898–1900*, 141, Fig. 53.
42. Stern, *Material Culture of the Land of the Bible in the Persian Period*, 492–4.

Item	Dimensions	Material	Original Publication	Comments and Parallels
Figurine of a grotesque face (R, p77, replica P), the back side is not worked. The nose is flattened, the ears are large and the beard is long. It is not clear whether there is hair or a hat on the head.	4.5x3cm	Pottery	Rough figurine of a satyr with a hoof and horns, painted scarlet red.[43]	No parallels were found for this item, although the grotesque style and its location in the rubbish heap place it securely in the Persian period. It may be a depiction of the god Bes.
Head of a statue (I, s196) remains of red paint on the face. The face is of a man wearing a pointy hat with a broken nose.	8cm	Limestone	Cypriot-style statue dated to the 6th century BCE.[44]	At Tel Zippor, the head of a female statue with a conical headdress and lines of curls was found. The item is made of soft limestone, which is incised. It is dated to the end of the 6th century/mid-4th century BCE.[45] It is also similar to item in pl. 3.3.

43. Bliss and Macalister, *Excavations in Palestine During the years 1898–1900*, 40, 141, Fig. 14a.
44. Bliss and Macalister, *Excavations in Palestine During the years 1898–1900*, 146, Pl. 75a. 3.
45. Negbi, *A Deposit of Terracotta's & Statuettes from Tel Sippor*, 8, 21, pl. XXVI. 114.

Item	Dimensions	Material	Original Publication	Comments and Parallels
Head of a statue (I, s191) with hair reaching the neck, wearing a pointy hat.	12cm	Limestone	In the second interim report, the head of a female statue with a pointy hat and scarf down to the shoulders is published. In the final report, the excavators add that the statue is of Cypriot style.[46]	This statue is very similar to item 60, both having lines of curls and a pointy hat. This item also has a scarf down to its shoulders. Both are similar to an example from Tel Zippor, dating to the Persian period.[47]
Head of a statue (I, s193, replica P) with hair arranged around the head and a broken nose.	12.5cm	Limestone	In the second interim report, the excavator reports this item as a head of a female statue, probably placed on a door hinge ('part of a corbel'). The nose is broken, and around the head is the mane of a lion. In the final report, the excavators add that the statue is of Cypriot style and dates to the 6th century BCE.[48]	Stern states that this head is a depiction of Herakles, according to the mane of the lion. He also states that this is a typical style of the Persian period.[49]

46. Bliss, 'Second Report on the Excavations at Tell Es-Safi', 329–30; Bliss and Macalister, *Excavations in Palestine During the years 1898–1900*, 146, Pl. 75a. 4.
47. Negbi, *A Deposit of Terracotta's & Statuettes from Tel Sippor*, 8, 21, pl. XXVI. 114.
48. Bliss, 'Second Report on the Excavations at Tell Es-Safi', 329–30; Bliss and Macalister, *Excavations in Palestine During the years 1898–1900*, 146, Pl. 75a. 2.
49. Stern, *The Material Culture of Israel during the Persian Period*, 161.

Item	Dimensions	Material	Original Publication	Comments and Parallels
Head of a statue (I, s192) with hair arranged in curls around the head, with a ribbon on the hair. The nose is broken, the eyes are marked and inset, the mouth is closed.	10cm	Stone	Not recorded	At Byblos a similar item was found, where the items are marked in indents, the nose is broken, the lips are furrowed, with the hair wrapped and a ribbon on it. This is an example of a Cypriot statue from the 4th–3rd centuries BCE.[50]
Head of a statue (I, s194) with a very worn-out face and hair arranged in curls around the head.	11x9.5	Stone	Not recorded	Despite the worn-out state, it is possible to see that this is almost identical to item 63, placing it in the 4th–3rd centuries BCE.

50. Dunand, *Fouilles de Byblos*, 689, Pl. CL-14382.

Item	Dimensions	Material	Original Publication	Comments and Parallels
Lower part of statue wearing a dress or toga, with both feet sticking out from under the dress. The statue stands unsupported.	14x10.5cm	Limestone	Cypriot-style statue from the 6th century BCE.[51]	A similar figurine was found at Tel Zippor, made of soft limestone, depicting a standing figure wrapped in a toga. The statue is dated to the 6th/mid–4th centuries BCE.[52] Stern compares this item with the next two items (nos. 66–67), and notes that all three are of women wearing very long dresses, that cover them from neck to toe. The horizontal lines are meant to represent the folds of the cloth, as it would be worn on the human body. Stern agrees that these items are of the Cypriot style, dating to the 5th century BCE.[53]

51. Bliss and Macalister, *Excavations in Palestine During the years 1898–1900*, 146, Pl. 75b.1.
52. Negbi, *A Deposit of Terracotta's & Statuettes from Tel Sippor*, 21, Pl. XV, 108.
53. Stern, *The Material Culture of Israel during the Persian Period*, 20, 162–3.

Item	Dimensions	Material	Original Publication	Comments and Parallels
Upper part of a statue (I, s177) from the shoulders until the hip. The figure wears a dress with folds, with the right hand extended out of the dress.	16x14cm	Limestone	Figure wearing a toga, of the 6th century BCE, and in Cypriot style. [54]	A similar figurine was found in Elyachin, of Cypriot style, dated to the 5th century BCE according to the pottery found with it. Stern notes that these items are Cypriot, dating to the 5th century BCE. [55]
Statue of a female body (I, s179), wearing a dress with folds. There is a necklace around the neck, and the left hand is in the dress.	18x10cm	Stone	In the second interim report, and in the final report, the excavators note that this statue is unique in the careful design of the dress, to the point where one can see the contour of the breasts, as well as the careful design of the necklace beads, which are pear-shaped. The statue is Cypriot style dating to the 6th century BCE.	At Vouni, Cyprus, a statue of a female body with no head, wearing a dress and a bead necklace was found. The beads are leaf-shaped. The left hand is resting on the side of the body. The statue is assigned to type III-2, since the dress follows the contour of the body (despite the folds). It is dated to the 5th century BCE. [56]

54. Bliss and Macalister, *Excavations in Palestine During the years 1898–1900*, 146, Pl. 75b. 2.
55. M. Bosheri, 'Persian Period Statuettes from Elyachin', *Hadashot Archaeologiot* 14 (1965), p.10 (Hebrew).
56. E. Gjerstad, *The Swedish Cyprus Expedition – Finds and Results of the Excavations in Cyprus 1927–1931* Volume III (Stockholm: The Swedish Cyprus Expedition, 1937), p. 267, Pl. LXVIII. 497.

Item	Dimensions	Material	Original Publication	Comments and Parallels
Body of a statue (I, s173), wearing a straight dress, with its arms resting on either side.	28x15cm	Stone	The excavators assign this to the 6th century BCE, and as being of Cypriot style.[57]	At Byblos, a similar statue was found, with a straight dress and right hand resting on the side of the body. The only difference between this and item no. 68 is that at Byblos, the left hand is bent.[58]

57.　Bliss and Macalister, *Excavations in Palestine During the years 1898–1900*, 146, Pl. 75b.2.
58.　Dunand, *Fouilles de Byblos*, 521, Pl. CLXXXIX.

Item	Dimensions	Material	Original Publication	Comments and Parallels
Glass drop (R, j457) of a grotesque face, painted white and yellow	2.8x1.6cm	Blue stone	In the second interim report the amulets of grotesque figures are assigned to the Phoenician style. They are made of blue or black paste with yellow or white ends respectively. One of the items lost an ear. Later the excavators add that the pendants were found in the rubbish heap, and were made grotesque and ugly in order to protect whomever wears them from the evil eye.[59]	Barkay found an amulet of a grotesque head of a male with a beard in Cave 24, Room 25 at Ketef Hinnom in Jerusalem. The amulet is dark blue and decorated with yellow and light blue lines. The item dates to the Persian period.[60] Stern points out that glass drops of this sort are common in the Persian period, from the 6th to the 4th Centuries BCE. They come in various forms, as male and female heads. The males have a beard. The figures are grotesque and of eastern style. They are primarily found in the Phoenician regions and those that had contacts with them.[61]
Drops (I, 1843). 1. Grotesque face, broken from the nose down. It is decorated with white bands around the face and eyebrows. The pendant hole is above the head. 2. Grotesque face. It is decorated with white bands around the face and eyebrows. The eye is of black stone and protrudes. The pendant hole is above the head.	1. 5x1.5 2. 2x2.1	1. Black stone 2. blue stone		

59. Bliss, 'Second Report on the Excavations at Tell Es-Safi', 332; Bliss and Macalister, *Excavations in Palestine During the years 1898–1900*, 154, Fig. 19.
60. G. Barkay, 'Excavations at Ketef Hinnom in Jerusalem', in H. Geva (ed.), *Ancient Jerusalem Revealed* (Jerusalem: Israel Exploration Society, 1994), pp. 85–106 (97–8).
61. Stern, *The Material Culture of Israel during the Persian Period*, 153–4.

Item	Dimensions	Material	Original Publication	Comments and Parallels
Right eye amulet (I 1857), with decoration around the eye to accentuate it. The back side is not worked, and the hole for the pendant runs through the entire back.	3x2.1cm	White stone	In the second interim report, it is noted that these pendants were found in the rubbish heap. These are only 2 of the 12 Egyptian pendants made of paste in the shape of an eye, which vary in colour and size. In the final report, the excavators add that the eyes represent the eternal eye of *wd't*.[62]	Cahill states that the pendants of the eye of Horus or Wedjat are a typical Egyptian motif represented by a human eye with aspects of an eagle eye. The eye can be divided into six parts: the sclera, the pupil, the brow (human), the back of the eye, the front plume and the rear plume (eagle). This pendant is a representation of the head of the Egyptian pantheon, Ra and later Horus. The purpose of the pendant is protection from the evil eye.[63]
Left eye amulet (I, 1861), with a decoration around the eye to accentuate it. The posterior is identical to the front, and the hole for the pendant runs through the entire back.	1.6x1.3cm	White stone		At Lachish eye pendants were found, described as combining human and eagle aspects, and representing Horus. The excavator explains that the eye appears on both sides of the pendant, in order to protect the bearer day and night.

62. Bliss, 'Second Report on the Excavations at Tell Es-Safi', 330, Pl. V. 10; Bliss and Macalister, *Excavations in Palestine During the years 1898–1900*, 154, Pl. 84. 5, 8.

63. J. M. Cahill, 'Horus Eye Amulets', in T. A. Donald and A. De Groot, *Excavations at the City of David 1978–1985, Vol. IV* (Qedem 35; Jerusalem: The Institute of Archaeology, The Hebrew University of Jerusalem, 1996), pp. 291–7 (291).

Item	Dimensions	Material	Original Publication	Comments and Parallels
				Additional examples from the Persian period were found at Tell el-Hesi, Stratum V and Cave 24, Room 25 at Ketef Hinnom in Jerusalem.[64]
Monkey pendant (I, 1856) with protruding ears. The monkey holds a round object. The hole for the pendant is located under the ears.	3x1.4cm	Light blue stone	The excavators report that the find was discovered in the rubbish heap. They believe that it was a representation of the god Bes, made of paste and green enamel.[65]	The monkey pendant (*papio anubis*) was also found in Megiddo Stratum VA dating to the Persian period.[66] The monkey is considered the sacred animal of the god Thoth. Herrmann notes that the figure is placing its hand on its face, and actually dates to the Iron Age II. She also states that the item is lost and could not be found.[67]

64. Tufnell, *Lachish III*, 379, Pl. 34. 8, 9, 10; W. J. Bennett and J. A. Blakely, *Tell el-Hesi, The Persian Period (Stratum V)* (Winona-Lake: Eisenbrauns, 1989), pp. 277–8; Barkay, 'Excavations at Ketef Hinnom in Jerusalem', 99–100.

65. Bliss, 'Second Report on the Excavations at Tell Es-Safi', 331, Pl. V. 2; Bliss and Macalister, *Excavations in Palestine During the years 1898–1900*, 154, Pl. 84. 2.

66. Tufnell, *Lachish III*, 380, Pl. 35. 31, 32.

67. C. Herrmann, *Ägyptische Amulette aus Palästina/Israel* (Orbis Biblicus et Orientalis; Freiburg: Universität Verlag, 1994), p. 490, fig. 702.

Item	Dimensions	Material	Original Publication	Comments and Parallels
Pendant of Bes (I, 1855) with both hands resting on the stomach. Behind the ears is the necklace hole. The pendant is very worn.	2.7x1.5cm	Light blue stone	The excavators report that this find was discovered in the rubbish heap and it is a representation of the god Bes.[68]	At Lachish a similar pendant of Bes was found. Tufnell explains that the god began as protector of mother and baby, but later evolved into the protector of all women and children.[69]
				At Dor, parallels were also found, although slightly different. Bes is usually described as a dwarf with long arms, short crooked legs, and a tail. He has a wide face and a long nose, messy beard, large eyes, thick eyebrows, protruding ears, and short horns. Sometimes he is depicted with a crown of feathers. The items are dated to the Persian period.[70] Herrmann notes that the figure places its hand on its face, and actually dates it to the Iron Age II. She also states that the item is lost and could not be found.[71]

68. Bliss and Macalister, *Excavations in Palestine During the years 1898–1900*, 154, Pl. 84. 1.
69. Tufnell, *Lachish III*, 379, Pl. 34. 12.
70. Stern, 'Clay Figurines, Popular Cult Objects, and Sculpture', 448–51, Fig. 7.6–3, 8.
71. Herrmann, *Ägyptische Amulette aus Palästina/Israel*, 490, fig. 702.

Item	Dimensions	Material	Original Publication	Comments and Parallels
Mould for making a bell (R, s215, replica P), with apparent faces of Bes.	8x5cm and 4cm diameter for the bell.	Limestone	The find was found in the rubbish heap and described as a very intricate mould for a bell.[72]	Moorey notes that the hot metal was poured into moulds of fired material. Molds of two parts were already used in the 4th millennium BCE, although they were generally used for thick tools.[73] It is therefore not possible to use technological factors to date the bell mould, and as no parallels were found, it seems that the only datable evidence is the find spot – the rubbish heap of the Persian period. See also Braun for a discussion of bells from ancient Israel. Although he states that this bell is pre-Hellenistic, he does not suggest a definite date.[74]

72. Bliss and Macalister, *Excavations in Palestine During the years 1898–1900*, 43, 145, Fig. 20.
73. P. R. S. Moorey, *Ancient Mesopotamian Materials & Industries* (Oxford: Oxford University, Press 1994), pp. 269–70.
74. J. Braun, *Music in Ancient Israel/Palestine: Archaeological, Written, and Comparative Sources* (trans. D. Stott; Grand Rapids: Eerdmans, 2002), p. 196, fig. V.5.

Finds not Located

Item	Dimensions	Material	Original Publication	Comments and Parallels
Piece of an Attic Lekythos	Not marked	Pottery	Piece of a Lekythos found in the garbage heap, with a figure drawn on it in gold and brown on white. The dress of the figure is pink.[75]	Stern states that this type of vessel is part of the Attic/Greek repertoire that was imported to this region at the end of the 6th Century BCE.[76] The upper part of the vessel is decorated with a geometric motif, and the scene is usually painted in red and black.[77] It is important to note that no such gold and brown decoration has ever been reported in our region.[78] It should be mentioned that because we did not see the pottery itself, we cannot be sure about the painting on it.
Lamp	11cm diameter	Pottery	Seven-wicked lamp, dating to the 'Jewish Period'.[79]	Lamp from the late Iron Age III-Persian period (7th–6th centuries BCE). A similar lamp was found at Tell El-Kheleifeh, although with an addition on the base.[80]

75. Bliss and Macalister, *Excavations in Palestine During the years 1898–1900*, 101, 102, Fig. 40.
76. Stern, *Archaeology of the Land of the Bible*, 518–22.
77. A. Stewart and S. R. Martin, 'Attic Imported Pottery at Tel Dor, Israel: An Overview', *BASOR* 337 (2005), pp. 79–94.
78. Dr. Sonia Klinger, personal communication.
79. Bliss and Macalister, *Excavations in Palestine During the years 1898–1900*, 131, 102, Pl. 66.11.
80. N. Glueck, 'The Third Season of Excavation at Tell El-Kheleifeh', *BASOR* 79 (1940), pp. 2–18 (fig.10.869); idem, 'Kheleifeh, Tell el-', *NEAEHL* 3 pp. 867–9 (869).

Item	Dimensions	Material	Original Publication	Comments and Parallels
Kernos	Each lamp is 5x2cm	Pottery	Identified as part of a holemouth jar, well known in the later periods. The rim is decorated with small lamps, placed next to – but not touching – each other.[81]	Stern notes that this is in actuality a *kernos*, with small lamps attached. He dates it to the Persian period.[82] A similar find is located in the collection of the Hebrew University, Jerusalem (Cat. HUJ6734), dating to the Iron Age II.
Stamp seal		Stone	In the second interim report, it is noted that a seal was found in the rubbish heap, made of agate stone, with a depiction of a priest in front of an altar. In the final report, the excavators add that this is a Babylonian seal of a priest standing before a holy tree.[83]	Keel and Kuchler state that on the seal there is a depiction of a priest standing before the gods Marduk and Nabu. Above him is a star. This is a Neo-Assyrian-style stamp from the 7th–6th centuries BCE.[84]

81. Bliss and Macalister, *Excavations in Palestine During the years 1898–1900*, 131, 102, Pl. 66.11.
82. E. Stern, 'The Material Culture of Israel during the Persian Period' (Ph.D. dissertation, Hebrew University in Jerusalem, 1969), Pl. 37, 39 (Hebrew).
83. Bliss, 'Second Report on the Excavations at Tell Es-Safi', 332; Bliss and Macalister, *Excavations in Palestine During the years 1898–1900*, 41, 153; fig.16.
84. Keel and Kuchler, *Orte und Landschaften der bibel*, 842, Fig. 547.

Item	Dimensions	Material	Original Publication	Comments and Parallels
Figurine		Pottery	The neck of a handmade vessel with a clear rim. It is painted red, and has accentuated eyes and breasts. The vessel was found in the rubbish heap, although it is very early and probably an import.[85]	The figurine is not clear enough to discuss.

85. Bliss and Macalister, *Excavations in Palestine During the years 1898–1900*, 135–6, Pl. 67.1.

Item	Dimensions	Material	Original Publication	Comments and Parallels
Figurine		Pottery	Part of a female figurine, with her hand bent under her breasts, where she holds an adder snake. This was discovered in the rubbish heap.[86]	It is not clear what the figure is holding or whether the line decoration is part of the figure's dress or something that the figure is holding. It is possible that this is part of a female or nude goddess, which is common in the Late Bronze Age and Early Iron Age I. In this period, it is common to find standing figurines, whose hands are either supporting the breasts, holding the breasts, along the body, in a V form in front of the body, or touching the genitals. It is widely agreed that the depiction of nudity and the placement of the hands, denote fertility, power, beauty and erotica.[87] Another possibility is to compare this to a figurine from Dor, where the figure is holding her breasts. This dates to the Persian period and is in the eastern style.[88]
Figurine		Pottery	Part of figure holding an adder snake to its thigh.[89]	This item is not sufficiently clear. It is possible that, once again, this item is a Late Bronze Age figurine, or, possibly, a Persian-period, eastern-style figurine (see above).

86. Bliss and Macalister, *Excavations in Palestine During the years 1898–1900*, 138, Pl. 70.4.
87. O. Keel and C. Uehlinger, *Gods, Goddesses, and Images of God in Ancient Israel* (Minneapolis: Fortress, 1998), p. 104.
88. Stern, 'Clay Figurines, Popular Cult Objects, and Sculpture', 443, Fig. 7.4.1.
89. Bliss and Macalister, *Excavations in Palestine During the years 1898–1900*, 138, Pl. 70.5.

Item	Dimensions	Material	Original Publication	Comments and Parallels
Figurine		Pottery	A hand grasping a breast.[90]	The sherd is small and unclear, although it seems that the best comparison is to the two items above.
Figurine		Pottery	The figure of a woman, covered from the hips down, holding the legs of a child that sits on her shoulders. The figure is sloppily made, and dated to Seleucid times, as a parallel was found from Seleucid levels at Mareshah.[91]	Stern notes that figurines of women with children on their shoulders are common in the Land of Israel during the Persian period. They are of eastern-style, and were possibly brought as an offering before the gods.[92] An identical figurine was found in the *favissa* at Tel Erani, dating to the 5th century BCE.[93]

90. Bliss and Macalister, *Excavations in Palestine During the years 1898–1900*, 138, Pl. 70.6.
91. Bliss and Macalister, *Excavations in Palestine During the years 1898–1900*, 153, Pl. 83.3.
92. Stern, *The Material Culture of Israel during the Persian Period*, 167, Pl. 169.8.
93. Ciasca, 'Un Deposito di Statuette da Tell Gat', 59–63.

Item	Dimensions	Material	Original Publication	Comments and Parallels
Amulet		Paste	Pendant of a lion head. Green, with the facial structure and eyebrows marked in yellow. This is a typical depiction of the god Seth, although since the image is grotesque, it may be Bas.[94]	Herrmann states that the pendant is made partially by hand and partially by mould. The lion has a mane, and he claims that the figure is grotesque, due to the facial hair, which does not appear to be of human type.[95] The hole for the pendant is intricate. The pendant is not to be seen as a representation of Bas, since from the Iron Age IIb onward, Bas is represented with a feather headdress, unlike this example. As the item was found in the rubbish heap which cannot be earlier than the Iron III, the figure cannot represent Bas.
Amulet		Paste	It is noted that this amulet, which was found in the rubbish heap, is green, and depicts Bes with black eyes and green and black feathers.[96]	Rowe believes that the pendant is the head of Bes, wearing a feather crown. Herrmann only refers to Rowe's figure, as the item was already missing at the time. She notes that the pendant was mould-made and dates to the Iron Age IIB.[97] At Dor, a similar faience pendant was found, with the head of Bes wearing a feather crown. This latter item dates to the Persian period.[98]

94. Bliss and Macalister, *Excavations in Palestine During the years 1898–1900*, 153, Pl. 83.2.
95. Herrmann, *Ägyptische Amulette aus Palästina/Israel*, 549, Fig. 801, *contra* Stern, 'Clay Figurines, Popular Cult Objects, and Sculpture'.
96. Bliss, 'Second Report on the Excavations at Tell Es-Safi', 331, Pl. V.16; Bliss and Macalister, *Excavations in Palestine During the years 1898–1900*, 153, Pl. 83.3.
97. Rowe, *A Catalogue of Egyptian Scarabs*, 269, Pl. XXX:A2; Herrmann, *Ägyptische Amulette aus Palästina/Israel*, 386, 459.
98. Stern, 'Clay Figurines, Popular Cult Objects, and Sculpture', 448, Fig. 7.6.3.

Item	Dimensions	Material	Original Publication	Comments and Parallels
Amulet		Blue Paste	Amulet depicting Bes.[99]	This item is similar to the previous one, depicting the head of the god Bes and dating to the Persian period.
Amulet		Green paste	Amulet depicting Bes.[100]	This item is similar to the previous ones, dating to the Persian period, but depicts the entire body of Bes.
Amulet		Green Paste	Amulet of El.[101]	This item depicts the head of Bes and is similar to the previous ones such as pl.4.7, and dates to the Persian period.
Eye Amulet			Eye amulet – *wḏ't* – the eye of god.[102]	This is an amulet of the eye of Horus, typical of the Persian period. See description of plates 4.4 and 4.5.

99.   Bliss, 'Second Report on the Excavations at Tell Es-Safi', 331, Pl. V.25.
100.   Bliss, 'Second Report on the Excavations at Tell Es-Safi', 331, Pl. V.24.
101.   Bliss, 'Second Report on the Excavations at Tell Es-Safi', 331, Pl. V.7; Bliss and Macalister, *Excavations in Palestine During the years 1898–1900*, 153–4, Pl. 84.3.
102.   Bliss, 'Second Report on the Excavations at Tell Es-Safi', 331, Pl. V.4; Bliss and Macalister, *Excavations in Palestine During the years 1898–1900*, 153–4, Pl. 84.6-7.

Item	Dimensions	Material	Original Publication	Comments and Parallels
Bronze Amulet		Bronze	Amulet depicting the god Seth.[103]	Similar amulets were found at Dor, where they were interpreted as symbols of the goddess Taweret. Stern notes that this goddess is decorated with cow horns (although in the drawing of the item from Tell eṣ-Ṣâfi, it seems that there is only one horn). The goddess is sometimes adorned with a depiction of heavenly light (the sun or moon), and at times is depicted as pregnant and/or with breasts. At Dor, the items are dated to the Persian period.[104]

103. Bliss, 'Second Report on the Excavations at Tell Es-Safi', 331, Pl. V.13; Bliss and Macalister, *Excavations in Palestine During the years 1898–1900*, 153–4, Pl. 84.11.

104. Stern, 'Clay Figurines, Popular Cult Objects, and Sculpture', 448–51, Fig. 7.6.6, 8, 9.

Item	Dimensions	Material	Original Publication	Comments and Parallels
Amulet		Black Paste	Amulet of the goddess Isis holding the baby Horus. Only the baby's legs remain.[105]	Rowe notes that it seems the goddess Isis is sitting and caring for the baby Horus. She is wearing a tunic and her crown is broken. The throne on which she sits is decorated with a chequerboard pattern.[106] Stern notes that the image of Isis caring for the baby Horus stresses the Egyptian influence on the local cult practices during the Persian period. He also notes that similar amulets were found at both Dor and Machmish.[107] Herrmann notes that this item is made of red pottery with a green glaze upon it. Furthermore, she notes that it is the image of Isis caring for baby Horus, which dates to the Persian period.[108] It is interesting to note that she found the item in the Rockefeller Museum in Jerusalem.

105. Bliss, 'Second Report on the Excavations at Tell Es-Safi', 331, Pl. V.18; Bliss and Macalister, *Excavations in Palestine During the years 1898–1900*, 153–4, Pl. 84.14.
106. Rowe, *A Catalogue of Egyptian Scarabs*, 272, Pl. XXXI:A23.
107. Stern, *Archaeology of the Land of the Bible*, 496–8.
108. Herrmann, *Ägyptische Amulette aus Palästina/Israel*, 119–20.

Item	Dimensions	Material	Original Publication	Comments and Parallels
Amulet		Granite	Crocodile-shaped amulet depicting Seth.[109]	Herrmann notes that the item depicts a crocodile, which according to the method in which the granite was worked, she dates to the Iron Age III-Persian period.[110] It is interesting to note that she found the item in the Rockefeller Museum in Jerusalem.
Metal Bowl		Metal	Bowl decorated with a relief, restored from 25 pieces.[111]	Stern notes that metal bowls are an Assyrian tradition that began to appear in the Assyrian period, but reach their peak during the Persian period. The Persian bowl is round and deep, with a concave base, decorated with a botanic motif, usually the lotus flower.[112] Keel and Kuchler note that the bowl is of a Cypriot style, dating to 550 BCE.[113]

109. Bliss, 'Second Report on the Excavations at Tell Es-Safi', 331, Pl. V.23; Bliss and Macalister, *Excavations in Palestine During the years 1898–1900*, 153–4, Pl. 84.15.

110. Herrmann, *Ägyptische Amulette aus Palästina/Israel*, 600.

111. Bliss and Macalister, *Excavations in Palestine During the years 1898–1900*, 149.

112. Stern, *The Material Culture of Israel during the Persian Period*, 146–7; idem, *Archaeology of the Land of the Bible*, 525–7.

113. Keel and Kuchler, *Orte und Landschaften der bibel*, 843, Fig. 549.

Chapter 5

HELLENISM IN THE LAND OF ISRAEL FROM THE FIFTH TO THE SECOND CENTURIES BCE IN LIGHT OF SEMITIC EPIGRAPHY

Hanan Eshel

Many finds discovered over the past few years in various sites in Israel shed light on the degree to which the Land of Israel was Hellenized between the fifth and second centuries BCE.[1] This article will focus on the Semitic-script epigraphic discoveries from the Persian period, discussing their significance to the above question.

Morton Smith, in his book on 'Palestinian Parties and Politics' noted that Nehemiah's actions in Jerusalem in the middle of the fifth century BCE can be understood in light of the activities carried out by the leaders of Greek *poleis* established in various places around the Mediterranean during the same period. According to Smith, dividing the wall of Jerusalem among builders from the local population and forcing one-tenth of them to move to Jerusalem was done according to the Greek model of establishing a new *polis*.[2]

In the excavations conducted by Y. Magen at Mt Gerizim, hundreds of fragments of inscriptions on building stones were discovered. Some of the inscriptions are in Aramaic, while others are written in the Palaeo-Hebrew script. These inscriptions are dated to the second century BCE. Most of these inscriptions were found near the base of the walls of the *temenos*. They mention various groups of builders and they document which part of the sacred wall was built by whom. Thus, the walls around the *temenos* of Mt Gerizim were probably built in the same way as the walls of Jerusalem at the time of Nehemiah.[3] The implications are obvious – the construction of both fifth-century BCE Jerusalem and second-century BCE Mt Gerizim were executed according to Greek organizational models.

Greek inhabitants' presence in the Land of Israel of the Persian period is first documented in a Phoenician inscription found in 1994 during the

---

1. E. Ambar-Armon, 'The Greek World and the Coastal Plain of Eretz Israel Prior to the Macedonian Conquest', *Cathedra* 116 (2005), pp. 5–30 (Hebrew).

2. M. Smith, *Palestinian Parties and Politics that Shaped the Old Testament,* (2nd ed.; London: SCM Press, 1987), pp. 103–9.

3. Y. Magen, H. Misgav and L. Tsfania, *Mount Gerizim Excavations I: The Aramaic, Hebrew and Samaritan Inscriptions* (Jerusalem: Israel Antiquities Authority, 2004).

excavation of a Persian-period cemetery in Jaffa. A small juglet discovered in one of the graves bears the inscription כד הרמש, 'The juglet of Hermes'. Based on palaeography, the juglet was dated to the fifth century BCE, at least a century before the time of Alexander the Great.[4] From the Ashmunazar Inscription we learn that at that time Jaffa was under Sidonian rule.[5] The owner of that juglet, who may have been cremated and buried in that juglet, bore the Greek name 'Hermes'. Thus we may assume that already in the fifth century BCE there were some Greek inhabitants in Jaffa.

Greek Influence in Samaria

By the fourth century BCE, Greek influence can be found not only along the shore, but also inland, in the city of Samaria. This influence can be found on the bullae found at Wadi ed-Daliyeh and Samaria, as well as on coins struck in Samaria, all dated to the fourth century BCE. In Wadi ed-Daliyeh, 128 bullae were discovered, some of which were still attached to the ancient documents, but the majority of which were found disconnected from their documents.[6] Remains of seal impressions were found on less than half of the bullae; the others were poorly preserved, making it impossible to tell whether they had no impression or whether the impression was worn out.[7]

Three bullae from Wadi ed-Daliyeh bear inscriptions. The first, no. 22 reads:

[יהו בן סנבאלט פחת שמרין], ']YHW son of Sanballat, governor of Samaria', written in Palaeo-Hebrew script. This bulla was sealed by a seal with no glyptic decoration.[8] Bulla no. 23 bears the inscription: ל יש[ו]ע, to Jeshua.[9] Bulla no. 54 depicts Perseus dressed in a knee-length *chlamys*, wearing a travelling cap. In his upraised left hand he grasps a staff that rests on the ground beside his left foot, while in his lowered right hand he

---

4. R. Avner and E. Eshel, 'A Juglet with a Phoenician Inscription from a Recent Excavation in Jaffa, Israel', *Transeuphratène* 12 (1996), pp. 59–63.

5. *KAI* 1, p. 3, no. 14, lines 18–19.

6. In the first report about the Wadi ed-Daliyeh finds, F. M. Cross wrote: 'About seventy of the bullae are in good condition. The seals were normally engraved either after Persian fashions or with familiar Attic motifs. One is particularly struck with the vivacity of Attic Greek influences in the glyptic art of Samaria in the era before the coming of Alexander'. See F. M. Cross, 'The Discovery of the Samaria Papyri', *BA* 26 (1963), pp. 110–21 (115).

7. The bullae from Wadi ed-Daliyeh were published by M. J. W. Leith, *Wadi Daliyeh Seal Impressions* (DJD 24; Oxford: Clarendon, 1997).

8. F. M. Cross, 'The Papyri and their Historical Implications', in P. W. Lapp and N. L. Lapp (eds), *Discoveries in the Wadi ed-Daliyeh* (AASOR 41; Cambridge, Mass: American Schools of Oriental Research, 1974), pp. 17–29 (18, pl. 61).

9. Leith, *Wadi Daliyeh Seal Impressions*, 184–7.

A Time of Change

holds the looped handle of a triangular bag. Beside the figure there is a Phoenician inscription: אדן.[10] This image is in Greek style, a style found in an additional 38 bullae. Thus, 39 seal impressions can be labelled as 'Greek', compared with only 21 bullae with Achaemenian motifs or in Near-Eastern style.[11] Among the Greek-style seals Leith identified three describing Herakles. In nos. 11c and 39 a nude figure identified as Herakles is supported by a club. In no. 42 Herakles wrestles the Namean lion.[12] In addition, Perseus is depicted on two bullae. On bulla 56, as on no. 54 mentioned above (on which the name אדן was depicted) the figure of Perseus holding the Gorgon's head can be seen.[13] Bulla no. 43 was identified by Leith as Achilles helping Penthesilea, queen of the Amazons.[14]

Some other bullae have Dionysian themes: bulla 21B has a dancing satyr which is part of the Dionysian cult. No. 2 depicts a satyr with a heron, a common description of Greek seals. Nos. 5 and 16B portray a bearded satyr, and no. 44 has a satyr playing knucklebones with a nymph.[15] The Wadi ed-Daliyeh seal impressions have animals from Greek mythology as well: no. 45 portrays the winged protome of a flying boar, while no. 35 has a winged Hippocamp.[16] In addition to these Greek-style bullae there are also seal impressions which include figures in Greek style, the most common one being a naked warrior, who sometimes holds a spear or a shield. No. 32 shows a warrior in Greek battle costume and no. 7 shows a youth with a *chlamys*.[17]

Some of the bullae from Wadi ed-Daliyeh are done in Greek style, but have Persian figures on them, that is, figures dressed in Achaemenid style. Such is the case with no. 27, which shows a Persian dancer. Leith is of the opinion that this bulla was done in a workshop in southwest Asia Minor.[18] Bulla no. 6 bears a seal impression with a Persian warrior and a Greek woman, while in no. 52 both the man and the woman are dressed in Persian style.[19] Other bullae have animal descriptions made in Greek style: no. 55 depicts a lion scratching his ear, and no. 30 has a running quadruped.[20] These bullae prove that by the end of the Persian period, the

10. Leith, *Wadi Daliyeh Seal Impressions*, 77–9.
11. Leith, *Wadi Daliyeh Seal Impressions*, 20–4.
12. Leith, *Wadi Daliyeh Seal Impressions*, 85–94.
13. Leith, *Wadi Daliyeh Seal Impressions*, 77–81.
14. Leith, *Wadi Daliyeh Seal Impressions*, 145–50.
15. Leith, *Wadi Daliyeh Seal Impressions*, 107–34.
16. Leith, *Wadi Daliyeh Seal Impressions*, 167–172, 188–90.
17. Leith, *Wadi Daliyeh Seal Impressions*, 39–41, 74–6.
18. Leith, *Wadi Daliyeh Seal Impressions*, 121–3.
19. Leith, *Wadi Daliyeh Seal Impressions*, 151–61.
20. Leith, *Wadi Daliyeh Seal Impressions*, 173–5, 182–3.

inhabitants of the city of Samaria were heavily influenced by Greek culture.

After the preliminary publication of the Wadi ed-Daliyeh seal impression, another hoard from the Persian-period bullae, found in the Samaria region, was published by E. Stern.[21] This hoard includes 44 bullae, on 42 of which the impression is still visible. The majority of the bullae bear no inscriptions, with the exception of two bullae with a winged griffin and the inscription ישמעאל, 'Ishmael'.[22] Stern was able to distinguish between eastern-local and Greek styles of bullae. The first group includes 24 eastern-style bullae with griffins, lions, horses and riders, a bird and a lotus,[23] and the second group includes 18 bullae which bear Greek-style images – all with human figures. 13 bullae depict male figures, usually standing. The figures are partially naked, in nine cases are completely nude, while in other bullae only the upper part of their bodies is bare.[24] Some of these men carry weapons: swords or bows. One of the nude men holds a winged sceptre and thus can be identified as Hermes, while on another bulla there is a bearded man standing, wearing a *kition* and *himation*, holding the signs of thunder and lightning and thus identified as Zeus.[25] Women are depicted on five bullae, always fully dressed, four of them are standing. The fifth bulla describes a woman sitting on a footstool, holding a bird in her hand, probably a hawk.[26] This hoard of bullae bears testimony to the mixture of Persian and Greek cultures in the city of Samaria at the end of the Persian period.

The coinage of Samaria from the fourth century BCE is also proof of Greek influence. Ya'akov Meshorer and Shraga Qedar published two monographs on these coins. In their first book 106 types of coins minted in the city of Samaria were included, while the second includes 224 coin types (including the 106 of the first volume).[27] Greek influence in the city of Samaria during the fourth century BCE can be seen, for example, in a coin which bears on its obverse side the inscription בר, with the date: 'year fourteen', while its reverse side has a Greek inscription: ΒΑΓΑΒΑΤΑC. Based on the Greek inscription, it became clear that

21. E. Stern, 'A Hoard of Persian Period Bullae from the Vicinity of Samaria', *Michmanim* 6 (1992), pp. 7–30 (Hebrew); idem, 'A Hoard of Persian Period Bullae from the Vicinity of Samaria', in E. Stern and H. Eshel (eds), *The Samaritans* (Jerusalem: Yad Ben-Zvi, 2002), pp. 82–103 (Hebrew).

22. Stern, 'A Hoard of Persian Period Bullae from the Vicinity of Samaria', 82.

23. Stern, 'A Hoard of Persian Period Bullae from the Vicinity of Samaria', 85–7.

24. Stern, 'A Hoard of Persian Period Bullae from the Vicinity of Samaria', 88–90.

25. Stern, 'A Hoard of Persian Period Bullae from the Vicinity of Samaria', 99.

26. Stern, 'A Hoard of Persian Period Bullae from the Vicinity of Samaria', 101.

27. Y. Meshorer and S. Qedar, *The Coinage of Samaria in the Fourth Century BCE* (Jerusalem: Numismatic Fine Arts International, 1991); Y. Meshorer and S. Qedar, *Samarian Coinage* (Jerusalem: Israel Numismatic Society, 1999).

בת is an abbreviation of B(agaba)T. This coin was minted in the fourteenth year of Artaxerxes III, 346/5 BCE. If we assume that Bagabat was a local governor Samaria, then the Greek inscription on his coin would confirm that at least some of the inhabitants of Samaria were able to read Greek even before the Macedonian conquest.[28] Another coin also shows Greek influence: on its obverse side it depicts a Persian king seated on a throne, smelling a flower he is holding in his right hand and resting his left hand on his sceptre, an Achaemenian fire altar in front of him, with the Greek inscription IEYΣ, which Meshorer and Qedar read as Zeus. On the reverse side of that coin a rider on a horse is found, galloping to the right, wearing a Persian tiara and holding a sword. Below the figure is the inscription יהועגה. A local governor who on one hand bears the Israelite theophoric name יהועגה, but on the other hand does not hesitate to include the Greek god Zeus on his coin, is of great significance.[29]

In their second book, Meshorer and Qedar included coins with the Greek name Pharanabazos, who was the governor of Abr-Naharain between the years 413 and 373 BCE.[30] Another coin depicts Herakles wearing a lion's skin, and a Greek inscription which may be reconstructed as 'Herakles'.[31] Although no detailed study of the art-descriptions found in the Samaria coinage has hitherto been published, nor has there been a study of its connection with the bullae, it is already clear that many of these finds include Greek descriptions, which in turn confirms that during the fourth century BCE, before the Macedonian conquest, there was a significant Greek influence on the city of Samaria.[32]

Leith has argued that finding figures like Herakles or Perseus on the bullae from Wadi ed-Daliyeh does not necessarily attest to the religious beliefs of the people of Samaria during the fourth century BCE. She believes that the people of Samaria were unable to distinguish between the descriptions of Herakles and the salvation scenes that were common on the Achaemenian bullae, or between a nude Greek human male and Perseus.[33] However, despite Leith's minimalistic explanations, finding a coin bearing the Greek inscription 'Zeus' which was minted at Samaria, proves, in my opinion, that already before Alexander the Great's conquest of the Levant, people of the higher classes in the city of Samaria had adopted Greek religion and cults.

28. Meshorer and Qedar, *Samarian Coinage*, 83, no. 4.
29. Meshorer and Qedar, *Samarian Coinage*, 90, no. 40.
30. Meshorer and Qedar, *Samarian Coinage*, 83, nos. 1–2.
31. Meshorer and Qedar, *Samarian Coinage*, 104, no. 114.
32. Meshorer and Qedar, *Samarian Coinage*, 32–68.
33. Leith, *Wadi Daliyeh Seal Impressions*, 24–8.

Aramaic in Judah

Since the 1960s, hundreds of Aramaic ostraca dated to the fourth century BCE have been discovered in the southern part of Israel. The first of these were discovered by Yohanan Aharoni at the excavation he conducted at Arad. These ostraca are mainly short notes with orders concerning grains – chiefly barley – to be given to soldiers serving as horsemen or donkey-keepers in the Persian army.[34] An additional 54 Aramaic ostraca were discovered during the excavations held by Aharoni at Tell Beer-Sheba. These ostraca were found in silos and were probably used as tags, attached to grain-sacks that were brought as taxes to the Persian government.[35] Four ostraca were discovered at Tell Jemmeh – two of which are similar to those of Arad, while the other two were wine tags.[36] Other sporadic ostraca dated to the fourth century were discovered at Tell el-Far'ah (south), Tell 'Ira, Raphah and the region of Yatta.[37] During a salvage excavation conducted in 1971 at Khirbet el-Kôm, seven Aramaic ostraca were found, one of them bilingual Aramaic and Greek.[38] During the 1980s more than 1,600 Aramaic ostraca were discovered in illegal excavations at Khirbet el-Kôm. These documents were soon scattered all over the globe, in various museums and private collections. In 1996 two monographs were published about this collection: one was written by Joseph Naveh and Israel Eph'al,[39] and the other by Andre Lemaire.[40] A third book was published by Lemaire in 2002.[41] In those books more than 800 of these Ostraca were published. Most of the ostraca found during the 1980s at el-Kôm are tags attached to

34.   J. Naveh, 'The Aramaic Ostraca from Tel Arad', in Y. Aharoni, *Arad Inscriptions* (Jerusalem: Israel Exploration Society, 1981), pp. 153–76.

35.   J. Naveh, 'The Aramaic Ostraca', in Y. Aharoni (ed.), *Beer-Sheba I, Excavations at Tel Beer-sheba 1969–1971* (Tel Aviv: Tel Aviv University – Institute of Archeology, 1973), pp. 79–82; idem, 'The Aramaic Ostraca from Tell Beer Sheba (Seasons 1971–1976)', *Tel Aviv* 6 (1979), pp. 182–98.

36.   Idem, 'Aramaic Ostraca and Jar Inscriptions from Tell Jemmeh', *Atiqot* 21 (1992), pp. 49–53.

37.   Idem, 'Published and Unpublished Aramaic Ostraca', *Atiqot* 17 (1985), pp. 114–21.

38.   L. T. Geraty, 'Third Century B.C. Ostraca from Khirbet el-Kom', *HTR* 65 (1972), pp. 595–6.

39.   I. Eph'al and J. Naveh, *Aramaic Ostraca of the Fourth Century BC from Idumaea*, (Jerusalem: Magnes Press, 1996).

40.   A. Lemaire, *Nouvelles Inscriptions Araméennes d'Idumée au Musée d'Israël* (supplément n. 3 à Transeuphratène; Paris: Gabalda, 1996).

41.   Idem, *Nouvelles Inscriptions Araméennes d'Idumée Tome II* (supplément n. 9 à Transeuphratène; Paris: Gabalda, 2002); more ostraca from this collection were published by H. Lozachmeur and A. Lemaire, 'Nouveaux Ostraca Araméens d'Idumée', *Semitica* 46 (1996), pp. 123–42; S. Ahituv, 'An Edomite Ostracon', in Y. Avishur and R. Deutsch (eds), *Michael: Historical, Epigraphical and Biblical Studies in Honor of Prof. Michael Heltzer* (Tel Aviv-Jaffa: Archaeological Center Publications, 1999), pp. 33–7; S. Ahituv and A. Yardeni, 'Seventeen Aramaic Texts on Ostraca from Idumea: The Late Persian to the Early Hellenistic

sacks or jars with agricultural content that were submitted to the Persian or Macedonian government as taxes. The great part of that tax was paid in wheat or barley, submitted during the summer months, that is, during the Babylonian months of Sivan, Tammuz or Ab, during which the crop is harvested.[42] We may conclude, that the documents found at Tell Beer-Sheba and el-Kôm show how the agricultural products were handed to the government, while those of Arad concern their usage.[43]

As for the date of these ostraca, it should be noted, that some of the Aramaic ostraca from el-Kôm should be dated to the end of the Persian period (from 362 BCE), while others are dated to the Macedonian period, to the reigns of Alexander the Great (the III), Philip Arrhidaeus, Alexander IV and Ptolemy I. The latest ostracon published in the three monographs is dated to 311 BCE,[44] while the latest published separately by Ahituv and Yardeni is dated to after 306 BCE.[45] These collections show, that during the first years after the Macedonian conquest, the administration in the southern part of the Land of Israel was still conducted in Aramaic.

A papyrus discovered in Ketef Jericho (Jer Pap 1) in 1986 is also a proof of the usage of Aramaic after the Macedonian conquest. This document was brought to the cave where it was discovered probably around the year 312 BCE. It includes a list of loans taken by people with Jewish names written on side A of the document, while the returns of these loans were listed on side B.[46]

The linguistic continuity between the end of the Persian period and the beginning of the Hellenistic period is also attested in the silver coins minted in Jerusalem during the Ptolemaic period, which continued to mint the Aramaic inscription יהדה, 'Judah'. There is no consensus among numismatists about whether these coins were minted during the reign of Ptolemy I (310–285 BCE) or II (285–246 BCE).[47]

David Amit published an Aramaic dedication inscription discovered in

---

Periods', *Maarav* 11 (2004), pp. 7–23; A. Lemaire, 'New Aramaic Ostraca from Idumea and their Historical Interpretation', in O. Lipschits and M. Oeming (eds.), *Judah and the Judeans in the Persian Period*, (Winona Lake: Eisenbrauns 2006), pp. 413–456.

42.   Eph'al and Naveh, *Aramaic Ostraca*, 18.

43.   For a different interpretation of the Khirbet el-Kôm ostraca see B. Porten and A. Yardeni's contribution to the present volume.

44.   Eph'al and Naveh, *Aramaic Ostraca*, 16–17; Lemaire, *Nouvelles Inscriptions I*, 136; idem, *Nouvelles Inscriptions II*, 199–201.

45.   Ahituv and Yardeni, 'Seventeen Aramaic Texts', 9.

46.   H. Eshel and H. Misgav, 'A Fourth Century BCE Document from Ketef Yeriho', *IEJ* 38 (1988), pp. 158–76; H. Eshel and H. Misgav, '1. Jericho papList of Loans ar', in J. Charlesworth and others, *Miscellaneous Texts from the Judaean Desert* (DJD 38; Oxford: Clarendon, 2000), pp. 21–30.

47.   Y. Meshorer, *A Treasury of Jewish Coins* (Jerusalem and New York: Yad Ben-Zvi and Amphora, 2001), pp. 18–21.

1993, which probably originated in the pagan temple of Mazor (south of Aphek). This inscription is dated, based on palaeography, to the first half of the third century BCE. The Mazor inscription testifies, that not only the Idumean but also the pagan population living along the coastal area continued to write in Aramaic during the third century BCE.[48]

Bilingual in Idumea

The bilingual ostracon found at Khirbet el-Kôm in 1971 was discovered on the floor of a room, together with an additional five ostraca, four of which were written in Aramaic, and one in Greek. All six ostraca belonged to Qosyada' son of Hanan, who was a moneylender. Based on palaeography, the bilingual ostracon was dated to the beginning of the third century BCE. Due to the fact that it bears the date 'year six', it was suggested that this ostracon was written in 279 BCE, year six of the reign of Ptolemy II. This document records a loan, in which the lender bears the Idumean name קוסידע, while the borrower has a Greek name ניקרתם. That is probably also the reason for using both languages – for the lender probably spoke Aramaic, while the borrower used Greek.[49]

The question to be asked is when the shift actually occurred, when the administration started to be handled in Greek. Since we do not have enough epigraphic information from the third century BCE we cannot offer an accurate answer to this question.

In the excavations conducted by Amos Kloner at Mareshah, which started in 1989 and continue to this day, more than 300 ostraca were discovered. These ostraca were written prior to the destruction of Mareshah in 112 or 111 BCE.[50] 250 of these ostraca were written in Greek, while about 50 were written in Aramaic.[51]

The Mareshah ostraca are probably evidence of the shift from Aramaic to Greek; it seems that statistically most of the Aramaic ostraca are earlier than the Greek ones. Especially important among these Aramaic ostraca is a marriage contract, written in Aramaic and dated to 176 BCE, which was discovered in 1993.[52] This contract documents a marriage of two

---

48. D. Amit, 'An Aramaic Inscription from the Hellenistic Period at Horvat Mazor', *Eretz-Israel* 26 (1999), pp. 129–31 (Hebrew).

49. L. T. Geraty, 'The Khirbet el-Kom Bilingual Ostracon', *BASOR* 220 (1975), pp. 55–61.

50. D. Barag, 'New Evidence on the Foreign Policy of John Hyrcanus I', *INJ* 12 (1993), pp. 1–12; G. Finkielsztejn, 'More Evidence on John Hyrcanus I's Conquests: Lead Weights and Rhodian Amphora Stamps', *BAIAS* 16 (1998), pp. 33–63.

51. I would like to express my gratitude to Prof. Amos Kloner for sharing this information with me.

52. E. Eshel and A. Kloner, 'An Aramaic Ostracon of an Edomite Marriage Contract from Maresha, Dated 176 BCE', *IEJ* 46 (1996), pp. 1–22.

Idumean families who lived in Mareshah. The name of the groom is
קוסרם son of קוסיד, while the bride's name is אסרנה daughter of קוסיד
son of קוסיהב. As we can see, the bride bears a Greek name which was
common in Egypt during the Ptolemaic period. In line 5 of the contract,
the Greek word נומוס is used. As of now, this is the earliest instance of a
Greek word which found its way into a Semitic language to be attested in
the epigraphic finds from the Land of Israel. The Mareshah marriage
contract proves that even in the second century BCE the inhabitants of
Idumea continued to use Aramaic in their legal documents. We may
assume that while the administration probably shifted to Greek during the
third century BCE, some people preferred to continue to use Aramaic in
private correspondence and in their legal documents.

It is our hope, that with the full publication of the Mareshah ostraca in
the near future, we will be able to better understand the process and the
timeframe of the shifting of the administration of the Land of Israel from
Aramaic to Greek.

Chapter 6

MAKKEDAH AND THE STOREHOUSE IN THE IDUMEAN OSTRACA[*]

Bezalel Porten and Ada Yardeni

One of the few topographical terms that courses through all three sections of the Hebrew Bible (Torah, Prophets and Writings) is ערי מסכנות. The Israelites built them for Pharaoh (Exod. 1.11). Solomon built them along with chariot towns and cavalry towns (1 Kings 9.19). Jehoshaphat built them along with fortresses (2 Chron. 17.12). Commentators are divided on the translation. Some favour 'store cities' with the Targum and others 'garrison cities' with the Septuagint; one commentator has blended the two, proposing 'fortified storage cities'.[1] The determinative passage would seem to be 2 Chron. 32.27-28, which describes the activities of Hezekiah. It contrasts אוצרות, 'treasuries' which are for silver and gold and מסכנות which are for the 'produce of grain, wine and oil', proving that the only suitable translation for מסכנות is 'storehouses'. This translation is strengthened if we consider the word a loan from Akkadian *maškattu/ maškantu*, 'storehouse'. It occurs some dozen times in Neo-Babylonian texts where *kor*s of grain are being paid *ina muḫḫi maškattum*, 'into the storehouse'.[2] Now, for the first time, the word appears in a group of Aramaic ostraca from Idumea, in the determined form מסכנתא and in the construct מסכנת מנקדה. Since these are the depositories of wheat and barley, their meaning is patent. So while the Bible does not name any of the store cities in the land of Israel, from these ostraca we learn of 'the storehouse of Makkedah'.

[*] This paper was first presented in preliminary form on July 31, 2005 in a session entitled 'The Bible and the Ancient East' at the Fourteenth World Congress of Jewish Studies. Research of these documents has been made possible, in part, by a grant from The Israel Science Foundation. Appreciation is extended to our research assistants Jacqueline Vayntrub and Barak Givon.

1. W. H. C. Propp, *Exodus 1–18* (AB; New York; Doubleday, 1999), p. 133.

2. See *CAD* M/I (Chicago: The Oriental Institute, 1977), pp. 375–6; P. V. Mankowski, *Akkadian Loanwords in Biblical Hebrew* (Winona Lake: Eisenbrauns, 2000), pp. 99–100. We are grateful to Laurie Pearce for reviewing these texts with us.

Figure 1: Judah and Idumea in the Fourth Century BCE

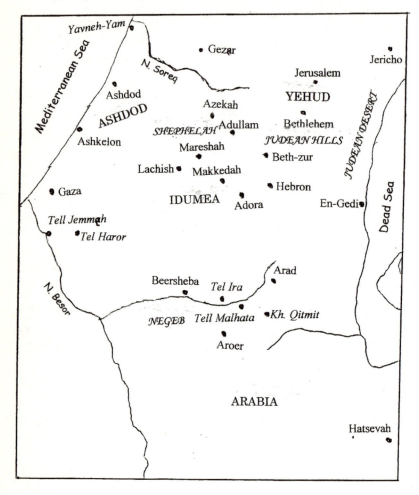

As is known, the Greek word *ostracon* gives us the verb 'ostracize', because the ancient Athenians periodically recorded the name of their least favourite person on broken pottery sherds. Whoever got the most votes was 'ostracanned'. Otherwise, ostraca were the scrap paper of Egypt, Greece, and the Levant. The corpus of Idumean ostraca numbers some 1,700 legible pieces,[3] acquired from dealers and believed to come

---

3. The ostraca have been published over the past decade by several scholars. See: I. Eph'al and J. Naveh, *Aramaic Ostraca of the Fourth Century BC from Idumaea* (Jerusalem: Magnes, 1996) (=EN); nos. 160 and 161 are concave and convex of the same piece as are

from Khirbet el-Kôm (map reference 147.104), identified with biblical Makkedah, some 7 miles SE of Lachish and some 9 miles due west of Hebron (Figure 1).[4] With a grant from the Israel Science Foundation, we are preparing a corpus of all these ostraca. Most of them are little pieces you can hold in the palm of your hand and are what we call commodity chits. Usually written on the convex side of the sherd, they contain (1) a date (day, month, year, rarely ruler); (2) occasionally a verb, like היתי, 'he brought'; (3) a personal name plus a patronym or a family/clan name, such as Baalrim; (4) possibly the name of a recipient (preceded by the preposition *lamed*) and an agent (preceded by the compound preposition על יד, 'by the hand of'); (5) and name and amount of a commodity, such

---

196, 197 and 198 of another piece; A. Lemaire, *Nouvelles inscriptions araméennes d'Idumée au Musée d'Israel* (Supplément no 3 à *Transeuphratène*; Paris: Gabalda, 1996) (=L); H. Lozachmeur and A. Lemaire, 'Nouveaux ostraca araméens d'Idumée (Collection Sh. Moussaieff)', *Semitica* 46 (1996), pp. 123–52 (=LL); A. Lemaire, 'Quatre nouveaux *ostraca* araméens d'Idumée', *Transeuphratène* 18 (1999), pp. 71–4 (=S=ISAP1231–1234); A. Lemaire, 'Der Beitrag idumäischer Ostraka zur Geschichte Palästinas im Übergang von der persischen zur hellenistischen Zeit', *ZDPV* 115 (1999), pp. 14–15 + Plate 2 [note that R 37 = AL19, R 20 = AL88, R 21 = AL91, R 6 = AL73, and R 1 = AL9]; S. Ahituv, 'An Edomite Ostracon', in Y. Avishur and R. Deutsch (eds), *Michael: Historical, Epigraphical and Biblical Studies In Honor of Prof. Michael Heltzer* (Tel Aviv-Jaffa: Archaeological Center Publications, 1999), pp. 33–7, one of 58 ostraca held by an anonymous collector; A. Lemaire, *Nouvelles inscriptions araméennes d'Idumée Tome II* (Supplément no 9 à *Transeuphratène*. Paris: Gabalda, 2002) (= AL); S. Ahituv and A. Yardeni, 'Seventeen Aramaic Texts on Ostraca from Idumea', *Maarav* 11 (2004), pp. 7–23 (ISAP 703, 705, 706, 709–712, 716, 721–728, 751). Nine new texts have been published with handcopies in B. Porten and A. Yardeni, 'In Preparation of a Corpus of Aramaic Ostraca from the Land of Israel: The House of Yehokal,' R. Deutsch (ed.), *Shlomo: Studies in Epigraphy, Iconography, History and Archaeology in Honor of Shlomo Moussaieff* (Tel Aviv-Jaffa: Archaeological Center Publications, 2003), pp. 207–23 (ISAP 111–112, 408, 424, 429, 702, 704, 1658, 1712); 19 new texts in B. Porten and A. Yardeni, 'On the Problems of Identity and Chronology in the Idumean Ostraca', in Michael Heltzer and Meir Malul (eds), *Tᵉshûrôt LaAvishur: Studies in the Bible and in the Ancient Near East, in Hebrew and Semitic Languages* (Tel Aviv-Jaffa: Archaeological Center Publications, 2004), pp. 162*-165* (ISAP 2, 113, 277, 430, 432, 464, 616, 703, 722, 724, 1404, 1419, 1454, 1481, 1573, 1609, 1652, 1739, 1741); and 30 new texts in A. Lemaire, 'New Aramaic Ostraca from Idumea and Their Historical Interpretation', in O. Lipschits and M. Oeming (eds), *Judah and Judeans in the Persian Period* (Winona Lake: Eisenbrauns, 2005), pp. 413–56 (ISAP 1652–1665, 1757–1761, 1798) (=LW); B. Porten and A. Yardeni, 'Social, Economic, and Onomastic Issues in the Aramaic Ostraca of the Fourth Century', in O. Lipschits and M. Oeming (eds), *Judah and Judeans in the Persian Period* (Winona Lake: Eisenbrauns, 2005), pp. 457–88. For working purposes, all the pieces have received temporary ISAP (Institute for the Study of Aramaic Papyri) numbers. New numbers will be assigned in the final publication. The abbreviations refer to our tables 1–8, allowing the reader to cross-reference our ISAP numbers with the collection or original publication of each item.

4.　In the Bible, Makkedah is mentioned only in the book of Joshua, where it is stated that the five Canaanite kings fleeing from Joshua holed up in a cave there, from whence they were removed and impaled. The city itself was captured and its king and people put to the sword

as wheat or barley, and so many *kors*, *seahs*, and *qabs*, usually abbreviated. Just under 100 texts relate to the subject at hand. For the purposes of this study, we have divided them into three main groups and several sub-groups. Group I, with five sub-groups, contains 55 texts, several bunched together chronologically and written by the same scribe, which state that the commodity was headed 'to the storehouse' (למסכנתא) (Nos. 1–29a) or 'to the storehouse of Makkedah' (למסכנת מנקדה, alternately מסכנה למנקדה) (Nos. 30–44, 48–51); *varia* (Nos. 45–47, 52–55). Group II, with two sub-groups, states that the commodity is simply 'to' (Nos. 56–70) or 'from' 'Makkedah' (Nos. 71–91). Group III contains a few miscellaneous texts (Nos. 92–96). We've arranged our material in tables to facilitate comprehension of patterns.

Sub-groups Ia-b: 'To the Storehouse' and 'To the Storehouse of Makkedah'

Nos. 1–44 (Tables 1–2): in our discussion of this group, we shall consider the scribe, the storehouse, the depositor and the venue.

1. The Scribe: First is the question of scribal identity. Since the Idumean scribes did not sign their chits, as the Elephantine scribes did their contracts, how do we identify chits written by the same scribe? We work with six interrelated and often overlapping criteria: palaeography, terminology, prosopography, chronology, provenance and ceramics. What follows is a guided tour through the workshop of the ostracologist, if we may coin such a word. All the drawings herein were handcopied

---

(Josh. 10.10–29, 12.16). In the list of the towns of Judah, Makkedah appears as the last of 16 sites in the second district of the Shephelah (Josh. 15.41). Until the discovery of the present corpus, Makkedah was not known from any extra-biblical sourses, and its identification was long considered a puzzle in biblical historical geography. Eusebius stated that Makkedah was 8 miles east of Eleutheropolis (see G. S. P. Freeman-Grenville, R. L. Chapman III and J. E. Taylor, *Palestine in the Fourth Century A.D.: The Onomasticon by Eusebius of Caesarea* (Jerusalem: Carta, 2003), p. 71. Based on this, several scholars, such as Alt and Abel, suggested identifying Makkedah with Khirbet Sheikh Maqdum, east of Mareshah. In his monumental 1963 Hebrew commentary on Joshua, Y. Kaufmann rejected all previous identifications, but refrained from providing his own (*Sefer Yehoshua* [Jerusalem: Kiryat Sefer, 1963], p. 143 [Hebrew]). In 1980, David Dorsey conclusively argued for identifying Makkedah at Khirbet el-Kôm, not far from Sheikh Maqdum. See D. A. Dorsey, 'The Location of Biblical Makkedah', *Tel Aviv* 7 (1980), pp. 185–93, and also J. C. de Vos, 'Das Los Judas. Über Entstehung und Ziele der Landbeschreibung in Josua' (unpublished Ph.D. dissertation, Rijkuniversiteit Groningen, 2002), pp. 249, 252, 255–6, 397, 399 and references there. The ostraca under discussion seem to prove Dorsey's suggestion. Sometime between the fall of the kingdom of Judah in 586 and the late fourth century BCE, Makkedah, together with large parts of the southern Shephelah and hill country, was inhabited by Idumeans, Arabs and members of other groups, eventually being included in the province of Idumea (for which see the contributions by I. Stern and Y. Levin in this volume).

directly from the ostraca by Yardeni. Our emphasis on detail requires careful concentration.

a. PALAEOGRAPHY: The first two sub-groups in group I were the largest – 29/30 for the storehouse (למסכנתא) (Nos. 1–29a) and 15/16 for the storehouse of Makkedah (למסכנת מנקדה) (Nos. 30–44).[5] Initial examination inclined us to see two identifiable scribal hands at work, one which we identified as Scribe A (Table 1 Nos. 3–4, 7–10, 12–19, 41) and the other as Scribe B (Table 2 Nos. 34–38, 40–41). We cite here six distinctive peculiarities which enabled us to fingerprint Scribe B: (1) the letter *he* was written with a long wavy upper stroke drawn to the left (3A3, 3B3, 2B4, 2C3, and perhaps 3C2); (2) in the abbreviated combination שׂכ, 'b(arley), k(ors)' the *kaph* is a particularly long stroke that does not curve to the left at the bottom (3A4, 3B4; also 2A4 though it lacks the wavy *he*) in contrast to a short *kaph* in חֿך, 'w(heat), k(ors)' (8A4) and in שׂך, 'b(arley), k(ors)' (9C2) that *does* turn to the left at the bottom – both probably by different scribes; (3) a *samekh* with a long vertical upper stroke and a bottom stroke curved to the right (3A1, 3, 4, 2C1–4, 3B1, 3, 4, 2B1); (4) a final *lamed* that turns sharply to the right (3A2, 2C3, 3B2); (5) a very similar impression given off by a single word – e.g. the name עבדאדה (2B2, 3C2); (6) similarity of line and letter spacing.

b. TERMINOLOGY: Putative Scribe A wrote eleven chits (Nos. 3–4, 7–10, 12–19) for deposit of wheat in the storehouse (למסכנתא) and one chit (No. 41) for deposit of barley in the storehouse of Makkedah (למסכנת מנקדה), while putative Scribe B wrote six chits (Nos. 34–38, 40) for deposit of barley in the storehouse of Makkedah.

c. PROSOPOGRAPHY: Fourteen chits are for a single family, the members of the clan of Baalrim (Nos. 5–10, 12, 15–18, 37, 40–41).[6]

d. CHRONOLOGY: The 14 chits are concentrated chronologically. Scribe A wrote all his chits during a month in year 5 – two at the end of Sivan (the 26th and the 29th [Nos. 3 and 4]) and 12 in Tammuz (from the 1st to the 27th [Nos. 7–10, 12–19]).[7] Putative Scribe B wrote five chits (Nos. 34–38)

---

5.   The number in the first column of Tables 1–8 is the serial number of the ostracon (1, 2, 3, etc.). The number below that is the Figure number, followed by a letter, indicating the ostracon (e.g. '3' below which is '5A'). The number(s) following the letter in the body of the text is/are the line numbers of the ostracon (e.g. 3A3 = Figure 3, ostracon A, line 3, to be found under No. 36). For simplicity of citation, in the course of the article, ostraca will be cited by their serial numbers (e.g. No. 5).

6.   See our extensive treatment of this clan in the forthcoming B. Porten and A. Yardeni, 'The House of Baalrim in the Idumean Ostraca' in M. Lubetski (ed.), *New Seals and Inscriptions, Hebrew, Idumean and Cuneiform*, Sheffield: Sheffield Phoenix Press (forthcoming).

7.   Three appeared at first sight to be dated to year 4 (Nos. 15–17) but considerations of palaeography, chronology, and prosopography argue for their being assigned to year 5: (1) all three belong to Baalrim; (2) all three dates are in Tammuz, and all the other Tammuz

during a week and a day of Sivan (16th to 24th), year 3 and one six months later, on 26 Kislev (No. 40).[8]

e. PROVENANCE: For us, provenance means not archaeological find spot but the dealer's. In this case, it turns out that nine of the 14 chits for Scribe A came to us in a single batch and were reported to have been found at the bottom of a well (Nos. 4, 7–10, 12, 16–17, 41), along with three out of the six for Scribe B (Nos. 37–38, 40).

f. CERAMICS: The two chits from 18 Tammuz (Nos. 16–17) were exceptionally written not on the convex but on the concave and most likely came from the same piece of pottery; notice the striations. This would help explain the scribal ellipses. Having just written year five on the first one (No. 16), the scribe felt he need not write it on the second. But the instruction ליד שעדאל, 'to the hand of Saadel' could not be assumed and so he wrote it supralinearly.

In sum, we have nine chits found together at the bottom of a well, eight sending wheat to the storehouse for members of the clan of Baalrim, written in under three weeks – one on 29 Sivan (No. 4), two on 1 Tammuz (Nos. 7–8), two on 5 Tammuz (Nos. 9–10) and two on 18 Tammuz (Nos. 16–17), the latter two on sherds from the same vessel (7A and B). Here is Scribe A. In making this identification, we are sensitive to the fact that ostraca differ from papyri. As a flat surface, papyrus allows for a consistent uniformity in writing. But rapid writing on uneven convex surface, albeit by trained scribes, will result in frequent variation in the shape and size of letters. Palaeographical determination will thus depend as much on general impression of whole words and the spacing between lines and letters as on the form and shape of individual letters. Our isolation of Scribe A is based mainly upon general impression, yet for Scribe B we were able to isolate six distinctive peculiarities.

However, the more we studied these texts, the more we recognized that the outstanding feature was not distinctiveness but variation; for example, putative Scribe B had three forms of *samekh* in as many lines in a single ostracon (2B1, 3–4) and one day after another he wrote the clan name now *plena* יהוכל (2C3) and now abbreviated יוכל (3A2). A chit is not a coin, and variation of letters, even within the same text, proved a stumbling block to positive identification, since many features typical of Scribe B were also to be found in Scribe A. We thus became uncertain whether we could confidently distinguish Scribe A from Scribe B. On the other hand, the similarities among these texts were all the more striking

---

dates fall in year five; (3) we may assume that the fifth stroke was cut off at the edge of No. 16 while the reading of the date in No. 15 is uncertain; (4) written on the same day as No. 16 and, like it, assigning the goods to Saadel, No. 17 should likewise be dated to year five.

8. For absolute dating of these texts see our treatment in Porten and Yardeni, 'The House of Baalrim'.

when set against the background of other texts that are truly different. See, for example, a large accounting text with a distinctly early *samekh* (Figure 10.1–3, 4–10, 12) and a nearly unvarying hand; so, too, contrast the name עבדאדה in line 6 with that in 2B2 and 3C2. So, going with our initial intuition and functional convenience, but with reservation, we preserve the distinction between the two scribes, yet melding them as one, Scribe AB, with now (A) in parentheses and now (B) in parentheses, to preserve recollection of the initial stages in our research.

2. The Storehouses: Having dealt with the identity of the scribes, we now turn to the identity of the storehouses. Was there a difference between מסכנתא, 'the storehouse' and מסכנת מנקדה, 'the storehouse of Makkedah'? Two pivotal pieces suggest that there was. Both were written on the same day, 19 Tammuz, year 5 by our Scribe A(B), though only one was said to have been found at the bottom of the well (No. 41). In the first he recorded a full name, Qosyinqom from the sons of Baalrim (No. 18); in the second he sufficed with Qosyinqom (No. 41). The first ostracon records 13 + *seah*s of *wheat* for מסכנתא, 'the storehouse'; the second, 5 + *seah*s of *barley* for the מסכנת מנקדה, 'the storehouse of Makkedah'. If both grains went to the same place, why did the scribe not suffice with a single chit? We may thus assume that two chits were necessary because each grain was deposited in a different place. Indeed, in the narrow time frame of Scribe A(B), the end of Sivan and almost all of Tammuz in year 5, eleven chits were written for wheat to be deposited in 'the storehouse' (Nos. 3, 7–10, 12–14, 16–18), a twelfth for a wheat-barley exchange (No. 19), while two more exchanges were recorded on the above (Nos. 13, 17). In like fashion, there were five chits for Sivan and one for Kislev, year 3 by Scribe (A)B, and they all record barley for 'the storehouse of Makkedah' (Nos. 34–38, 40). Other evidence, however, complicates this apparent pattern. On the same day (29 Sivan, year 5) that other scribes deposited, according to pattern, wheat in the storehouse for members of Baalrim (Nos. 5–6), our Scribe A(B) sent *barley* for a certain Qoskhair (no patronym) to the storehouse, specifically to Saadel (No. 4). The storehouse, it turns out, was not just a depository but a place of transaction. In the month of Tammuz, when wheat was in abundance, it was exchanged for barley, perhaps for animal fodder, at the standard exchange rate of 1 measure for 2 (Nos. 11, 13, 17, 19). This ratio reflected both their monetary (see 2 Kings 7.1 [time of Elisha]) and nutritional values (Peah 8.5 [poor man]; Ketubot 5.8 [wife]), which remained constant down through the centuries This transaction was expressed by the single letter preposition *beth*, with the meaning '(in exchange) for'. As implied above, a chit might express a double transaction – (1) a deposit of wheat in the storehouse and an exchange of wheat for barley (Nos. 11, 13, 17); (2) an unexpected exchange of *barley* for *wheat* in the *storehouse*, at the standard 2 for 1 rate, and a deposit of barley in the storehouse of Makkedah, as expected (No. 20). But when a *second* chit

records a barley for wheat exchange in the *storehouse*, also at the standard rate (No. 23), the earlier transaction ceases to be unique. The second of such double transactions was often introduced by an internationally recognized accounting term בב, 'entry' (*TAD* C3.28: Nos. 13, 17, 20, 11 [here the scribe forgot the second *beth* in front of the *ḥeth* for 'wheat']);[9] (3) here Scribe A(B) divides the deposit into the storehouse in two: the first by Samitu of *x kor*s of wheat; the second, following בב, by Samitu of 9 *seah*s of wheat]). Two other chits recording double transactions will be discussed below.

This double capacity of both storehouses is borne out when we examine the chits of other scribes. While seven chits for the storehouse recorded wheat – five dated (29 Tammuz, year1 [No. 1], 2 Tammuz, year 2 [No. 2], 10 Sivan, year 7 [No. 21], 24 Sivan, year 7 [No. 22], 11 Ab, year 8 [No. 25] and two undated [Nos. 27, 29]); three other chits recorded barley – two dated (29 Sivan, year 5, as seen [No. 4], and 28 Adar, year7 [No. 24], and a third undated [No. 28]). Likewise, six dated chits for the 'storehouse of Makkedah' all recorded wheat – (29 Marcheshvan, year 43 [No. 30]), 7 Tebeth, year 14 [No. 31], *x* Kislev, year 16 [No. 32], 20 Tammuz, year 1 [No. 33], 28 Marcheshvan, year 3 [No. 39], 12 Tammuz, year 8 [No. 44]); and only one, the expected barley (7 Elul, year 6 [No. 42]). Yet, one consistency is noteworthy – all four wheat/barley exchanges and the two barley/wheat exchanges (Nos. 11, 13, 17, 19; 20, 23) take place in 'the storehouse' and not 'the storehouse of Makkedah'. Evidence for proximity and/or unified administration of these two places may be found in the person of Saadel. Three times he is the recipient of barley and wheat at 'the storehouse' and also effects a barley/wheat exchange there (Nos. 4, 16–17) and of fifteen chits directed 'to Makkedah' he is the only individual also mentioned, as the recipient of roosters (No. 65). He is in 'the storehouse' and in Makkedah! (see further below).[10]

3. The Depositors: While we continue to ponder whether 'the storehouse' and 'the storehouse of Makkedah' were two separate places or one and the same, let us have a look at the depositors and their amounts. Several items catch our attention.

(1) The prominence of members of five clans – (1) Baalrim (Qosghayr, Dikru, Qosyinqom [4x], Adarbaal and Zabdiel, Ammiqos, Ani, Zaydi[?], Ammiel, Saadel [2x], Ahyaqim/Aḥiqam [10/11 persons]); (2) Gur (Qosyeypa, Qosrim, Al[i]qos, Qosnaqam [4 persons]), (3) Y(eh)okal (Qosner, Qoslanṣur [2 persons]); (4) Al(i)baal (Aydu, Laadiel [2 persons]); and (5) Qoṣi (Al[i]qos [1 person]).

9. B. Porten and A. Yardeni, *Textbook of Aramaic Documents from Ancient Egypt* (Jerusalem: Academon, 1986–1999), 4 volumes (henceforth referenced as *TAD*, A-D).

10. For a full discussion of the dossier of Saadel, see Porten and Yardeni, 'Social, Economic and Onomastic Issues', 466–73.

(2) Grain is measured out with great precision – 1 *kor* = 30 *seah*s, 1 *seah* = 6 *qab*s, and a *qab* may be divided into halves, quarters and even eighths. One is reminded of the biblical injunction to 'have completely honest weights and completely honest measures' (Deut. 25.15). Our ancient sources – Josephus (*Ant.* IX.4.4, 62; XV.9.2, 314), the Talmud (Eruv. 4b, 83a), and Epiphanius[11] – come together to show that there existed at the same time three different *seah* measures, known in the Talmud as the desert *seah* (8.1 litres), Jerusalem *seah* (9.72 litres), and Sepphoris *seah* (11.664 litres).[12] In seeking modern equivalents, many scholars, taking their cue from Josephus, took their lead from Greco-Roman sources and came up with equivalents in the range of the Sepphoris *seah*.[13] Others have taken their lead from the Talmud and came up with equivalents in the range of the desert *seah*.[14] And still others have adopted an archaeological approach and arrived at an equivalent at the lowest end of the scale (7.3 litres).[15] Since the Greek New Testament and the Peshitta (Mt. 5.15; Mk. 4.21; Lk. 11.23), and the Mishnah (*Kelim* 17.11) equate the *seah* with Italian *modius*, which we know lies in the range of 8 litres, we may assume that it was the desert measure that applied in Idumea of the fourth century BCE.[16]

(3) Patterns of payment are elusive. Qosyinqom of the sons of Baalrim made four payments within just three weeks, three of wheat and the fourth of barley – 8 *seah*s, 4 *qab*s on 29 Sivan (No. 5); 17 *seah*s, 1 *qab* on the next day, 1 Tammuz (No. 8); and two payments on 19 Tammuz, 13 *seah*s, 4.5 *qab*s of wheat and 5.75 *seah*s of barley (Nos. 18, 41). On 26 Tebeth, (no year), Qosyinqom made a fifth and very large payment of wheat 'to Makkedah': 3 *kor*s, 7 *seah*s, 5.5 *qab*s (No. 58). On the other hand, five/six other members of the Baalrim clan (Adarbaal and Zabdiel acting together, Ammiqos, Qosyinqom, Ani, Zaydi[?]) brought roughly the same amount

11.   J. E. Dean, *Epiphanius' Treatise on Weights and Measures, The Syriac Version* (Chicago: University of Chicago Press, 1935), pp. 40–1, 46. We are grateful to Shlomo Naeh for detailed discussion of these metrological problems.

12.   Calculations on the basis of H. Lewy, 'Assyro-Babylonian and Israelite Measures of Capacity and Rates of Seeding', *JAOS* 64 (1944), p. 69 n. 34.

13.   F. Hultsch, *Griechische und Römische Metrologie* (2nd ed.; Berlin: Weidmann, 1882), pp. 416, 447–56; W. Nowack, *Lehrbuch der Hebräischen Archäologie* (Leipzig: Akademische Verlagsbuchhandlung Mohr, 1894), pp. 202–6; I. Benzinger, *Hebräische Archäologie* (3rd. ed.; Leipzig: J. C. B. Mohr [P. Siebeck], 1927), pp. 192–5; M. A. Powell, 'Weights and Measures', *ABD* VI, pp. 904–5.

14.   Y. Feliks, *Agriculture in Eretz-Israel in the Period of the Bible and the Talmud* (2nd ed.; Jerusalem: Magnes, 1990), pp. 144–5 (Hebrew); Lewy, 'Assyro-Babylonian and Israelite Measures of Capacity', 65–73.

15.   W. F. Albright *et al.*, *The Excavation of Tell Beit Mirsim. Vol. III: The Iron Age*, (AASOR 21–22; New Haven: American Schools of Oriental Research, 1943), pp. 58–9; E. Stern, 'Measures and Weights', *Encyclopedia Biblica* IV (Jerusalem: Bialik, 1962), pp. 846–78 (852–5) (Hebrew).

16.   See Lewy, 'Assyro-Babylonian and Israelite Measures of Capacity', 65–73.

of grain (16–18 *seah*s of wheat) to the same duty scribe for the storehouse within a six-day period, 29 Sivan to 5 Tammuz, year 5 (Nos. 6–10), a second scribe also serving on the first day (No. 6). This equal amount is particularly noteworthy because there is otherwise no standard deposit amount, figures as low as 2 *seah*s (No. 1) and as high as seven/eight *kor*s (Nos. 37, 40) being encountered. Is it coincidental that a member of the Gur clan made a 10/20 *seah* wheat/barley exchange in the storehouse on 6 Tammuz (No. 13) and another member of that clan made a 5/10 *seah* wheat/barley exchange in the storehouse on 27 Tammuz, three weeks later (No. 19)? We would assume that deliveries were made by donkey, or, less likely, by camel. The regular donkey load was said to be 15 *seah*s/*modii* while the camel could support twice that amount (*Bab. Meṣ* 6.5).[17] Thus, these 16–18 *seah* shipments would constitute overloading. Furthermore, contrasts could be most stark (see Tables 9 and 10 at the end of this article).[18] For example, a week in July, year 3 could bring in to the 'storehouse of Makkedah' 554 $\frac{1}{24}$ *seah*s while a month in June/July, year 5 would only produce 180 $\frac{7}{12}$ *seah*s, mostly of wheat, for 'the storehouse'. Shipments of 7–9 *kor*s would ordinarily require an equivalent number of camels or double that of donkeys. The litre equivalent for the week in July would vary between 4,700+ and 4,000 litres while for a month in the summer only between under 1,600 and over 1,300.[19]

To get an idea as to the nutritional value of these *seah* measures we see that in Mishnaic times a poor man on the road was expected to receive no less than a loaf of a half *qab* of wheat or 1 *qab* of barley from the threshing floor, while the portion for the Sabbath *eruv* was also a loaf of a half *qab* of wheat, apparently meant to cover two meals (*Peah* 8.5–7; *Eruvin* 8.2). Similarly, the weekly allowance a husband was obligated to provide for his wife was 2 *qab*s of wheat or 4 of barley (*Ketuboth* 5.8). Thus, the five barley deposits for the 'storehouse of Makkedah' during a week in July would provide 3324.25 daily allotments for a poor man, that is, enough to last over nine years or to feed 475 persons for a week, while 831.06 weekly grain allotments for a wife were enough for almost 16 years. The one barley and 15 wheat deliveries to the 'storehouse' during a month in summer would provide 2209.5 daily allotments for a poor man, that is, enough to last only 6.5 years or to feed 317 persons a week, while 552.375 weekly grain allotments for a wife were enough for ten and a half years. 'The ancient norm for a daily food ration seems to have been widely regarded as ca. 1

17. Dean, *Epiphanius' Treatise on Weights and Measures*, 40.
18. The numbers in the first, left-hand, vertical column in each chart correspond to the numbers in the first column in Tables 1–2.
19. More precisely from 4731.5 (Feliks), 4593 (Naeh), 4487.73 (Lewy), to 4060.7 (Albright) litres; and from 1384.09 (Feliks), 1343.67 (Naeh), 1312.87 (Lewy), to 1183.7 (Albright) litres.

liter, usually of barley, ... throughout the entire history of Babylonia and two *sextarii* [= 1 liter] (Roman) or one *choinix* in the Mediterranean area'.[20]

(4) Saadel of the sons of Baalrim, especially, draws our attention. On 24 Sivan and 26 Kislev, year three, six months apart, he brings to the storehouse of Makkedah huge quantities of barley, at first 7 *kor*s, 18 *seah*s, 2 *qab*s (No. 37) and later 8 *kor*s (No. 40). Is he the same Saadel into whose hand will be paid, on 29 Sivan and 18 Tammuz, year five very small amounts of wheat and barley, 2–6 *seah*s, and who effects an exchange of a *seah* or so of wheat for barley (Nos. 4, 16–17)? Is he a dealer and the storehouse not merely a granary but also a market?[21]

Table 1: 29/30 deliveries to the storehouse (למסכנתא)

In this and the following tables, the second number and the letter in the left-hand column refer to the drawings in Figures 2–12, at the end of the article. Also, the following abbreviations are used: db = date at beginning; dm = date in middle; de = date at end; nd = no date; e = in exchange for; f = from; o = of; ss = sons of.

No.	ISAP	Babylonian date	Julian Date	Scribe	Payer	Payee	Commodity
1.	1249 = AL16 = JA76	29 Tammuz, 1 [Philip III?] db	9 August, 323?		Qosadar \n\n from Zabdi		to the storehouse wheat: 8 seahs \n\n wheat: 2 seahs
2.	2420 = JA131	2 Tammuz, 2 [Philip III?] db	2 July, 322?		Abdidah		to the storehouse wheat: 6 seahs, 3 qabs
3. 4A	2516 = JA235	26 Sivan, 5 [Philip III?] db	24 June, 319?	A(B)	Samitu *entry*: Sam- itu		to the storehouse wheat: [x] kor(s), [...] wheat: 9 seahs
4. 4B	890 = GCh90	29 Sivan 5 [Philip III?] db	27 June, 319?	A(B)	Qoskhair	to Saadel	to the storehouse barley: 2 seahs, 4.5 qabs
5. 4C	893 = GCh93	29 Sivan, 5 [Philip III?] db	27 June, 319?	?	Qosyinqom f ss Baalrim		to the storehouse wheat: 8 seahs, 4 qabs
6. 8A	908 = GCh108 = JA474	29 Sivan, 5 [Philip III?] db	27 June, 319?	?	Adarbaal and Zabdiel f ss Baalrim		to the storehouse wheat: 1 kor, 3 seahs, 4.5 qabs

20. Powell, 'Weights and Measures', 904; see further, Z. Safrai, *The Economy of Roman Palestine* (London : Routledge, 1994), p. 106.

21. The evidence for this assumption has been discussed elsewhere. See Porten and Yardeni, 'Social, Economic, and Onomastic Issues', 466–73.

No.	ISAP	Babylonian date	Julian Date	Scribe	Payer	Payee	Commodity
7. 5B	889 = GCh89	1 Tammuz, 5 [Philip III?] db	28 June, 319?	A(B)	Ammiqos f ss Baalrim		to the storehouse wheat: 17 seahs, 4 qabs
8. 5A	924 = GCh124 = JA488	1 Tammuz, 5 [Philip III?] db	28 June, 319?	A(B)	Qosyinqom f ss Baalrim		to the storehouse wheat: 17 seahs, 1 qab
9. 5C	928 = GCh128	5 Tammuz, 5 [Philip III?] db	2 July, 319?	A(B)	Ani f ss Baalrim		to the storehouse wheat: 18 seahs, half qab
10. 5D	932 = GCh132 = JA493	5 Tammuz, 5 [Philip III?] db	2 July, 319?	A(B)	Zaydi f [ss Baalrim]		to the storehouse wheat: 18 seahs, half qab
11.	1050 = L50	5 Tammuz, 5 [Philip III?] db	2 July, 319?	??	Laadiel f ss Al(i)*b*[aa]l		to the storehouse wheat: 4 seahs, 5 qabs, en\<try\> :wheat: 3 seahs, 2 qabs e barley: 6 seahs, 4 qabs
12. 6A	927 = GCh127	6 Tammuz, 5 [Philip III?] db	3 July, 319?	A(B)	Ammiel f ss Baalrim		to the storehouse wheat: 4 seahs
13. 6C	2436 = JA148	6 Tammuz, 5 [Philip III?] db	3 July, 319?	A(B)	Qosyeypi f ss Gur		to the storehouse wheat: 1 seah entry: wheat: 10 seahs e barley: 20 seahs
14. 6B	13 = JTS13	9 Tammuz, 5 [Philip III?] db	6 July, 319?	A(B)	Zubaydu		to the storehouse wheat: 16 seahs Palaqos
15. 6E	1766 = Zd38 = JA524	14 Tammuz, [5?] [Philip III?] db	11 July, 319?	A(B)	Aḥyaqim/ Aḥiqam f ss Baalrim		to the storehouse . . .
16. 7A	904 = GCh104	18 Tammuz, [5] [Philip III?] db	15 July, 319?	A(B)	Qosghayr f ss Baalrim	to the hand of Saadel	to the storehouse wheat: 5 seahs
17. 7B	914 = GCh114 = JA479	18 Tammuz, [5 Philip III?] db	15 July, 319?	A(B)	Dikru o ss Baalrim	to the hand of Saadel (supralinear)	to the storehouse wheat: 6 seahs, 1 qab; entry: wheat: 1 seah, 1.5 qabs e barley: 2 seahs, 3 qabs
18. 6D	543 = FCO 6	19 Tammuz, 5 [Philip III?] db	16 July, 319?	A(B)	Qosyinqom f ss Baalrim		to the storehouse wheat: 13 seahs, 4.5 qabs

No.	ISAP	Babylonian date	Julian Date	Scribe	Payer	Payee	Commodity
19. 7C	1532 = AL44 = M247	27 Tammuz, 5 [Philip III?] db	24 July, 319?	A(B)	Qosrim o ss Gur		to the storehouse wheat: 5 seahs e barley: 10 seahs
20.	1857 = EN58 = JA400	7 Elul, 6 [Philip III?] db	21 Sept., 318?	?	Abdidah	Ḥanniel/ Ḥazael	to the storehouse barley: 12 seahs e wheat: 6 seahs entry: to the storehouse of Makkedah barley: 4 seahs, 4.5 qabs
21.	1237 = AL54 = JA67	10 Sivan, 7 [Philip III?] db	16 June, 317?		Samitu		to the storehouse wheat: 1 kor, 7 seahs, 4 qabs
22.	2452 = JA165	24 Sivan, 7 [Philip III?] db			Aydu f *ss* Al(i)baal	to the head of Qosmalek/ Mosmilk	to the storehouse wheat: 24 seahs, 4 qabs
23.	2431 = JA142	22 Elul, 7 [Philip III?] db	24 Sept., 317?		Samitu		to the storehouse barley: 1 kor, 5 seahs, 4 qabs e wheat: 17 seahs, 5 qabs
24. 9A	1463 = AL55 = M175	28 Adar, 7 [Philip III?] db	26 March, 316?		Zabdi	to Qoskahel	to the storehouse barley: 14 seahs ?
25. 12B	1886 = EN92	11 Ab, 8 [Philip III?] db	4 August, 316?		Al(i)qos o ss Qoṣi	to the hand of Ḥazael	from the loan wheat: 10 seahs to the storehouse wheat: 20 seahs
26.	1268 = AL137 = JA94	[x +]3 Tebeth, y db	—	—	—	[… b]y/[… t]o the hand of Qosmilk/ malak	*to* the storehouse [… .]ʿ and Natanmaran
27.	2531 = JA254	2 [x] db			Qosadar …		to [the] storehou[se] wheat: 1 kor, 7 seahs, [x] qabs
28. 9C	906 = GCh106 = Zd72 = JA472	— nd	—	—	Qosrai		to the storehouse barley: 2 kors, 13 seahs, 4.5 qabs
29.	2507 = JA225	—	—	—	—		to the storehouse wheat: 22 seahs

No.	ISAP	Babylonian date	Julian Date	Scribe	Payer	Payee	Commodity
29a.	19 = JTS19 = 159272	10 Elul, [x] db	—	?	Hazira s [...]		to the storehou[se] ...

Scribe A(B): 13 chits, 11 wheat, 1 barley, 1 uncertain (2x Sivan, year 5, 11x Tammuz, year 5).
24 chits: wheat, 3 also exchange; 4 chits: barley, 3 of these not by Scribe A(B), 1 also
exchange; 4 chits: exchange, 3 of these w/b and 1 b/w, 2 of these also wheat deposit and 1
barley deposit; 1 chit: b/w to storehouse and barley to storehouse of Makkedah; 1 also from
the loan; 6 (maybe 7) have recipients

Table 2: 15/16 deliveries to the storehouse of Makkedah (ל מסבנת מנקדה)

No.	ISAP	Babylonian date	Julian Date	Scribe	Payer	Payee	Commodity
30.	2445 = JA157	29 [Marcheshvan], 43 [Artaxerxes II] db	17 November, 362		Suaydu		[to the storehouse of] Makkedah wheat: [x] seahs [...]
31.	1032 = L32	7 Tebeth, 14 [Artaxerxes III] db	14 January, 344		Ḥanina		to the storehouse of Makkedah wheat: 5 seahs, 1.5 qabs
32.	1263 = AL63 = JA89	[x] Kislev, 16 [Artaxerxes III] db	November 19 - December 17, 343		[Qos]yatub [by] Yetiah		to the storehouse of Makkedah wheat: 7 seahs, 1.5 qabs 15 [seahs]
33.	1275 = AL14	20 Tammuz, 1 [Philip III?] db	31 July, 323?		Al(i)qos o ss Gur		to the storehouse of Makkedah wheat: 5 seahs, 5.5 qabs
34. 2B	542 = FCO5	16 Sivan, 3 [Philip III?] db	5 July, 321?	(A)B	Abdidah s Ghayran/ Aydan		to the storehouse of Makkedah barley: 12 seahs, 2 qabs, 1 q(uarter)
35. 2C	1604 = M406 = AL35	18 Sivan, 3 [Philip III?] db	7 July, 321?	(A)B	Qosner o ss Yehokal		to the storehouse of Makkedah barley: 12 seahs
36. 3A	1875 = EN81 = JA9	19 Sivan, 3 [Philip III?] db	8 July, 321?	(A)B	Qoslanṣur o ss Jokal		to the storehouse of Makkedah barley: 9 kors, 10 seahs
37. 3B	903 = GCh103	24 Sivan, 3 [Philip III?] db	13 July, 321?	(A)B	Saadel o ss Baalrim		to the storehouse of Makkedah barley: 7 kors, 18 seahs, 2 qabs

No.	ISAP	Babylonian date	Julian Date	Scribe	Payer	Payee	Commodity
38. 3C	909 = GCh109 = JA475	24 Sivan, 3 [Philip III?] db	13 July, 321?	(A)B	Abdidah (s Ghayran/ Aydan?)		to the storehouse of Makkedah barley: 21 seahs, 2 qabs
39.	2509 = JA227	28 Marcheshvan 3 [Philip III?] db	13 December, 321?		Anael/ Ḥanael		to the storehouse of Makkedah wheat: 1 kor, 1 seah, 3[+?] qabs
40. 2A	899 = GCh99	26 Kislev, 3 [Philip III?] db	9 January, 320?	(A)B	Saadel f ss Baalrim		brought to the storehouse of Makkedah barley: 8 kors
41. 7D	917 = GCh117	19 Tammuz, 5 [Philip III?] db	16 July, 319?	A(B)	Qosyinqom <f ss Baalrim>		to the storehouse of Makkedah barley: 5 and 3/4 seahs
42.	1857 = EN58 = JA400	7 Elul, 6 [Philip III?] db	21 Sept., 318?	?	Ab[didah]		entry: to the storehouse of [Ma]kke[dah] barley: 4 seahs, 4.5 qabs
42a.	19 = JTS19 159272	10 Elul, [x] db	—	?	Hazira s [...]		to the storehou[se of Makkedah?] ...
43.	1027 = L27	21 Elul db	—	?	Qoslaaqub		to the storehouse of M[akkedah] [...]
44. 8C	1225 = LL4 = SM11	12 Tammuz, 8 [Philip III?] db	6 July, 316?		Qosnaqam o ss Gur		to the storehouse of Makkedah wheat: 9 seahs, 3.5 qabs for the buyer: wheat: 9 seahs, 3.5 qabs

Scribe (A)B: 6 chits, all for barley (16–24 Sivan, 26 Kislev); Scribe A(B): 1 chit, barley; 4 chits: wheat, 1 of these also for the buyer.

Sub-group Ic: From the Grain of the Storehouse

Nos. 45–47 (Table 3) – These three dated chits seem to be about disbursing grain. The first one reads, 'Vanay, from the grain of the storehouse: wheat, 11 *seahs*' (No. 45). The next two were drawn up by Samitu, the first on 23 Tebeth, year 6 (No. 46) and the second on 23 Elul, without a year (No. 47). The amounts of wheat are small, five *seahs* and some. On 26 Sivan, year 5 and again on 10 Sivan, year 7, a Samitu, likewise without filiation, sends more than a *kor* of wheat to the storehouse each time (Nos. 3, 21). In one of the texts in this section we appear to have a reference to an agent (No. 46), but in none of the three texts is a recipient indicated. May we conjecture that Samitu himself (and Vanay) is the recipient, drawing on the amounts he had earlier deposited? In any case, we should conclude that once wheat had been deposited in the storehouse, it became known as עבור מסכנתא, 'grain of the storehouse'. We look further. Two storehouse (of Makkedah) chits record double deposits that allude to market transactions:

(1) In the first half of the first chit, Al(i)qos of Qosi gives to the hand of Hazael 'from the loan' (מן זפתא) 10 *seah*s of wheat. In the second half of the chit he sends 20 *seah*s of wheat to the storehouse (No. 25). The term מן זפתא seems to be an abbreviation for the term מן עבור זפתא, 'from the grain of the loan', also found elsewhere, both for barley and wheat (ISAP 806, 1710, 1847 = EN 47). Elephantine has yielded a loan document for emmer (*TAD* B3.13) which suggests that 'grain of the loan' is grain which one acquired through borrowing.

(2) In the second chit, Qosnaqam of Gur sent 9 *seah*s, 3.5 *qab*s of wheat to the storehouse of Makkedah and in the second half of the chit records an equal amount for an unnamed 'buyer' (זבונא; alternately זבינא, 'sale') (No. 44). Close to ten chits refer to wheat and occasionally barley as coming מן עבור זבינתא, 'from the grain of the purchase' (ISAP 2.3, 10.2-3, 15.3, 45.3, 918.2, 1575.3, 1576.2, 1632.4 [Figure 8B], 1866.2-3). The prophet Amos speaks of a lively trade in grain that barely gave way to Sabbath observance (Amos 8.5). In short, grain was harvested, borrowed, and bought. Some of this made its way to the מסכנתא or the מסכנת מנקדה, where it was traded.

Table 3: Three deliveries from the grain of the storehouse (מן עבור מסכנתא)

No.	ISAP	Babylonian date	Julian Date	Scribe	Payer	Payee	Commodity
45. 12A	1876 = EN82 = JA10	20 Ab, 4 db	—	—	Vanay	—	from the grain of the storehouse wheat: 11 seahs
46.	2532 = JA255	23 Tebeth, 6 db	1 February, 317?	—	Samitu	by the hand of [PN]	from the grain of the storehouse wheat: 5 seahs, 4.5 qabs
47.	1589 = M305 = AL99	23 Elul db	—	—	Samit[u]	—	from the grain of the storehouse wheat: 5 seahs

Sub-group Id: Idiosyncratic Formulation

Nos. 48–51 (Table 4) – Four chits bear an alternate formulation – מסכנה למנקדה, to be rendered '(to the) storehouse of Makkedah'. Written by the same scribe (Scribe C) in close proximity, they demonstrate scribal individuality. They are much earlier than the ones dealt with above – 5 Sivan, 9 and 20 (2x) Tammuz, year 18 (June 5, July 9 and 20, 341 [Nos. 48–51]). They all carry the verb 'brought in' (הנעל), record small to medium amounts of wheat, not for the 'storehouse', as did the texts discussed above, but for the 'storehouse of Makkedah' [so restore in No. 48]. In this, they follow the same pattern as the three early chits for the 'storehouse of Makkedah' (November 17, 362, November 19–December 17, 343, January 14, 344 [Nos. 30–32]), which send wheat there and not barley, as do most of the late chits, especially those of scribes (A)B and A(B) (Nos. 34–42). There are only three exceptions among these late chits, sending wheat and not barley (Nos. 33, 39, 44).

Table 4: '(to the) storehouse of (ל) Makkedah' (מסכנה למנקדה)

No.	ISAP	Babylonian Date	Julian Date	Scribe	Payer	Payee	Commodity
48.	1267 =JA93 =AL84	5 Sivan, 18 [Artaxerxes III] db	5 June, 341	C	[PN s] *Rufayu*		*brought in* (to the) storehouse [of Makkedah] [...: *x* seahs], 1.5 qabs
49.	1034 =L34	9 Tammuz, 18 [Artaxerxes III] db	9 July, 341	C	Qosmil[k]/mala[k]s Qayne[l]		brought in (to the) storehouse of Makkedah wheat: 2 seahs
50. 9B	1578 =M294 =AL85	20 Tammuz, 18 [Artaxerxes III] db	20 July, 341	C	Labiel		brought in (to the) storehouse of Makkedah wheat: 19 seahs
51.	2552 =JA277	20 Tammuz, 18 [Artaxerxes III] db	20 July, 341	C	Ḥazira		brought in (to the) storehouse of Makkedah wheat: 3 seahs

Was 'the Storehouse' a tax-collection centre?

4. Venue – Can archaeology shed any light on the מסכנא and its purpose? We cite three possible models:

(1) Subterranean storage pits – In 1971 Lawrence E. Stager noted that during the Persian period such pits were to be found everywhere. At Tell el-Hesi, for example, they were usually 1.00–2.00 m. in diameter and 2.00–2.5 m. in depth.[22]

(2) The NW Storeroom in the first century BCE/first century CE administrative centre at Kedesh in the Galilee measured 4.9x5.4 m. and contained 15 large storage jars.[23]

(3) Tripartite pillared buildings – It was Zeev Herzog who, in 1973 first argued that similarly constructed pillared buildings in six Iron Age sites were storehouses that should be identified with the biblical מסכנות and these 'should definitely be linked with the system of tax collection and distribution for which evidence is found in the Samaria, Arad and Beersheba ostraca'.[24] The Beersheba storehouse measured 10x18 m. Fifteen years later, in 1988, Larry Herr brought the total sites up to nine, cited Herzog's reference to מסכנות, and argued that these constructions were markets with a storage capacity where farmers would bring their surplus goods for sale.[25] Carrying the argument further, Moshe Kochavi 'had counted 35 of these buildings at 12 sites' by 1999 and dubbed them 'the ancient equivalent of shopping malls!'[26] Some such explanation is certainly attractive, since our ostraca lack the royal trappings we would associate with Hezekiah's מסכנות. We may contrast the terminology found in the Persian-period Elephantine papyri, where the imperial presence is keenly felt. The storehouse or treasury, or whatever we call it, is designated אוצר מלכא, 'treasury of the king' (*TAD* B 3.4:9, 3.7:7, 11:4,

---

22.   L. E. Stager, 'Climatic Conditions and Grain Storage in the Persian Period,' *BA* 34 (1971), pp. 86–8.

23.   S. C. Herbert and A. M. Berlin, 'A New Administrative Center for Persian and Hellenistic Galilee: Preliminary Report of the University of Michigan/University of Minnesota Excavations at Kedesh', *BASOR* 329 (2003), pp. 13–59 (27–8), figures 12–13.

24.   Z. Herzog, 'The Storehouses' in Y. Aharoni (ed.), *Beer-Sheba I: Excavations at Tel Beer-Sheba, 1969–1971 Seasons* (Tel-Aviv: Tel Aviv University Institute of Archaeology, 1973), pp. 23–30, especially pp. 24, 27, 30, figure 1.

25.   L. G. Herr, 'Tripartite Pillared Buildings and the Market Place in Iron Age Palestine', *BASOR* 272 (1988), pp. 47–66, especially figure 1 and pp. 63–4.

26.   M. Kochavi, 'Tripartite Buildings: Divided Structures Divide Scholars', *BARev* 25/3 (1999), pp. 44–50 (45). At Tell en-Naṣbeh, J. R. Zorn noted in Stratum 2 (6th/5th centuries) in the south-central part the remains of two long rooms connected to each other diagonally at the corner; 'Such long rooms are often used for storage, which might then be the function of these rooms' ('Tell en-Naṣbeh and the Material Culture of the Sixth Century' in O. Lipschits and J. Blenkinsopp, *Judah and the Judeans in the Neo-Babylonian Period* [Winona Lake: Eisenbrauns, 2003], pp. 413–47 [423–24]).

13:4) or בית מלכא, 'house of the king' (*TAD* B 3.13:6; 4.4:12, 16; 5.5:8), while the large-size weight and capacity denominations are the Persian *karsh* and *ardab* respectively.[27] Tribute collected throughout the Persian empire would be denominated in standard Persian measures not in local measures. The contrast to our ostraca could not be starker. There is no glimpse of a royal storehouse and the measure of capacity is not the Persian *ardab* but the native *kor*. It is clear that our chits are not reporting tax collection![28]

Sub-group Ie: In/Of Makkedah

Nos. 52–55 (Table 5) – Coming together in a group by itself are four chits where Makkedah is an identity tag. Two chits are dated only by day and month. The first (No. 54) was written on 28 Elul by 'Qoshanan from the sons of Baa<l> rim who is/are in Makkedah' (זי במנקדה). Unlike the Elephantine contracts, where it was regular practice to identify a party by his ethnicon and origin, e.g. 'PN, Jew of Elephantine' (זי יהב) (*TAD* B2.4:2), this is the only time in our ostraca that the origin of the payer is identified. Moreover, it is not unequivocally clear whether the particle זי, 'who', refers to Qoshanan or to the sons of Baalrim. The second chit (No. 55) was written on 1 Nisan by 'Baani and Sammuk of the citizens of Makkedah' (מנקדה לבעלי) (less likely 'to the citizens of Makkedah'). In plural construct followed by GN, this expression was well known in Hebrew, Aramaic, and Phoenician to designate 'citizens of GN'.[29] In our texts, however, it occurs but once. In neither of the two chits is the payee mentioned.

While over a dozen Aramaic ostraca from Arad mention horses and donkeys and four mention camels,[30] in the more than 1,700 Idumean ostraca there are only two references to donkeys (ISAP 1085.1, 1648.3) and two to camels (ISAP 672.2, 1648.1) Yet renewed palaeographical examination discovered young female camels hidden in chits signed by Saadel and sealed with an archaic *aleph* in the heat of summer, on 20

---

27.   See the 96 entries for ארדב and the 282 entries for כרש in B. Porten and J. A. Lund, *Aramaic Documents from Egypt: A Key-Word-in-Context Concordance* (Winona Lake: Eisenbrauns, 2002), pp. 28–9, 172–75.

28.   A. Lemaire makes a valiant attempt to extract from our ostraca, particularly from the difficult-to-read-and-interpret land registry texts, evidence for the payment of various and sundry taxes, but he skates on thin ice; see 'Taxes et impôts dans le sud de la Palestine (IVᵉ s. av. J.-C.)', *Transeuphratène* 28 (2004), pp. 133–42.

29.   E.g. Jericho (Josh. 24.11), Shechem (Judges 9.2), Gibeah (Judges 20.5), Keilah (1 Sam. 23.11), Jabesh-Gilead (2 Sam. 21.12); Arpad and *Ktk* (Sefire 1A4 = *KAI* 1, p. 42, no. 222), Elephantine (*TAD* A 4.7:22 = 4.8:22); and Sidon (*KAI*, 60.6, p. 13).

30.   J. Naveh, 'The Aramaic Ostraca from Tel Arad', in Y. Aharoni, *Arad Inscriptions* (Jerusalem: The Israel Exploration Society, 1981), pp. 153–76, Nos. 24.1, 25.2, 42.7, 70.1 (only the first was recognized by Naveh).

Tammuz and 3 Ab, year 46 (August 8 and 21, 359) (Nos. 52 and 53). The first should not read that Ḥalfat dispatched ליד קצא זי במנקרה, 'to the hand of Qoṣa which is in (the) pit', as the document's editors would have it, but לינקתא זי במנקדה, 'for the young female camels who are in Makkedah'. And what he sent was not a *kor* and 3 *seah*s of wheat but תבן פחל \ ץ, '1 bale of chaff', that is, fodder for the animals.[31] The second one was only very partially clear to the original editors from their photo, but much was evident from examination of the piece itself (in the Jeselsohn collection [JA4]). We can confidently read and restore the phrase לי[נ]קתא] זי במנקדה, while the products sent were '1 bale of STALKS' (עצה) and probably '1[+?] bales of chaff'. As the grazing land dries up in the heat of summer, the camels need food prepared by man. Camels figure prominently in our written and monumental sources. One of the earliest occurrences is in the tale of Abraham's servant's stay in the house of Laban, where they are provided with chaff and feed to eat (Gen. 24.25, 32).[32] In the final decades of the monarchy, Jeremiah chose a young female camel (בכרה) in heat as a striking image for wanton Israel (Jer. 2.23). Our ינקתא evokes this saucy image since the Targum of that passage is our only source for the Aramaic word. As beast of burden the camel, laden with water jars, figures on the wall reliefs in Sennacherib's Nineveh palace. It accompanies the inhabitants of Lachish (Room XXXVI [B. M. 129697]) and perhaps of Ashkelon (Room X) on their journey into exile.[33] Returning from exile, the repatriates were accompanied by 435 camels (Ezra 2.66 = Neh. 7.68) and Deutero-Isaiah foretold that young male camels (בכר) from Midian, Ephah and Sheba would haul spices and gold to restored Judah (Isa. 60.6). The female camel was highly prized, for her milk and reproductive capacity and as means of

---

31. A rare document, which seems to be part of a letter, records a payment order: 'Beldalani thus said, "Give to Menaḥem for the rams of Qoskahel 1 *kor* of barley from the grain of the loan which is mine ..."' (ISAP 1710). Barley was known as animal feed (Sotah 2.1) and along with chaff, as fodder for horses (1 Kings 5.8); see G. Dalman, *Arbeit und Sitte in Palästina* II, (Gütersloh: C. Bertelsmann, 1933; photographic reproduction: Hildesheim: G. Olms, 1964), pp. 252, 254 n. 7 (we are further grateful to Mordecai Kislev and Marc Hirshman for sharing their thoughts on this subject with us).

32. For further references to chaff as food for other animals see Dalman, *Arbeit und Sitte in Palästina* III, 136–8; Y. Feliks, *Agriculture in Eretz-Israel in the Period of the Bible and Talmud: Basic Farming Methods and Implements* (Jerusalem: Magnes, 1990), pp. 257–60 (Hebrew), cites some seven uses to which chaff was put.

33. R. D. Barnett, 'Lachish, Ashkelon and the Camel: A Discussion of its Use in Southern Palestine', in J. N. Tubb (ed.), *Palestine in the Bronze and Iron Ages: Papers in Honour of Olga Tufnell* (London: University of London, Institute of Archaeology, 1985), pp. 15–30.

payment.[34] It is certainly striking that the city known for its granaries of wheat and barley was also home to those nubile creatures that so caught Jeremiah's eye. Equally striking is the verbal association that echoes from the Passover ostracon at Elephantine (*TAD* D7 = *CoS* 3.87A).[35] Here, Ḥalfat and Laadiel provide chaff for the ינקתא to eat as the natural pasture dries up. At Elephantine, a correspondent advises Hoshaiah to personally look after the ינקיא (not camels but 'babes') and prepare for them bread before their mother arrives. Both Idumean summer chits bore the signatory of Saadel. Is he the same Saadel who dealt with small quantities of wheat and barley in the storehouse or the Saadel of Baalrim who brought huge quantities of barley to the storehouse of Makkedah? Or perhaps his papponymous grandfather?

Makkedah, let us not forget, was a dozen kilometres or so slightly southeast of Lachish.

Table 5: 'To ... who are (who is) in Makkedah' (לל ־ זי במנקדה)/ 'to/of men of Makkedah' (לבעלי מנקדה) pl = *plene*

No.	ISAP	Babylonian date	Julian Date	Scribe	Payer	Payee	Commodity
52. 11B	1802 = EN2	20 Tammuz, 46 [Artaxerxes II] archaic *aleph*	8 August, 359	D	Ḥalfat	young female camels	who are in Makkedah (payee) chaff: 1 bale Saa[de]l
53. 11A	1853 = EN54 = JA4	3 Ab, [4]6 [Artaxerxes III] archaic *aleph*	21 August, 359	D	Laadiel	young female camels	who are in Makkedah (payee) stalks (עצה): 1 bale chaff (תבן): [?+]1 bales Saadel
54.	1244 = AL127	28 Elul	—		Qoshanan f ss Baa<l> rim	—	who is/are in Makkedah (payer) chaff: 1 bundle

34. See H. Gauthier-Pilters and A. I. Dagg, *The Camel: Its Ecology, Behavior and Relationship to Man* (Chicago: University of Chicago Press, 1981), pp. 93, 135–7; P. Wapnish, 'Camel Caravans and Camel Pastoralists at Tell Jemmeh', *JANES* 13 (1981), pp. 101–21 (108–9, n. 30).

35. W. W. Hallo (ed.), *The Context of Scripture* III (Leiden: Brill, 2002), no. 3.87A, pp. 208–9.

No.	ISAP	Babylonian date	Julian Date	Scribe	Payer	Payee	Commodity
55.	1941 = EN150 = BLM690	1 Nisan	—		Baani and Sammuk	pl	of the men of Makkedah wine: 20 seahs; LAUREL: 2 qabs by the hand of Gar(a)pa and Reimaran

Group II: To and From Makkedah

Nos. 56–70, 71–91 (Tables 6–7) – Just as מסבנתא and מסבנת מנקדה are paired off against each other, so למנקדה, 'to Makkedah' and מן מנקדה, 'from Makkedah', are correlatives. The 14/15 texts marked 'to Makkedah' (Nos. 56–70) have a very different complexion from the texts marked 'to the storehouse of Makkedah'.

(1) For one, the only goods that went 'to the storehouse of Makkedah' were wheat and barley whereas items directed 'to Makkedah' included, in addition to barley (five chits [Nos. 57, 59–61, 63]) and wheat (2 chits [Nos. 56, 58]), semolina (No. 68), wine (No. 67), roosters (No. 65), goat hide (No. 69), loads (No. 64), and logs (No. 70). Whereas six or seven of the 29 items directed to the storehouse are also directed to a specific person, especially Saadel (Nos. 4, 16, 17), only one of the 15 items directed just 'to Makkedah', namely the roosters, is also directed to a person, and that person is Saadel (No. 65). If the wheat and barley were deposited in one or the other storehouse and the roosters went to Saadel in Makkedah, who received the other items? Strikingly, Saadel himself is a payer who sends semolina 'to Makkedah' (No. 68). To whom did he send it? The same may be asked of Saadi, whose name may be an abbreviation of Saadel and who sent wine 'to Makkedah' (No. 67). As for many of the chits, the recipient remains a mystery.

(2) Secondly, two ostraca from the dossier of Ḥalfat make plain that the preposition מן, 'from', identifies the source of the commodity and not the origin of the payer, though he, too, may have come from Makkedah. They read, 'Ḥalfat *delivered* (המטא) from Makkedah semolina' (No. 77); 'There brought in (הנעל) Ḥalfat from Makkedah to Ab(i)yatha by the hand of PN wheat ... barley' (No. 78). This later sentence is freely composed, containing all the elements of the transaction – verb, payer, source, payee, agent, product and amount. But among the 20-some relevant chits, those without the verb, the source (מן מנקדה) followed the payer eleven times (Nos. 71, 75–78, 80–81, 83, 88–90), but the payee only five times (Nos. 72–

73, 79, 84–85). We should not assume that now the payer originated in Makkedah and now the payee did. The normal elliptical sentence followed the model of 'Ḥalfat (brought in) from Makkedah to Ab(i)yatha' but occasionally the scribe would follow an alternate word order and write 'Ḥalfat (brought in) to Ab(i)yatha from Makkedah'. It may not be coincidental that a verb connoting transport is not to be found in any of the 15 ostraca addressed 'to Makkedah' but four different verbs are found in five of the 21 ostraca directing items 'from Makkedah' – הֵיתִי, 'brought' (Nos. 74, 82), הַמְטָא, 'delivered' (No. 77), הַנְעַל, 'brought in' (No. 78), הַנְחַת, 'brought down' (No. 86). Were they synonyms or did each have its own nuance?

   (3) Truth to tell, one of the texts listed along with the 'to' (-לְ) texts lacks the preposition (No. 56, figure 13a). It has an unusual order: day and month, 'Makkedah', payer, payee, clan of payer, commodity and amount. The natural order would have been: date, payer, clan of payer, 'Makkedah', payee, commodity and amount. We have recently come upon a pertinent Hebrew ostracon (figure 13b) dated palaeographically to the end of the seventh or the beginning of the sixth century BCE. This ostracon is one of four that originated in an unknown site in the Judean hills and includes a word read מֻודְרה by the original editors but corrected to מקדה (Makkedah) by André Lemaire.[36] It is striking that our Idumean ostracon follows the Hebrew spelling for the toponym. The normal spelling in the Aramaic ostraca (some 70 times!) is מנקדה, 'Mankedah', because Aramaic generally retains the *nun* before the *qoph* whereas Hebrew tends to assimilate it. The Aramaic thus reveals that the source of the name is *n-q-d*. This has been related to *noqed*, 'sheeptender' or the like (2 Kings 3.4; Amos 1.1).[37] It has been suggested, then, that Makkedah was a place of sheeptenders, a matter yet to be explored.[38] Be that as it may, the Hebrew ostracon is, indeed, a commodity chit, and as such, unique among the several Hebrew ostraca that have so far come to light from that unknown source believed to be Khirbet el-Kôm. The commodity is none other than semolina (סלת), with the amount translated by the editors as '50' (what?), though this is not certain. The day, payer and payee are not noted. The order is: 1. year and month (06.vii); 2. Makkedah; 3. commodity and amount. Here too, מקדה appears without preposition. May we assume an ellipsis in both the

---

36.   R. Deutsch and M. Helzer, *New Epigraphic Evidence from the Biblical Period* (Tel Aviv-Jaffa: Archaeological Center Publications, 1995), no. 76, pp. 81–3; A. Lemaire, 'Hebrew and Aramaic in the First Millenium BCE in the Light of Epigraphic Evidence (Socio-Historical Aspects)', in S. Fassberg and A. Hurvitz (eds), *Biblical Hebrew in its Northwest Semitic Setting* (Jerusalem - Winona Lake: Magnes - Eisenbrauns, 2006), pp. 177–96 (187 n. 42) – this was already recognized in 1997.

37.   BDB (p. 667a) gives three alternate translations: 'sheepraiser, -dealer or -tender'.

38.   We are thankful to Ran Zadok for his discussion of this toponym.

A Time of Change

Aramaic and the Hebrew ostraca, and that in both the commodity was headed *for* Makkedah, probably for the storehouse? In any case, there was already some depository for grain at the site when it was controlled by Judahites, three centuries before our Idumean documents.

Table 6: To Makkedah (למנקדה)

No.	ISAP	Babylonian date	Julian Date		Payer	Payee	Commodity
56.	1723 = TM8	18 Ab archaic *aleph* db	—		Qosghayr f h Al(i)baal	Zubaydu	Makkedah wheat: 4.5 seahs
57.	1716 = TM2 = M427 = AL28	26 Elul, 2 [Philip III?] db	24 September, 322		Ḥamiyu/ Ḥumayu o ss Baalrim (OR: of Makkedah)		to Makkedah barley:14 kors, 22 seahs
58.	1645 = OG?11	26 Tebeth db	—		Qosyinqom o ss Baalrim		to Makkedah wheat: 3 kors, 7 seahs, 5.5 qabs *Elimilk/malak*
59.	1017 = L17	27 Elul, 5 db	—		Zaidilahi s Ḥal(a)fu		to Makkedah *barley*: [x] qab
60.	53	7 Tammuz, 7 [Philip III?] db	12 July, 317?		Q[ra]bel	by the hand of Ḥalfan	to Makkedah barley: 26 seahs [? + 1] בשחל ן גזיר
61.	1900 = EN108	18 Tammuz, 5 Antigo-nu[s] db	9 July, 313		Nahru; Qosmilk/ malak?	by the hand of [...]u in Malḥat(?)	to Makkedah barley: 2 kors barley: 1 seah
62.	227 = IA11802	20 [x], [y] Antigonus db	—		[PN] o ss [PN]		to Makkedah ... 3
63.	240 = IA11817	22 Tammuz db	—		[PN]		to Makkedah barley: [...]
64.	2610 = JA346	8 E[lul]/ A[dar]/ I[yyar]/A[b] db			Al(i)qos		to Makkedah loads: 4
65.	921 = JA485	year 2	—		Bayyun	to Saadel by the hand of Ašmu/iel to PN	to Makkedah roosters: 2
66.	458 = IA11321	—	—		Ab(i)šalam		to Makkedah 212 [...?]

No.	ISAP	Babylonian date	Julian Date		Payer	Payee	Commodity
67.	919 = GCh119 = JA483	—	—		Saadi		to Makkedah wine:14 seahs
68.	920 GCh120 = JA484	20 [x]	—		Saadel		to Makke[dah] semolina: 8 seahs
69.	1942 = EN151 = BLM678	—	—		[...]y		to Makkedah goat [hi]de: 1
70.	915 = GCh115 = JA480	—	—		Qosyinqom		let there be unloaded (יתפרק) for Makkedah logs: 2 logs: 2

Table 7: From Makkedah (מן מנקדה)

No.	ISAP	Babylonian date	Julian Date		Payer	Payee	Commodity
71.	837 = GCh37 = IA12445	—	(5th century BCE?)		Gadi	Abdram	(from) Makkedah men: [x]
72.	1849 = EN49 = JA104	26 Nisan, 44 [Artaxerxes II] archaic *aleph* de	10 May, 361		Abdbaal	Marṣaat s Qoṣi	from Makkedah barley groats: 5 seahs yazidu
73.	1286 = AL6 = B1 = JA497	26 Marcheshvan, 44 [Artaxerxes II] archaic *aleph* db	2 Dec., 361		Qosnaqam	Samitu	from Makkedah from the grind o ss Malka/ the king barley groats: 2 seahs, 2 qabs *Yazidu*
74.	2511 = JA229	30 Sivan, 46 [Artaxerxes II] archaic *aleph* db	July 20, 359		Laedielf ss Allifbael		[brou]gh[t] from Makkedah semolina: 2 seahs, 2 qabs, 1 quarter flour: 2 seahs, 3 qabs *Yazidu*
75.	1809 = EN9	4 Sivan, 2 [Artaxerxes III] db	1 June, 357		Ḥalfat	Baalghayr	from Makkedah barley: 1 kor, 26 seahs, 5 qabs

No.	ISAP	Babylonian date	Julian Date		Payer	Payee	Commodity
76.	1815 = EN15	4 Shebat, 4 [Artaxerxes III] db	1 February, 354		Ḥalfat	—	from Makkedah wheat: 12 seahs, 1 qab Qos [... ...]
77.	1826 = EN26	—	—		Ḥalfat	—	delivered from Makkedah semolina: 1[+?] seah flour: [x]
78.	1834 = EN34	—	—		Ḥalfat	Ab(i)yatha by the hand of [PN]	brought in from Makkedah wheat: 2 kors, [x seahs], 3 qabs barley: 6 kors
79.	1838 = EN38	13 Sivan, [43 Artaxerxes III] de	June 7, 362		Zabdi	Baalghayr	from Makkedah 2 bales
80.	1430 = AL184	—	—		Maš(i)ku f ss Qoṣi	—	from [Ma]kkedah chaff: 1 b[a]le
81.	1429 = AL225	—	—		Zubaydu s Qoskahel	—	from Makkedah DRIED FIGS (גרגר): 36
82.	2527 = JA250	—	—		Shammu	—	who brought, who is from Makkedah DRIED FIG[S] ([ג]רגר[ן]): 10
83.	1458 = M170 = AL36	19 [x], 3 de	—		???	by the hand of *Hanan*	from Makkedah wheat: 9 seahs, 2 qabs, 1 q(uarter) 2[+?] seahs
84.	2430 = JA141	—	—		Qosyahab	Udayd/ru	from Makkedah 3 logs
85.	1608 = M410 = AL213	—	—		1. Ḥalfan 2. [PN]	1. Haggai 2. Qosami	from Makkedah barley groats: 13 seahs, [x] qabs
86.	1563 = M278 = AL288	—	—		[PN]	???	brought down from Makkedah bundles: [x]
87.	248 = IA11812	???	???		???	???	from Makkedah [...]: 3 seahs
88.	2418 = JA128	—	—		Yaadarel		from Makkedah 30 [?]

No.	ISAP	Babylonian date	Julian Date		Payer	Payee	Commodity
89.	2533 =JA256	—	—		Lubayu	by the hand of [...]	from Makkedah [...]:
90.	1038 =L38	26 Sivan, 2 Alexander db	10 July, 315		Hanziru	—	from Makkedah barley: 21 seahs
91.	867= GCh67 =JA453	—	—		[... o s]s Baalrim		[from] Makkedah 1 wood

The Steppe and the 'Horse-Ranch'

There are several other geographical sites, all known as 'steppe of PN' ערבת\חנזרו) [ISAP 1039, 1535,1893]; ערבת חגי [ISAP 1553]; ערבת\ זמרו נמרו [ISAP 1254, 1654, 2491]).[39] The word ערבה is not otherwise known in Aramaic but in Biblical Hebrew it occurs frequently in parallel with מדבר, 'wilderness' (e.g. Deut. 1.1; 1 Sam. 23.24; Isa. 35.6; Jer. 2.6, 3.12). In construct plural it is attached to a GN, 'the steppes of Jericho' (Josh. 4.13, 5.10; 2 Kings 25.5 = Jer. 52.8) or 'the steppes of Moab' (Num. 22.1 etc.), not to a PN. Likewise the parallel מדבר occurs in some 20 construct combinations, but always with a GN, including towns (e.g. Beersheba [Gen. 21.14], Damascus [1 Kings 19.15], Ein-gedi [1 Sam. 24.1], Gibeon [2 Sam. 2.24], Tekoa [2 Chron. 20.20], Zif [1 Sam. 26.2] etc.), and never with a PN. Yet unlike the biblical combinations, which are traditional place names, ours, based as they are on PN's, are contemporary. Most of them are explicitly dated to the reign of Alexander IV (year 2 [ISAP 1039 = L39], 23.iii.2 = July 7, 315; [ISAP 1535 = AL87], 8.iv.2 = July 21, 315 [ISAP 1254 = AL88], 6.i.3 = April 10, 314 [ISAP 2410]; 25.iii.5 = July 5, 312 [ISAP 2491]). Hanziru, the first name mentioned above, is also associated with the word רכשת (likewise in construct), rendered by Eph'al and Naveh elsewhere as 'horse-ranch' (EN 97.3), or, alternately, 'property' of some sort. Both texts are dated to the reign of Philip III (27.v.5 = August 23, 319 [ISAP 1255 = AL91], 12.ix.7 = December 11, 317 [ISAP 1890 = EN97]). What is relevant for our discussion above is that all these place names fill the slot elsewhere held by Makkedah. They are always preceded by the preposition מן 'from'. As with מנקדה the phrase usually comes at the beginning, following the name of the payer, but in one ostracon it follows directly on the date and *precedes* the name of the payer – 'year 2 of [Alexa]nder the king from the

---

39. It is uncertain if the first letter should be read *zayin* or *nun*.

steppe of Ḥanziru, Palṭi/Pilṭi son of Qosgad to the hand of Akbor: wheat, 7 *seah*s' (ISAP 1039 = L39). It would seem clear, then, that the place name refers to the source of the transaction and not the origin of the payer. In two instances, however, the text *does* identify the origin not only of the payer but even of the agent. One text, undated, reads [... זי איתי מנקדה גרגר]ן שמוע זי מן, 'that which Shammu', who is from Makkedah, brought: [x] DRIED FIGS' (No. 82). The relative pronoun following the PN requires that the preposition מן, 'from' refer to it and not to the commodity. The second text, dated to Alexander (6.i.3 = April 10, 314 [ISAP 2412]), after mentioning the payer, Uzayzu, and the product, 1 *kor*, 23 *seah*s, 2 1/2 *qab*s of wheat, concludes with reference to the agent, 'by the hand of Qosi (who is) of (זי) the steppe of Ḥanziru.' Why in these two texts the origin of a party was recorded remains unclear. What is clear is that in all but one of the texts there is no relationship between the parties and the PN in the construct רבשת or ערבת. This exception is dated 6.iv.8 = June 30, 316 (ISAP2 497: IA14), written on the same date and by the same scribe as one attributed to Philip III on prosopographical and chrono-logical grounds (ISAP 1530 = AL57). After the date it reads 'Ḥazael son of Zabdi from the steppe of Qosner son of Zabdi: wheat, 7 *seah*s, 4 *qab*s'. Ḥazael is bringing wheat from the steppe of his brother Qosner. In this instance alone we witness a personal relationship between the payer and the 'steppe' but also sense the possibility that the origin of the payer is the 'steppe' itself.

As barley and wheat went 'to Makkedah' by a ratio of 5:2, so they were brought 'from Makkedah', but in equal proportion, 3:3 (Nos. 75, 78, 90; 76, 78, 83). Just as some scribes reported items other than barley and wheat going 'to Makkedah', so too, several scribes saw fit to report that a commodity was coming *from* Makkedah, e.g., semolina and flour (Nos. 74, 77), barley groats (Nos. 72–73, 85), DRIED FIGS (Nos. 81–82), bales, usually of chaff (Nos. 79–80), and bundles (No. 86), logs and wood (Nos. 84, 91). Except for logs (No. 70) and semolina (No. 68), none of these items was reported as going 'to Makkedah', nor do roosters, wine and goat hide (Nos. 65, 67, 69) ever come 'from Makkedah'. We know only one of the 15 recipients (Saadel) of the products sent 'to Makkedah' but we know some eight recipients of the products sent 'from Makkedah' (Nos. 71–73, 75, 78–79, 84–85). Just as we do not know the destination of the items being sent 'to Makkedah' so we cannot fathom why some 15 out of several hundred documents saw fit to record that their commodities were coming '*from* Makkedah'. Clearly, we have more information than we have explanation.

Group III: Miscellaneous Makkedah and Storehouse

Nos. 92–96 (Table 8) – These are four very fragmentary texts that mention Makkedah but without any clear indication of context. One fragmentary land description text headed by the word חלקתא, 'the portions', mentions מסכנתא, 'the storehouse' at the beginning of line 2; 'the vineyard of Baalš[...]' at the beginning of line 3; and 'a third of the חלת' at the beginning of line 4 (ISAP 2474). This is the only indication of the location of this building. At Elephantine, the אוצר מלכא, 'treasury of the king' adjoined the private house of Ananiah (*TAD* B3.4.9). Proximity to private property is one thing these two public buildings *do* seem to have in common.

Table 8: Miscellaneous Makkedah

No.	ISAP	Julian Date		Scribe	Payer	Payee	Commodity
92.	445 = IA11314	—	—		*Qosi*	to [...]	]Makkedah
93.	1769 = Zd41 = JA527	[? +]2 Elul	—		—	—	[Mak]kedah
94.	880 = GCh80 = JA466	—	—				[...]... *Makke-dah* [...]1 [qa]b the half of/which [...] [...]3 seahs, 1 qab, [the] hal[f] ... [...]1, from...[...] [...]...[...]
95.	1915 = EN124 = JA28	—	—		[...]*wy*	Dael/Raiel	[to/from] Makkedah oil: [*x* seahs], 5.5 qabs
96.	17 = JTS17 = 159270	9 Ab, [*y*] db	—		Qo[s...]	—	[*to-the-store-house-of/from*] Makkedah barley: [*x*]

Summary

The Idumean ostraca were locally produced and barely mention a toponym. The one that is mentioned some 50 times was not even recognized by one pair of early editors. It was the other editor, André Lemaire, who recognized that the uncertain word was to be read מנקדה,

biblical Makkedah. In our commodity chits, the word appears in three combinations – (1) a commodity, usually wheat, is sent to the 'storehouse of Makkedah'; (2) a commodity, including items other than wheat or barley, is sent 'to Makkedah'; (3) a commodity is sent 'from Makkedah'. There is also a fourth destination – 'to the storehouse'. We addressed two main areas:

(1) Was there a distinction, in terms of commodities deposited, between the 'storehouse' and the 'storehouse of Makkedah'? The affirmative answer that emerged showed that the early texts, those of the Achaemenid period, recorded only wheat for the 'storehouse of Makkedah', while the later texts, those of the Macedonian period, made a distinction, though not an absolute one, between wheat, which was sent to the 'storehouse', and barley, which went to the 'storehouse of Makkedah'. Furthermore, we learned that the storehouse was also a place of exchange, barley for wheat and wheat for barley at a standard, well-attested, historical rate. We also examined various archaeological models for the 'storehouse', determined the value of the ancient measurements (*kor*, *seah*, *qab*), and concluded that the deliveries were not tax payments.

(2) The second half of our investigation left more questions than answers. Items sent 'to Makkedah' included – besides barley and wheat – wine, semolina, goat hide, logs, and loads of chaff. Yet the recipient of these items is recorded in only one case – two roosters to Saadel. Who received the other things? We were able to determine that the designation 'from Makkedah' usually referred to the source of the commodity and not to the origin of the sender. As 'to' Makkedah, so 'from' Makkedah, a variety of commodities was sent. But were these 20 transactions the only ones whose commodities were sent from Makkedah that they alone were so designated? Hard to imagine!

The still unanswered question is what purpose these, and the hundreds more, commodity chits served.

Table 9: Amount of Commodities for the 'Storehouse' and their Equivalents in Litres and Food Allotments: 29 Sivan - 27 Tammuz, Year 5 (A Month in Summer)

No.	ISAP	Babylonian Date	Payer (and Payee)	Commodity	Kor	Seah	Qab	Total in Seahs	Total in Litres Feliks (1 seah = 8.54 litres)	Total in Litres Mikveh (1 seah = 8.29 litres)	Total in Litres Lewy (1 seah = 8.1 litres)	Total in Litres Albright (1 seah = 7.3 litres)	Total Daily Allotments for Poor Man	Number of Persons Fed per Week	Weekly Grain Allotments for Wife
4.	890	29 Sivan, 5	Qoskhair to Saadel	Barley	0	2	4.5	$2\frac{3}{4}$	23.47	22.798	22.275	20	16.5	2	4.125
5.	893	29 Sivan, 5	Qosyinqom f ss Baalrim	Wheat	0	8	4	$8\frac{2}{3}$	74	71.847	70.2	63.2	104	15	26
6.	908	29 Sivan, 5	Adarbaal and Zabdiel f ss Baalrim	Wheat	1	3	4.5	$33\frac{3}{4}$	288.21	279.788	273.378	247.3	405	58	101.25
7.	889	1 Tammuz, 5	Ammiqos f ss Baalrim	Wheat	0	17	4	$17\frac{2}{3}$	150.86	146.457	143.1	128.9	212	30	53
8.	924	1 Tammuz, 5	Qosyinqom f ss Baalrim	Wheat	0	17	1	$17\frac{1}{6}$	146.6	142.312	139.05	125.3	206	29	51.5
9.	928	5 Tammuz, 5	Ani f ss Baalrim	Wheat	0	18	0.5	$18\frac{1}{12}$	154.43	149.911	146.475	132	217	31	54.25
10.	932	5 Tammuz, 5	Zaydi f [ss Baalrim]	Wheat	0	17	0.5	$17\frac{1}{12}$	145.89	141.621	138.375	124.7	205	29	51.25

No.	ISAP	Babylonian Date	Payer (and Payee)	Commodity	Kor	Seah	Qab	Total in Seahs	Total in Litres Feliks (1 seah = 8.54 litres)	Total in Litres Mikveh (1 seah = 8.29 litres)	Total in Litres Lewy (1 seah = 8.1 litres)	Total in Litres Albright (1 seah = 7.3 litres)	Total Daily Allotments for Poor Man	Number of Persons Fed per Week	Weekly Grain Allotments for Wife
11.	1050	5 Tammuz, 5	Laaadiel f ss Al(i)b[aa]l	Wheat	0	4	5	$4^5/_6$	41.26	40.068	39.15	35.2	58	8	14.5
11.	1050	5 Tammuz, 5	Laaadiel f ss Al(i)b[aa]l	Wheat	0	3	2	$3^1/_3$	28.46	27.633	27	24.3	40	6	10
12.	927	6 Tammuz, 5	Ammiel f ss Baalrim	Wheat	0	4	0	4	34.16	33.16	32.4	29.2	48	7	12
13.	2436	6 Tammuz, 5	Qosyeypi f ss Gur	Wheat	0	11	0	11	93.94	91.19	89.1	80.3	132	19	33
14.	13	9 Tammuz, 5	Zubaydu	Wheat	0	16	0	16	136.64	132.64	129.6	116.8	192	27	48
16.	904	18 Tammuz, 5	Qosghayr f ss Baalrim	Wheat	0	5	0	5	42.7	41.45	40.5	36.5	60	9	15
17.	914	18 Tammuz, 5	Dikru o ss Baalrim	Wheat	0	7	2.5	$7^5/_{12}$	63.34	61.48	60.8	54.14	89	13	22.25

No.	ISAP	Babylonian Date	Payer (and Payee)	Commodity	Kor	Seah	Qab	Total in Seahs	Total in Litres Feliks (1 seah = 8.54 litres)	Total in Litres Mikveh (1 seah = 8.29 litres)	Total in Litres Lewy (1 seah = 8.1 litres)	Total in Litres Albright (1 seah = 7.3 litres)	Total Daily Allotments for Poor Man	Number of Persons Fed per Week	Weekly Grain Allotments for Wife
18.	543	19 Tammuz, 5	Qosyinqom f ss Baalrim	Wheat	0	13	4.5	$13\frac{3}{4}$	117.41	113.988	111.375	100.3	165	24	41.25
19.	1532	27 Tammuz, 5	Qosrim o ss Gur	Wheat	0	5	0	5	42.7	41.45	40.5	36.5	60	9	15
								Total $180^{7}/_{12}$	1584.07 litres	1537.79 litres	1503.275 litres	1354.64 litres	2209.5 a-llotments	317 people	552.375 allot-ments

Table 10: Amount of Commodities for the 'Storehouse of Makkedah' and their Equivalents in Litres and Food Allotments: 16 Sivan–24 Sivan, Year 3 (A Week in July)

No.	ISAP	Babylonian Date	Payer (and Payee)	Commodity	Kor	Seah	Qab	Total in Seahs	Total in Litres Feliks (1 seah = 8.54 litres)	Total in Litres Mikveh (1 seah = 8.29 litres)	Total in Litres Lewy (1 seah = 8.1 litres)	Total in Litres Albright (1 seah = 7.3 litres)	Total Daily Allotments for Poor Man	Number of Persons Fed per Week	Weekly Grain Allotments for Wife
34.	542	16 Sivan, 3	Abdidah s Ghay-ran/ Aydan	Barley	0	12	2.25	$12\frac{3}{8}$	105.675	102.589	100.238	90.3	74.25	11	18.56
35.	1604	18 Sivan, 3	Qosner o ss Yehokal	Barley	0	12	0	12	102.48	99.48	97.2	87.6	72	10	18
36.	1875	19 Sivan, 3	Qoslan- s-ur o ss Yokal	Barley	9	10	0	280	2391.2	2321.2	2268	2053	1680	240	420
37.	903	24 Sivan, 3	Saadel o ss Baal-rim	Barley	7	18	2	$228\frac{1}{3}$	1949.96	1892.883	1849.5	1673.8	1370	196	342.5
38.	909	24 Sivan, 3	Abdidah s Ghay-ran/ Aydan	Barley	0	21	2	$21\frac{1}{3}$	182.18	176.853	172.8	155.7	128	18	32
							Total	$554\frac{1}{24}$	4731.495 litres	4593.005 litres	4487.738 litres	4060.7 litres	3324.25 allotments	475 people	831.06 allotments

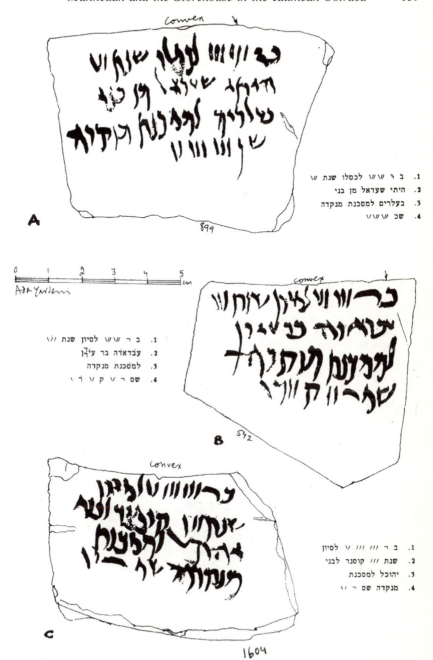

1. ב ר ש\ש\ לכסלו שנת ש\
2. היתי שעדאל מן בני
3. בעלרים למסכנת מנקדה
4. שכ ש\ש\ש\

1. ב ר ש\ש\ לסיון שנת ז\\
2. עבדאדה בר עז\ין\
3. למסכנת מנקדה
4. שס ר ע ק ע ד י

1. ב ר \\\ //// ע לסיון
2. שנת //// קוסנר לבני
3. יהוכל למסכנת
4. מנקדה שס ר \ ז\

Figure 2.

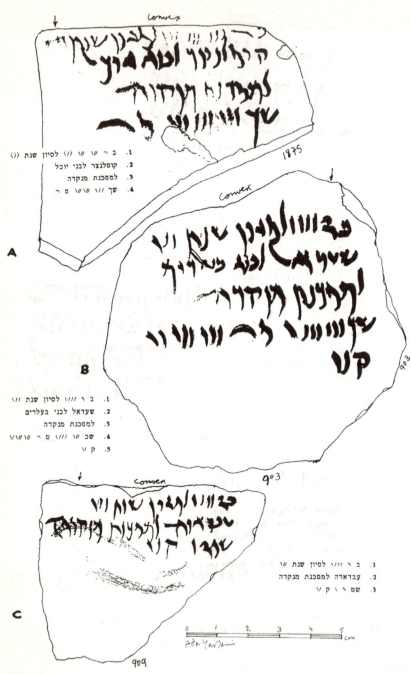

1.   ב ר ש׳ש ///ׁ לסיון שנת ///ׁ
2.   קוסלנצר לבני יוכל
3.   למסכנת מנקדה
4.   שך /// ש׳ש ס ר

1.   ב ר ////׳ לסיון שנת ///׳
2.   שעדאל לבני בעלרים
3.   למסכנת מנקדה
4.   שכ ש׳ ////ׁ ס ר ש׳ש׳ש
5.   ק ע

1.   ב ר ////׳ לסיון שנת ש׳
2.   עבדאדה למסכנת מנקדה
3.   שס ר י ק ע

Figure 3.

1. ‫ב ‏‪ר‬‎ ‏‪/‏‪//‪/‬‬ לסיון שנת ‏‪//‪/‬‏ ‪ע‬
2. שמתו ‫|‬   ‫|‬ ‏‪ו‬‎ למסכנתא‏‪א‬
3. חכ ‫|‬   ‫|‬ בב שמתו
4. חס ‫‏//‪/‬ ‪ש‬‎ ‏‪/‪ש‬

1. ‫ב ‏‪ר‬‎ ‏‪ש/ש/ש‬ לסיון שנת ‏‪///‪ע‬
2. קוסחיר לשעראל למסכנתא
3. שס ‪ע‬‎ ק ‏‪///‪ ‪פ‬

1. ‫ב ‏‪ר‬‎ ‏‪//‪/‬ ‏‪//‪/‬ לסיון שנת ‏‪ש/ש‬
2. קוסינקם מן בני בעלרים
3. למסכנתא חס ‏‪//‪/‬ ‪ע‬
4. ק ‏‪////‪‬

Figure 4.

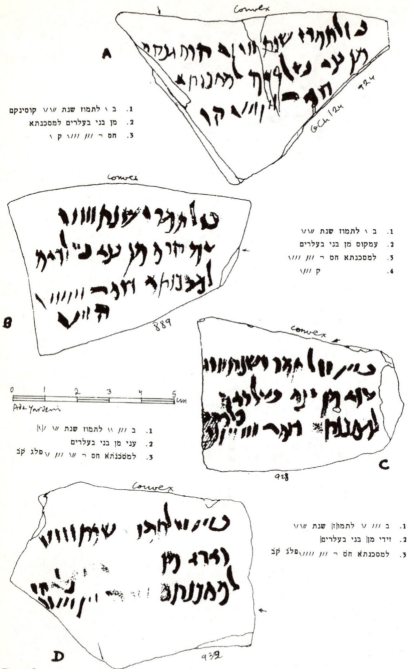

Figure 5.

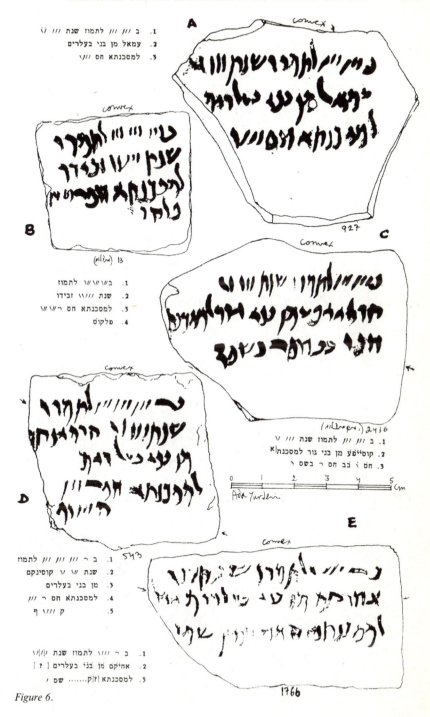

1. ב זוו זוו לתמוז שנת ווו וֹ
2. עמאל מן בני בעלרים
3. למסכנתא חס ווון

1. בשוֹשֹוֹש לתמוז
2. שנת וווווו זבידו
3. למסכנתא חס רשֹוֹש
4. פלקוֹס

1. ב זוו זוו לתמוז שנת ווו ע
2. קוסייֹסֹע מן בני גור למסכנתֹא
3. חס ו זב חס ר בשס ו

1. ב ר זוו זוו זוו לתמוז
2. שנת ש ע קוסינקם
3. מן בני בעלרים
4. למסכנתא חס זוו
5. ק וווו ף

1. ב ר וווו לתמוז שנת וֹוֹוֹוֹ
2. אחיקם מן בנֹי בעלרים [?]
3. למסכנתא [?]ק........ שס ו

Figure 6.

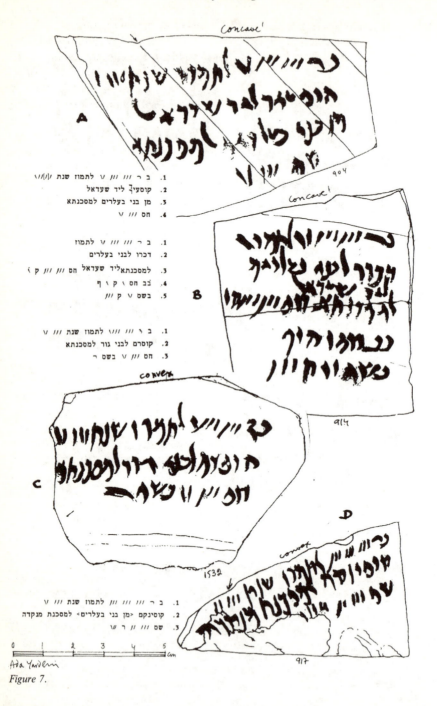

1. ב ר //// //// ע לתמוז שנת //////
2. קוסעיך ליד שעדאל
3. מן בני בעלרים למסכנתא
4. חס //// ע

1. ב ר //// //// ע לתמוז
2. דכרו לבני בעלרים
3. למסכנתאליד שעדאל חס //// ק ///
4. בב חס // ק | ף
5. בשס ע // ק ///

1. ב ר //// //// לתמוז שנת //// ע
2. קוסרם לבני גור למסכנתא
3. חס //// ע בשס ר

1. ב ר //// //// לתמו שנת //// ע
2. קוסינקם <מן בני בעלרים> למסכנת מנקדה
3. שס //// ר ש

Figure 7.

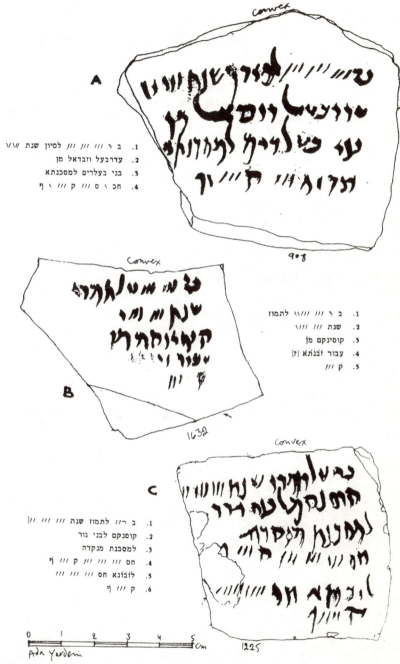

1. ב ר ////// //// לסיון שנת ש/ע
2. עדרבעל וזבדאל מן
3. בני בעלרים למסכנתא
4. חכ ׳ ס //// ק //// ף

1. ב ר //// ///// לתמוז
2. שנת //// ////
3. קוסינקם מן
4. עבור זבנתא [?]
5. ק ///

1. ב ר// לתמוז שנת //// //// ///
2. קוסנקם לבני גור
3. למסכנת מנקדה
4. חס //// //// ק //// ף
5. לבונא חס //// //// ////
6. ק //// ף

Figure 8.

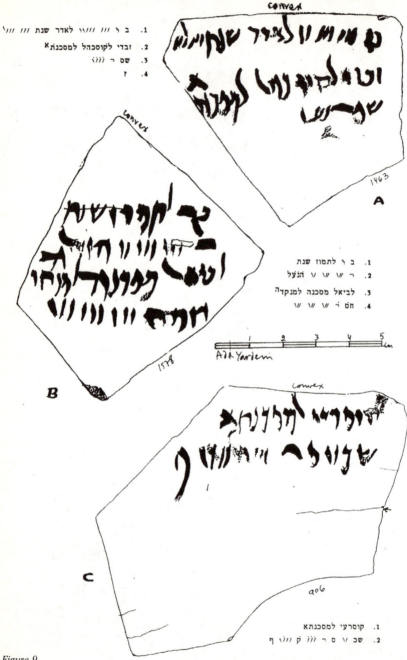

1. ב ר ////// לאדר שנת ///// ///
2. זבדי לקוסכהל למסכנתא
3. שס ר (///)
4. ?

1. ב ר לתמוז שנת
2. ר ש/ש/ע הנעל
3. לביאל מסכנה למנקדה
4. חס ר/ ש/ ש/ ש/

1. קוסרעי למסכנתא
2. שכ ע/ ס ר /// ק ///// ף

Figure 9.

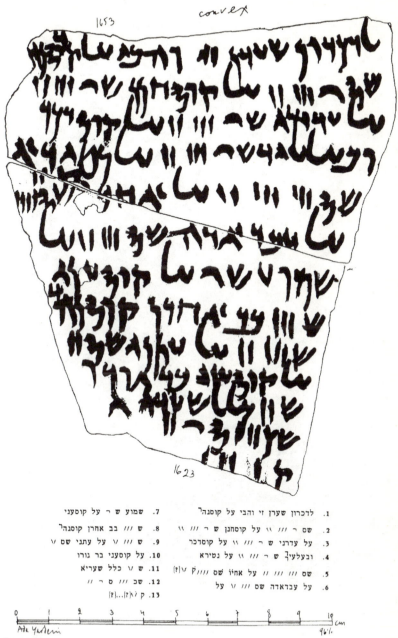

1653

convex

1623

1. לדכרון שערן זי והבי על קוסנה‎ר‎
2. שס ר /// וו על קוסחנן ש ר /// וו
3. על עדרני ש ר /// וו על קוסדכר
4. ובעלעיך ש ר /// וו על נטירא
5. שס /// ווו // על אחוו שס ////ק ז[?]
6. על עבדאדה שס /// ו על

7. שמוע ש ר על קוסעני
8. ש /// בב אהרן קוסנה‎ר‎
9. ש /// ז על עתני שס ז
10. על קוסעני בר גורו
11. ש ז כלל שעריא
12. שכ /// ס ר //
13. ק /ז[?]...[?]‎

Figure 10.

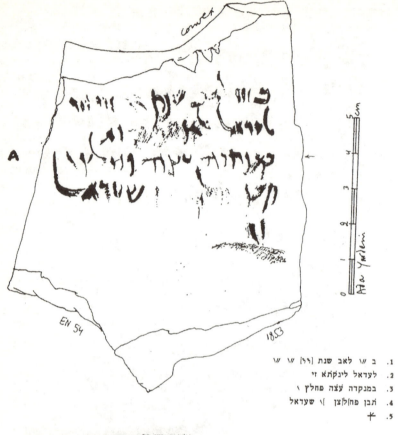

1. ב ⸍/ לאב שנת [רי] ⸍/ ⸍/
2. לעדאל לינקתֹא זי
3. במנקדה עצֹה פֹחלץ ו
4. תֹבן פֹח[ל]צֹן ו| שעדאל
5. ✝

Figure 11.

1. ב ר לתמוז שנת רר ⸍/ ⸍//
2. חלפת לינקתֹא זי
3. במנקדה תֹבֹן פֹהֹלֹץ ו
4. שעֹרֹאל ✝

1. ב ר לאב שנת ////
2. וני מן עבור מסכנתא
3. חס ר

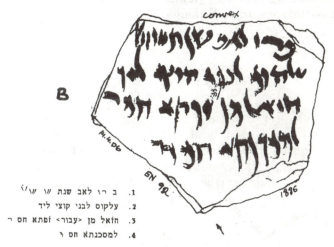

1. ב רו לאב שנת ש/ ש/ו
2. עלקוס לבני קוצי ליד
3. חזאל מן ‹עבור› וסתא חס ר
4. למסכנתא חס ר

Figure 12.

Hebrew ostracon — A receipt, "slt" flour of high quality.

Figure 13.

Chapter 7

TWO ARAMAIC OSTRACA FROM MARESHAH

Esther Eshel

This article discusses two Aramaic ostraca discovered at Mareshah (Marisa). These ostraca are part of the 72 inscribed sherds and ostraca written in Semitic script discovered at Mareshah, 68 of which can be dated to the Persian and Hellenistic periods, between the fifth and the second centuries BCE. Of these inscriptions, 64 are written in the Aramaic script and language, two are written in the Aramaic script and in the Edomite language, and two are written in Phoenician language and script.[1]

The inscriptions from Mareshah are dated to the Persian and Hellenistic periods and resemble three other major corpora of inscriptions dated to the same periods – those found in the excavations held at Beersheba and Arad, and another large corpus which has come more recently through the antiquities market, presumably originating at Khirbet El-Kôm, commonly identified with Makkedah in Idumea.[2]

Inscription No. 1 discovered in subterranean complex 128 is partly preserved and includes what seems to be the remains of a letter. What is preserved from Inscription No. 2 found in subterranean complex 147 seems to be a list of personal names and probably their place of origin. Both inscriptions are dated, based on palaeography, to the end of the fourth or the beginning of the third centuries BCE.

1. E. Eshel, 'Inscriptions in Hebrew, Aramaic, and Phoenician Scripts from Mareshah (IAA Report)' (in print). I would like to express my gratitude to Professor Amos Kloner who entrusted me with the publication of the Semitic ostraca from Mareshah and to Professor Emile Puech, with whom I consulted concerning the decipherment of these inscriptions.

2. I. Eph'al and J. Naveh, *Aramaic Ostraca of the Fourth Century BC from Idumaea* (Jerusalem: Magnes and Israel Exploration Society, 1996); A. Lemaire, *Nouvelles Inscriptions Araméennes d'Idumée au Musée d'Israël* (Supplément n° 3 à Transeuphratène; Paris: Gabalda, 1996); idem, *Nouvelles Inscriptions Araméennes d'Idumée* Tome II (Supplément n° 9 à Transeuphratène; Paris: Gabalda, 2002) and see the papers by I. Stern, B. Porten and A. Yardeni in this volume.

Inscription No. 1

The author of this fragmentary text uses the first person singular ואנה (and I), addressing the second person: [. . .] מה חוית על (what do you say about [. . .]), referring to a third person: לא נתן (he did not give), and [וֹהי אנפֹ]ועזה (and he turned (?) [his?] face). Thus it might be suggested that this ostracon is part of a letter. It reads as follows:

Figure 1.

[אׄנׄ]	.1
[מׄ/בכ אמר בֹ]	.2
(?) הׄי[וׄ]אנפֹ ועזה א°[	.3
[מׄא]צל אנה נׄא[	.4
[עלׄן חוית מה מנני[הׄי]	.5
[שׄין ושׄ משאׄי כל הׄן]	.6
[ ] מׄן תׄתׄן לׄא [	.7

Translation

1. [. . .]*n*²[. . .]
2. [. . .]]*b* said *bk/m*[. . .]
3. [. . .]°° he turned (?) [his?] face [. . .]
4. [. . .]*n*', and I [. . .] *the* idol [. . .]
5. [. . .PN] believed me (of) what you have said concerning [X. . .]

6. [...]*hn* all the hidden things/treasures (?) and[...]
7. [...]*l*-do not give t[...]

Notes on the Reading

Based on the palaeographical study of the letters (e.g. the shape of the letters *ṣade* and *ṭeth*), this inscription should be dated to the end of the fourth or the beginning of the third centuries BCE.

Line 1

One can see a long base, probably of an *aleph*, and a stroke turning to the left before it, of a *nun* or a *beth*.

Line 2

Starting with remains of a long final beth. After the word אמר one can see a beth, followed by a *mem* or a *kaph*. If we read a *kaph*, it might be reconstructed as: בכ]ל; if a mem it might be: במ]לין or במ]לתא etc.

Line 5

After the word על one might read a *he* or a *beth*.

Commentary
Line 3

ועזה – Might be derived from the root עזז, found both in Hebrew and Aramaic; see העזה פניה ותאמר לו, 'Brazenly she says to him' (Prov. 7.13) and העז איש רשע בפניו, 'The wicked man is brazen-faced' (Prov. 21.29) and also the Hebrew term עז פנים (Deut. 28.50; Dan. 8.23). In Old Aramaic one can find this root used as a verb meaning 'to be strong', as found in the Sefire Inscription, reading: יעז מנך is [...], '[...] (who) will be stronger than you [...]' (II B: 20).[3] In Official Aramaic it is used as an adjective, עזיז, 'strong', as in Aramaic Ahiqar 83: ארב פם מן ארב מלחם כי עזיז, 'for mightier is ambush of mouth than ambush of battle'.[4]

The less probable reading of this word is ועוה. The root עוי is found in Hebrew, meaning 'to twist, commit iniquity', thus it might be understood as 'he turned his face'.

---

3.   J. A. Fitzmyer, *The Aramaic Inscriptions of Sefîre* (Rome: Pontifical Biblical Institute, 1967), pp. 82–3; 89.

4.   B. Porten and A. Yardeni, *Textbook of Aramaic Documents from Ancient Egypt. Volume 3: Literature, Accounts, Lists* (Jerusalem: The Hebrew University, 1993), pp. 36–7. See also ibid. 84, 143.

אנפ[והי '[his] face' – we might reconstruct other suffixes of the first, second or third person, as a construct form, or as an emphatic form.

Line 4

ואנה צלמא – probably the remains of the noun and the accusative, followed by a verb: 'and I [+ VERB] the idol'. צלמא is the emphatic form of צלם, meaning the image or statue of a deity or a human.

Line 5

מנני[– Might be reconstructed as הי[מנני, '[PN] believed me'.

] מה חוית על 'what you have said' – חוי in *pa'el* means 'to show, to make known, to report' or 'to tell' – the last meaning might be preferable because the verb is followed by an indirect object of על, 'about (something or someone)'. Thus, we might translate this line as: '[PN] believed me (of) what you have said concerning [X]'.

Line 6

הן[– might either be a suffix or a conjunction – 'if. . .'.

טשאי – the meaning of the root טשא in Qumran Aramaic is 'to hide'. Since טשאי is preceded by כל, 'all', followed by a *waw*, it seems to be used as a plural form. This root can be found in 4Q561 3.9 [ותחתשא ותהך בלבב], 'and you will go and hide in the heart of [. . .]'; and 11Q10 14.2, [ו]חזוני עלומין טשו, which is a Targum of Job 29.8 ראוני נערים ונחבאו, '[And] when youth saw me, they hid', where the Peshitta also uses the same root, reading יאתמטשיו.[5] In Syriac the root טשא means: 'to hide, to conceal', as well as 'hidden or secret sins, treasures'.[6] This can be compared with Ben Sira 16.21 (MSA):

אם חטאתי לא תראני עין
או אם אכזב בכל סתר מי יודע

'If I sin, no eye will see me;
if all in secret I am disloyal, who is to know?'[7]
Which is translated into Syriac as: בכל אתר דמטשי מנו ידע.

5. F. García Martínez, E. J. C. Tigchelaar and A. van der Woude, *Qumran Cave 11: II, 11Q2–18, 11Q20–31* (Oxford: Clarendon, 1998), pp. 113–15.

6. J. Payne Smith, *A Compendious Syriac Dictionary* (Founded upon the Thesaurus Syriacus of R. Payne Smith; Oxford: Clarendon, 1903), pp. 183–4; K. Brockelmann, *Lexicon Syriacum* (2nd ed; Halle: Niemeyer, 1928), p. 292.

7. P. W. Skehan and A. A. Di Lella, *The Wisdom of Ben Sira* (AB; New York: Doubleday, 1987), p. 269.

The same meaning, 'to hide', is found in later Babylonian Aramaic טשי,
e.g. כי היכי דטשאי אנא, 'Just as I hide...' (b. *Avoda Zara* 70a).[8]

Discussion

Two additional letters, Ostraca Nos. 199 and 196 in the collection
published by Eph'al and Naveh, are of great importance to our discussion
of the ostraca found in Mareshah, since they originate from the same area,
Idumea, and are dated to around the same period, that is the late fourth
century BCE. These letters have recently been published by J. M.
Lindenberger as part of a corpus of 79 letters written in Hebrew and
Aramaic.[9]

The first ostracon (No. 199) is a note concerning a debt.[10] This
document, written on both sides of the sherd, does not include an address
or greeting formula.[11] The second inscription (No. 196) is a short note
concerning the release of a woman, saying: 'If my lord please, let them free
the daughter of Haggai'.[12] To these one might add two partly preserved
letters which were written by the same scribe as that who wrote No. 196.
The two letters, Nos. 197 and 198, were addressed to one Qausmalak, the
second of which mentions 'a servant in your hand'.[13]

Another group of four ostraca, also from Idumea and dated to the same
period, were entitled by their editor as 'Fragments de message'.[14] These
ostraca are very fragmentary, but in each of them we can read words such
as: '[...] did not come' or '[...]/' came' (No. 96.2); or ל', 'to me' (No.
97A.2); כען, 'now' (97B.2); ואנת, 'and you' (98.2), and]עֹנוּ לשמה[, '[...]
and they spoke in his name(?)' (99.3); all of which can be seen as indicating
their being notes or parts of letters.

Our newly published ostracon is the only letter found at Mareshah. As
such it is an important contribution to our small corpus of ancient
Aramaic letters.

8. M. Sokoloff, *Dictionary of the Jewish Babylonian Aramaic of the Talmudic and Geonic Periods* (Ramat-Gan: Bar Ilan University, 2002), p. 520.

9. J. M. Lindenberger, *Ancient Aramaic and Hebrew Letters* (Leiden and Boston: Brill, 2003), Nos. 71–72, pp. 139–141.

10. Eph'al and Naveh, *Aramaic Ostraca*, 90–1.

11. Eph'al and Naveh, *Aramaic Ostraca*, 90.

12. Eph'al and Naveh, *Aramaic Ostraca*, 88–9.

13. Eph'al and Naveh, *Aramaic Ostraca*, 88–9.

14. Lemaire, *Nouvelles Inscriptions* 1, 77–9.

Inscription No. 2

This inscription includes the remains of four lines of writing. It reads as follows:

Figure 2.

[ ]°א̇[ ].1

ש[ב̇]עו בר ותרו בפט̇[ר]ה] .2

[ ]ק̇ במצפרי] .3

[ ]ש̇ו במות א] .4

Translation

1. [...]ʾ [
2. ... S]BʿW son of WTRW, in Pet[ra
3. ...]Q in MṢPRY
4. ...]SW in MWTʾ

From this Aramaic inscription only a fragment of the left side has been preserved. It is written with the elongate shapes of letters and a typical ductus, especially in the case of the *aleph* and the *yod*. It resembles the Nabatean script.

This inscription seems to include a list of proper names. Since the first three letters after the name ותרו (WTRW) at the end of line 2 are beth, *pe* and *teth*, it can be reconstructed as: בפט[ר]ה 'in Pet[ra'. Another geographical name preceded by a *beth* is found in line 4: ב̇מ̇ותא (in MWTʾ). Thus, we might expect the last name in line 3, also starting with a *beth*, to be a place name as well. If this interpretation is correct, all three lines include proper names followed by geographical names.

Notes on the Reading

Based on the palaeographical study of the letters (e.g. the shape of the letters *beth* and *taw*), this inscription should be dated to the end of the fourth or the beginning of the third centuries BCE.

Line 1

Remains of the base of a letter at the break on the right, then the base of another letter and the axis of an *'aleph*.

Line 2

On the right border compacted letter with a long basis: *beth*, then *'ayin*, waw/yod, two letters in a pseudo-ligature of which the second one begins with a slanted stroke to the left turning to the horizontal, probably a *beth*.

Line 3

The resh has a large head, followed by a final *yod*. The ṣade could also be read as a *taw*.

Line 4

Light remains of three strokes of which the right ones begin with the curve of a shin. The last letter is an *'aleph* with the left and right strokes curvilinear on both sides of the axis or in an inverse 'S' shape put at an angle of 45° to the right.

Commentary

Line 2

שֱ[עׄבׄו] (Š]BʿW) – An Arabic name.[15]

ותרו (WTRW) – An Arabic name.[16]

Line 3

במצפרי – Probably to be identified with the site of el-Mussafar in northern Moab.[17]

---

15. A. Negev, *Personal Names in the Nabatean Realm* (Qedem 32; Jerusalem: The Hebrew University, 1991), No. 1100, p. 62.

16. Negev, *Personal Names*, No. 365, p. 25.

17. N. Glueck, *Explorations in Eastern Palestine III*, see the common name שבע, No. 1099 there. (AASOR Vols. XVIII-XIX; New Haven: American School of Oriental Research, 1939), p. 247.

Line 4

ושׁ[()ŠW) – Can be reconstructed with an Arabic name, such as: אישׁו, במשׁו, אשׁו etc.

מׄותׁא (MWT') – A place name in Arabia: Μότους (ed-Môte) located south of Karak.[18]

Discussion

As we learn from the study of the onomasticon of Mareshah from the Persian and Hellenistic periods,[19] Mareshah was populated by various ethnic groups, the majority of whom were Edomites and Arabs. Other groups had West-Semitic names and very few had Babylonian or Egyptian names. This partly preserved ostracon adds two Arabic names (and another one, partly preserved), but its main significance is in the three geographical names of the places from which these people originated: the first is the well-known Petra, and the other two are מותא, which is in Arabia, located south of Kerak, and מצפרי, located in northern Moab. Thus we learn that some of the Arabic inhabitants of Mareshah originated in various places in Transjordan.

The question of the origin of the Idumean population has engaged the scholarly world for a long time.[20] One of the accepted notions is that the Idumeans had migrated from Transjordan to the Negev and from there to the southern parts of Judah and later to the Judean Shephelah. Ostracon No. 2, published here, shows us that at least some of Mareshah's inhabitants probably came to the city directly from Transjordan.

18. R. E. Brünnow and A. V. Domaszewski, *Die Provincia Arabia* Vol. I (Strassburg: K. J. Trübner, 1904), p. 104; idem, *Die Provincia Arabia*, Vol. III (Strassburg: K. J. Trübner, 1909), p. 280.

19. E. Eshel, 'The Onomasticon of Mareshah in the Persian and Hellenistic Periods' in O. Lipschits, G. N. Knoppers and R. Albertz (eds.), *Judah and the Judeans in the Fourth Century* BCE (forthcoming).

20. See a recent study of B. Porten, 'Theophorous Names in Idumean Ostraca', M. Mor, J. Pastor, I. Ronen and Y. Ashkenazi (eds), *For Uriel: Studies in the History of Israel in Antiquity Presented to Professor Uriel Rappaport* (Jerusalem: The Zalman Shazar Center for Jewish History, 2005), pp. 105*–130*.

Chapter 8

FROM XENO-PHILIA TO -PHOBIA – JEWISH ENCOUNTERS WITH THE
OTHER[*]

Lisbeth S. Fried

The goal of this study is to trace the attitude toward the resident alien, the *gēr*, across the two hundred years of Persian hegemony as it is revealed in the biblical text.[1] A profound change in attitude can be traced in the biblical corpus across this short time frame. Writings from the early Persian period exhibit an optimism toward the foreigner, which later turns to doubt, fear and hostility. This paper traces the change in attitude toward the non-Jew living in Judah and searches for the source of the change.

A. *The Foreigner in the Biblical Corpus*

1. *Pre-Exilic Texts*

Although the focus of this article is on attitudes toward the resident alien, the *gēr*, that are reflected in Persian-period writings, some mention of earlier texts is warranted. J refers to the *gēr* only twice (Gen. 15.13 and Exod. 2.22).[2] In the first instance, Abraham is told that his descendants will be *gērîm* in the land of Egypt and they will be oppressed and enslaved there for 400 years. In the second, Moses names his son Gershom, because

---

[*]   I am indebted to Yigal Levin for broaching this subject with me, and for his comments as well as those of V (A.) Hurowitz, M. Fried, D. Lamm, B. Porten, and L. Schiffman on an earlier draft.

1.   For recent discussions of the meaning and use of the term *gēr* in the MT, see C. van Houten, *The Alien in Israelite Law* (JSOTSup. 107; Sheffield: Sheffield Academic Press, 1991); C. Bultmann, *Der Fremde im antiken Juda* (FRLANT 153; Göttingen: Vandenhoeck & Ruprecht, 1992); R. Rendtorff, 'The *Gēr* in the Priestly Laws of the Pentateuch', in Mark G. Brett (ed.), *Ethnicity and the Bible* (Leiden: Brill Academic Publishers, 1996), pp. 77–87; J. E. R. Kidd, *Alterity and Identity in Israel* (BZAW 283; Berlin: de Gruyter, 1999); J. Milgrom, 'Excursus N: Reflections on the Biblical *Gēr*,' in J. Milgrom, *Leviticus 17–22* (AB; New York: Doubleday, 2000), pp. 1416–20.

2.   Document attribution is approximately according to R. E. Friedman, *Who Wrote the Bible?* (New York: Summit Books, 1987).

he has been an alien there in a foreign land (*'ereṣ nôkrîah* – J's only use of the word 'foreign,' *nkr*). For J, the *gēr* is a resident alien, a stranger residing in a land not his own.

E uses the term *gēr* four times (Exod. 18.3; 22.20; 23.9, 12). The first is a doublet of J's Exod. 2.22, in which Moses names his son Gershom (Exod. 18.3). The other instances are more properly assigned to the Covenant Code. By stating that 'you shall not wrong or oppress the *gēr* for you were *gērîm* in the land of Egypt' (Exod. 22.20; 23.9) and by requiring the *gēr* to observe the Sabbath (Exod. 23.12), the Code adumbrates the issues brought out more fully in D and P.

D, Core Deuteronomy (Deuteronomy 12–26.15), is the Deuteronomic law code. Its narrative framework (Deuteronomy 1–4; and 29–34) as well as numerous homiletic expansions throughout the book, are the work of the exilic or post-exilic deuteronomistic historians.[3] Deuteronomy 5–11 and 26.16–28.68 frame the law code as a treaty similar to Esarhaddon's Vassal Treaty (672 BCE) and for that reason Deuteronomy 5–28 has been assigned to the mid-seventh century.[4] I have suggested that Deuteronomy's law code, Core Deuteronomy, may be dated as early as 701, when all that was left of the kingdoms of Judah and Samaria was a small rump state centred at Jerusalem.[5] The treaty framework is later than the core. The core refers to the *gēr* in a stereotyped phrase in which the *gēr*, along with the orphan, the widow, and sometimes the Levite, form a defenceless class which is to be protected by the state (Deut. 14.29; 16.11, 14; 24.17, 19, 20, 21; 26.12, 13).[6] Core Deuteronomy does not require that you 'love the *gēr*', as does the treaty framework (10.19), but it does state that 'you shall not abhor any of the Edomites, for they are your kin; you shall not abhor the Egyptians, because you were a *gēr* in his land' (23.7).

This compassionate attitude toward the stranger is reflected in other pre-exilic and exilic texts. Jeremiah (7.6; 22.3) and Ezekiel (14.7; 22.7, 29;

---

3. For discussions of the composition of Deuteronomy, see M. Noth, *The Deuteronomistic History* (trans. E. W. Nicholson; JSOTSup. 15; Sheffield: Sheffield Academic Press, 1991); M. Weinfeld, *Deuteronomy and the Deuteronomic School* (Reprint of Oxford University Press 1972, Winona Lake: Eisenbrauns, 1992); R. D. Nelson, *The Double Redaction of the Deuteronomistic History* (JSOTSup, 18; Sheffield: Sheffield Academic Press, 1981); idem, *Deuteronomy* (OTL; Louisville: Westminster John Knox Press, 2002); idem, *Deuteronomy 1–11* (AB; New York: Doubleday, 1991); R. F. Person Jr., *The Deuteronomic School* (Studies in Biblical Literature 2; Atlanta: Society of Biblical Literature, 2002).

4. M. Weinfeld, *Deuteronomy and the Deuteronomic School*, 1, 7; idem, *Deuteronomy 1–11*, 1–2, 4–16.

5. L. S. Fried, 'The High Places (Bamôt) and the Reforms of Hezekiah and Josiah: An Archaeological Investigation', *JAOS* 122 (2002), pp. 437–65.

6. *Pace* C. Bultmann, *Der Fremde im antiken Juda*. For the meaning of the *gēr* in Deuteronomy, see J. Milgrom, *Leviticus 17–22*, 1416–20.

47.22-23), like D, include the alien with the widow and the orphan, the poor and the needy, who must not be oppressed.

In sum, texts that can be dated to the pre-exilic period illustrate the *gēr* as a protected class, like the widow, the orphan – and the Levite. Similar Greek attitudes toward the stranger can be seen in the tales of Homer, dating to about the same time period.[7]

2. *Exilic and Post-Exilic Texts – The Deuteronomistic Historian*

Deuteronomic expansions in the book of Deuteronomy and throughout the so-called deuteronomistic history (DH) reveal an attitude toward the seven Canaanite nations different from that toward the *gēr*. The *gēr* lives within the gates of Judean or Israelite cities. Members of the seven proscribed nations live elsewhere. These you must destroy (Deut. 7.1-2; 20.17), and you certainly must not marry them (or the Ammonites and Moabites, Deut. 23.3, 4) for that would lead you to apostasy (7.1-6; so also Exod. 34.15-16). The wife from one of the seven proscribed nations will turn your heart to serve other gods, and YHWH will turn you over to serve foreign rulers. A good example is Judges 3:

> So the Israelites lived among the Canaanites, the Hittites, the Amorites, the Perizzites, the Hivites, and the Jebusites; and they took their daughters as wives for themselves, and their own daughters they gave to their sons; and they worshiped their gods. The Israelites did what was evil in YHWH's sight, forgetting YHWH their God, and worshiping the Baals and the Asherahs. Therefore YHWH's anger was kindled against Israel, and he sold them into the hand of King Cushan-rishathaim of Aram-naharaim; and the Israelites served Cushan-rishathaim eight years (Judges 3.5-8).

According to the DH, moreover, the northern kingdom was lost to Judah because Solomon took wives from among these proscribed nations who turned his heart after other gods:

> King Solomon loved many foreign women along with the daughter of Pharaoh: Moabite, Ammonite, Edomite, Sidonian, and Hittite women,[8] from the nations concerning which YHWH had said to the Israelites, 'You shall not enter into marriage with them, neither shall they with you; for they will surely incline your heart to follow their gods'; Solomon clung to these in love. And when Solomon was old, his wives turned away his heart after other gods; and his heart was not true to YHWH his God, as was the heart of his father David (1 Kings 11.1-5).

7. C. Auffarth, 'Protecting Strangers', *Numen* 39 (1992), pp. 193–216.

8. M. Cogan, *I Kings* (AB; New York: Doubleday, 2001), p. 329, sees in the addition of the Sidonites an old tradition in which Solomon married one of Hiram's daughters.

Marriage to these women was prohibited because it leads to apostasy. Solomon is the proof of it.

Except for the attitude toward these proscribed nations, the deuteronomistic history exhibits a positive attitude toward the foreigner, and does not exclude him from an important role in public life.[9] Individuals such as Doeg the Edomite (1 Sam. 21.8; 22.9) and Zelek the Ammonite (2 Sam. 23.37) achieve high levels at court. Hiram of Tyre is in charge of decorating Solomon's temple (1 Kings 7.14).[10] The DH predicts, moreover, that foreigners will recognize YHWH's greatness and stream to Jerusalem to worship him. Deut. 28.10 reads: 'All the peoples of the earth (*kol ʿammê hāʾāreṣ*) shall see that you are called by YHWH's name and be afraid of you.' Josh. 4.24 reads, 'that all the peoples of the earth (*kol ʿammê hāʾāreṣ*) may know that YHWH's hand is mighty.' DH makes the confident assertion that foreigners will come to Jerusalem to pray at YHWH's temple, and includes this motif in Solomon's prayer (1 Kings 8.43, cf. 60).

> Likewise when a foreigner (*nôkrî*), who is not of your people Israel, comes from a distant land because of your name – for they shall hear of your great name, your mighty hand, and your outstretched arm – when a foreigner comes and prays toward this house, then hear in heaven your dwelling place, and do according to all that the foreigner calls to you, so that all the peoples of the earth (*kol ʿammê hāʾāreṣ*) may know your name and fear you, as do your people Israel, and so that they may know that your name has been invoked on this house that I have built (1 Kings 8.41-43).

It seems likely that this positive strand (toward the individual *gēr* and toward the foreigners who come to Jerusalem to worship YHWH) stems from the early Persian period, and is later than the strand which perceives the proscribed nations as a threat. Arguments for a second deuteronomistic redaction of the deuteronomistic history during the Persian period have been put forward by several scholars and need not be repeated here.[11]

---

9. So noted by Milgrom, *Leviticus 17–22*, 1417.

10. The Deuteronomist assigns his mother to the tribe of Naphtali, but this does not make him Israelite in his eyes.

11. For example, R. Rofé, 'Joshua 20', in Jeffrey H. Tigay (ed.) *Empirical Models for Biblical Criticism* (Philadelphia: University of Pennsylvania Press, 1985), pp. 131–47; idem, 'The Monotheistic Argumentation in Deuteronomy IV 32-40', *VT* 35 (1985), pp. 434–45; R. Smend, *Die Entstehung des Alten Testaments* (Stuttgart: Kohlhammer, 1981); W. Dietrich, *David, Saul und die Propheten* (BWANT 7; Stuttgart: Kohlhammer, 1987); R. F. Person Jr., *The Kings-Isaiah and Kings-Jeremiah Recensions* (BZAW 252; Berlin: de Gruyter, 1997); idem, *The Deuteronomic School*.

3. *Persian Period Texts*
a. *The Priestly Writer*

I turn now to P, the priestly writer, probably among the earliest of Persian-period texts.[12] P's attitude toward the foreigner can be observed first in the table of nations, Genesis 10.[13] P's genealogy begins with one man, Adam (Gen. 5.1). The various peoples of the earth do not have separate ancestors. They all descend from the first created human, in fact from the three sons of Noah. This genealogical organization of mankind implies no dichotomy between Jew and Gentile. Differences are only a matter of degree. This web of relations structures both the unity and the diversity of mankind.

P's law codes concretize these relationships. The command is far-reaching: There shall be one law for the native and the alien, the *ezraḥ* and the *gēr* (Exod. 12.49; Lev. 24.22; Num. 15.16, 29). P forbids the resident alien and the native equally from eating leavened bread during the Passover (Exod. 12.19), the *gēr* must abstain from all work on the Sabbath (Exod. 20.10) and on the Day of Atonement (Lev. 16.29). He may offer a burnt offering or a sacrifice, just as the Israelite (Lev. 17.8; 22.18ff.), and he too will be cut off if he eats the blood. The *gēr*, like the Israelite, is enjoined from defiling himself by any of the practices of the nations whom God is casting out of the land (Lev. 18.24). Like the Israelite, the *gēr* shall be put to death if he consigns his children to Molech (Lev. 20.2), and he, like the Israelite, shall be stoned if he profanes God's name (Lev. 24.16).

H is even more emphatic than P. Not only shall there be one law, but H requires you to *love* the *gēr*, for you were *gērîm* in the land of Egypt (Lev. 19.34). This does not mean that the *gēr* is an Israelite or a proselyte; important differences between the *gēr* and the Israelite are retained. The model of the *gēr* for P is Abraham. He lives among the Hittites, but is not a Hittite and does not own land. Special permission must be sought before he can purchase a cave to bury his wife (Gen. 23.4).[14] The separate status of the *gēr* is exemplified in the laws of the Jubilee. According to Leviticus 25.39-40, an Israelite may not be enslaved. He shall work as a paid

---

12. For discussions of the ongoing controversy surrounding the date of P see J. Milgrom, *Leviticus 1–16* (AB; New York: Doubleday, 1991), pp. 3–35; A. Levine, *Numbers 1–20* (AB; New York: Doubleday, 1993), p. 101–9 plus references cited there.

13. I am indebted for this discussion to F. Crüsemann, 'Human Solidarity and Ethnic Identity: Israel's Self-definition in the Genealogical System of Genesis', in M. G. Brett (ed.), *Ethnicity and the Bible* (Leiden: Brill Academic Publishers, 1996), pp. 57–76.

14. E. A. Speiser, *Genesis* (AB; New York: Doubleday, 1964), p. 167–73 and G. von Rad, *Genesis* (Philadelphia: Westminster Press, 1961), p. 249 see this as P built upon earlier material; D. M. Carr, *Reading the Fractures of Genesis: Historical and Literary Approaches* (Louisville: Westminster John Knox Press, 1996), pp. 111–22 sees a P story with later expansions; B. A. Levine (personal communication) understands it as P.

servant, and go out in the Jubilee. In contrast, Leviticus 25 permits the *gēr* to be enslaved (Lev. 25.45) and handed down as an inheritance like other property (Lev. 25.46). He does not go out in the Jubilee. This distinction between the *gēr* and the Israelite contradicts the primary admonition in P and H, not to have a separate law. This exception is made because neither P nor H allow the *gēr* to own land; they have no property to return to. Ezekiel disagrees and demands that land be allotted to the alien among the holdings of the tribe in which he resides (Ezek. 47.21-23). The *gēr* who is allotted land, however, is only the resident alien who has 'begotten children among you', among the people Israel.[15] He is the one who lives in the land of Israel and whose family is there, the one for whom Israel is his permanent residence. Only that person may own land, and as Rendtorff realizes, become a citizen.[16] Ezekiel does not require that land be allotted to the itinerant merchant or labourer who resides in Israel but whose family lives elsewhere. That person remains a *gēr*. Ezekiel does not abolish the concept of the *gēr*, therefore, and the *gēr* who does not own land is classified with the widows and orphans as a protected group.

b. *Haggai and Zechariah*

The texts of Haggai and Zechariah, dated to the reigns of Darius I and Zerubbabel, like the DH, exhibit an optimistic attitude toward foreigners. All the world's peoples and all its riches will follow the Jew to Jerusalem to worship YHWH at his temple. Haggai quotes YHWH as saying:

> I will shake all the nations, so that the treasure of all nations shall come, and I will fill this house with splendour, says YHWH of hosts (Hag. 2.7).

Zechariah has YHWH say:

> Sing and rejoice, O daughter Zion! For lo, I will come and dwell in your midst, says YHWH. Many nations shall join themselves to YHWH on that day, and shall be my people; and I [YHWH] will dwell in your midst (Zech. 2.14-15).

Zechariah quotes God further:

> Thus says the YHWH of hosts: Peoples shall yet come, the inhabitants of many cities; the inhabitants of one city shall go to another, saying, 'Come, let us go to entreat the favour of YHWH, and to seek YHWH of hosts; I myself am going.' Many peoples and strong nations shall come to seek YHWH of hosts in Jerusalem, and to entreat the favour of

---

15. The likely assumption is that he has acquired his children by an Israelite wife. This is similar to Solon's citizenship laws, promulgated in 594 BCE, around the time of Ezekiel (and see my discussion on Solon below, and in note 59).

16. R. Rendtorff, 'The *Ger* in the Priestly Laws of the Pentateuch', in M. G. Brett, (ed.) *Ethnicity and the Bible* (Leiden: Brill Academic Publishers, 1996), pp. 77–87.

YHWH. Thus says YHWH of hosts: In those days ten men from
nations of every language shall take hold of a Jew, grasping his garment
and saying, 'Let us go with you, for we have heard that God is with you'
(Zech. 8.20–23).

c. *Deutero-Isaiah*

This optimistic attitude toward the foreigner apparent in early Persian-
period texts is echoed in the prophecies of Deutero-Isaiah.[17] Deutero-
Isaiah must be dated from the time of Darius I and the completion of the
temple in Jerusalem.[18] The predictions of the advent of Cyrus, the
rebuilding of the city and the temple, the return of the temple vessels, are
not true predictions, but prophecies after the fact, *vaticinia ex eventu*. Like
Haggai and Zechariah and other texts from the time of Darius, the
writings of Deutero-Isaiah portray the peoples of the world flowing into
Jerusalem to worship Judah's God. Isaiah 45.14 is typical:

> Thus says YHWH: The wealth of Egypt and the merchandise of
> Ethiopia, and the Sabeans, tall of stature, shall come over to you and be
> yours, they shall follow you; they shall come over in chains and bow
> down to you. They will make supplication to you, saying, 'God is with
> you alone, and there is no other; there is no god besides him' (Isaiah
> 45.14).

Scholars see the pen of Deutero-Isaiah in other Isaianic texts, for example
Isaiah 14.1:[19]

> For YHWH will take pity on Jacob and will once again choose Israel,
> and will set them in their own land; and the alien (*gēr*) will join them
> and attach themselves to the house of Jacob (Isaiah 14.1).

Isaiah 2.2-4 (=Micah 4.1-3) may also stem from the time of Deutero-
Isaiah, if not from his pen:

> In days to come the mountain of YHWH's house shall be established as
> the highest of the mountains, and shall be raised above the hills; all the
> nations shall stream to it. Many peoples shall come and say, 'Come, let
> us go up to the mountain of YHWH, to the house of the God of Jacob;

---

17. For recent discussions of the literature on Deutero-Isaiah, see J. D. W. Watts, *Isaiah 34–66* (WBC 25; Waco: Word Books, 1987), pp. 69–75; H. G. M. Williamson, *The Book Called Isaiah: Deutero-Isaiah's Role in Composition and Redaction* (Oxford: Oxford University Press, 1994); J. Blenkinsopp, *Isaiah 40–55* (AB; New York: Doubleday, 2000), pp. 41–126; K. Baltzer, *Deutero-Isaiah: a Commentary on Isaiah 40–55* (ed. P. Machinist, trans. M. Kohl; Minneapolis: Fortress Press, 2001), p. 597; L. S. Fried, 'Cyrus the Messiah? The Historical Background of Isaiah 45.1', *HTR* 95 (2002), pp. 373–93.

18. Fried, 'Cyrus the Messiah?', 375–9.

19. For example O. Kaiser, *Isaiah 13–39, A Commentary* (trans. R. A. Wilson; OTL; Philadelphia: Westminster Press, 1974), p. 25; Williamson, *The Book Called Isaiah*, 165–6; Blenkinsopp, *Isaiah 1–39*, 281; idem, *Isaiah 40–55*, 53, 257.

that he may teach us his ways and that we may walk in his paths'. For out of Zion shall go forth torah, and the word of YHWH from Jerusalem. He shall judge between the nations, and shall arbitrate for many peoples; they shall beat their swords into ploughshares, and their spears into pruning hooks; nation shall not lift up sword against nation, neither shall they learn war any more.

Duhm's famous commentary on Isaiah has led scholars to routinely date chapters 1–39 of Isaiah to Isaiah ben Amoz of eighth-century Jerusalem.[20] Recently, however, many have begun to look at the book of Isaiah as a whole and to recognize the pen of Deutero-Isaiah in all parts of the book.[21] Various arguments have been proposed suggesting that this passage too may be seen as a composition of Deutero-Isaiah which was then inserted into both Isaiah 2 and Micah.[22] Anderson and Freedman argue that Micah 4.1-3 is authentic to Micah however, but they also maintain that the theology reflected in Micah 7.7-12 finds full expression only in the theology of Deutero-Isaiah, and is appropriate for that prophet's period.[23] This admits not only to a post-exilic redaction of the book, but also to a redaction by the Deutero-Isaianic school. Williamson points out that Isaiah 2.2-4 represents a reversal of Proto-Isaiah's thought elsewhere, in which the eighth century prophet speaks of nations coming to Jerusalem to attack it, never to worship at its temple.[24] Nor are the foreign nations in Isaiah 2 forcibly disarmed by God as elsewhere in Proto-Isaiah; here they come to learn, they do not submit in fear. This

20. B. Duhm, *Das Buch Jesaja*, (HKAT 3/1; Göttingen: Vandenhoeck & Ruprecht, 1922).

21. For example, J. Becker, *Isaias – der Prophet und sein Buch* (SBS 30; Stuttgart: Verlag Katholisches Bibelwerk, 1968); P. R. Ackroyd, 'Isaiah i-xii: Presentation of a Prophet', in *Congress Volume: Göttingen 1977* (VTSup 29; Leiden: Brill, 1978), pp. 16–48; idem, 'Isaiah 36–39: Structure and Function', in W. C. Delsman *et al.* (eds), *Von Kanaan bis Kerala: FS J. P. M. van der Ploeg* (AOAT 211; Neukirchen-Vluyn: Butzon & Bercker, 1982), pp. 3–21; R. Rendtorff, 'Zur Composition des Buches Jesaja', *VT* 34 (1984), pp. 295–320; idem, 'Jesaja 6 im Rahmen der Komposition des Jesajabuches', in J. Vermeylen (ed.), *The Book of Isaiah* (Leuven: Leuven University Press, 1989), pp. 73–82; M. Sweeney, *Isaiah 1–4 and the Post-Exilic Understanding of the Isaianic Tradition* (BZAW 171; Berlin: de Gruyter, 1988); Williamson, *The Book Called Isaiah*; Blenkinsopp, *Isaiah 1–39*, 73–4.

22. For example, Blenkinsopp, *Isaiah 1–39*, 190–1; Sweeney, *Isaiah 1–4 and the Post-Exilic Understanding*, 164–9; Williamson, *The Book Called Isaiah*, 143–54. S. L. Cook notes a post-exilic Levitical redaction of Micah, increasing the likelihood of a Deutero-Isaianic passage included in the text; see 'Micah's Deuteronomistic Redaction and the Deuteronomist's Identity', in L. S. Schearing and S. L. McKenzie (eds), *Those Elusive Deuteronomists: The Phenomenon of Pan-Deuteronomism* (Sheffield: Sheffield Academic Press, 1999), pp. 216–31.

23. F. I. Anderson and D. N. Freedman, *Micah* (AB; New York: Doubleday, 2000), p. 576.

24. Williamson, *The Book Called Isaiah*, 148–55.

thought has its parallels only in the ideas of Deutero-Isaiah, Haggai and Zechariah.

Moreover, the notion of the law (*torâ*) going forth from Zion out to the entire land seems to be declared first in Zechariah 5:

> Again I looked up and saw a flying scroll. And he said to me, 'What do you see?' I answered, 'I see a flying scroll; its length is twenty cubits, and its width ten cubits.' Then he said to me, 'This is the curse [of the covenant] that goes out over the face of the whole earth; for everyone who steals shall be cut off according to the writing on one side, and everyone who swears falsely shall be cut off according to the writing on the other side. I have sent it out', says YHWH of hosts, 'and it shall enter the house of the thief, and the house of anyone who swears falsely by my name; and it shall abide in that house and consume it, both timber and stones' (Zech. 5.1-4).

This is a literal image of a Torah scroll, a law scroll, going forth from YHWH, in particular from his temple on Mt Zion. It goes forth to judge the entire land. This is a concrete expression of Zechariah's vision of a world in which the high priest rules from Zion (Zech. 3.7; 6.11). The literal presentation comes first, followed by the metaphoric ideal, its poetic description, as in Isaiah 2 (and Micah 4).

The theme of Torah/law going out from God to the entire world is repeated again in Isaiah 51.4 (cf. Isa. 42.21 and Isa. 24.6, a post-exilic passage) and does not occur elsewhere in Micah, nor indeed elsewhere in the book of Isaiah. It seems most likely therefore that these verses in Isaiah 2 and Micah 4 belong to the period of Deutero-Isaiah if not from the pen of the prophet himself.

d. *Trito-Isaiah*

Isaiah 56–66 is conventionally labelled Trito-Isaiah, and the date assigned to these passages has varied widely.[25] However, as Blenkinsopp suggests, Isaiah 60.10 seems to imply that the walls of Jerusalem have not yet been built.[26]

> Foreigners shall build up your walls, and their kings shall minister to you; for in my wrath I struck you down, but in my favour I have had mercy on you (Isaiah 60.10).

Thus, we can, with Blenkinsopp, date Trito-Isaiah to the period between Darius I and Nehemiah, i.e., between 520 and 445, the first century of Persian rule. The theme of foreigners streaming to Jerusalem to rebuild that is expressed in this verse is repeated throughout Trito-Isaiah:

---

25. See the recent review in Blenkinsopp, *Isaiah 56–66*, 27–90.
26. Blenkinsopp, *Isaiah 56–66*, 42.

> Do not let the foreigner joined to YHWH say, 'YHWH will surely separate me from his people' . . .. for the foreigners who join themselves to YHWH, to minister to him, to love YHWH's name, and to be his servants, all who keep the Sabbath, and do not profane it, and who hold fast to my covenant – these I will bring to my holy mountain, and make them joyful in my house of prayer; their burnt offerings and their sacrifices will be accepted on my altar; for my house shall be called a house of prayer for all peoples. Thus says lord YHWH, who gathers the outcasts of Israel, I will gather others to them besides those already gathered (Isaiah 56.3, 6-8).

Also:

> Arise, shine; for your light has come, and YHWH's glory has risen upon you. For darkness shall cover the earth, and thick darkness the peoples; but YHWH will arise upon you, and his glory will appear over you. Nations shall come to your light, and kings to the brightness of your dawn. Lift up your eyes and look around; they all gather together, they come to you; your sons shall come from far away, and your daughters shall be carried on their nurses' arms. Then you shall see and be radiant; your heart shall thrill and rejoice, because the abundance of the sea shall be brought to you, the wealth of the nations shall come to you. A multitude of camels shall cover you, the young camels of Midian and Ephah; all those from Sheba shall come. They shall bring gold and frankincense, and shall proclaim YHWH's praise. (Isaiah 60.1-6).

And further:

> For I know their works and their thoughts, and I am coming to gather all nations and tongues; and they shall come and shall see my glory, and I will set a sign among them. From them I will send survivors to the nations, to Tarshish, Put, and Lud – which draw the bow – to Tubal and Javan, to the coastlands far away that have not heard of my fame or seen my glory; and they shall declare my glory among the nations. They shall bring all your kindred from all the nations as an offering to YHWH, on horses, and in chariots, and in litters, and on mules, and on dromedaries, to my holy mountain Jerusalem, says YHWH, just as the Israelites bring a grain offering in a clean vessel to YHWH's house. And I will also take some of them as priests and as Levites, says YHWH. For as the new heavens and the new earth, which I will make, shall remain before me, says YHWH; so shall your descendants and your name remain. From new moon to new moon, and from Sabbath to Sabbath, all flesh shall come to worship before me, says YHWH (Isaiah 66.18-23).

These texts reflect the euphoria of the days of the rededicated temple in the early years of Persian rule. They portray the peoples of the world and the wealth of nations flowing to Jerusalem in recognition of Israel's God.

e. *Ezra 1 and 2*

Ezra 1 and 2 also likely stem from the time of Darius.[27] Evidence suggests that Ezra 1 is derived from the Second Temple's actual building inscription.[28] If so, it can be dated to 516, the sixth year of Darius the Great, the year when the temple was dedicated and the building inscription written (Ezra 6.15). The list of repatriates in Ezra 2 seems to be a census of the repatriated community at the time of Zerubbabel, and if so, should be dated to around 500 BCE.[29] These two chapters (Ezra 1 with its list of vessels brought to the temple as well as Ezra 2 with its list of repatriates) portray the world's peoples and resources flowing into Jerusalem to rebuild the temple of YHWH. Importantly, this list of returnees in Ezra 2, i.e., this list of the legitimate population of Judah, includes 652 men who could not prove their descent from Israel (Ezra 2.59-60), being unable to name either the house of their father or their lineage (בית-אבותם וזרעם). This early Persian-period text assumes that non-Israelites, non-Jews, went up to Jerusalem with the *golâ* and were joined to the assembly of the people Israel (cf. Ezra 6.21).

4. *Late Persian Period Texts: Ezra 3 – Nehemiah 13*
a. *Ezra 3–4*

The positive welcoming attitude toward the foreigner that we see in early Persian period texts disappears suddenly in Ezra 3. Instead of celebrating the multitudes of peoples in Jerusalem, now the Jews are in dread of them:

> They set up the altar on its foundation, because they were in dread of the neighboring peoples (*'ammê hā'araṣôt*)[30] and they offered burnt offerings upon it to YHWH, morning and evening (Ezra 3.3).

Instead of rejoicing in the flow of the world's people to worship YHWH in Jerusalem, there is fear. We read further:

> When the enemies of Judah and Benjamin heard that the returned exiles were building a temple to YHWH the God of Israel, they approached Zerubbabel and the heads of families and said to them, 'Let us build with you, for we worship your God as you do, and we have been sacrificing to him ever since the days of King Esarhaddon of Assyria

---

27. L. S. Fried, *Ezra-Nehemiah, A Commentary* (Eerdmans Critical Commentary Series; Grand Rapids: Eerdmans, forthcoming).

28. L. S. Fried, 'The Land Lay Desolate: Conquest and Restoration in the Ancient Near East,' in O. Lipschits and J. Blenkinsopp (eds), *Judah and the Judeans in the Neo-Babylonian Period* (Winona Lake: Eisenbrauns, 2003), pp. 21–54.

29. Fried, *Ezra-Nehemiah*.

30. Evidence suggests this is the appropriate translation of *'ammê hā'araṣôt*. See L. S. Fried, 'Because of the Dread Upon Them – Fear and Uncertainty in the Persian Empire', in F. Hakimzadeh (ed.), *The Forgotten Empire – Persia Under the Achaemenids* (London: The Iran Heritage Foundation, forthcoming).

who brought us here.' But Zerubbabel, Jeshua, and the rest of the heads
of families in Israel said to them, 'You shall have no part with us in
building a house to our God; but we alone will build to YHWH, the
God of Israel, as King Cyrus of Persia has commanded us.' So the
people of the land (ʿam hāʾareṣ)[31] discouraged the people of Judah, and
made them afraid to build (Ezra 4.1-3).

Contrary to expectations, the idea that non-Judeans might join with the
returnees and help build the temple of YHWH is met with hostility instead
of joy. Their recognition of YHWH and their plea to participate in
building his temple is not interpreted by the redactor as fulfilment of
prophetic predictions. What is the source of this abrupt about-face? The
scene in Ezra 3 and 4 is set in the initial years of the return, the years of
Cyrus and Darius I. Is this when the text was written? Ezra-Nehemiah as a
whole must be dated from the early Hellenistic period. Numismatic and
other considerations lead to the conclusion that the Jaddua of Nehemiah
12.11 and 22 is the Jaddua who greeted Alexander the Great and that the
Darius the Persian in 12.22 is Darius III.[32] This implies a redaction after
the fall of the Persian Empire. In agreement with Williamson,[33] it seems
likely that Ezra 7–Nehemiah 13 was compiled first and that Ezra 1–6 was
added later. If Ezra 7–Nehemiah 13 was redacted after the fall of the
Persian Empire, the redaction of Ezra 1–6 must have been later still. This
second historian would have had Ezra 7–Nehemiah 13 among his sources,
and probably the second temple's actual building inscription as well.[34] He
very likely also had letters to and from the kings Darius, Xerxes and
Artaxerxes, some lists, the biblical books Haggai and Zechariah, and other
biblical texts.[35] He does not seem to have had a source for Ezra 3 and 4.1-4.
These passages conflict with Haggai and Zechariah which know of no
friction between social groups. They were likely composed by the second
Hellenistic redactor to provide a narrative context for the letters.[36] Ezra 3

    31.   I discuss the identity of these non-Judeans in L. S. Fried, 'The ʿAm Hāʾāretz in Ezra
4.4 and Persian Imperial Administration', in O. Lipschits and M. Oeming, eds *Judah and
Judaeans in the Achaemenid Period* (Winona Lake: Eisenbrauns, 2006), 123–45. The referent
of the singular term is different from that of the plural.
    32.   J. C. VanderKam, *From Joshua to Caiaphas: High Priests after the Exile*
(Minneapolis: Fortress Press, 2004), pp. 54–111; L. S. Fried, 'A Silver Coin of Yoḥanan
Hakkôhēn', *Transeuphratène* 26 (2003), pp. 65–85, Pls. II–V.
    33.   H. G. M. Williamson, 'The Composition of Ezra i-vi', *JTS* [ns] 34 (1983), pp. 1–30;
idem, *Ezra, Nehemiah* (WBC 16; Waco: Word Books, 1985), pp. xxiii–iv, xxxiii–vi.
    34.   L. S. Fried, 'The Land Lay Desolate'.
    35.   Williamson, *Ezra, Nehemiah*, xxiii–xxxiii.
    36.   Williamson, 'The Composition of Ezra i-vi', idem, *Ezra, Nehemiah*, 43–5; P. R.
Bedford, *Temple Restoration in Early Achaemenid Judah* (Leiden: Brill, 2001), pp. 11–39; 85–
111; Fried, 'The ʿam hāʾāreṣ in Ezra 4.4 and Persian Imperial Administration', 124, 134–5,
136–7.

and 4.1-4 express the views of this second late redactor. They do not relate actual events or conversations.[37]

b. *Nehemiah's Memoir*

The negative attitude toward the foreigner visible in Ezra 3 and Ezra 4.1-4 is apparent throughout Ezra 7–Nehemiah 13. Since Ezra must be dated to after Nehemiah,[38] the earliest source in this section of text (Ezra 7–

37. For a recent discussion of the non-historicity of Ezra 3 and 4.1-5, see Bedford, *Temple Restoration*, 94–181.

38. The historical order of Ezra and Nehemiah has been a vexatious problem since 1890 when first brought up by A. V. Hoonacker, 'Néhémie et Esdras, une nouvelle hypothèse sur la chronologie de l'époque de la restauration', *Muséon* 9 (1890), pp. 151–84, 317–51, 389–400. See also H. H. Rowley, 'Nehemiah's Mission and Its Background', in H. H. Rowley (ed.), *Men of God: Studies in Old Testament History and Prophecy* (London: Nelson, 1963), pp. 211–45; A. Lemaire, 'La fin de la première période perse en Égypt et la chronologie judéenne vers 400 av. J.-C.', *Transeuphratène* 9 (1995), pp. 51–61. To attempt a solution I first assume that portions of Ezra 7.21-26 contain the original Artaxerxes' Letter and that Ezra was sent to appoint the royal judges of the satrapy Beyond the River (Ezra 7.14, 25, 26); see L S. Fried, 'You Shall Appoint Judges: Ezra's Mission and the Rescript of Artaxerxes', in J. W. Watts (ed.), *Persia and Torah: The Theory of Imperial Authorization of the Pentateuch* (SBL Symposium Series; Atlanta: Society of Biblical Literature, 2001), pp. 63–89; R. C. Steiner, 'The MBQR at Qumran, the *Episkopos* in the Athenian Empire, and the Meaning of LBQR in Ezra 7.14: On the Relation of Ezra's Mission to the Persian Legal Project', *JBL* 120 (2001), pp. 623–46. I discuss the so-called Artaxerxes Rescript at length in my *Priest and the Great King*, 221–7.

I assume second that (probably as a favour to Ezra) the king remitted taxes and tribute for the cultic personnel of the temple of YHWH in Jerusalem; i.e., that Ezra 7.24 is genuine although the specific list of temple personnel may have been added by the redactor. This type of remission of taxes on temple priesthoods has precedent. Cyrus remitted the taxes and corvée labour for Babylon because the city opened its gates to him (Cyrus Cylinder, lines 25–26). Gadatas, probably the governor of Lydia, had exacted tribute and corvée labour from the priests of Apollo, contrary to Darius's wishes 'on behalf of the god who spoke only truth to the Persians' (lines 19–29). Evidently he had promised them exemption from both. The priest of the Carian god at Xanthus in Lycia was granted exemption from public burdens, i.e., taxes and corvée labour, by Pixadarus, last satrap of Caria and Lycia (Xanthus Stele, line 11, Greek text). If Ezra 7.24 is genuine, as seems likely, the remission of taxes and tribute promised in the Artaxerxes' Letter would have included remission of the duty of corvée labour as well, as was the case everywhere throughout the empire (temple priests were a common source of corvée labour; in fact, the Persians built their fabulous gardens, *paradēsū*, near temples just to have labourers nearby). Nehemiah, however, imposed corvée labour on the people of Judah – including the priests – when he had them build the city wall (Neh. 3.1, 17, 22, 26, 28). In spite of the alacrity that Nehemiah attributes to the builders, it is still corvée labour. Nehemiah admits his reluctance to inform those who would be doing the work of his plans (Neh. 2.6). It does not seem possible that the priests, especially the *high* priest,

Nehemiah 13) is Nehemiah's memoir.[39] The memoir, consisting of portions of Neh.1.1–7.5, of 12.27-43; and of 13.4-31, can reasonably be attributed to Nehemiah himself.[40] Although hostile to Nehemiah's enemies (Sanballat, Tobiah and Geshem), the memoir does not reveal antipathy to the non-Judean in general until Nehemiah 13, a description of events taking place upon Nehemiah's return from his visit to the king (between 432 and 424 BCE). The first passage in that chapter describes Nehemiah's fury at Tobiah's being granted living accommodations in the temple. Whether this is because of his personal animosity toward Tobiah or because Tobiah is a foreigner, is not clear:

> When I returned to Jerusalem, I realized the evil that Eliashib had done on behalf of Tobiah, preparing a room for him in the courts of the house of God. I was very displeased, and I sent all the personal property of Tobiah out of the room. Then I gave orders and they purified the apartment, and I returned the vessels of the house of God, with the grain offering and the frankincense (Nehemiah 13.7-9).

To Nehemiah, Tobiah's furniture profaned the temple. Only after Tobiah's property was removed could the temple be purified, and only then would Nehemiah order the vessels of the house of God returned. This may be similar to Udjaḥorresnet's demand of Cambyses that the Persian soldiers be ordered out of the House of Life, the Temple of Neith in Sais Egypt.[41] Nevertheless, there is a difference between a contingent of foreign soldiers bivouacked in the temple, as in the case of Udjaḥorresnet, and one foreign dignitary staying in a temple apartment, as in the case of Nehemiah and Tobiah.

A second passage which relates an event upon Nehemiah's return to Judah describes a run-in between Nehemiah and some Tyrian merchants.

> Tyrians dwelt in [the city] bringing fish and all kinds of merchandise and selling them on the Sabbath to the people of Judah ... in Jerusalem.

---

would have worked on the city wall had they been given an exemption from corvée labour 13 years before. Ezra must have arrived with his remission of public burdens after Nehemiah, not before him, in the seventh year of Artaxerxes II, 398.

39. Williamson (*Ezra, Nehemiah*, xxvii–xxxii) and Blenkinsopp, (*Ezra-Nehemiah*, 45–6) provide reviews of the discussion, although they reach conclusions opposite to my own.

40. This according to the 'minimalist' scholar, L. L. Grabbe, *Ezra-Nehemiah* (Old Testament Readings; London: Routledge, 1998), pp. 154–6. See also S. Mowinckel, *Studien zu dem Buche Ezra-Nehemia II* (Oslo: Universitetsforlaget, 1964), pp. 154–6; U. Kellermann, *Nehemia: Quellen, Überlieferung, und Geschichte* (Berlin: Töpelmann, 1967), pp. 4–56; T. Reinmuth, *Der Bericht Nehemias: Zur literarischen Eigenart, traditionsgeschichtlichen Prägung und innerbiblischen Rezeption des Ich-Berichts Nehemias* (OBO 183; Göttingen: Vandenhoeck & Ruprecht, 2002). J. L. Wright, *Rebuilding Identity* (BZAW 348; Berlin: de Gruyter, 2004) for additional discussions.

41. So D. J. Clines, *Ezra, Nehemiah, Esther* (NCB; Grand Rapids: Eerdmans, 1984), p. 240.

> ...When it began to be dark at the gates of Jerusalem before the Sabbath, I commanded that the doors should be shut and gave orders that they should not be opened until after the Sabbath. And I set some of my servants over the gates, to prevent any burden from being brought in on the Sabbath day. Then the merchants and sellers of all kinds of merchandise spent the night outside Jerusalem once or twice (Nehemiah 13.16, 19, 20).

Merchants from Tyre, residing in Jerusalem, were evidently selling fish on the Sabbath. These men are *gērîm par excellence*, but Nehemiah forces them to spend the night outside the city walls (v. 16). This is a strange way to treat the *gēr*, even the *gēr* who sells merchandise on the Sabbath (after all, he does not force anyone to buy).

A third passage relates Nehemiah's anger at learning that some Judeans had married women from Ashdod.

> In those days also I saw Jews who had married Ashdodite [Ammonite Moabite] women; and their children are half speaking Ashdodite,[42] and none know how to speak Judean [...][43] (Nehemiah 13.23-25).

Neither of the words 'Ammon' or 'Moab' is preceded by the conjunction 'and' (*waw*) and the phrase seems to have been added later. The rest of the passage refers only to the language of Ashdod. The words 'Ammon Moab' were likely added by the same redactor who added Neh. 13.1-3 and most scholars exclude them.[44] The passage continues:

> And I contended with them and cursed them and beat some of them and pulled out their hair (Neh. 13.25a).

M. Heltzer has shown that flogging and plucking hair from the head and beard were official sanctions in the Achaemenid Empire. According to a cuneiform text from the Murašû archive (CBS 5213) two men agreed by contract to do groundbreaking on the land of Rimuūṭ-Maš. The text then states:

> If they have not completed the groundbreaking by the first day of the fifth month, they shall be beaten one hundred times with a *niṭpu*, their

---

42. This alternative translation is proposed by A. Lemaire, 'Ashdodien et Judéen à l'Époque Perse: Ne 13,24', in K. van Lerberghe and A. Schoors (eds), *Immigration and Emigration within the Ancient Near East: FS E. Lipínski* (Leuven: Peeters Publishers, 1995), pp. 153–63.

43. The rest of the phrase, ובלשון עם ועם, 'and as a language of a people and a people,' is practically unintelligible. It is absent from the LXX.

44. L. Batten, *The Books of Ezra and Nehemiah: A Critical and Exegetical Commentary*, (ICC; Edinburgh: T & T Clark, 1913), p. 299; S. Mowinckel, *Studien zu dem Buche Ezra-Nehemia II* (Oslo: Universitetsforlaget, 1964), p. 41; U. Kellermann, *Nehemia: Quellen, Überlieferung, und Geschichte* (Berlin: Töpelmann, 1967), 53–4; Williamson, *Ezra, Nehemiah*, 397; Blenkinsopp, *Ezra-Nehemiah*, 363.

beards and hair (of the head) shall be plucked out, and Rībat, son of Bēl-irība, servant of Rimūṭ-Ninurta, shall keep them in the work-house.[45]

The text is dated to the fifth year of Darius II, 420 BCE. Rather than an impetuous act, Nehemiah was applying normal Persian sanctions to violations of an edict, an edict that he must have pronounced prior to his departure in 432.

These passages in Nehemiah's memoir reveal a significant change in attitude toward the foreigner. Tobiah the Ammonite is expelled from the temple precincts, Tyrian merchant *gērîm* are expelled from the city, and men who married Ashdodite women are beaten. In summarizing his activities, Nehemiah commends himself to God because he 'purified them from everything foreign', טהרתים מכל נכר (Neh. 13.30).

If this last passage is genuine to Nehemiah's memoir, it is the earliest indication in the book of Ezra-Nehemiah, and indeed in the biblical corpus, of an antipathy to all that is foreign. This change in attitude, if authentic to the memoir, must be dated at least to 445. Nehemiah was governor of Judah from 445 to 433 when he visited the king (Neh. 5.14), and continued in that role an unknown number of years after his return to Judah (Neh. 13.6-7). P, the Deuteronomic Historians, Haggai and Zechariah, Deutero- and Trito-Isaiah, all evidently written prior to Nehemiah's governorship, do not exhibit this general antipathy to the foreigner. In fact, as reviewed above, many of these texts seem to exult in all the world's peoples and all the world's resources streaming in to enrich Jerusalem.

B. *Attitudes toward the Foreigner in Mesopotamia and Greece*

1. *The Attitude toward the Foreigner in Mesopotamia*
Was the about-face in the attitude toward the non-Judean that is evident upon Nehemiah's return from Susa influenced by Mesopotamian or Persian attitudes? A great deal is known about the status of foreigners in Mesopotamia. Although some who entered Assyria as deportees from conquered enemy areas were retained as slaves and cruelly treated, others were settled in border areas and enrolled in the defensive forces there on a par with native Assyrians.[46] They did not constitute a specific social or

---

45. M. Heltzer, 'The Flogging and Plucking of Beards in the Achaemenid Empire and the Chronology of Nehemiah', *Archäologische Mitteilungen aus Iran* 28 (1995–96), pp. 305–7.

46. G. Cardascia, 'Le statut de l'étranger dans la Mésopotamie ancienne', *Recueils de la société Jean Bodin: L'Étranger* IX (première parte) (Bruxelles: Institut de sociologie Solvay, 1958), pp. 105–17; B. Oded, *Mass Deportations and Deportees in the Neo-Assyrian Empire* (Wiesbaden: Reichert, 1979), pp. 75–115; M. Dandamayev, *Slavery in Babylonia, 626–331* (trans. V. Powell; Dekalb, IL: Northern Illinois University Press, 1984), p. 46 (on p. 103,

judicial category. The stereotyped phrase used by Assyrian kings at least prior to Sennacherib is 'I have counted them with the people of the land of Assyria' (*itti niše* ^{kur}*Aššur amnūšunūti*). Although originally settled with their families on lands from which they could not leave, eventually the deported had all the rights of free persons.

Deportees were not the only source of foreigners. Foreigners entered Assyria voluntarily as fugitives from war or for economic reasons, perhaps as merchants or, like the Amorites, as nomadic peoples. Examination of the Assyrian onomastica reveal foreign names in abundance, but do not reveal how they came to be living in Assyria. The onomastica show that foreigners were well integrated into the life of the empire. They are seen owning and inheriting property, buying and selling real estate, acting as creditors and debtors, engaging in litigation and approaching the court.[47] They engaged in commerce and business, witnessed contracts and suits, and maintained their ancestral traditions. Foreigners, perhaps even deportees or their descendants, served as officials in the royal court both in the capital in Assyria proper and in the provinces; many district governors and eponym holders bore non-Akkadian names.[48]

Under the Neo-Babylonians, deportees were assigned crown land, first becoming tenant farmers, but this land soon became their heritage, passing from father to son.[49] As Cardascia argues:

> In a world without a civil state, without an identity card, without a passport, the quality of being a foreigner is a fact, and purely a fact. One may attach juridical consequences, but these consequences disappear with the fact itself. As soon as the foreigner absorbs the language, the national customs, and this will often be the case for his descendants, the law ceases to consider him a foreigner.[50]

Dandamayev points out that the majority of slaves in Babylon under the Achaemenids were not foreign, but Babylonian); K. L. Younger, 'Give Us Our Daily Bread: Everyday Life for the Israelite Deportees', in M. W. C. Richard, E. Averbeck, and David B. Weisberg (eds), *Life and Culture in the Ancient Near East* (Bethesda: CDL Press, 2003), pp. 269–88; M. C. Poo, *Enemies of Civilization: Attitudes toward Foreigners in Ancient Mesopotamia, Egypt, and China* (SUNY Series in Chinese Philosophy and Culture; Albany: State University of New York Press, 2005), p. 102.

47. Oded, *Mass Deportations*, 49–83.

48. Cardascia, 'Le statut de l'étranger dans la Mésopotamie ancienne', pp. 105–17; Oded, *Mass Deportations*, 87–99.

49. B. Oded, 'Observations on the Israelite/Judaean Exiles in Mesopotamia during the Eighth-Sixth Centuries', in K. van Lerberghe and A. Schoors (eds), *Immigration and Emigration within the Ancient Near East: FS E. Lipiński* (Leuven: Peeters Publishers, 1995), pp. 205–12.

50. Cardascia, 'Le statut de l'étranger', 114 (translation mine).

Cardascia thinks that this was especially true for the later periods and in particular that of the Achaemenid. 'Primarily in the Achaemenid Empire, Mesopotamia became a crucible of races and one can say that there were no longer foreigners there, since the empire absorbed every nation'.[51] The equality demanded in the law codes for the *'ezraḥ* and the *gēr* seems to reflect Mesopotamian ideas in which the foreigner is assured of equality, both *de jure* and *de facto*. No law in any of the extant law codes of Mesopotamian prescribes a separate status for the alien.[52] A man's status depends only upon his relationship to the land. Free citizens, slaves and serfs are differentiated in the codes, not the foreigner. Dandamayev had once defined what it meant not to be a full citizen in Babylon:

> Free-men deprived of civil rights consisted of . . . persons [who] did not own property within the city's lands. [Therefore they] had no access to the Babylonian temples, and consequently could not become members of the popular assembly.[53]

In his recent study of the *mār banê* however, Dandamayev had reason to revise his earlier view.[54] The term *mār banê* is used in the texts to refer to the men who sat in the city and temple assemblies. Dandamayev has recently examined 291 men who are explicitly referred to by this title one or more times over several years (sometimes over 40 years) and in thousands of economic, legal and administrative documents. He has determined that the *mār banê* included every stratum of the free inhabitants of a city, even those who rented or leased land, but did not own it, and even those who did not work in the temple at all or have temple prebends. Thus, any free male (*awīlum*) who was a permanent resident in the city could participate in the city or temple assemblies if he desired. This included foreigners. The Murašû archive from fifth-century Nippur reveals the many foreigners and fugitives from all parts of the Empire, perhaps even deportees, as well as native Babylonians, who, as citizens, *awīlū*, leased estates on crown land called *ḫatrus*. *Ḫatrus were labelled in the Murašû archive by the common ethnicity, city of origin, or occupation of the lessees and rarely, by the name of their pater familias.*[55]

---

51.   Cardascia, 'Le statut de l'étranger', 114 (translation mine).

52.   C. van Houten, *The Alien in Israelite Law*, (JSOTSupp. 107; Sheffield: Sheffield Academic Press, 1991), pp. 23–36.

53.   M. A. Dandamayev, 'The Neo-Babylonian Elders', in M. A. Dandamayev (ed.), *Societies and Languages of the Ancient Near East: FS I. M. Diakonoff* (Warminster: Aris & Phillips, Israel Exploration Society, 1982), pp. 38–41.

54.   M. A. Dandamayev, 'Babylonian Popular Assemblies in the First Millennium B. C.', *Bulletin of the Canadian Society for Mesopotamian Studies* 30 (1995), pp. 23–9.

55.   M. Stolper, *Entrepreneurs and Empire: The Murašû Archive, the Murašû Firm, and Persian Rule in Babylonia* (Leiden: Nederlands Instituut voor het Nabije Oosten, 1985), pp. 72–9; G. Cardascia, *Les archives des Murašû, une famille d'hommes d'affaires à l'époque perse*

We read about *ḥatru*s leased by 'people from Asia', 'men from Caria', as well as about native 'leather workers', or the 'estate of the Babylonian ^mItti-^dŠamaš-balāṭu'. The lessees, all called *awīlu* in the texts, were free citizens. They would have had equal access to the temple, and to participation in city and temple assemblies. They were all obligated to furnish men for the king's army, as well as provide horses with their gear. The texts do not distinguish between foreign and Babylonian *ḥatru*s; obligations and rights were identical. There was one law for both.

2. *Attitudes Toward the Foreigner Visible in Persian Royal Inscriptions*
The texts of Haggai and Zechariah, the writings of Deutero- and Trito-Isaiah, the passages of the post-exilic Deuteronomic historian, as well as Ezra Chapters 1 and 2, reflect this Mesopotamian attitude toward the foreigner. They also reflect the literary motifs of Persian royal inscriptions. Like the biblical texts, these inscriptions portray all the world's peoples and resources flowing into the empire, here because of the greatness of Darius's god, Ahura Mazda. In one of Darius's inscriptions from Susa (DSf), Darius presents himself as the recipient of all the world's resources. He names the peoples from all over the empire who come to build his palace. He lists the materials which flow in for its construction, and stresses their rarity and the great distances they travelled. They do not flow in as a result of the might of Darius's army, in contrast to Assyrian building inscriptions; rather, they flow in voluntarily. This voluntary inflow of human and material wealth is characteristic of Achaemenid texts. According to this inscription:

> ll. 1–5. A great god is Ahuramazda, who created this earth, who created yonder sky, who created man, who created happiness for man, who made Darius king, one king (over) many kings, one lord (over) many (lords).

> ll. 5–8. I am Darius the Great King, King of Kings, King of countries, son of Hystaspes, an Achaemenian, who built this palace.

> ll. 8–12. Thus says Darius the King: Ahuramazda, the greatest of the gods – he created me; he made me king; he bestowed upon me this great kingdom, possessed of good horses, possessed of good men.

> . . .

> ll.22–27. This palace which I built at Susa, from *afar* its *ornamentation was brought*. Downward the earth was dug, until I reached rock in the earth. When the excavations had been made, then rubble was packed

---

(455–503 av. J.-C.) (Paris: Centre National de la Recherche Scientifique, 1951); G. Cardascia, 'Le statut de l'étranger'; I. Eph'al, 'The Western Minorities in Babylonia in the 6th-5th Centuries B. C.: Maintenance and Cohesion', *Orientalia* 47 (1978), pp. 74–90.

down, some 40 cubits in depth, another [part] 20 cubits in depth. On
that rubble the palace was constructed.

ll.28–30. And that the earth was dug downward, and that the rubble was
packed down, and that the sun-dried brick was molded, the *Babylonian*
people, they did it [these tasks].

ll. 30–35. The cedar timber, this – a mountain by name *Lebanon* – from
there was brought. The *Assyrian* people, it brought it to *Babylon*; from
Babylon the *Carians* and the *Ionians* brought it to Susa. The yaka
timber was brought from *Candara* and from *Carmania*.

ll.35–40. The gold was brought from *Sardis* and from *Bactria*, which
here was wrought. The precious stone lapis-lazuli and carnelian which
was wrought here, this was brought from *Sogdiana*. The precious stone
turquoise, this was brought from *Chorasmia*, which was wrought here.

ll. 40–45. The silver and the ebony were brought from *Egypt*. The
ornamentation with which the wall was adorned, that from *Ionia* was
brought. The ivory which was wrought here, was brought from *Ethiopia*
and from *Sind* and from *Arachosia*.

ll. 45–49. The stone columns which were wrought here, were brought
from a village by name *Abiradu*, in *Elam*. The stone-cutters who
wrought the stone, these were *Ionians* and *Sardians*.

ll. 49–55. The goldsmiths who wrought the gold, those were *Medes* and
Egyptians. The men who wrought the wood, those were *Sardians* and
Egyptians. The men who wrought the baked brick, those were
Babylonians. The men who adorned the wall, those were *Medes* and
Egyptians.

ll. 55. Thus says Darius the King: At Susa a very excellent [work] was
ordered, a very excellent [work] was [brought to completion]. May
Ahuramazda protect me, Hystaspes my father, and my country.[56]

Darius' art and architecture as well as that of his successors also portray
the Great King receiving tribute from all over the world. Visiting Darius
required climbing the dozens of steps of the Apadana audience hall, each
one flanked with a relief of a foreign subject in native costume bearing
tribute to the Great King. This common Achaemenid motif of all the
world's peoples coming to worship the Great King is reflected in biblical
texts from the first century of Persian hegemony in Judah where, however,
the Great King is YHWH.

3. Greek Influences on the Levant?
It does not seem likely, therefore, that the about-face seen for the first time
in Nehemiah's memoir could be due to Mesopotamian influences.

56.   R. G. Kent, *Old Persian: Grammar, Texts, Lexicon* (New Haven: American Oriental
Society, 1953), pp. 142–4. Emphases mine.

Mesopotamian texts, whether Assyrian, Babylonian, or Persian, indicate no distinction between native-or foreign-born. The change in attitude toward the foreigner may therefore reflect Greek influences. Ephraim Stern has recorded Greek presence in the Levant from before Alexander the Great. Greek pottery from as early as the end of the eighth century has been found, with large quantities appearing from the end of the sixth century on. Attic ware was an integral part of the pottery used throughout the Persian period. Coins on the Greek standard appear by the end of the sixth century and continue unabated (Ezra 2.69 records that temple contributions at the end of the sixth century were made in gold drachmas, a coin on the Greek standard.) Stern reports the presence of Greek colonies in Persian-period Akko, Jaffa, Tel Dor, Mesad Hashavyahu, and Migdol. Phoenician cities boasted a strong Greek element from the end of the sixth century. Greek trade and its material culture became prominent in the entire Levant from the end of the sixth century and continued throughout the Persian period, bringing with it Greek settlers, soldiers and traders.[57] Could Greek mores and attitudes toward the stranger also have become prevalent?

4. *Attitudes Toward the Foreigner in 5th–4th Century BCE Athens*[58]
Contemporary Athenian attitudes toward the stranger are revealed in the law codes of sixth-and fifth-century Athens. In 594 BCE, Solon, as archon, enacted a series of entitlements for Athenian citizens, i.e., those whose fathers were Athenian. They were entitled to own the land they worked on and they could not be enslaved by other Athenians. Loans to Athenians could no longer be taken on security of persons. Non-Athenians were not so protected. Moreover, aliens, *xenoi*, working or marketing their wares in Athens, were prohibited from working at the Agora, and this evolved into their obligation to pay a special tax, the *xenika*. Exemptions were granted to foreign artisans and tradesmen who would settle in Athens with their families to ply their trades, and who were, moreover, exiled permanently from their own countries.[59] These were granted citizenship; but no others.

This strict distinction between citizen and non-citizen was new with Solon. Prior to the sixth century, the categories of *xenos* (ξενος, stranger,

---

57. E. Stern, 'Between Persia and Greece: Trade, Administration and Warfare in the Persian and Hellenistic Periods (539–63 BCE)', in T. E. Levy, (ed.) *The Archaeology of Society in the Holy Land* (New York: Facts on File, Inc, 1995), pp. 432–45. See also the articles by H. Eshel, E. Ambar-Armon and A. Kloner in the present volume.

58. The following discussion is based on P. B. Manville, *The Origins of Citizenship in Ancient Athens* (Princeton: Princeton University Press, 1997); G. R. Stanton, *Athenian Politics c. 800–500 BC: A Sourcebook* (London: Routledge, 1990); I. A. Arnaoutoglou, *Ancient Greek Laws: A Sourcebook* (London: Routledge, 1998); and N. G. L. Hammond, *A History of Greece to 322 B. C.* (Oxford: Clarendon Press, 1991), pp.153–66, 179–91, 299–310.

59. This is similar to the requirements of Ezekiel, deported to Babylon in 597.

foreigner, non-resident guest) and *metoikos* (μέτοικος, resident alien,
sojourner) did not exist as legal statuses. As part of Solon's reforms,
foreign tradesmen were assigned to a guild, but not to a clan, and so had
no share in the land which was clan-owned. Solon divided everyone into
four income classes or *telé* with honours and duties dependent on class.
Even though the wealthier classes had the greatest number of privileges,
the right of members of the bottom class to participate in the assembly
and to have equal access to the law courts was established for the first time
(*Athenian Politeia,* 7.3, 8.1). Guild members (with no landed estates) were
assigned to classes on an equal footing with clansmen. Since wealth was
wealth in land, however, and since the clansmen controlled the land, their
power was not greatly affected by these reforms.

Solon's laws took practical effect during the revolution of Kleisthenes
at the end of the sixth century. Solon left Athens after his archonship, and
Athens degenerated into anarchy, civil war, and finally tyranny. The
tyranny was ended by Isagoras, Kleisthenes, the aristocratic families of
Athens, and their Spartan allies. After the Spartans withdrew in 510,
various aristocratic families vied for power. Isagoras was elected archon in
508/507 and subjected the Athenian population to a civic scrutiny or
diapsēphismos, διαψηφισμος, in which those of 'impure birth' (οἵ τῷ γένει
μὴ καθαροὶ) were purged from the citizenship rolls. Aristotle reports that:

> After the tyranny was overthrown, a revision was made of the citizen-
> roll on the ground that many persons were partaking in the franchise
> who were of impure birth. The names [of those removed] given to the
> respective parties were derived from the districts in which they held their
> lands [i.e., the *demes*] (*Athenian Politeia,* 13.5).[60]

Determination of citizenship status was carried out by a vote of the *deme*
to which a youth was registered when he turned 18. Every Athenian's
citizenship status was at the mercy of his *deme*, but appeal to a city-wide
jury, the *thesmothetai,* was possible. Winners of the appeal were
vindicated as citizens, losers were sold as slaves. Under Isagoras, 700
families were removed from the citizenship list and exiled (Herodotus,
Histories, V.72), an act carried out by a largely Spartan military force.

Isagoras' main opponent in the rivalry for power after the Spartan
withdrawal was Kleisthenes. As part of the democratic reaction against
Isagoras' purge, Kleisthenes was able to drive through a series of reforms
that solidified the definition of citizenship. He changed the basis of the
deme to a geographical unit rather than one based on lineage. Everyone
was newly enrolled in a *deme* according to his current place of residence
(*Ath. Pol.* 21). A family's residence in a *deme* in 507 was now the condition

---

60.   Whether Aristotle or Pseudo-Aristotle is beyond this writer's competence to judge.
In either case, the text is usually dated to the end of the fourth century.

of citizenship. Wherever a family lived thereafter, it was a member of the *deme* in which it had been living in 507. Kleisthenes moreover randomly assigned these *deme*s to one of ten newly created 'tribes'. To avoid being labelled 'impurely born' and removed from the citizenship rolls, men had only to trace their lineage back to their father's house (*oikos*), to the *deme*, and to the tribe to which his family was assigned in 507. Every citizen – and every non-citizen resident alien – now had a systematic and tangibly defined place in society. *Metoikia* became a securely attested legal status, identifying the foreigner who lived in Athens but who was not a citizen. *Metoikoi* registered as such in the *deme* in which they resided.

60 years later, in the mid-fifth century (451–450), Pericles persuaded the Athenians to restrict their definition of Athenian citizenship further. According to Aristotle:

> In the archonship of Antidotus, in consequence of the great increase in the number of citizens, it was resolved, on the motion of Pericles, that no one should be admitted to the franchise who was not of citizen birth by both parents (*Ath. Pol.* 26).

For the first time Athenian citizens had also to prove descent from an Athenian mother, that is, a woman whose father was a citizen. The decree of 451/450 was followed by another scrutiny (διαψηφισμος) in 445 when the Egyptian king sent grain to be distributed to Athenian citizens.[61] Five thousand Athenians were struck from the citizenship rolls then as being of 'impure birth', not entitled to the grain. Of these, some were put to death, others were exiled, some were allowed to live in Attica, but deprived of their rights, *atimia* (Andocides, *On the Mysteries* 1.106).[62] Deprived of their rights as citizens, they had no recourse to the protection of the courts; if murdered, their family had no right of vengeance. Confiscation of property and often loss of life followed even those allowed to remain in Athens. Those who sued for their citizenship rights and lost their suit were executed. These laws were allowed to lapse during the Peloponnesian Wars, but in 403 they were reinforced and strengthened. Another census and mass exile ensued. Manville characterizes these periodic 'scrutinies' as 'reigns of terror'.[63]

Laws prohibiting intermarriage between Athenians and foreigners followed closely upon Pericles' citizenship law. Two laws in particular are noteworthy. Both date from the end of the fifth century:

> If a foreign man lives as husband with an Athenian woman in any way or manner whatsoever, he may be prosecuted before the *thesmothetai* by

---

61.   C. B. Patterson, *Pericles' Citizenship Law of 451/50 B.C.* (New York: Arno Press, 1981), p. 96 connects the law to the grain shipment.

62.   Manville, *The Origins of Citizenship*, 183.

63.   Manville, *The Origins of Citizenship*, 184.

any Athenian wishing and entitled to do so. If he is found guilty, both
he and his property shall be sold and one-third of the money shall be
given to the prosecutor. The same rule applies to a foreign woman who
lives with an Athenian as his wife, and the Athenian convicted of living
as husband with a foreign woman shall be fined a thousand drachmas
(Demosthenes LIX.16).

This implies a mandatory divorce for all marriages between an Athenian
and non-Athenian. The foreigner living as spouse with an Athenian shall
be sold into slavery, and his or her property confiscated (with one-third
given to the man who brings the suit). Since women did not give
themselves in marriage, anyone giving a foreign woman to an Athenian in
marriage was also subject to sanctions:

> If any Athenian gives a foreign woman in marriage to an Athenian
> citizen, as being his relative, he shall lose his civic rights and his property
> shall be confiscated and one-third shall belong to the successful
> prosecutor. Those entitled may prosecute before the *thesmothetai,* as
> in the case of usurpation of citizenship (Demosthenes LIX.52).

5. *Judean and Athenian Laws toward the Alien Compared*

The promulgation of Athenian citizenship laws has striking parallels with
events in *Yehud*. The census list we find in Ezra 2 most likely dates to the
end of the sixth century BCE,[64] about seven years after the time of the first
'scrutiny' (διαψηφισμος), and seven years after Kleisthenes, as part of a
democratic revolt, granted every man in Athens citizenship and assigned
him and his family to a *deme* and a tribe. So too, according to Ezra 2,
those in *Yehud* not able to prove their fathers' house or their descent from
the people Israel were still counted in the assembly of the returnees, the
legitimate people of Israel (Ezra 2.59; 6.21). Pericles' citizenship laws
(451–450) were followed in 445 by a 'scrutiny' of the citizenship rolls,
expulsion of those of 'impure birth', and mass divorce. Nehemiah may
also have enacted his ruling against mixed marriages in 445, his first year
as governor of Judah, getting his idea from Athens. In Chapter 5,
Nehemiah states that he and his colleagues decided to buy back Judeans
who had been sold into slavery (5.8). He may have restricted the definition
of a 'Judean' at that point.[65] If he modelled his edict on that of Pericles' of

---

64. L. S. Fried, *Ezra-Nehemiah* (forthcoming).
65. Elsewhere ('The Political Struggle of Fifth Century Judah', *Transeuphratène* 24
(2002), pp. 9–21) I have suggested that Nehemiah forbade intermarriage to prevent dynastic
marriages of governors from the different provinces and the subsequent massing of wealth in
powerful families. While this may have been the cause, the idea for the solution derived from
the Athenian citizenship laws.

a few years before, he would have defined a Judean as one with two Judean parents who could trace their lineage to a father's house and to a tribe. When Nehemiah returned after his visit to Susa (Neh. 1.1) he saw that some Judeans had married Ashdodites. He resorted to beating the offenders and pulling out their hair (Neh.13.23-25), a recognized Persian sanction. If Nehemiah enacted his edict against intermarriage before he left for the king, it was evidently not enforced during his absence. The citizenship laws in Athens lapsed during the Peloponnesian Wars, but were tightened and strengthened again in 403. The laws against mixed marriages in Judah also lapsed again after Nehemiah's second tour of duty and they too were strengthened and solidified again when Ezra arrived in 398, the seventh year of Artaxerxes II. Ezra's mass divorce and expulsion in Judah would have been five years after the mass divorce and expulsion in Athens. As in Athens, Ezra required Judeans to divorce their foreign wives and banish the children of these unions or face exile and confiscation of property:

> They made a proclamation throughout Judah and Jerusalem to all the returned exiles that they should assemble at Jerusalem [to divorce their foreign wives], and that if any did not come within three days, by order of the officials and the elders all their property should be confiscated, and they themselves exiled from the community of the returnees (Ezra 10.7-8).

Ezra expresses his prohibition against intermarriage in language similar to that of Pericles. Citizenship in both the people of Athens and in *Yehud* was described as a holy thing, not to be adulterated.

> For the Athenian people, although they hold ultimate authority over all things in the state and have the power to act however they see fit, nonetheless regarded their citizenship to be something so worthy and holy (σεμνόν) that they passed laws strictly prescribing its bestowal (Demosthenes LIX.88; a speech given in 345 about the laws of 451/450).

In Athens these laws were described as an attempt to keep their citizenship holy and to weed out those of 'impure birth'. In Judah it was described as opposition to mingling the 'holy seed' with the peoples of the lands (Ezra 9.1-2).

Conclusions

The evidence suggests striking parallels between the changes in attitude toward the non-Athenian that are visible in the citizenship laws of Athens in the sixth and fifth centuries and the change in attitude toward the non-Judean which is exhibited in the book Ezra-Nehemiah. The laws and the consequent purges of the citizenship rolls in sixth-and fifth-century Athens seem to have had the same trajectory in contemporary *Yehud*, with the events in *Yehud* following those in Athens by a few years in every case. Could the events described in Ezra-Nehemiah have been influenced by the wider Hellenistic culture, a culture that was making itself felt across the continent of Asia Minor, down the Levantine coast, and into Egypt? Evidence for a Hellenistic influence on the Levantine material culture is described above and other papers in this volume discuss it at length. Material culture does not arrive by itself, however. It is brought by people, people who carry with them their ideas and attitudes as well as news of the events in their native lands. It may be that news of the citizenship laws in Athens provided Nehemiah with possibilities not previously apparent. Nehemiah's restriction of citizenship then seems to have later metastasized into an abhorrence of all things foreign which gave rise, in turn, to the words of the writer of the scenes posed in Ezra 3 and 4.

Chapter 9

THE POPULATION OF PERSIAN-PERIOD IDUMEA ACCORDING TO THE
OSTRACA:
A STUDY OF ETHNIC BOUNDARIES AND ETHNOGENESIS[*]

Ian Stern

None of the written sources that have come down to us from the Persian
period relate directly to the area we refer to as Idumea (although there are
of course earlier and later references). And while archaeological surveys
and excavations have provided us with valuable data regarding the
population of Idumea at this time as well as the possibility of drawing
tentative borders for the region,[1] a fuller, more accurate picture can be
achieved by analysing the contemporary epigraphic material from this
region that has come to light in recent years. During the past decade over
1,600 Aramaic ostraca that are identified as having a provenance
somewhere in Idumea have appeared on the antiquities market.[2] Only
1,380 of these were considered legible and approximately 800 have been
published to date. Other material has been discovered in the many
excavations conducted in the area. During the course of the past ten years
I have personally been involved with the Mareshah excavation and have
had the opportunity to discover a portion of that epigraphic material
myself. Access to this relatively large corpus (compared to other
excavated sites) of unpublished ostraca was kindly provided to me by

*   This paper is based upon my dissertation 'Idumaea in the Persian Period: The
Interaction between Ethnic Groups as Reflected in the Material Culture', (unpublished
doctoral dissertation, Bar Ilan University, Ramat-Gan, 2005), written under the direction of
Professor Amos Kloner of Bar Ilan University. I would also like to thank Dr Yigal Levin for
his many valuable comments and suggestions in this article.
    1.   For the purpose of this paper, the borders have been drawn from south of Beth Zur to
the Beersheba Valley. Persian period remains that I believe can be associated with Idumea
can be found as far west as Tell el Far'ah (south) and Tel Jemmeh. See I. Stern, 'Idumaea in
the Persian-Period', 241–91.
    2.   B. Porten and A. Yardeni, 'On the Problems of Identity and Chronology in the
Idumean Ostraca', in M. Heltzer and M. Malul (eds), T^eshûrôt LaAvishur: Studies in the Bible
and in the Ancient Near East, in Hebrew and Semitic Languages (Tel Aviv-Jaffa:
Archaeological Center Publications, 2004), pp. 161–83 (161).

A. Kloner and E. Eshel. The importance of ostraca from a known provenance, albeit a small percentage of the total number, cannot be overstated.

The Database

Until recently, most scholars have assumed that an entity or province of 'Idumea', known from Hellenistic-period sources, may have already existed in the Persian period, but there has been no attempt to quantify the material finds from this period or to define their parameters. I have attempted to gather relevant information into a single database in order to help define the borders of Persian-period Idumea as to well as to clarify the region's ethnic makeup at the time. The database is composed of a number of different components, each with its own nuances that help provide an overall picture of Idumea in the Persian period. These components include archaeological excavations, of which there are only a limited number, archaeological surveys with their own accompanying limitations, and epigraphic material.

The purpose of this paper is to explore the ethnic interactions within Persian-period Idumean society by means of the available epigraphic material, which was collected in a master database. In this paper, we will use the ostraca discovered and published in recent years to determine the onomasticon and prosopography of the population in the area. This should provide a picture of the ethnic makeup of the province and perhaps shed light on how these different groups interacted.

The database includes all sites in which Persian-period material was uncovered. I have differentiated between large and small sites, and, when the information was available, the sizes of the settlements and their relative populations calculated on the basis of an average of 25 people per dunam. We must remember, though, that the degree of accuracy in estimating populations from archaeological finds, while improved in recent years, is still very speculative.[3]

The evidence from excavations is based on the reports from Arad,[4]

3. O. Lipschits, 'Demographic Changes in Judah between the Seventh and the Fifth Centuries BCE' in O. Lipschits and J. Blenkinsopp, (eds) *Judah and the Judeans in the Neo-Babylonian Period* (Winona Lake: Eisenbrauns, 2003), pp. 323–76 (324–6); G. A. London, 'Tells: City Center or Home?' *Eretz-Israel* 23 (1992), pp. 71–9.

4.   J. Naveh, 'The Aramaic Ostraca from Tel Arad', in Aharoni, *Arad Inscriptions*, (Jerusalem: Israel Exploration Society, 1981) pp.153–76.

Beersheba,[5] and most importantly our first-hand data from Mareshah;[6] from smaller sites such as Tell Jemmeh and Tell el-Far'ah (south)[7] as well as the minor sites of Tell el-Kheleifeh[8] and the region of Yata.[9]

These sites not only revealed Persian-period material culture, but also provided valuable epigraphic information. Many Aramaic ostraca discovered at these sites provide insights into the ethnic makeup of the area as well as the economy of the period. In addition, excavations at Tel Lachish, Tell el-Ḥesi, Tel Erani, Tel Ḥalif and Ein Gedi, where Persian-period levels were uncovered, helped to define settlement patterns.

It is well known that the nature of archaeological surveys is problematic.[10] They tend to be inexact and interpreting the finds can be at times ambiguous or misleading. Nevertheless this data, when juxtaposed with full-scale excavations, can be helpful in reconstructing settlement patterns.

The survey material here is derived primarily from the extensive works of Ofer[11] in the Judean Highlands and Dagan[12] in the Judean Shephelah, or lowlands. Their work is supplemented by a number of other surveys including those conducted by Kochavi,[13] Govrin,[14]

5. Y. Aharoni, *Beersheva I: Excavations at Tel Beer Sheba 1969–71* (Tel Aviv: Tel Aviv University, Institute of Archaeology Publications 2, 1973), pp. 79–82; J. Naveh, 'The Aramaic Ostraca from Tel Beer-Sheba (Season 1971–76)', *Tel Aviv* 6 (1979), pp. 182–99.

6. A. Kloner, *Maresha Excavations Final Report I: Subterranean Complexes 21, 44, 70* (IAA Reports 17; Jerusalem: Israel Antiquities Authority, 2003).

7. J. Naveh, 'Published and Unpublished Aramaic Ostraca', *Atiqot* 17 (1985), pp. 114–21.

8. G. Pratico, 'Nelson Glueck's 1938–1940 Excavations at Tell el-Kheleifeh: A Reappraisal', *BASOR* 259 (1985), pp.1–32.; idem, *Nelson Glueck's 1938–1940 Excavations at Tell el-Kheleifeh: A Reappraisal* (Atlanta: Scholars Press, 1993).

9. Naveh, 'Published and Unpublished Aramaic Ostraca'.

10. P. Bienkowski, *Early Edom and Moab: The Beginnings of the Iron Age in Southern Jordan* (Sheffield: J. R. Collis Publications, 1992), p. 164; A. Faust, 'Judah in the Sixth Century BCE: A Rural Perspective', *PEQ* 135 (2003) pp. 37–53, (39); Lipschits, 'Demographic Changes in Judah between the Seventh and the Fifth Centuries BCE', 325.

11. A. Ofer, 'The Highland of Judah During the Biblical Period' (unpublished doctoral dissertation, Tel Aviv University, 1993).

12. Y. Dagan, 'The Settlement in the Judean Shephela in the Second and First Millennium B.C.: A Test-Case of Settlement Processes in a Geographic Region', (unpublished doctoral dissertation, Tel Aviv University, 2003).

13. M. Kochavi, 'The Land of Judah', in M. Kochavi (ed.), *Survey of Judah, Samaria and the Golan 1967–1968*, (Jerusalem: Carta, 1972) pp. 19–89.

14. Y. Govrin, 'Nahal Yattir Site –1987', *ESI* 77/78 (1988/89), pp.142–3.

Govrin and Dorfler,[15] Cohen,[16] Dagan,[17] Rahmani,[18] Gazit[19] and Beit
Arieh.[20]

The most critical element in the database is the epigraphic material. The
onomastic material from Persian-period Idumea reflects a certain socio-
logical and demographic reality of the region that is difficult to ascertain
from most other material finds. This is especially instructive when we look
at ostraca that represent more than one generation, or include information pertaining to group identity. Many of the ostraca covered in this
study contain theophoric names as well as names with ethnic combinations. These combinations appear to reflect a blending of cultures in an
environment of apparently minimal ethnic boundaries.

The database contains all the published ostraca of the Persian period
from the general region of Idumea. Whenever possible, the epigraphic
material is provided in relation to its specific origin. Most of the ostraca
however, are of unknown provenance and are marked accordingly. They
are parts of private collections that have surfaced in the last few years.
Most scholars have attributed the source of these to Khirbet el-Kôm
which has been identified with ancient Makkedah,[21] the most cited
toponym in our texts (16 times).

Ethnic Categories

For this purpose the onomasticon in the database is presented (when
possible) according to ethnic categories, usually based on the theophoric
elements contained in the names.[22] In some cases the ostraca even shed
light on intergenerational relationships and from these it is sometimes
possible to understand the prosopography of some of the families/clans.
Charts and tables are provided (see below) to analyse acculturation

15. Y. Govrin and S. Dorfler, 'Nahal Yattir', *ESI* 88/89 (1986), pp. 84–5.
16. R. Cohen, *Map of Sede Boqer – West (167)* (Archaeological Survey of Israel;
Jerusalem: Department of Antiquities and Museums, 1985), pp. 93–107; R. Cohen and R.
Cohen-Amin, 'The End of the Iron Age and the Persian Period', in R. Cohen and R. Cohen-
Amin (eds), *Ancient Settlement of the Negev Highlands II: The Iron Age and the Persian
Period* (Jerusalem: Israel Antiquities Authorities, 2004), pp. 159–202.
17. Y. Dagan, *Map of Lakhish (98)* (Archaeological Survey of Israel; Jerusalem: Israel
Antiquities Authorities, 1992).
18. L. Rahmani, 'A Partial Survey of the Adullam Area', *Yediot* 28 (1964), pp. 209–31
(Hebrew).
19. D. Gazit, *Map of Urim (125)* (Archaeological Survey of Israel; Jerusalem: Israel
Antiquities Authorities, 1996).
20. I. Beit-Arieh, *Map of Tel Malhata (144)* (Archaeological Survey of Israel; Jerusalem:
Israel Antiquities Authorities, 2003).
21. For which see D. Dorsey, 'The Location of Biblical Makkedah', *Tel Aviv* 7 (1980),
pp. 185–93.
22. See Stern, 'Idumaea in the Persian Period', 375–432.

patterns within the region and comparisons with *Yehud*, Samaria and Elephantine (*Yeb*) have been drawn. These are provided in order to compare and contrast the social patterns, specifically probing the issue of ethnic boundary maintenance. The biblical text provides valuable information concerning Persian-period *Yehud*, Samaria and indirectly even Elephantine. This information is complemented by the important epigraphic materials uncovered in Wadi Daliyeh[23] and Elephantine.[24] It is often difficult to determine the exact origin of a particular name, since it can appear in similar forms in related Semitic languages. For this reason, at times the designation 'Western Semitic' has been given without further elucidation.

Derived primarily from publications of fifth- and more importantly fourth-century BCE Aramaic ostraca[25] the database contains a complete onomasticon of Idumea to date and is composed of all the published

---

23.   M. J. Leith, *Wadi Daliyeh I: The Wadi Daliyeh Seal Impressions* (Oxford, Clarendon Press, 1997); F. M. Cross, 'The Papyri and Their Historical Implications', *AASOR* 41 (1974), pp. 17–32.

24.   B. Porten, *The Elephantine Papyri in English: Three Millennia of Cross Cultural Continuity and Changes* (Leiden-New York: Brill, 1996).

25.   J. Naveh, 'The Scripts of Two Ostraca from Elath', *BASOR* 183 (1966), pp. 27–30; idem, 'The Aramaic Ostraca', in Y. Aharoni (ed.) *Beer-sheba I: Excavations at Tel Beer-sheba – 1969–71 Seasons* (Tel Aviv: Tel Aviv University, Institute of Archaeology Publications 2, 1973), pp. 79–82; idem, 'Two Aramaic Ostraca from the Persian Period', in B. Uffenheimer (ed.), *Bible and Jewish History, Studies Dedicated to the Memory of Jacob Liver* (Tel Aviv: Tel Aviv University 1972), pp. 184–89 (Hebrew); idem, 'The Aramaic Ostraca from Tel Beer-sheba (Season 1971–76)', *Tel Aviv* 6 (1979), pp. 182–99; idem, 'Published and Unpublished Aramaic Ostraca', *Atiqot* (English Series) 17 (1985), pp. 114–21; I. Eph'al and J. Naveh, *Aramaic Ostraca of the Fourth Century BC from Idumaea* (Jerusalem: Magnes Press and Israel Exploration Society, 1996); A. Lemaire, *Nouvelles inscriptions araméennes d'Idumée du Musée d'Israel* (Supplément no. 3 à Transeuphratène; Paris: Gabalda, 1996); idem, *Nouvelles inscriptions araméennes d'Idumée. II Collections Moussaieff, Jeselsohn, Welch et Divers* (Supplément no. 9 à Transeuphratène; Paris: Gabalda, 1996); idem, 'Der Beitrag idumäischer Ostraka zur Geschichte Palästinas im Ubergang von der persischen zur hellenistischen Zeit', *ZDPV* 115 (1999), pp. 12–13; idem, 'Quatre Nouveaux ostraca araméens D'Idumée', *Transeuphratène* 18 (1999), pp. 71–4; idem, *Nouvelles inscriptions araméenes d'Idumée du Musée d'Israel Tome II* (Supplément no. 9 à Transeuphratène, Paris: Gabalda, 2002); H. Lozachmeur and A. Lemaire, 'Nouveaux ostraca araméens d'Idumée (Collection Sh. Moussaieff)', *Semitica* 46 (1996), pp.123–42, pls. 11–14; S. Aḥituv, 'An Edomite Ostracon', in Y. Avishur, and R. Deutsch (eds), *Historical, Epigraphical and Biblical Studies in Honor of Prof. Michael Heltzer* (Tel Aviv-Jaffa: Archaeological Center Publications, 1999), pp. 33–7; B. Porten and A. Yardeni, 'In Preparation of a Corpus of Aramaic Ostraca from the Land of Israel: The House of Yehokal', in R. Deutsch (ed.), *Shlomo: Studies in Epigraphy, Iconography, History and Archaeology in Honor of Shlomo Mussaieff* (Tel Aviv: Archaeological Center Publications, 2003), pp. 207–23; B. Porten and A. Yardeni, 'On Problems of Identity and Chronology in the Idumean Ostraca' in M. Heltzer and M. Malul (eds), *Tᵉshûrôt LaAvishur: Studies in the Bible and in the Ancient Near East, in Hebrew and Semitic Languages* (Tel Aviv-Jaffa: Archaeological Center Publications, 2004), pp.161–84; E.

material available. No attempt has been made to reinterpret the names, but for the sake of clarity tables have been created that reflect the total number of distinct names in absolute terms. In the course of Klingbeil's study of the demographic makeup of the entire country, Klingbeil based his data on 'actual occurrences of a name-type and not on the basis of names types'.[26] He did this in order to prevent counting the same person's name that could theoretically appear on a number of different ostraca. While this system avoids the potential problem of counting someone more than once it is also problematic in that it precludes the distinct possibility that more than one person may have used the same name at the same time.

To resolve this potential problem, I have determined that when there is a very strong likelihood that the same name represents the same individual, the name is recorded only once. For example, Eph'al and Naveh refer to a specific corpus of 36 ostraca where a certain *Ḥalfat* provides goods to *Ba'alid*. Since these ostraca have been dated within a short time of one another (5 years) and contain some of the same signatures, the authors assume that these are the same individuals. Similarly the name *Zebadel* appears five times as a signatory, *Sha'adel* four times, *Yatua* and *Qosyeta* twice. Eph'al and Naveh concluded that these too were the same people,[27] and they have accordingly been recorded here only once.

The ethnic designations have been taken from the respective scholars who published the ostraca (Eph'al, Lemaire, Lozachmeur, Naveh, Porten and Yardeni). When no ethnic description was given, accepted norms or parallels from the other sites or collections included within the database were used, although in certain cases where there were no parallels the names were left without an ethnic designation.

The designation 'Arab' includes three separate categories: Arab, Nabataean and Palmyrene. The Palmyrene and Nabataean names have been in the database combined with the Arab names since they are generally characterized by the Arabic diminutive *qutayl* pattern combined with the final *waw* representing the typical 'u' ending.[28] Combining the three in the database simplifies the tables since it is often difficult to distinguish many names that overlap in two or three of these specific

Eshel, 'Three Inscriptions from Horbat Rogem' in R. Cohen and R. Cohen-Amin (eds), *Ancient Settlement of the Negev Highlands II: The Iron Age and the Persian Period* (Jerusalem: Israel Antiquities Authorities, 2004), pp. 16–17.

26.   G. Klingbeil, 'The Onomasticon of the Aramaic Inscriptions of Syro-Palestine During the Persian Period', *JNSL* 18 (1992), pp. 67–94.

27.   Eph'al and Naveh, *Aramaic Ostraca of the Fourth Century BC*, 10.

28.   Klingbeil, 'The Onomasticon of the Aramaic Inscriptions of Syro-Palestine During the Persian Period', 80; Naveh, 'The Aramaic Ostraca from Tel Beer-sheba', 185.

onomastica.[29] The other criteria for this category are parallel occurrences in other Arabic inscriptions.[30]

Idumean names were the most easily identified as those containing the unique Idumean theophoric *Qws* (*Qos*). Judahite names were identified primarily by the Yahwistic theophoric or from their occurrence in biblical or extra-biblical texts. The scholars who identified the Phoenician, Babylonian, Iranian and Egyptian names are indicated in the footnotes.

Of the approximately 200 ostraca published by Naveh and Eph'al, close to 150 personal names which were given a more specific designation were simply listed as 'Western Semitic'. We applied the same system to the other epigraphic collections.

The vast majority of the ostraca can be dated to the fourth century BCE. Eph'al and Naveh date their material from 363 to 311 BCE.[31] Lemaire's materials fall within the same chronological range. The Mareshah corpus considered here includes two fifth-century BCE ostraca; the remaining material from Mareshah is from the fourth century BCE.[32]

As Porten and Yardeni correctly point out, the format of these ostraca are variegated, presenting quite a few patterns.[33] They generally include a regnal date, the name of the individual purchaser/s, the person/s who received the payment and the amount of payment in goods. Occasionally a toponym is included, as are patronyms and/or familial/clan/tribal associations. No attempt has been made in the database to collate any dates of the personalities mentioned beyond the most general terms. Ostraca from earlier or later periods, at the respective excavated sites, have not been included in the database so as not to obfuscate the demographic conclusions.

In the future more ostraca will no doubt be published that could possibly alter the conclusions presented here. The nature of research, however, is that it can only be based upon currently available evidence, and the 1,300 names represented in this study are more than a representative sampling of the onomasticon of Idumea in the late Persian period.

---

29.   Klingbeil, 'The Onomasticon of the Aramaic Inscriptions of Syro-Palestine During the Persian Period', 74–8.

30.   Klingbeil, 'The Onomasticon of the Aramaic Inscriptions of Syro-Palestine During the Persian Period', 80.

31.   Eph'al and Naveh, *Aramaic Ostraca of the Fourth Century BC*, 18.

32.   This according to a personal communication from Amos Kloner and Esther Eshel.

33.   Porten and Yardeni, 'On Problems of Identity and Chronology in the Idumean Ostraca', 168.

The Provenance of the Ostraca

The vast majority of the ostraca are of unknown provenance but are believed by many scholars to originate in the area of Khirbet el-Kôm. This assumption is based upon rumours from local antiquities merchants that the ostraca originated there and is reinforced by the appearance of the name Makkedah on many of the ostraca; this site has been independently identified with Khirbet el-Kôm. Excavations at Khirbet el-Kôm itself have uncovered one bilingual Greek and Aramaic ostracon and eight Aramaic ostraca.[34]

The striking similarity between the ethnic breakdown at Mareshah and that of the ostraca of unknown provenance in Table 2.1 quickly becomes apparent. Both stand apart from the onomasticon of the two other major excavations that have also produced significant quantities of epigraphic material, those of Arad and Beersheba. The Mareshah figures (as well as those of other excavations) must be understood, however, in light of the fact that they are a small percentage of the total number of ostraca: there are approximately ten times as many unprovenanced names as there are names from Mareshah. The similarity between the two lists does not preclude Khirbet el-Kôm's being the source of this epigraphic corpus, but does suggest an alternative perspective.

Ethnic Analysis of the Population of Idumea According to the Ostraca

The epigraphic material presented here represents a very mixed ethnic population within late Persian-period Idumea. Approximately 1,300 names recorded from the published ostraca of the period to date are included. The breakdown of the main ethnic groups by identifiable ethnic names (primarily via their theophorics) is approximately 32% Arabs, 27% Idumeans, 25% Western Semitic, 10% Judahite, 5% Phoenician, with the remaining 1% being a mixture of smaller groups. The majority of the names that appear in Persian-period Arad are Judahite, followed by three other ethnic groups: Idumeans, Arabs and Western Semitic. The largest ethnic representation in Persian-period Beersheba are Arabs, with a large minority of Idumeans and smaller minorities of Judahite, Western Semitic and Iranian names. In the material from Mareshah and in the unprovenanced material, no single ethnic group was in the majority, but names from three groups were dominant: Arabs, Idumeans and Western Semitic, with other groups being represented only marginally. While it was assumed in the past that the ethnic majority in Idumea was comprised

---

34.   L. Geraty, 'The Khirbet El Kom Bilingual Ostracon', *BASOR* 220 (1975), pp. 55–61.

of Arabs and Idumeans,[35] here this assumption has been quantified into specific ethnic categories for the first time. In the following sections I will use the material in the database to investigate the ethnic makeup of Persian-period Idumea as well as to better understand what appears to be a very fast acculturation process within the province. Finally, in order to better understand the process in Idumea, I will briefly compare my findings to the situation known in *Yehud*, Samaria and Elephantine.

Table 2.1 Ethnic Breakdown of Idumean Ostraca

Ethnicity	Arad	Beersheba	Mareshah	Unknown Provenance	Total
Arab	12.24%	42.62%	30.68%	32.18%	31.73%
Aramaean	None	3.28%	None	None	0.19%
Babylonian	None	None	3.41%	0.36%	0.58%
Idumean	14.30%	24.59%	23.86%	28.49%	27.19%
Iranian	None	4.92%	None	None	0.29%
Judahite	61.22%	19.67%	9.09%	5.60%	9.35%
Phoenician	None	1.64%	4.55%	5.60%	5.01%
Western Semitic	12.24%	3.28%	28.41%	27.77%	25.65%
Total	100.00%	100.00%	100.00%	100.00%	100.00%

Ethnic Boundaries

Ethnic boundaries are maintained by symbols that emerge or develop in order to identify and separate.[36] Barth has shown that these boundaries exist despite the fact that groups interact both socially and economically and in fact ethnic distinctions can exist not due to any lack of interaction but many times as a result of it.[37] He maintains that 'cultural differences can persist despite inter ethnic contact and interdependence'.[38] These boundaries are usually accentuated in times of tension between

---

35. I. Eph'al, 'Changes in Palestine during the Persian Period in Light of Epigraphic Sources', *IEJ* 48 (1998), pp. 106–19; Naveh, 'The Aramaic Ostraca from Tel Beer-sheba', 194–5; M. Avi Yonah, *The Holy Land from the Persian to the Arab Conquests (536 B.C. to A.D. 640): A Historical Geography* (Grand Rapids: Baker Books, 1966), pp. 25–6.

36. I. Hodder, *Symbols in Action: Ethnoarchaeological Studies of Material Culture* (Cambridge: Cambridge University Press, 1982), pp. 11–35; R. McGuire, 'The Study of Ethnicity in Historical Archaeology', *Journal of Anthropological Archaeology* 1 (1982), pp. 159–78.

37. F. Barth, 'Introduction', in F. Barth (ed.) *Ethnic Groups and Boundaries: The Social Organization of Cultural Difference* (Bergen – London: Universitets Forlaget – George Allen and Unwin, 1969), pp. 9–13.

38. Barth, *Ethnic Groups and Boundaries*, 10.

different groups while the inverse is true at times when tensions between groups are minimal or when the tension is directed against a common 'other'. As we shall see, this appears to be the case in Idumea in the Persian period.

The conditions in Idumea during the 6th–4th centuries BCE and for that matter in *Yehud* as well, could be described as that of a 'post-collapse society'. This is a term that refers to a situation in which an existing socio-political entity experiences a fast and significant deterioration due to either internal, external or combination of reasons.[39] As Faust correctly points out, Tainter's model of post-collapse societies seems to mirror the way in which most scholars, working from the archaeological record, describe Idumea and *Yehud* in the Persian period: a territory denuded of most of its towns and cities and its population on the brink of total collapse.[40] As shown by archaeological surveys, following the Babylonian conquest, the population of the kingdom of Judah had been reduced to approximately one-third of its Iron Age II size, with certain areas suffering a decrease in settlement of up to 95%.[41] This is also in line with Tainter's thesis that collapse is often associated with depopulation. Current estimates however, especially those based upon surveys, can be very deceiving. The usual population estimate given is that of 25 people per dunam,[42] but this only applies as a basic average in 'normal' times, meaning when both urban and rural areas are included within the surveys. This was not the case in Persian-period Idumea where, it seems, there were no urban centres (with the possible exception of Mareshah) and therefore the estimate of 25 persons per dunam appears to be highly inflated. Even if urban centres were to be discovered, Fletcher has cast doubt on the notion that one can estimate the population size of a settlement based upon its physical size, pointing out that the density variable is difficult to define and therefore the numbers may always be inaccurate.[43] Finally, Tainter maintains that recovery from such a collapse

39.   J. Tainter, 'Post Collapse Societies', in G. Barker (ed.) *Companion Encyclopedia of Archaeology* 2 (London: Routledge, 1998), pp. 988–1039.

40.   A. Faust, 'Social and Cultural Changes in Judah during the 6th Century BCE and their Implications for our Understanding of the nature of the Neo-Babylonian Period', *UF* 36 (2004), pp. 157–76 (168–9). See also Lipschits, 'Demographic Changes in Judah between the Seventh and the Fifth Centuries BCE', 336–45.

41.   Lipschits, 'Demographic Changes in Judah between the Seventh and the Fifth Centuries BCE', 340.

42.   For a discussion see Lipschits, 'Demographic Changes in Judah between the Seventh and the Fifth Centuries BCE', 326.

43.   R. Fletcher, 'People and Space: A Case Study on Material Behavior' in I. Hodder, G. Isaac and N. Hammond (eds), *Pattern of the Past: Studies in Honour of David Clarke* (Cambridge: Cambridge University Press, 1981), pp. 97–128.

could take hundreds of years, which in our case would cover the entire Persian period.[44]

In light of this depopulation, this sparsely populated region could create social conditions that would be conducive for co-operation rather than competition over its limited resources, paving the way for low ethnic boundary maintenance. Hodder's contention is that during periods of competition and conflict over resources there are definite advantages in overtly stressing ethnic differences just as in times of insecurity and instability greater material and cultural uniformity within communities can be expected.[45] Ethnic borders, however, tend to blur when economic stress and competition are at an ebb. Alternatively, in times of threat there is an increased economic and physical dependence on the group. Therefore, due to the low population levels that characterize post-collapse societies such as that discussed here, this much smaller population probably had greater access, albeit limited and taxed, over available resources. In other words, since there were fewer people that needed to divide the economic pie, there was less competition. This situation is reflected in our onomasticon: a blurring of clear ethnic boundaries as expressed in intergenerational family lists which appears to be an expression of low boundary maintenance.

Aḥituv's Ostracon – A Case of Neighbours

While Table 2.1 above shows the total ethnic breakdown of the onomasticon in percentages, the implications of these statistics can be understood better by observing one individual ostracon, published by Aḥituv.[46] In many ways, this Idumean ostracon reflects a microcosm of inter-ethnic relationships in Idumea at the time. This ostracon is a memorandum that describes the borders of a vineyard that was made into an olive orchard, and reflects the daily economic life in a village with a mixed ethnic population in the fourth century BCE. The text relates to people who lived next to each other, a population that included Judahites and Idumeans and focuses upon the borders of a certain field. The field is located beneath the land of a man named *Qosdina* (an Idumean name), near the garden of *Qosleat* (another Idumean name). The field measures from the border of *Hanael* (possibly a Judahite name) as far as the border of *Hazir* (possibly a Judahite name) mentioning the vineyard of *Kinyo* (a Judahite name) and the field of *Galgala* which apparently also bordered the area. From this one ostracon it can be surmised that this village contained at least two ethnic groups that resided next to one another.

44. Tainter, *Post Collapse Societies*, 1022–4.
45. Hodder, *Symbols in Action: Ethnoarchaeological Studies of Material Culture*, 26.
46. Aḥituv, 'An Edomite Ostracon'.

However, just as Table 2.1 presents a breakdown of the onomasticon of the region but does not address the issue of interrelationships, the names of the residents on Ahituv's ostracon provide us with only limited information. In both cases ethnically identifiable names exist but we are missing a description of how the groups of people interacted and if there were significant ethnic barriers between them. In both cases there is simply not enough information provided here to make such a determination.

Are there any patterns that allow us to make certain generalizations about the demographic makeup of Idumea? As Ahituv's ostracon highlights, while the names alone allow us to better understand who lived there, it still does not clarify the nature of the ethnic relations. There are, however, ostraca that do provide intergenerational or clan-related information which reflect to some extent how these groups interacted.

Clan Relationships

Eph'al and Naveh[47] as well as Lemaire[48] observed that many of the personalities mentioned in the ostraca are defined by their connection to a family, clan or tribe. This is expressed as 'son of', 'sons of' or 'house of'. As Porten and Yardeni have noted, these designations are helpful in understanding the prosopography of the individuals mentioned.[49]

The idea of tribal, clan or family identity is more complex than appears at first since it is difficult to determine whether the use of a theophoric was the most important factor, or even a factor at all, in maintaining ethnic boundaries, especially in a period of little stress or low boundary maintenance. As stated by McGuire, 'What is important to the maintenance of such boundaries is not the totality of cultural traits contained by them but those traits that the groups utilize as symbols of their identity separate from other groups'.[50] Hodder has shown in his research that under certain circumstances members of one tribe (read 'ethnic group') may move into areas inhabited by another tribe, wear the garb of that tribe, yet still retain their own ethnic identity.[51] This does not imply that ethnic identity symbols no longer existed, but rather that there was less of a need to display *certain* symbols, usually due to a relative lack of conflict or stress. Stone, for example, considers the acculturation or cultural changes undergone by the Philistines during the Iron Age II not as

---

47.   Eph'al and Naveh, *Aramaic Ostraca of the Fourth Century BC*, 15.
48.   A. Lemaire, *Nouvelles inscriptions araméennes d'Idumée du Musée d'Israel*, 145.
49.   Porten and Yardeni, 'In Preparation of a Corpus of Aramaic Ostraca from the Land of Israel', 211.
50.   McGuire, 'The Study of Ethnicity in Historical Archaeology', 160.
51.   Hodder, *Symbols in Action: Ethnoarchaeological Studies of Material Culture*, 24–31.

assimilation (meaning a total fusion into another identity) but rather as adaptation or modification of certain ethnic traits.[52]

In their study of 180 ostraca, Porten and Yardeni identified eight families or clans, although they took the liberty of combining certain names into larger categories.[53] They show that the names *Baalrim*, *Baalrum* and *Baarim* are mentioned in approximately 60–62 ostraca; *Guru*, *Gur* and *Gir* in 45, *Qosi* in 37–39, *Alba'al* in at least 18, *Y[eh]okal* in 18, *Hori* in two and *Rawi* in one.

In our database, we have identified 124 clan or intergenerational relationships, some of which overlap. The overlapping can be attributed to a number of causes ranging from scribal error, legibility of the ostraca today, or perhaps, since the majority of the ostraca are dockets and not formal letters, shorthand, nicknames or different expressions of the same entity made in antiquity. It should be noted that this analysis of the family/clan names has been done only in respect to their interrelationships. That is to say, this is an observational analysis of intergenerational interrelationships in order to better understand intercultural relationships/ barriers or the lack thereof.

The Clan of Ye[ho]kal

Porten and Yardeni list 17 (or 18) documents in which the name *Y[eh]okal* and its variant spellings (*Yehokal, Yokal, Yakal*) appears. Nine of these were among the published material initially included in the database; the remainder come from the Institute for the Study of Aramaic Papyri (ISAP) under the direction of Bezalel Porten, located at the Institute of Archaeology of the Hebrew University. While the majority of these ostraca are still unpublished, Porten and Yardeni recently published eight additional ostraca from the ISAP. They also mention receiving an additional ostracon with an Idumean theophoric in connection to *Ye[ho]kal* after the proof for their article was submitted.[54] These additional nine ostraca have been added to our database for a total of 18 ostraca associated with the clan of *Ye[ho]kal*. Four of these ostraca do not include ethnically identifiable names, but only mention the *Ye[ho]kal* clan and are therefore not listed.[55] Porten and Yardeni classify *Ye[ho]kal*

52.   B. Stone, 'The Philistines and Acculturation: Cultural Change and Ethnic Continuity in the Iron Age', *BASOR* 298 (1995), pp. 7–32.

53.   Porten and Yardeni, 'In Preparation of a Corpus of Aramaic Ostraca from the Land of Israel', 211.

54.   Porten and Yardeni, 'In Preparation of a Corpus of Aramaic Ostraca from the Land of Israel', 215.

55.   Porten and Yardeni, 'In Preparation of a Corpus of Aramaic Ostraca from the Land of Israel', 214–5.

as a Judahite name with biblical associations. *Ye[ho]kal* is possibly identified as the Judahite progenitor of the clan, but all the sons associated with him have non-Judahite names, some containing the Idumean theophoric *Qws*.

Table 2.2 The Ye[ho]kal Clan

Family Tie	Arab Names	Idumean Names	Egyptian Names	Total
House of *Yehokal*		3		3
House of *Yokal*	2	1		3
Son of *Yehokal*	1	1		2
Sons of *Yehokal*	1	2	2	5
Sons of *Yokal*		1		1
Total	4	8	2	14

This data indicates that 57% of the sons or members of this 'Judahite' clan had clearly Idumean names, 29% had Arabic or Nabataean names, 14% had Egyptian names and none carried a clearly Judahite name. The authors ask whether this is 'an isolated case of a Jew settled in the midst of pagan Idumeans who gave his children the names of his neighbours or must we understand the Idumean name differently from its Hebrew homonym?'[56] Indeed, was *Ye[ho]kal* a Judahite or an Idumean?

The question itself is very revealing. It suggests that it was theoretically possible that an Idumean could take on a Judahite name with its respective theophoric. This seems plausible only within an environment that showed no signs of heightened ethnocentrism and boundary maintenance by either ethnic group. However, while this is possible, it seems more likely that the family of *Ye[ho]kal* was part of the remnant of the post-collapse Judahite society whose members experienced what Hodder described (in an African context) as a yearning for support, protection, and aid and were therefore drawn towards a more dominant group.[57] Hodder also cites a number of examples of members of one ethnic group moving temporarily or permanently within the ranks of another group, especially during periods of low-level tensions; a situation that appears to have existed at this time in Idumea. The onomastic statistics from our database indicate a clear Idumean dominance and it appears reasonable to assume that *Ye[ho]kal* was a Judahite who was in the process of acculturation into the more dominant Idumean society. This would also depend upon the importance attached at that time to

56.   Porten and Yardeni, 'In Preparation of a Corpus of Aramaic Ostraca from the Land of Israel', 212.

57.   Hodder, *Symbols in Action: Ethnoarchaeological Studies of Material Culture*, 25–35.

theophoric names. Under the circumstances, it seems more than likely that the *Ye[ho]kal* clan had a Judahite patriarch whose members and offspring either chose to identify with or included a variety of ethnic groups and identities that were expressed in at least one identifiable manner, via theophoric names.

The Clan of Gur/Guru/Gir

Porten and Yardeni group several ostraca referring to the 'son', 'sons' or 'house of' the Western Semitic names *Gur*, *Guru* and *Gir* together and categorize them as a clan.[58] Of the 45 names they mention, 17 names are included in the database while the others remain unpublished by the ISAP. Nevertheless these 17 names are certainly a representative sample and are listed here in Table 2.3.

Table 2.3 The Clan of Gur/Guru/Gir

Family Ties	Arab Names	Idumean Names	Phoenician Names	Western Semitic Names	Total Names
House of *Gur*		1			1
Son of *Gur*		3		1	4
Son of *Guru*		1	1		2
Sons of *Gir*	1				1
Sons of *Gur*				3	3
Sons of *Guru*	4			2	6
Total	5	5	1	6	17

Five of the names are distinctly Idumean (*Qosram, Qoskahel, Qos-ḥanan, Alqos,* and *Qosmalek*), five are Arabic (*Ubaydu* three times, Mashru and *Ḥabutu*), six are Western Semitic and one is possibly Phoenician (*Baal*). Those ostraca that do not contain a combination of both a name and the family tie/clan are not represented in this sampling. A number of tentative conclusions can be reached from this data. Only 32% of the members or descendants of this clan or family had Western Semitic names while approximately 31% had Arabic names, 31% had Idumean names and only one, comprising of approximately 6% of the total, could be identified as Phoenician.

---

58.   Porten and Yardeni, 'In Preparation of a Corpus of Aramaic Ostraca from the Land of Israel', 211.

The Clan of Alba'al

The Phoenician family name *Alba'al* occurs over 18 times in the ostraca if one includes the unpublished material from ISAP.[59] It appears 13 times in the database, of which three are names that have not been identified with a specific ethnic group. Of the ten that are left, the breakdown is interesting: three Idumean names, two Arabic names, one Judahite, three Western Semitic names, and only one Phoenician name are identified with this 'Phoenician' clan.

The Clan of Baalrim/Baalrum/Baarim

According to Porten and Yardeni the largest clan is that of the Phoenician *Baalrim/Baalrum/Baarim*, including over 60 names. In our database only 14 names met the requirements of being an ethnically identifiable name connected to this clan. Of these seven (50%) were Arab names; four Idumean, one Egyptian, one Western Semitic and only one Phoenician name were also identified.

Conclusions

It is interesting to note that the largest clan, or the family with the most people connected to it, carried a Phoenician name: *Baalrim/Baalram/ Baarim*. The Phoenician clan of *Alba'al* is also highly represented. This suggests a strong Phoenician presence that goes beyond the normal transient mercantile remains and points to a significant ethnic component within the area. In addition, the only non-Aramaic language Persian-period ostraca in the database are two fourth century BCE Phoenician ostraca discovered at Mareshah. The behaviour of this group, at least as far as can be understood from this prosopography, is similar to that of other ethnic groups in Idumea. In all the clans studied, the majority of names do not reflect the same ethnicity (or theophoric) as that of the clan's founder.

Low Boundary Maintenance: The Relationship of the Name Qos-ḥanan to Different Clans or Families

In addition to analysing the data from the perspective of the inner makeup of the larger clans or families it is also worthwhile to look at the ethnic interrelationships through an onomasticon containing easily identifiable theophorics. A case in point is the relationship of different

---

59.   Porten and Yardeni, 'In Preparation of a Corpus of Aramaic Ostraca from the Land of Israel', 211.

clans or tribes to the Idumean name *Qos-ḥanan*. The name appears 20 times in the texts, four of which are associated with families or clans.[60] The earliest of these, from the mid-fourth century BCE, is related to the 'house of *Baalrim*'.[61] By the end of that century, we have evidence of two other persons bearing the name *Qos-ḥanan*: one connected to the 'house of *Gur*' and the other to the 'sons of *Qosi*'. Finally, Eph'al and Naveh interpret a fourth ostraca (their #153) as *Qos-ḥanan* 'son of *Qoskahel*'.[62] Judging by the Idumean theophoric *Qos*, the named individuals are probably Idumean. However, of the four family/clan affiliations revealed in these ostraca, only two can be said to be Idumean: 'son of *Qoskahel*' and 'sons of *Qosi*', while the other two can be ascribed to other groups, possibly Phoenician ('house of *Baalrim*') and Western Semitic ('house of *Gur*').

Low Boundary Maintenance in 3rd–2nd Century BCE *Mareshah*

It is elucidating to observe how this process played itself out in the prosopography of Mareshah during the following centuries, the 3rd–2nd centuries BCE. The Hellenistic-period 'Sidonian' tomb inscriptions at Mareshah include a clear mixture of intergenerational names.[63] The most famous inscription from the tomb states that: '*Apollophanes*, son of *Sesmaios*, thirty-three years chief of the Sidonians at Mareshah, reputed the best and most kin-loving of all those of his time; died having lived seventy-four years.' In addition to identifying the origin of the family buried here, this and other inscriptions that mention a number of *Apollophanes*' relatives that have been found in the tomb provide us with his prosopography.

Proper names combined with 'Apollo' were common among the Phoenicians. *Thus Apollophanes* is possibly a Phoenician name, connected with the Greek god Apollo. This man was the son of *Sesmaios*, identified as a Semitic name. Another inscription in the same tomb mentions the 'grave of *Sabo*, daughter of *Sesmaios*'. *Sabo*, apparently the sister of *Apollophanes*, bears a name that can be recognized as Idumean, Palmyrene or Nabataean. Nearby is another inscription, '(grave) of *Demetrios*, son of *Meerbal*'. *Demetrios* is the Hellenistic name given to the son of *Meerbal*, a Graecized form of the Phoenician name *Maherbaal*.

---

60. Porten and Yardeni, 'On Problems of Identity and Chronology in the Idumean Ostraca', 162–4.

61. Porten and Yardeni, 'On Problems of Identity and Chronology in the Idumean Ostraca', 163.

62. Eph'al and Naveh, *Aramaic Ostraca of the Fourth Century BC*, 72.

63. J. Peters and H. Thiersch, *Painted Tombs in the Necropolis of Marissa (Mareshah)* (London: Palestine Exploration Fund, 1905), pp. 38–41.

A fourth inscription refers to '*Qosnatanos*, son of *Ammoios*, son of *Sesmaios*'. In this instance we have the Idumean name *Qosnatanos* borne by a son of *Ammoios*, an Egyptian name that has also been found in Phoenician contexts, who is the grandson of the above-mentioned *Sesmaios*. Thus of the three children of the Semitic-named *Sesmaios*, one (*Sabo*) bore an Idumean/Palmyrene/Nabataean name, one (*Apollophanes*) a Phoenician name with a Greek theophoric and the third (*Ammoios*) an Egyptian/Phoenician name. To broaden the list of ethnic groups, the last example mentions '*Babas* (a Judahite name), son of *Qosnatanos* (an Idumean name), son of *Ammoios*' apparently the great-grandchild of the above-named *Sesmaios*.[64]

These examples from the 3rd–2nd century BCE have been cited to provide a historical context for the processes depicted in the database from the late fifth and the fourth centuries BCE in the same region. The ethnic groups described in Persian-period ostraca more than a century earlier continued to reside and acculturate throughout the Ptolemaic period and into at least the beginning of the Seleucid era. Coexistence between different ethnic groups under the Persians and later the Ptolemies did not provoke or generate a competitive atmosphere that would have resulted in ethnocentrism.[65] This is visible in the prosopography of the various ostraca and inscriptions.

The above data on the ethnic relations of Idumea in the Hellenistic period give us insight into where the ethnic interrelationships in the Persian period were leading. In order to gain a broader picture of these interrelationships we must examine other families/clans as well as the intergenerational name sequences at our disposal. Of the close to 1,300 names gathered in this study, 104 names can be connected to the prosopography of Idumea. An additional 16 names contain prosopographic information, but the ethnic identity of these names has not been identified.

Low Boundary Maintenance in 'Arab' Names

Table 2.4 below contains a list of 35 names that are identified as belonging to the Arab ethnic group and its associations (including Nabataean,

---

64. Peters and Thiersch, *Painted Tombs in the Necropolis of Marissa (Mareshah)*, 38–45.

65. Hodder, *Symbols in Action: Ethnoarchaeological Studies of Material Culture*, 22–35; McGuire, 'The Study of Ethnicity in Historical Archaeology', 168–73 ; F. Barth and D. Noel, 'Conceptual Frameworks for the Analysis of Race Relations: An Evaluation', *Social Forces* 50 (1972), pp. 333–48 (344); E. Bloch-Smith, 'Israelite Ethnicity in the Iron Age: Archaeology Preserves What is Remembered and What is Forgotten in Israel's History', *JBL* 122 (2003), pp. 401–25 (403–5); G. Emberling, 'Ethnicity in Complex Societies: Archaeological Perspectives', *Journal of Archaeological Research* 5 (1997), pp. 301–4.

Table 2.4 *List of Arab Names*

Ethnicity of Family Tie	Family Tie	Name
Arab	Son of *Idrah*, Son of *Abdba'ali*	*Zubaydou*
Arab	Son of *Ahou*	*Wahabou*
Arab	Son of *Samuk*	*Neqamou*
Arab	Son of *Samouk*	*Halfat*
Arab	Son of *Samuk*	*Amou*
Idumean	Son of *Qoskahel*	*Zubaydou*
Idumean	Son of *Qosi*	*Mashikou*
Idumean	Son of *Qosani*	*Abdou*
Idumean	Son of *Qosmal*	*Naharah*
Judahite	House of *Yokal*	*Zubaydu*
Judahite	Son of *Malkiyah*	*Zabidou*
Judahite	Sons of *Yehokal*	*Zabdidah*
Judahite	Son of *Shema'aya*	*Tubyau*
Judahite	Son of *Yehokal*	*Nutaynu*
Judahite	House of *Yokal*	*Habibu*
Phoenician	Sons of *Baalrim*	*Zubayd*
Phoenician	Sons of *Baalrim*	*Zebadmelek*
Phoenician	Sons of *Alba'al*	*Zabdi*
Phoenician	House of *Alba'al*	*Zabadi*
Phoenician	Son of *Baal*	*Neqarou*
Phoenician	Son of *Baalram*	*Malikou*
Phoenician	Son of *Baalram*	*Malikou*
Phoenician	Son of *Baalram*	*Malikou*
Phoenician	Son of *Baalram*	*Hamyou*
Phoenician	Son of *Baalsamek*	*Hagou*
Phoenician	Son of *Baalsamek*	*Hagigou*
Phoenician	Son of *Baalram*	*Amtou*
Phoenician	Son of *Azizu*	*Nahari*
Western Semitic	Sons of *Idrah, Baalrim, Hanzir, Abda*	*Zubaydou*
Western Semitic	Sons of *Guru*	*Ubaydu*
Western Semitic	Sons of *Guru*	*Ubaydu*
Western Semitic	Sons of *Gir*	*Ubaydu*
Western Semitic	Sons of *RWY*	*Shu'aydu*
Western Semitic	Sons of *Guru*	*Mashru*
Western Semitic	Sons of *Guru*	*Habutu*

Palmyrene and Qedarite). An additional six Arab names did not have an ethnic clan/family designation and therefore are not included.

What is noteworthy about these names is that although all are Arab their ethnic clan/family associations are quite varied. Four are connected to the Judahite House of *Yehokal* and two others with other Judahite clans. Four belong to Idumean clans/families, seven to Western Semitic clans/families and thirteen to Phoenician clans/families. Only five continue to belong to Arab clans. This pattern is indicative of the pervasive acculturation process that took place in late fourth-century BCE Idumea.

An investigation of the prosopography of *all* the other major ethnic groups listed in the charts below will give us a more comprehensive picture of the province.

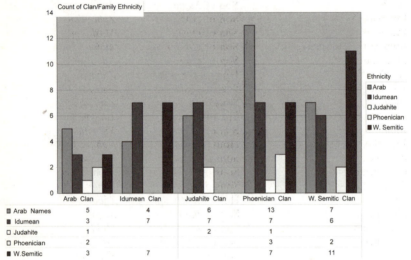

Table 2.5 Intergenerational/Familial Ties by Ethnic Groups

Table 2.6 Intergenerational/Familial Ties by Ethnic Groups in Absolute Numbers

Names	Arab Clans	Idumean Clans	Judahite Clans	Phoenician Clans	Western Semitic Clans	Total
Arab	5	4	6	13	7	35
Idumean	3	7	7	7	6	30
Judahite	1	0	2	1	0	4
Phoenician	2	0	0	3	2	7
W. Semitic	3	7	0	7	11	28
Total	14	18	15	31	26	104

Table 2.7 Intergenerational/Familial Ties by Ethnic Groups by
Percentages

Names	Arab Clans	Idumean Clans	Judahite Clans	Phoenician Clans	Western Semitic Clans	Total
Arab	14.29%	11.43%	17.14%	37.14%	20.00%	100%
Idumean	10.00%	23.33%	23.33%	23.33%	20.01%	100%
Judahite	25.00%	None	50.00%	25.00%	None	100%
Phoenician	28.57%	None	None	42.86%	28.57%	100%
W. Semitic	10.71%	25.00%	None	25.00%	39.29%	100%
Average	12.96%	17.59%	15.74%	29.63%	24.08%	100%

Initial Conclusions from the Epigraphic Evidence

From the data we have gathered it appears that there are many examples of intergenerational changes of names that reflect an atmosphere of low ethnic tension, which would be conducive for acculturation.

During the period under discussion, the disparity of power between the Idumeans, Judahites, Arabs, Phoenicians and others in Idumea was probably minimal and would have allowed a partial assimilation of cultures rather than a *Kulturkampf*, eliminating the need for the various groups to have demonstrative displays of separate identity symbols. This is reflected in many of the ostraca, in which ethnic distinctions are blurred.

These figures point to a process of intense integration. The majority of the second generation names are blended into a variety of ethnic affiliations with only a small percentage maintaining their progenitors' ethnic identity. This also suggests that these various ethnic groups resided in the area over a period of time, since the process of integration was not an instantaneous event but rather a slow process that took place over the course of at least a few generations. This is illuminating in that it has demographic implications *vis-à-vis* the region. The Judahite population may very well represent the descendants of the Iron Age Judahite population that did not perish, flee or suffer exile at the hands of the conquering Babylonians at the beginning of the sixth century BCE. References to this remnant may be what are referred to in Nehemiah 11.[66] Nevertheless the material remains at most excavated areas in the region testify to a gap in the sixth century BCE. Mareshah, Lachish, Tel Halif, Tel Arad, and Tel Beersheba indicate a settlement hiatus during this period, with a modest renewal occurring in the late fifth century BCE and

---

66. A. Rainey, 'The Biblical Shephelah of Judah', *BASOR* 251 (1983), pp. 1–22 (18).

accelerating slightly into the fourth century BCE. This is also reflected, according to the surveys of Ofer and Dagan, in the relatively high percentage of newly settled sites in the Persian period. The Arab population may represent an influx from the south, referred to in the Tell el-Maskhuta inscription (*Gashmu* the Qedarite, identified by some scholars as the Geshem mentioned in the book of Nehemiah).[67] Idumeans possibly represent those who gradually moved into the region after Nabonidus' conquest of Edom in 552 BCE.[68] What is very revealing is the information regarding the Phoenicians.

As shown above, the ethnic group that had the largest representation of clans was the Phoenicians. It should be noted that some of the families and names counted as Phoenician could be considered 'Western Semitic' since not all names with the theophoric *Ba'al* are automatically Phoenician, but they have, for the most part, been categorized as such in the database. Accepting the possibility of a certain margin of error, the Phoenicians still reflect the largest number of clans (31 out of 104).[69] This in itself is enlightening since it highlights a strong Phoenician presence in the region even before the time of *Apollophanes* of Mareshah in the third century BCE. Furthermore, since our ostraca date primarily from 363–311 BCE and it can be assumed that the integration process was not immediate, it is axiomatic to consider the possibility that the Phoenicians (as well as the other ethnic groups) began settling the region at least a generation or two earlier.

A number of scholars have pointed out that ethnicity must be regarded as a complex, dynamic, ever-changing and interactive multidimensional process.[70] In their view, ethnicity is a reflection of social interaction that

---

67.   I. Rabinowitz, 'Aramaic Inscriptions of the Fifth Century BCE from a North-Arab Shrine in Egypt', *JNES* 15 (1956), pp.1–9; W. J. Dumbrell, 'The Tell el-Maskhuta Bowls and the "Kingdom" of Qedar in the Persian Period', *BASOR* 203 (1971), pp. 33–44.

68.   S. Dalley and A. Goguel, 'The Sela' Sculpture: A Neo-Babylonian Rock Relief in Southern Jordan', *ADAJ* XLI (1997), pp. 169–76; P. Bienkowski, 'The Edomites: The Archaeological Evidence from Transjordan', in D. Edelman (ed.), *You Shall Not Abhor an Edomite for he is your Brother: Edom and Seir in History and Tradition* (Atlanta: Scholars Press, 1995), pp. 41–92 (60); A. Lemaire, 'Nabonidus in Arabia and Judah in the Neo-Babylonian Period', in Oded Lipschits and Joseph Blenkinsopp (eds), *Judah and the Judeans in the Neo-Babylonian Period* (Winona Lake: Eisenbrauns, 2003), pp. 285–98 (291); J. R. Bartlett, *Edom and the Edomites* (JSOTSup. 77; Sheffield: Sheffield Academic Press, 1989), pp. 148–61.

69.   Stern, 'Idumaea in the Persian Period', 72.

70.   M. Banks, *Ethnicity: Anthropological Constructions* (BAR International Series 87; London: Routledge, 1996), pp. 47–50; Hodder, *Symbols in Action: Ethnoarchaeological Studies of Material Culture*, 22–35; Z. Herzog and O. Bar Yosef, 'Different Views on Ethnicity in the Archaeology of the Negev', in E. Oren and S. Ahituv (eds) *Aharon Kempinski Memorial Volume: Studies in Archaeology and Related Disciplines* (Beer-sheva: Ben Gurion University of the Negev Press, 2002), pp. 151–81.

cannot be defined by a set of characteristics such as common language, territory, or shared biological origins but rather as a means by which groups adapt to shifting socio-environmental and socio-economic conditions.

It is clear from the epigraphic evidence cited above that ethnicity was not a constant attribute of the groups but perhaps reflects a conscious means by which individuals or clans freely chose to identify with a social unit for economic or social reasons (not necessarily known to us today). Theoretically, at a later date this interaction could be defined in more ideological terms, which may be inclusive or exclusive of others depending on the situation. Whether or not a group used its ethnicity as a means of exclusion or inclusion is difficult to ascertain from archaeological remains. As Herzog and Bar Yosef state: 'Ethnic, tribal, or national identities are social structures constructed in specific situations to serve economic, political, or cultural needs. In most cases, the population of a political unit consists of divergent ethnic elements, different social classes and varied life styles, stemming from diverse subsistence economy bases'.[71]

The behaviour of all of the ethnic groups examined above is generally consistent; there is almost a complete integration of ethnicities in Persian-period Idumea. Approximately 10% of the Idumean names are connected to an Arab clan or father, 23% to Judahites, 20% to Western Semites, 23% to Phoenicians and 24% to Idumeans. As with the Arab names, only a minority of this group showed ethnic continuity as expressed through their particular ethnic onomasticon. Each ethnic group eventually ceased to be a majority within their own clans; in other words, each ethnic group, for reasons still unknown to us, appears to have evolved into something different. The data related to the Phoenician families/clans is also instructive: almost 30% of the names in each of the ethnic groups represented in the region were somehow connected with a Phoenician clan/family. This warrants further investigation.

While our ostraca offer an important glimpse into this period in Idumea, the paucity of explicit epigraphic Idumean material makes it difficult to recreate the 'big picture' of the Idumeans' historical narrative. Bloch-Smith's example of the ethnogenesis of Iron Age I Israelite ethnicity is well taken.[72] Predicated upon Emberling's paradigm,[73] she reconstructs the evolution of early Israel from polytheism to monotheism that integrated new and different ethnicities within its new ethnos. In order

---

71. Herzog and Bar Yosef, 'Different Views on Ethnicity', 169.

72. Bloch-Smith, 'Israelite Ethnicity in the Iron Age', 401–425.

73. G. Emberling, 'Ethnicity in Complex Societies: Archaeological Perspectives', *Journal of Archaeological Research* 5/4 (1997), pp. 295–344 (301–4); see also P. Spickard and W. Burroughs, 'Introduction' in P. Spickard and W. Burroughs (eds), *We Are a People: Narrative and Multiplicity in Constructing Ethnic Identity* (Philadelphia: Temple University Press, 2000), pp. 8–9.

to better understand the pattern of acculturation within Idumea, we will now compare and contrast the patterns cited above concerning Idumea to those of two contemporary societies: *Yehud* to the north and Elephantine, far away to the south.

Comparison *to* Yehud

It seems clear that this phenomenon of acculturation or integration reflected in the ostraca in our database was not limited to the area of Idumea. Specifically, the biblical text makes it quite clear that fifth-century BCE *Yehud* and Samaria were experiencing similar processes regarding ethnic boundaries. Naveh and Magen mention a variety of ethnic names that appear in the onomasticon of Persian-period Samaria.[74] Zertal attributes the influx of different population groups to improved economic conditions.[75] Cross cites the fourth-century BCE papyri from Wadi Daliyeh that include Arabic, Idumean, Canaanite/Phoenician, Babylonian, Aramaic and of course Yahwistic names.[76] Many are identified by their respective theophoric elements. The fact that both Ezra and Nehemiah were involved in resolving issues of acculturation and intermarriage[77] is indicative of a process that appears to have been pervasive in the Levant at that time. It reflects, in fact, a contemporaneous process that the ostraca describe happening in Idumea. There was resistance to this process in *Yehud* at a certain point, at least by the appointed leadership and for a limited period of time. For this reason a closer look at the seemingly parallel events that were taking place in the province of *Yehud*, just north of Idumea, is warranted.

According to E. Stern, the seal impressions found in *Yehud* during the first half of the Persian period up to and including the time of Nehemiah (who took office in 445 BCE) were not distinguishable from the pagan motifs on seals discovered in other areas of the Persian Empire.[78] Stern maintains that the archaeological evidence in *Yehud* does not distinguish it from other provinces and therefore there is no evidence of *Yehud* even

---

74.   J. Naveh and I. Magen, 'Aramaic and Hebrew Inscriptions of the 2nd Century BCE at Mt. Gerezim', *Atiqot* 32 (1997), pp. 9–17.

75.   A. Zertal, 'The Pahwah of Samaria (Northern Israel) During the Persian Period: Types of Settlement, Economy, History and New Discoveries', *Transeuphratène* 3 (1990), pp. 9–30 (16).

76.   F. M. Cross, 'The Papyri and Their Historical Implications', *AASOR* 41 (1974), pp. 17–32 (20).

77.   Ezra 10.44; Nehemiah 13.23-31.

78.   E. Stern, 'Seal Impressions of the Achaemenid Style in the Province of Judah', *BASOR* 202 (1971), pp. 6–16.

functioning as a separate province at this time.[79] More importantly for our discussion, a process of integration and assimilation of cultures that was typical of provinces throughout the Persian Empire in general, and in Idumea in particular, was, according to the biblical text, also happening in *Yehud*. The biblical text relates that intermarriage was rampant; the situation resembled the conditions of a society with low ethnic boundary maintenance similar to Idumea at the time. Heltzer's analysis of a fifth-century BCE Babylonian tablet includes *Gadal(y)ama/Gedalyahu*, a clearly Yahwistic name, who is the son of *Banna-Ea*, a pagan name.[80] His claim that this was a well-known practice in Achaemenid Babylonia gives further context to this pattern of integration.

Archaeological remains in *Yehud* however, indicate that by the second half of the fifth century BCE, there was a change reflective of an internal striving to maintain continuity with the pre-exilic Kingdom of Judah. This manifested itself in the reintroduction of distinct identity symbols such as early royal emblems on stamps, ancient names on official weights (for example the 'shekel' symbol on weights and the rosette) and a revival of archaic Hebrew script.[81] Nostalgic reminders of the 'glory days gone by' that Tainter discusses are another characteristic of 'post-collapse societies'.[82] Variations of *yhd* stamps and coins in Aramaic and Hebrew script begin to emerge in places from Beth Zur to Tell en-Nasbeh and from Jericho and Ein Gedi to Gezer. It is Stern's contention that the appearance of the name *Yehud* on its coins and seals was an assertion of prominence and a renewal of national pride that was unusual at that

---

79. E. Stern, 'The Province of Yehud: the Vision and the Reality', in L. I. Levine (ed.), *The Jerusalem Cathedra* (Jerusalem: Yad Yitzhak Ben Zvi, 1981), pp. 9–21 (14–15). (The idea that Judah was annexed to Samaria and was not a province until the governorship of Nehemiah originated with Alt and has since been adopted by some and rejected by many. See: A. Alt, 'Die Rolle Samarias bei der Entstehung des Judentums', *Kleine Schriften* II (Munich, 1953), pp. 316–37. P. Briant, *From Cyrus to Alexander: A History of the Persian Empire* (trans. Peter T. Daniels; Winona Lake: Eisenbrauns, 2002), p. 47. For the opposite position see: S. E. McEvenue, 'The Political Structure in Judah from Cyrus to Nehemiah', *CBQ* 43 (1981), pp. 353–64 and more recently J. W. Betlyon, 'Neo-Babylonian Military Operations Other Than War in Judah and Jerusalem', in Oded Lipschits and Joseph Blenkinsopp (eds), *Judah and the Judeans in the Neo-Babylonian Period* (Winona Lake: Eisenbrauns, 2003), pp. 263–83 (267); for a summary of the debate see H. G. M. Williamson, *Ezra and Nehemiah* (Old Testament Guides; Sheffield: JSOT Press, 1987), pp. 48–50; L. S. Fried, 'The Political Struggle of Fifth Century Judah', *Transeuphratène* 24 (2002), pp. 9–21 (10) and citations there.

80. M. Heltzer, 'A Recently Published Babylonian Tablet and the Province of Judah after 516 BCE', *Transeuphratène* 5 (1992), pp. 58–61.

81. E. Stern, *Archaeology of the Land of the Bible, Vol. II: The Assyrian, Babylonian, and Persian Periods* (ABRL; New York: Doubleday, 2001), pp. 332–9.

82. J. Tainter, 'Post-Collapse Societies', 1025; Faust, 'Social and cultural Changes in Judah during the 6th Century BCE', 168 (my thanks to Dr Avraham Faust for his valuable comments and suggestions on this subject.)

time in Persian provinces.[83] I believe that this rise in ethnic awareness should be understood in the context of Samaritan-Jewish tensions.

The political tensions between Samaria and *Yehud* were expressed to some degree with the ethnic symbols mentioned above; the concomitant ethnic boundaries becoming more and more prevalent as political tensions increased. The biblical text of both Ezra and Nehemiah provide numerous examples of this. The rejection of the Samaritan offers to help rebuild the wall (Nehemiah 2.19-20), rebuild the altar (Ezra 3.1-3), or rebuild the temple (Ezra 4.1-24) and the subsequent Samaritan reaction to this rejection, were all clear attempts at establishing boundaries between the Judahites and other ethnic groups residing near them. Klein has suggested that these 'other groups' may have included Idumeans and others,[84] while Breneman states that these enemies are from Ashdod, Samaria, Moab and Edom.[85] What seems apparent is that *Yehud*, like many other provinces, was a heterogeneous society at the beginning of the Persian period, containing many ethnic groups, and that under the leadership of Ezra and Nehemiah there was an attempt to transform *Yehud* into a monolithic community. Klein understands Nehemiah 2.20 as stating that non-members will have no political share in the new society,[86] and Blenkinsopp argues that this may have been a declaration of political, economic and religious independence from their neighbours.[87] Nehemiah's and Ezra's attempts at imposing Sabbath observance, along with Ezra's banishment of 'foreign' wives (Ezra 9.1–10.44; Nehemiah 13.1-3, 23-28) should be understood in this light as well. Statements such as 'You have nothing in common with us' (Ezra 4.3), or 'the sons of Israel who returned from exile and all those who had *separated* themselves from the impurity of the nations . . .' (Ezra 6.21) are clearly aimed at separation. In short, this behaviour reflects high ethnic boundary maintenance that was predicated on political tensions between the Judahites and their neighbours.

A closer analysis of the biblical evidence suggests varied opinions concerning relations with Samaria. The minimal information available suggests that both Nehemiah and the editor of Ezra 1–6 were hostile towards the Samaritans.[88] Eshel, however, notes that the Chronicler wrote sympathetically of the Samaritans in the fourth century BCE; at the same

83. Stern, *Archaeology of the Land of the Bible*, 562–70.

84. R. Klein, 'The Books of Ezra and Nehemiah', in L. Kech (ed.), *The New Interpreter's Bible* 3 (Nashville: Abingdon Press, 1999), pp. 661–852 (691).

85. M. Breneman, *Ezra, Nehemiah, Esther* (New American Commentary 10; Nashville: Broadman and Holman, 1993), pp. 192–6.

86. Klein, 'The Books of Ezra and Nehemiah', 761.

87. J. Blenkinsopp, *Ezra-Nehemiah* (Philadelphia; Westminster Press, 1988), pp. 226–7.

88. H. G. M. Williamson, *Ezra, Nehemiah* (WBC 16; Waco: Word Books, 1985), p. 36, dates most of the book of Nehemiah to the last third of the fifth century BCE.

time that Ezra 1–6 was written.[89] Governor Bagoas, whom Eshel believes took over for Nehemiah after the latter returned to Babylon, had cordial relations with Samaria, which is reflected in his co-ordinating political issues with Deliah, son of Sanballat I, governor of Samaria.[90] Eliashib, the high priest at the time of Nehemiah, married his son to the daughter of Sanballat I (Nehemiah13.29). The high priest obviously did not seem to perceive the Samaritan as a 'foreigner'. Nehemiah 13.23, when listing the 'foreign' women that the Judahites were forbidden to marry, includes the women of Ashdod, Ammon and Moab, but not those of Samaria.

Eshel suggests that the sensitivity of the issue of mixed marriages may be derived from the collective experience of the Babylonian exile, a perspective represented by Nehemiah but which was not necessarily shared by those who had never left.[91] Furthermore, Eshel implies that the grouping of Philistines, Edomites and Samaritans together negatively in Obadiah 1.19 may mean that these ethnic groups were perceived to have taken over territories that formerly belonged to Judah.

The epigraphic material from Elephantine suggests that the Jewish colony there had good relations with Bagohi governor of *Yehud* and with Deliah of Samaria. Deliah and Bagohi answered the Judahites of Elephantine together in 407 BCE. This was done despite the fact that the high priest in *Yehud* had chosen to ignore the questions sent from Elephantine indicating differences of opinion in Jerusalem, not only concerning Elephantine but probably also concerning Samaria.[92] In any case, Nehemiah's reforms were evidently not totally successful. It is possible that the choice of Bagohi as governor by the Persian authorities was a deliberate one in order to fit better into their inclusive *Weltanschauung* more than the exclusive philosophy promulgated by Ezra and Nehemiah.[93]

The vacillation of positions by the leadership of *Yehud* towards the Samaritans can be understood better if we divide their arguments into those who favoured isolation, including ethnic boundaries, versus those who were in favour of low boundary maintenance. Eshel cites Nehemiah 9 and Psalms 20, suggesting that both were written north of *Yehud* and adapted by writers in Jerusalem during this period, indicating the possibility of literary connections or co-operation between scribes and writers in both *Yehud* and Samaria. According to both Mildenberg and

---

89. H. Eshel, 'The Samaritans in the Persian and Hellenistic Periods: The Origins of Samaritanism' (unpublished doctoral dissertation, Hebrew University in Jerusalem, 1994), p. 61. See also M. Mor, *From Samaria to Shechem: The Samaritan Community in Antiquity*, (Zalman Shazar Center, Jerusalem, 2003), pp. 33–53 (Hebrew).

90. Eshel, 'The Samaritans in the Persian and Hellenistic Periods', 7.

91. Eshel, 'The Samaritans in the Persian and Hellenistic Periods', 61.

92. Eshel, 'The Samaritans in the Persian and Hellenistic Periods', 68.

93. Eshel, 'The Samaritans in the Persian and Hellenistic Periods', 67.

Meshorer, the earliest *Yehud* coins date to 360–350 BCE.[94] The earliest coins from Samaria date to ca. 400.[95] Although both Samaria and *Yehud* were among the few provinces in the Fifth Satrapy to have provincial coins,[96] some of which contained clear ethnic symbols, the numismatic evidence from the fourth century BCE shows no economic ties between the two provinces. No Samarian coins have been found in *Yehud* nor have *Yehud* coins been found in the two hoards discovered in Samaria (with a total of 1,299 coins), even though the treasury of Shechem did include three coins from distant Anatolia.[97] The tension between the two provinces was such that by the late Persian period it is believed that there were virtually no economic ties between them.

Eshel claims that this breakdown in relations may be a reaction to the fact that the Samaritans at this point decided to build a temple on Mt Gerizim, a structure that would compete with that in Jerusalem. He believes that 2 Kings 17.24-33 was added in at this time and edited back to the eighth century BCE.[98] Thus, while there appear to have been ties and communication between Samaria and *Yehud* during the fifth century BCE, by the fourth century this was no longer the case.

The case of the relationship between *Yehud* and Samaria is illuminating on a number of levels. First, the initiatives of Ezra and Nehemiah reflect a reaction to a situation in *Yehud* that Barth describes as a process of identification and differentiation.[99] Their opposition to the process of integration that was happening in *Yehud* is also instructive. The interruption of this process during the time of Ezra and Nehemiah may have reflected the ideology of the 'returnees': the perspective of people who had roots as a minority in Babylon and whose group identity was threatened by the low boundary maintenance they observed in *Yehud*. This perspective was poignantly different from that of those who had never been in exile. As shown above, it was not surprising, despite all the efforts of Ezra and Nehemiah, that not all of their initiatives reached fruition. Tendencies to keep ethnic barriers low were consistent until the fourth century BCE. Nevertheless, by the fourth century, perhaps abetted

94. L. Mildenberg, 'Yehud – A Preliminary Study of the Provincial Coinage of Judaea', in O. Morkholm and N. Waggoner (eds), *Greek Numismatics and Archaeology: Essays in honor of Margaret Thompson* (Wetteren: Numismatique Romaine, 1979), pp. 183–96 (183–90); Y. Meshorer, *Ancient Jewish Coinage: The Persian Period to the Hasmoneans* (New York: Amphora Books, 1982), pp. 17–18.

95. Y. Meshorer and S. Qedar, *Samarian Coinage* (Jerusalem: Israel Numismatic Society, 1999), p. 17.

96. Stern, *Archaeology of the Land of the Bible*, 565–70; I. Eph'al, 'Changes in Palestine during the Persian Period in Light of Epigraphic Sources', *IEJ* 48 (1998), pp. 106–19.

97. Eshel, 'The Samaritans in the Persian and Hellenistic Periods', 71.

98. Eshel, 'The Samaritans in the Persian and Hellenistic Periods', pp.71–2.

99. F. Barth, *Ethnic Groups and Boundaries*, 9–38.

by the construction of an alternative shrine that could theoretically compete with Jerusalem, the rift or barriers that Ezra and Nehemiah strove to establish had certainly been created.

Comparison to Elephantine (Yeb)

The other contemporary community that can be compared to Idumea is the Jewish military colony at Elephantine, also known as *Yeb*. This community in Upper Egypt left a large corpus of Aramaic epigraphic material that reflects the same time period but very different circumstances. The majority of the Aramaic papyri were written at the turn of the 6th–5th century BCE; the latest date from 407–400 BCE. Unlike most of the ostraca found in Idumea, these were documents written by skilled scribes who wrote for a variety of peoples living in Elephantine.[100]

The Jewish community in Elephantine was a small minority residing in a far-off land, representing and simultaneously dependent upon the foreign ruling power, Persia. Its primary function as a military colony lay in defending the interests of the Persian overlords. While there was interaction with other ethnic groups on different levels, including commercial ties, the main identity symbols of the community were not infringed upon. Observance of the Sabbath and Passover, the worship of *Yhw* as well as the community's onomasticon testify to the apparent importance of these symbols. The events at the end of the fifth century BCE, when the Elephantine temple was destroyed by the priests of the local god Khnum were a prelude to the final destruction of the community as a whole (and for that matter the parallel Arab military colony at Tell el-Maskhuta). These events may reflect, to some extent, the relations that had previously existed between these foreign communities and the local Egyptians and their leadership.

While there was clearly interaction between the colony and the indigenous population, there were also definite barriers, and this is strongly expressed in the onomasticon of the community. Johnson points out that wherever there is sufficient information regarding the ethnic identity of people in Persian-period Egypt, the various communities, including that of Elephantine, were seen as being comprised of a mix of different ethnic groups.[101] She goes on to suggest that some people may have taken on dual ethnic identities, taking on one or the other depending on their specific contexts.

In Elephantine, of the 160 different names of Judahites, only a few were

---

100. B. Porten, *The Elephantine Papyri in English*, 74–84.

101. J. H. Johnson, 'Ethnic Considerations in Persian Period Egypt', in E. Teeter and J. Larson (eds), *Gold of Praise: Studies on Ancient Egypt in Honor of Edward F. Wente* (Chicago: University of Chicago Oriental Institute, 1999), pp. 211–22 (218).

non-theophoric.[102] The rest contained the *Yhw* theophoric almost exclusively.

The propensity to use Hebrew names was so great that Porten stated that if both the praenomen and patronymic were not Hebrew it could be assumed that the person was most likely pagan.[103] Approximately 60 non-Hebrew names are known from these papyri and approximately 15 people who bore non-Hebrew names had children with Hebrew names. The assumption is that these were probably non-Judahites who married Judahites and assimilated into the Jewish community. In 12 instances the parent had a Hebrew name while the child did not: Porten suggests this may reflect the parent marrying a non-Judahite spouse.

In a number of cases Porten was able to reconstruct three generations of names in a family. Unlike the processes that we saw in Idumea or *Yehud*, Porten discerned from the onomasticon of Elephantine that the vast majority of Jewish parents gave their children Hebrew names, while Persian parents gave their children Persian names. Aramaeans, on the other hand, tended to give their offspring very mixed names ranging from Egyptian to Akkadian to Aramaic. The one Egyptian name discovered amongst the 65 Jewish document witnesses is probably a result of intermarriage; a person by the name of *Petekhnum*, the father of Hosea, married a Jewish woman.[104] It is interesting to note that the epigraphic material reflects that no Jewish sons had Egyptian names.

From the above discussion, one can conclude that there was a high level of boundary maintenance by the Elephantine Jewish community, by the indigenous population or by both. Ray states that while most immigrant or foreign groups living in Persian-period Egypt assimilated into Egyptian society, the Jewish community was a major exception.[105] The picture, however, is even more complex. While the Jewish community apparently maintained clear ethnic boundary symbols, it also expressed a few syncretistic elements in its identity, which Porten concludes was inevitable in light of the intense social contact they had with their non-Jewish neighbours and their occasional intermarriages. In such cases it is plausible to assume that the spouse that 'converted' would have brought some elements of their former religion with them. A case in point was the collection of monies by the leader of the community *Jedaniah* from members of the Jewish community and distributing these funds to both

---

102.   B. Porten, *Archives from Elephantine* (Berkeley: University of California Press, 1968), pp. 133–5.

103.   Porten, *Archives from Elephantine*, 148–50.

104.   B. Porten, *The Elephantine Papyri in English*, 85.

105.   J. D. Ray, 'Jews and Other Immigrants in Late Period Egypt', in J. H. Johnson (ed.), *Life in a Multi Cultural Society: Egypt from Cambyses to Constantine and Beyond* (Studies in Ancient Civilization 51; Chicago: University of Chicago Oriental Institute, 1992), p. 273.

Yhw and to two other deities. Porten cautiously extrapolates that this may imply Jewish communal worship of both *Anathbethel* and *Eshembethel* alongside the worship of *Yhw*.[106] Reference to the worship of the 'Queen of Heaven' in Jeremiah (7.16; 44.15) may later have become that of Anath or the syncretized Anathyahu. While oaths may have been sworn to Anathyahu, her importance, judged from the onomastic absence, was less communal and perhaps more domestic.

In summation, unlike Idumea, and for that matter fifth-century BCE *Yehud*, there was minimal acculturation in the Elephantine community. The very different circumstances caused the members of the community to maintain the ethnic barriers that separated them from the other inhabitants in the region. In Elephantine it appears the nature of the community caused it to define itself in opposition to the sometimes hostile indigenous population, while at times adopting and adapting some of the local traditions.

Conclusions

It should be remembered that Judah's conquest by the Babylonians in 586 BCE was followed by Nabonidus' conquest of Edom on his campaign into Arabia in 552 BCE. While this paper is not concerned with the developments in Edom proper, the upheavals cited above would have certainly also affected those Edomites who had immigrated into Southern Judah. It seems probable that after these groups had been defeated any disparity of power between the two ethnic groups would have been negligible. Hence, using McGuire's paradigm, the relationship between Judahites and Idumeans (and for that matter any other ethnic groups still residing in the area) at this point would not have manifested itself in strong, well-defined borders. A glance at the archaeological remains north of Beth Zur reflects a similar post-collapse scenario. In fact all groups in the region would have existed in a post-collapse situation. Moreover, the drastic decrease in populations following these conquests and destruction would have been such as to create a non-competitive atmosphere *vis-à-vis* the resources. This most likely applied to the ethnic interrelationships within Idumea throughout the period and perhaps even between the two provinces until the fourth century BCE. The archaeological evidence for the 6th–5th centuries shows that the area was sparsely populated. There does not seem to be any distinctly ethnic ceramic repertoire, the Persian-period material continuing for the most part the late Iron Age traditions and/or imitating various imports.[107] Distinctly ethnic linguistic elements,

106. Porten, *Archives from Elephantine*, 173–9.
107. Stern, *Archaeology of the Land of the Bible*, 516.

figurines, and even ceramic material are not for the most part distinguishable.

It is interesting to consider the observations made at Lachish where the bulk of the pottery in stratum I was attributed primarily to the Late Persian period of the fourth century BCE. Fantalkin and Tal relate that 'the appearance of "coastal" types at the site, together with the high occurrence of different pottery types, may also indicate a 4th century BCE date, *a time when regional frontiers in terms of material culture (especially pottery) were blurred*' (italics mine).[108] Their observation at Lachish reinforces the epigraphic information described earlier.

From an administrative point of view, it is very possible that in the beginning of the Persian period the area we term Idumea was not yet organized as a province and certain territories were simply under the control or influence of the Qedarites. Written reference to the Qedarites was discovered in Subterranean Complex 128 at Mareshah where Qedarites are mentioned in an ostracon.[109] They appear as part of a list that also includes the 'sons of *ZRD*', which is the ancient name of what is now called the Wadi al-Hasi on the border between Moab and Edom, that Eshel suggests may be these people's place of origin.[110] The Qedarite influence and possible control of the region was related to the assistance these people gave to Cambyses during his campaign into Egypt in 525 BCE. Their area of influence may have included the poorly populated Negev, a wilderness that was seemingly unimportant and contained very few settlements.[111] The primary concern of the ruling Persians would have been to maintain the lucrative trade routes, a concern that was mutually beneficial to both them and the Arab Qedarites.

It appears that political circumstances in the mid-fifth century BCE caused the central government to become more involved in the Negev and the southern Shephelah. At that time Egypt successfully rebelled against Persia; it would be several decades before Persia re-established permanent control. During this period, the southern Levant was an imperial frontier and would have been the logical location for the concentration of invasion and supply efforts for Persian military campaigns launched against

108.   A. Fantalkin and O. Tal, 'Persian and Hellenistic Pottery of Level I', in D. Ussishkin (ed.), *Lachish IV* (Tel Aviv: Tel Aviv University Institute of Archaeology, 2004), pp. 2174–96 (2188).

109.   In an area I excavated, by the author of this article; information on the ostracon from personal communication with Esther Eshel.

110.   Personal communication.

111.   Lipschits, 'Demographic Changes in Judah between the Seventh and the Fifth Centuries BCE', 355–66; C. H. de Geus, 'Idumaea', *Jaarbericht Van Het Vooraziatisch-Egyptisch Genootschap Ex Oriente Lux* 26 (1980), pp. 53–74 (71). Also see Y. Levin's article in this volume.

Egypt.[112] The Egyptians successfully revolted again at the beginning of the fourth century BCE and temporarily took over parts of the southern Levant. At Gezer a broken stone tablet with the name of Pharaoh Nepherites I (399–393) was found by Macalister.[113] This Egyptian success may have been made easier due to the civil war in Persia, and facilitated by Athenian help. The Persians eventually regained control over the area and renewed investment in the defences and infrastructure of the region. These included supply depots that were established enroute to Egypt for the Persian army. In general, it seems that the fourth century BCE was a period of economic expansion in the region.[114]

The preponderance of Phoenician family/clan names in the ostraca strongly suggests that Phoenicians played a central role in the region. Three of the most commonly found storage jars from this period discovered at Mareshah were prevalent in Persian-period Ashkelon, and called 'Phoenician jars' by the excavator.[115] 70 to 80 per cent of the storage jars found at Ashkelon were similar to a twisted-handled jar found at Mareshah.[116] Historical sources also relate that the Phoenicians, especially from Sidon and Tyre, had been given control of a number of coastal cities in return for abetting the Persians with their fleet,[117] and epigraphic sources (see pseudo-Scylax and the Eshmun'ezer inscription),[118] confirm that the transition from residing in coastal areas to residence further inland was widespread.

The epigraphic finds from Idumea can give us insight into the social norms of the period. These norms can be better understood as reflecting a more universal process that was also transpiring in *Yehud* and Samaria as well. This in turn can help us understand the biblical description of the Jewish population's shift from low to high ethnic boundary maintenance within the *Yehud* province. As stated by Hodder: 'where there is strong competition there is a corresponding increase in the marking of boundaries'.[119] Cultural differences are maintained or created in order to insure security and justify competitive access to resources. When there

112. W. Bennett and J. Blakely, *Tell el Hesi: Persian Period (Stratum V)* (Eisenbrauns, Winona Lake, 1989) pp. 354–5.

113. Stern, *Archaeology of the Land of the Bible*, 439–41.

114. A. Fantalkin and O. Tal, 'Redating Lachish Level I: Identifying Achaemenid Imperial Policy at the Southern Frontier of the Fifth Satrapy', in O. Lipschits and M. Oeming (eds), *Judah and the Judeans in the Persian Period* (Winona Lake, Eisenbrauns, 2006), pp. 167–98 (177–90); Stern, *Archaeology of the Land of the Bible*, 581–2.

115. Stern, 'Idumaea in the Persian Period', 91, as well as personal communications from Amos Kloner, Adi Ehrlich and Ross Voss.

116. Amos Kloner, Adi Ehrlich and Ross Voss, personal communication.

117. Stern, *Archaeology of the Land of the Bible*, 580–1.

118. L. Grabbe, *A History of the Jews and Judaism in the Second Temple Period* 1 (London: T & T Clark International, 2004), pp. 64, 159–62.

119. Hodder, *Symbols in Action: Ethnoarchaeological Studies of Material Culture*, 28–30.

is a relative lack of conflict, as was the case within Idumea, there is less of a need to display clear identity symbols.

The process whereby shared interests that are often economic or political can cause unrelated clans or groups to amalgamate into an ethnic nucleus is referred to as 'ethnogenesis'[120]. This process is given legitimacy by creating a common ancestry which incorporates normative behaviour and defines it as tradition; a process referred to as an 'ideology of authenticity'. New institutions are invented to perpetuate the group after the original purpose fades; these institutions continue to function in order to maintain the cultural norms of the group. Groups incorporate circumstantial features into their collective consciences creating 'collective memories'.

While the onomasticon of Idumea allows us certain insights into the ethnic makeup of the region, the actual epigraphic corpus is too small to allow for a *detailed* reconstruction of what we, using Bloch-Smith's terminology, might call 'the Idumean ethnogenesis'. The fact that the province of Idumea was clearly recognized as such by Diodorus Siculus (Diodorus 19.25.2) in the Ptolemaic period allows one to infer that it was during the Persian period that the various ethnic groups amalgamated into an Idumean identity. This affiliation would have been founded upon a common deity (*Qws*), a common territory (Idumea), and possibly certain 'collective memories' that would eventually (probably in the late Hellenistic period, perhaps after their conversion in the time of John Hyrcanus) be created in order to connect this ethnic group to Abraham and Esau, legitimizing the group's past whether imagined or real. This may have become part of the self-perception of those zealous 'Idumeans' in later centuries. It is not surprising however to see that there is a clear correlation between the provenance of ethno-cultural names and the geographic-territorial regions. Most of the names from Idumea are Idumean and Arab while those from *Yehud* are Jewish and those from the coastal plain are Phoenician.

From our investigation of ethnic boundaries in fourth-century BCE Idumea, it would seem that this period witnessed the ethnogenesis of the Idumeans. While it is outside the scope of this paper, it would seem that the same process was also happening in Samaria and to a lesser extent even in *Yehud*.

The comparison to Elephantine is also significant. There the ethnic interaction between Judahites and Egyptians was very tense, reflecting a situation of high ethnic boundary maintenance that resulted in limited acculturation (at least as reflected in the onomasticon).

---

120. E. Bloch-Smith, 'Israelite Ethnicity in the Iron Age', 403.

Chapter 10

THE SOUTHERN FRONTIER OF *YEHUD* AND THE CREATION OF IDUMEA

Yigal Levin

The two-and-a-half centuries beginning with the Neo-Babylonian take-
over of the Levant in 605 BCE and ending with the region's conquest by
Alexander in 333 BCE were a time of huge changes. These changes were
manifest in the region's geopolitics, administration, demography, society,
economics, settlement patterns and in the ethnic composition and self-
identification of the inhabitants of the region. The Neo-Babylonian
empire completed the process of dismantlement of the Iron Age kingdoms
that was begun by the Assyrians; the Persians allowed some of the region's
states a measure of autonomy under local kings (as in the case of the
Phoenicians), priests (as in the case of the Jews, at least during part of the
period),[1] or governors, some of whom were chosen from the local
population. Populations shifted, some states were given preferential status
or granted land by the Persian kings, administrative units were combined
or separated, at times in accordance with the needs or wishes of the local
population and its leaders, at other times despite their wishes. We,
however, must remember, that whether the locals liked the changes or not,
the paramount consideration was that of the needs, real or perceived, of
the imperial administration. Like any empire, the Persians wished to
conquer, to rule, and to collect taxes that enriched the royal coffers and
those of the regional and local satraps, and they wished to do so with a
minimum expenditure of efforts and resources. All other considerations
were secondary.

The purpose of this paper is to trace the geopolitical and administrative
changes on the southern border of the province of Judah, or *Yehud*,
during this period, and to connect those changes to the creation of what
would become Judah's southern neighbour, the '*hyparchia*' of Idumea,
which, at least during the Early Hellenistic, or Ptolemaic, period, included

---

1. *Contra* the opinion expressed by L. S. Fried, *The Priest and the Great King: Temple-
Palace Relations in the Persian Empire* (Winona Lake: Eisenbrauns, 2004), pp. 227–33.

the southern part of the hill-country and the Shephelah, as well as parts of the Negeb.

Since we do not possess a single written document that specifically describes the administrative history of the area during the Neo-Babylonian and Persian periods, we must, of necessity, turn to the various other sources that are available to us: sources that inform us about the region in previous and in subsequent periods, as well as relevant archaeological and epigraphic evidence.

As all of our sources seem to indicate, the southern frontier of the kingdom of Judah during the late seventh and early sixth centuries BCE ran approximately from the southern tip of the Dead Sea, through the Ascent of Akrabbim and the wilderness of Zin, and then in a northwestern direction towards the Mediterranean Sea, meeting the boundaries of the Philistine city-states Gaza and Ashkelon along the way.[2] Its southern point was at Kadesh-barnea, usually identified with the oasis of 'En el-Qudeirat and the nearby 'En el-Qudeis, first visited in 1842 by John Rowland.[3] A large Iron Age II-Persian period fortress, apparently a part of the southern defenses of the kingdom of Judah, was excavated by Dothan in 1956 and then again by Cohen in 1972–82.[4] This southern border is recorded as that of 'the Land of Canaan' in Num. 34.3-5 and as that of 'the inheritance of Judah' in Josh. 15.2-5.[5] The ostraca discovered at Arad prove that that site was an important post on the southern frontier during the final days of the Judahite kingdom,[6] one of a series of such fortified sites.[7]

To the south and east of that boundary, lay the kingdom of Edom. While Edomite origins may be obscure,[8] the existence of an independent Edomite kingdom during the late Iron Age (the seventh and sixth

2. For which see N. Na'aman, 'The Boundary System and Political Status of Gaza under the Assyrian Empire', *ZDPV* 140 (2004), pp. 55–72 (60–4).

3. For the story of its discovery see H. C. Trumbull, *Kadesh Barnea: Its Importance and Probable Site* (London: Hodder & Stoughton, 1884), pp. 237–99, and Y. Roman, 'The Kadesh Controversy', *Eretz Magazine* 3.2 (1988), pp. 45–57.

4. M. Dothan, 'The Fortress at Kadesh Barnea', *IEJ* 15 (1965), pp. 134–51; R. Cohen, *Kadesh Barnea – A Fortress from the Time of the Judean Kingdom* (Jerusalem: The Israel Museum, 1983).

5. For the interrelationship of these two texts and their dating to this period see Y. Levin, 'Numbers 34.2-12, The Boundaries of the Land of Canaan and the Empire of Necho', *JANES* 30 (2006), pp. 55–76.

6. Y. Aharoni, *Arad Inscriptions* (Jerusalem: Israel Exploration Society, 1981), pp. 141–51.

7. I. Beit Arieh, 'The Edomites in Cisjordan', in D. Edelman (ed.), *You Shall Not Abhor an Edomite for he is your Brother: Edom and Seir in History and Tradition* (Atlanta: Scholars Press, 1995), pp. 33–40 (35).

8. For an in-depth discussion see J. R. Bartlett, *Edom and the Edomites* (JSOTSup. 77; Sheffield: Sheffield Academic Press, 1989), pp. 67–145.

centuries BCE) is attested in the Bible, in contemporary Assyrian inscriptions, in a small number of seal impressions mentioning kings of Edom, in a few of the Arad ostraca and by what seems to be a distinctive Edomite material culture, on both sides of the Arabah valley.[9]

The border, of course, was not sealed, and there is ample evidence of Edomite settlement in the Negeb as early as the seventh century.[10] It would seem that a sizeable Edomite population lived within southern Judah by this time,[11] perhaps worshipping at the shrine at Qitmit, southwest of Arad,[12] as well as that at 'En Ḥaṣeva.[13] At some point, the Judahites came to view these Edomites as 'invaders' and their country of origin as 'the enemy'.[14]

The kingdom of Judah was abolished by the Neo-Babylonians in several stages over the first two decades of the sixth century BCE. After the destruction of Jerusalem and the death of Zedekiah in 586, the Babylonians chose to transform the country into a province, to construct a new capital at Mizpah and to appoint a local nobleman, Gedaliah, as governor. According to the view expressed most recently by Lipschits, this arrangement was kept in place even after Gedaliah's assassination and into the Persian period.[15] The alternative view, proposed by Alt,[16] is that the province was abolished and annexed to Samaria, to be re-established

9.   P. Bienkowski, 'The Edomites: The Archaeological Evidence from Transjordan', in D. Edelman (ed.), *You Shall Not Abhor an Edomite for he is your Brother: Edom and Seir in History and Tradition* (Atlanta: Scholars Press, 1995), pp. 41–92; I. Beit Arieh, *Horvat Qitmit: An Edomite Shrine in the Biblical Negev* (Tel Aviv: Tel Aviv University, 1995).

10.   Beit Arieh, 'The Edomites in Cisjordan'; idem, 'Judean-Edomite Rivalry in the Negev', *Qadmoniot* 36 (126) (2003), pp. 66–76 (Hebrew). For the problematic definition of 'borders' in the reality of the biblical world see J. W. Rogerson, 'Frontiers and Borders in the Old Testament', in E. Ball (ed.), *In Search of True Wisdom: Essays in Old Testament Interpretation in Honor of Ronald E. Clements* (JSOTSup. 300; Sheffield: Sheffield Academic Press, 1999), pp. 116–26.

11.   I. Eph'al, 'The Origins of Idumaea', *Qadmoniot* 36 (126) (2003), pp. 77–9 (77) (Hebrew).

12.   For which Beit-Arieh, *Horvat Qitmit*.

13.   For which see R. Cohen and Y. Yisrael, 'The Iron Age Fortresses at 'En Haseva', *BA* 58 (1995), pp. 223–35; for a survey of 'Edomite' finds in the Negeb see J. R. Bartlett, 'Edomites and Idumaeans', *PEQ* 131 (1999), pp. 102–14 (103–5).

14.   For a survey of Judahite attitudes to Edom as reflected in the Bible see Bartlett, *Edom and the Edomites*, 175–86.

15.   Oded Lipschits, 'Nebuchadrezzer's Policy in "Hattu-Land" and the Fate of the Kingdom of Judah', *UF* 30 (1998), pp. 467–87 (482–3).

16.   A. Alt, 'Die Rolle Samarias bei der Entstehung des Judentums', *Kleine Schriften* II, Munich (1953), pp. 316–37.

Map no. 1: Southern Judah and Neighbours, 586-539 BCE

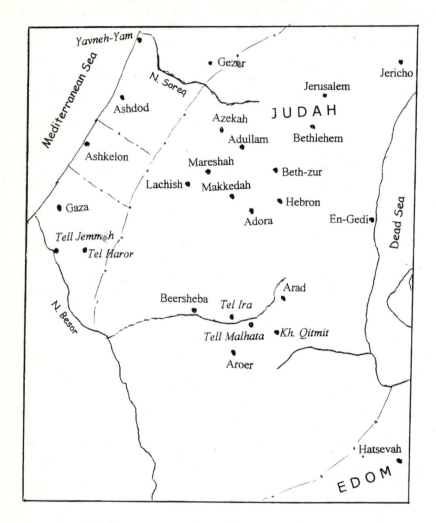

either by Cyrus[17] or by Artaxerxes I.[18] In any case, while Arad and the

17. So, for example, P. Briant, *From Cyrus to Alexander: A History of the Persian Empire* (trans. Peter T. Daniels; Winona Lake: Eisenbrauns, 2002), p. 47.

18. So S. E. McEvenue, 'The Political Structure in Judah from Cyrus to Nehemiah', *CBQ* 43 (1981), pp. 353–64 and more recently J. W. Betlyon, 'Neo-Babylonian Military Operations Other Than War in Judah and Jerusalem', in O. Lipschits and J. Blenkinsopp (eds), *Judah and the Judeans in the Neo-Babylonia Period* (Winona Lake: Eisenbrauns, 2003), pp. 263–83 (267); for a summary of the debate see H. G. M. Williamson, *Ezra and Nehemiah* (OTG; Sheffield: JSOT Press, 1987), pp. 48–50; L. S. Fried, 'The Political Struggle of Fifth Century

other fortresses along the southern frontier were destroyed at this time,[19] we have no evidence of any changes in the official boundaries of the local political units.[20]

However, it is also fairly well established that by the mid-fifth century BCE, the southern boundary of the province of *Yehud* had shifted considerably northward. Assuming, as do most scholars,[21] that 'the list of the wall-builders' in Nehemiah 3 is, in fact, authentic and does indeed reflect the extent of the province during the governorship of Nehemiah (445–433 BCE), the southernmost towns mentioned are Beth-zur, Keilah and Tekoa. This would seem to reflect a Judahite 'withdrawal' from the Negeb and the southern Shephelah and hill-country, including towns as far north as Hebron and Mareshah, the later Marisa. The southern limit of finds of '*Yehud*' stamp-impressions and later of coins more-or-less corresponds with this limit,[22] although one should exercise caution, since small objects such as coins and small vessels with stamp-impressions may have also 'wandered' outside the limits of the province through trade.

Since we possess little written evidence of events in Judea during the late Persian and early Hellenistic periods, the next period for which we have evidence is that of the Maccabean revolt. According to 1 Macc. 4.61, after Judas had finished his cleansing of the temple he fortified Mount Zion; 'he also fortified Beth-zur to guard it, so that the people might have a stronghold that faced Idumea' (NRSV). After Judas' death, Bacchides fortified a series of towns surrounding Jerusalem; Beth-zur is the southernmost and gets special mention (9.52). When Jonathan took over Judea and dismantled Bacchides' forts, Beth-zur remained 'a refuge' for 'those who had forsaken the law and the commandments' (10.14). 'Beth-zur on the borders of Judea' was eventually fortified by Simon (14.33).

All of this makes it obvious, that during the Hellenistic period, there

---

Judah', *Transeuphratène* 24 (2002), pp. 9–21 (10); L. L. Grabbe, *A History of the Jews and Judaism in the Second Temple Period: Vol. 1. Yehud – A History of the Persian Province of Judah* (London: T&T Clark, 2004), pp. 140–2 and citations there.

19.   E. Stern, *Archaeology of the Land of the Bible, vol. II: The Assyrian, Babylonian and Persian Periods, 722–332 BCE* (New York: Doubleday, 2001) p. 325.

20.   Y. Aharoni *The Land of the Bible – A Historical Geography* (2nd ed.; trans. A. F. Rainey; Philadelphia: Westminster, 1979), p. 410, considered the list of Judean towns preserved in Nehemiah 11.25-35, most of which were clearly outside the boundaries of the province during the time of Nehemiah, to reflect 'a permanent Judean population that had avoided deportation in the Babylonian period and had remained in the land.' For different views see O. Lipschits, 'Literary and Ideological Aspects of Nehemiah 11', *JBL* 121 (2002), pp. 423–40.

21.   Such as Aharoni, *The Land of the Bible*, 418; A. Lemaire, 'Histoire et Administration de la Palestine À L'Époque Perse', in Ernest-Marie Laperrousaz (ed.), *La Palestine À L'Époque Perse* (Paris: Les Éditions du Cerf, 1994), pp. 11–53 (19–20).

22.   Stern, *Archaeology of the Land of the Bible*, 246.

existed an administrative unit called 'Idumea'; its northern border was just south of Beth-zur. This unit is first mentioned in Diodorus Siculus' description of the events that occurred in the area in the year 312 BCE (xix 94–95, 98, actually quoting the third century Hieronymus of Cardia).[23] A group of papyri from Cairo record the journey of a Ptolemaic tax-collector named Zenon through Idumea; he travelled from the port of Gaza through Marisa to Adoreon (Adora, southwest of Hebron) in 259 BCE.[24] From further references in 1 Maccabees and in various quotes by Josephus, it is clear that the region south of Beth-zur was known by the name of Idumea, and was considered to be separate from Judea, at least until it was taken over by John Hyrcanus sometime after the death of Antiochus VII in 129 BCE (Ant. 13.256–257; War 1.63). Our question, then, is: when was this district formed, under what circumstances, and who were its inhabitants and rulers?

The 'classic' view, as portrayed by such scholars as Avi-Yonah, is that as early as the Persian period, 'south of Judah was the province of Idumaea, inhabited by Edomite Arabs who moved there after the fall of Jerusalem in 586 B. C. It included all southern Judah, from Beth-zur to Beersheba, except for the coastal plain. Its capital may have been Lachish ... Mareshah ... or even Hebron, the ancient capital of Judah. Nehemiah omits to refer to the ruler of this province, unless he sees in him "Geshem the Arabian"... We know of Arabs "free from tax" from Herodotus, possibly their rulers also had some authority over the Idumaeans, who were of Arabian stock.'[25] But what evidence is there for these claims?

That the Edomites were not 'of Arabian stock' has since been proven by the (admittedly few) written documents from both sides of the 'Arabah that have come down to us. As Vanderhooft has concluded, the Edomite dialect was Northwest Semitic, 'in the Canaanite linguistic group'.[26] Our question, however, is not ethnic or linguistic, but geopolitical: what evidence is there for the existence of an 'Idumean' province during the Persian period? When was such a province created?

While there is no direct evidence, the kingdom of Edom seems to have

---

23. Although one should note that the second reference is geographical, meant to elucidate the position of the 'Asphaltic Lake' (the Dead Sea), and cannot be taken as positive evidence that the political unit of Idumea already existed at this time.

24. Bartlett, 'Edomites and Idumaeans', 106.

25. M. Avi-Yonah, *The Holy Land from the Persian to the Arab Conquests (536 B.C. to A.D.640) – A Historical Geography* (revised ed.; Grand Rapids: Baker Books, 1977), pp. 25–6.

26. D. S. Vanderhooft, 'The Edomite Dialect and Script: A Review of the Evidence', in D. Edelman (ed.), *You Shall Not Abhor an Edomite For He is Your Brother: Edom and Seir in History and Tradition* (Atlanta: Scholars Press, 1995), pp. 137–57 (137).

been abolished by Nabunidus during his 552 BCE campaign to Arabia.[27] Bienkowski shows that there is almost no evidence of direct continuity of Edomite settlement east of the 'Arabah through the sixth century and into the Persian period.[28] The area that had been Iron-Age Edom was now a part of 'Arabia';[29] Bartlett may well be correct in his assumption that some of the remaining Edomites there were assimilated into what eventually became the Nabateans, although these are only attested over two centuries later. The chief area in which an Edomite-speaking population, many of whom bore names that included reference to the deity QWS, continued to flourish, was the former southern Judah – the Negeb, the southern Shephelah and the southern hill country. This is made clear by the many Edomite names found on ostraca from this period from both the Negeb and the Southern Shephelah.[30]

But who ruled this area? As already stated, by the mid-fifth century, during Nehemiah's governorship of *Yehud*, this area was outside his jurisdiction. For several decades now, it has been recognized that the area south of Beth-zur, rather than being ruled by Edomites/Idumeans, was actually ruled by an Arabic-speaking group known as the Qedarites. The eponym of this group (spelled 'Kedar' in most English translations)

27. S. Dalley and A. Goguel, 'The Sela' Sculpture: A Neo-Babylonian Rock Relief in Southern Jordan', *ADAJ* XLI (1997), pp. 169–76; Bienkowski, 'The Edomites: The Archaeological Evidence from Transjordan', 60; A. Lemaire, 'Nabunidus in Arabia and Judah in the Neo-Babylonian Period', in Oded Lipschits and Joseph Blenkinsopp (eds), *Judah and the Judeans in the Neo-Babylonian Period* (Winona Lake: Eisenbrauns, 2003), pp. 285–98 (291); Bartlett, *Edom and the Edomites*, 148–61. Bartlett, 'Edomites and Idumaeans', 105, attributes the 'collapse and subsequent decay' of Edom to the disruption of trade following the destruction of Judah.

28. Bienkowski, 'The Edomites: The Archaeological Evidence from Transjordan', 60–1, this *contra* an earlier study by J. B. Bartlett, 'From Edomites to Nabataeans: A Study in Continuity', *PEQ* 111 (1979), 53–66, who writes of continuity of settlement through the entire period and up to the Nabateans.

29. Cf. Lemaire, 'Nabunidus in Arabia and Judah in the Neo-Babylonian Period', 290.

30. Cf. I. Eph'al and J. Naveh, *Aramaic Ostraca of the Fourth Century BC from Idumaea* (Jerusalem: Magnes, 1996); A. Lemaire, *Nouvelles Inscriptions Araméennes d'Idumée au Musée d'Israël* (supplément n. 3 à Transeuphratène; Paris: Gabalda, 1996); R. Zadok, 'A Prosopography of Samaria and Edom/Idumea', *UF* 30 (1998), pp. 781–828 (785–822); B. Porten and A. Yardeni, 'On the Problems of Identity and Chronology in the Idumean Ostraca', in Michael Heltzer and Meir Malul (eds), *Tᵉshûrôt LaAvishur: Studies in the Bible and in the Ancient Near East, in Hebrew and Semitic Languages* (Tel Aviv-Jaffa: Archaeological Center Publications, 2004), pp. 161–83; S. Ahituv and A. Yardeni, 'Seventeen Aramaic Texts on Ostraca from Idumea: The Late Persian to the Early Hellenistic Period', *Maarav* 11 (2004), pp. 7–23; B. Porten, 'Theophorous Names in Idumean Ostraca', M. Mor, J. Pastor, I. Ronen and Y. Ashkenazi (eds), *For Uriel: Studies in the History of Israel in Antiquity Presented to Professor Uriel Rappaport* (Jerusalem: The Zalman Shazar Center for Jewish History, 2005), pp. 105*–130*. See also the contributions of E. Eshel, I. Stern, B. Porten and A. Yardeni in the present volume and the many references therein.

appears in the Bible as Ishmael's second son, after Nebaioth (Gen. 25.13).[31] The Qedarites are well attested in the Bible and in Assyrian inscriptions from the late eighth century onward.[32] It would seem that by the mid-fifth century at the latest, these Qedarite Arabs had established their control over the Negeb and Sinai, as well as the old land of Edom. As already stated, 'Geshem the Arab' is mentioned as Nehemiah's southern neighbour and enemy in Nehemiah 2.6. His name and that of his son QYNW, designated 'king of Qedar', has been found on inscriptions from Tell el-Maskhutah in the eastern Nile delta and at Dedan.[33] Arabic names have been found on ostraca at Tell el-Kheleifeh, Arad, Beer-sheba, Sheikh Zuweid and Tell el-Far'ah (South),[34] as well as at Lachish[35] and in the recently published 'Makkedah' ostraca,[36] which will be further discussed below.

At what stage, then, was this area detached from Judah and 'handed over', either by design or by default, to the Qedarites? There have been various suggestions. Aharoni assumed that the 'Negev district' was detached from Judah by the Babylonians in 597 BCE.[37] Lemaire believes that the area was detached from Judah during Nabunidus' conquest of Edom and in turn became part of 'Arabia'.[38]

However, there is no actual documentation for any of these events. Nor, really, would there have been a motive for either the Babylonians or for Cyrus to have made such changes. Whatever the administrative status of Judah was from 586 to Cyrus' death in 529, southern Judah and Philistia were an imperial frontier, facing the Egyptian enemy and the desert nomads. Some of the fortresses, such as Arad and Kadesh-barnea, were reoccupied, but there is no evidence of any major changes in the boundaries of administrative units. Despite Nabunidus' sojourn in Tema, there is no evidence of a Neo-Babylonian 'province of Arabia', and certainly not one that controlled southern Judah.

The next known major event in the area, one that changed the geo-political reality of the region, was Cambyses' campaign to Egypt in the

31. The connection between Nebaioth and the later Nabateans is often assumed but is problematic; cf. I. Eph'al, *The Ancient Arabs* (Jerusalem: Magnes, 1982), pp. 221–3, who rejects it on both historical and linguistic grounds.

32. For which see Eph'al, *The Ancient Arabs*, 223–7; Bartlett, *Edom and the Edomites*, 168–72.

33. See I. Rabinowitz, 'Aramaic Inscriptions of the Fifth Century BCE from a North-Arab Shrine in Egypt', *JNES* 15 (1956), pp. 1–9; W. J. Dumbrell, 'The Tell el-Maskhuta Bowls and the "Kingdom" of Qedar in the Persian Period', *BASOR* 203 (1971), pp. 33–44.

34. Stern, *Archaeology of the Land of the Bible*, 251.

35. For which see A. Lemaire, 'Un nouveau roi arabe de Qédar dans l'inscription de l'autel à encens de Lakish', *RB* 81 (1974), pp. 63–72.

36. Zadok, 'A Prosopography of Samaria and Edom/Idumea', 785–822.

37. Aharoni, *The Land of the Bible*, 410.

38. Lemaire, 'Nabunidus in Arabia and Judah in the Neo-Babylonian Period', 290–1.

summer of 525. Our main source for the events of Cambyses' campaign is Herodotus' *Histories* book III, sections 1–37.[39] According to Herodotus, as Cambyses was preparing to cross the desert from Kadytes (Gaza) to Egypt, a Halicarnassian named Phanes, who had fallen out with the Egyptian king, 'counseled Cambyses to send and ask the king of the Arabians for a safe passage' (III. 4). After he did so, the Arabian 'filled camel-skins with water and loaded all his live camels with these; which done, he drove them into the waterless land and there awaited Cambyses' army' (III. 9).[40] As Cruz-Uribe has shown, many of the way-stations uncovered along the ancient 'Ways of Horus' had cisterns and stores of jars, which could also have been used for stocking water.[41]

Of course, such tactics were hardly new. The admittedly incomplete annals of Esarhaddon describe his 671 BCE invasion of Egypt in similar vein: '... I caused my army to drink well water from pails ... the camels which all of the kings of Arabia had brought ... I put upon them'.[42] Cambyses' innovation, however, was in establishing a permanent relationship with the Arabs. In his well-known description of the 'fifth satrapy' as it was during the days of Darius I, Herodotus notes that 'the part belonging to the Arabians paid no tribute' (III. 91). The question is, at what stage was this 'tax-free' Arab territory established, and what area did it include? In his description of Cambyses' campaign, Herodotus (III. 5) tells us:

ἀπὸ γὰρ Φοινίκης μέχρι οὔρων τῶν Καδύτιος πόλιος ἥ ἐστι Σύρων τῶν Παλαιστίνων καλεομένων· ἀπὸ δὲ Καδύτιος ἐούσης πόλιος, ὡς ἐμοὶ δοκέει, Σαρδίων οὐ πολλῷ ἐλάσσονος, ἀπὸ ταύτης τὰ ἐμπόρια τὰ ἐπὶ θαλάσσης μέχρι Ἰηνύσους πόλιος ἐστὶ τοῦ Ἀραβίου.

This sentence, however, is ambiguous. In the Loeb translation, Godley renders: 'The road runs from Phoenice as far as the borders of the city of Cadytis, which belongs to the Syrians of Palestine, as it is called. From Cadytis ... to the city of Ienysus the seaports belong to the Arabians.'[43] In other words, Gaza/Kadytis was Syrian, but the coast beyond its (southwestern) border was Arab territory.[44] However Rainey, following

39.   Another oft-cited source is the 'autobiographical' statue inscription of the Egyptian official Udjahorresnet, but it has no bearing on our discussion. For this source see E. Cruz-Uribe, 'The Invasion of Egypt by Cambyses', *Transeuphratène* 25 (2003), pp. 9–60 (10–15) and references there.

40.   A. D. Godley, *Herodotus, Books III-IV* (LCL; Cambridge – London: Harvard University Press, 1938), pp. 7–11.

41.   Cruz-Uribe, 'The Invasion of Egypt by Cambyses', 22–4.

42.   D. D. Luckenbill, *Ancient records of Assyria and Babylonia* II (Chicago: University of Chicago Press, 1927), p. 220; see also Eph'al, *The Ancient Arabs*, 137–42.

43.   Godley, *Herodotus*, 9.

44.   So, for example, H. J. Katzenstein, 'Gaza in the Persian Period', *Transeuphratène* 1 (1986), pp. 7–86 (71).

Hude, renders: 'For from Phoenicia to the boundaries of Kadytis it belongs to the Syrians known as "Palestinian": from Kadytis ... the seaports as far as Ienysus belong to the Arabian.' In his view, 'the boundaries of Kadytis' refers to its boundary with Ashkelon to the north; his conclusion being 'that Gaza is in the hands of an Arabian.'[45] Mittmann suggested that while Gaza was controlled by Arabs, its military commander was Persian.[46] Na'aman, agreeing with Mittmann, Rainey and others on this, points out that this description obviously reflects the reality of Herodotus' own time. In his opinion, Gaza's rise as the major southern seaport was connected to the fall of Ashkelon in 604[47] 'and from its prominent place in the south Arabian trade and the commerce with Egypt under the Babylonian and Persian Empires'.[48] Katzenstein describes Gaza in 597, with its port and caravan trade, as 'the only surviving city of the once flourishing Philistine pentapolis'.[49] The king of Gaza was probably exiled by Nebuchadnezzar, but under Babylonian rule the city 'became a Babylonian watchtower against Egypt'.[50]

I would like to take this line of reasoning one step further and suggest that the city of Gaza and its environs was actually given to the Arabs by Cambyses, in return for their aid during his Egyptian campaign. This, too, is not without precedent. From the Eshmunazar inscription, for example, we learn that 'the Lord of Kings' (presumably the king of Persia) granted the areas of 'Dor and Jaffa, great lands of grain that are in the field of Sharon' to the ruler of Sidon, 'because of the great deeds which I have done', apparently in aiding Persian naval operations.[51]

However, if what the Phoenicians needed most was not only port cities, but also their grain-producing hinterlands, what the Arabs needed along with the port were the trade routes that led to it. As noted by Bartlett, the Gaza-Ienysus coastal district 'appears to have provided the Arabs with trade access to the Mediterranean.'[52] Especially since the development of

45. A. F. Rainey, 'Herodotus' Description of the East Mediterranean Coast', *BASOR* 321 (2001), pp. 57–63 (59); C. Hude, *Herodoti Historiae* (3rd ed.; Oxford: Clarendon Press, 1927).

46. S. Mittmann, 'Die Küste Palästinas bei Herodot', *ZDPV* 99 (1983), pp. 130–40 (132).

47. For which see L. E. Stager, 'Ashkelon and the Archaeology of Destruction: Kislev 406 BCE', *Eretz-Israel* 25 (1996), 61*–74*; according to Stager, *Ashkelon Discovered: From Canaanites and Philistines to Romans and Moslems* (Washington: Biblical Archaeology Society, 1991), p. 22, Ashkelon was resettled around 500 BCE.

48. Na'aman, 'The Boundary System and Political Status of Gaza under the Assyrian Empire', 66–7.

49. H. J. Katzenstein, 'Gaza in the Neo-Babylonian Period (626–539 BCE)', *Transeuphratène* 7 (1994), pp. 35–49 (43).

50. Katzenstein, 'Gaza in the Neo-Babylonian Period', 47.

51. Cf. K. Galling, 'Eschmunazar und der Kerr der Könige', *ZDPV* 79 (1963), 140–51.

52. Bartlett, *Edom and the Edomites*, 164.

the spice trade in the seventh century, Gaza had become the terminus of several increasingly important routes, including the En Gedi – Hebron – Lachish – Gaza road and the Zoar – Arad – Beersheba – Gaza road.[53] In 525 these routes were within the territory of an underpopulated and weakened minor province – Judah. And so the entire area was detached from Judah and handed over to Cambyses' Arab allies, chief among which were the Qedarites.

The region was not, of course, totally unpopulated. Gaza itself was probably still inhabited, mostly by the descendants of the Philistines, now identified by Herodotus, like their Ashdodite cousins to the north, as 'Syrians known as "Palestinian"'. The increase in trade in the area into the late fifth and fourth centuries, is reflected in an increase of use of the so-called 'Philisto-Arabian' coins of Gaza, Ashdod and what is usually assumed to be Ashkelon (with the '*aleph-nun*' mint mark). Of these, the mint at Gaza was the most prolific, and may even have minted the other cities' coins as well.[54] According to Mildenberg, these coins were also found in the Hebron area, showing Gaza's ties to this area.[55] Inland, the situation did not remain static either. Mareshah replaced Lachish as the major urban centre of the southern Shephelah, and slightly to the east, Makkedah[56] seems to have become an administrative centre, as it appears to be mentioned in several of the hundreds of ostraca that have been published in recent years, most of which are economic in nature.[57] As these ostraca and those found at Arad, Beersheba and other places show, the population of the area included Arabs, Edomites/Idumeans, Jews and others.[58] Over time, the Idumeans became the dominant component of the population of the southern hills and Shephelah.

Was there, however, an autonomous province of Idumea during the Persian period? As we have seen, there was certainly not one during the

53. For the road system in this area see D. A. Dorsey, *The Roads and Highways of Ancient Israel* (Baltimore and London: John Hopkins University Press, 1991), pp. 193–201.

54. L. Mildenberg, 'On Fractional Silver Issues in Palestine', *Transeuphratène* 20 (2000), pp. 89–100 (95–6).

55. Idem, 'On the Money Circulation in Palestine from Artaxerxes II till Ptolemy I. Preliminary Studies of the Local Coinage in the Fifth Persian Satrapy. Part 5', *Transeuphratène* 7 (1994), pp. 63–71 (70).

56. Identified as Khirbet el-Kôm; cf. D. A. Dorsey, 'The Location of Biblical Makkedah', *Tel Aviv* 7 (1980), pp. 185–93.

57. Cf. A. Lemaire, 'Taxes et impôts dans le sud de la Palestine (IVᵉ s. av. J.-C.)', *Transeuphratène* 28 (2004), pp. 133–42; actually Eph'al and Naveh, *Aramaic Ostraca of the Fourth Century BC from Idumaea*, 15, originally read the word as מקרה/מנקרה, which they understood as 'cistern, cavity or pit' but later recognized it as the toponym מקדה/מנקדה; cf. Eph'al, 'The Origins of Idumaea', 78. See also the paper by B. Porten and A. Yardeni in the present volume.

58. Zadok, 'A Prosopography of Samaria and Edom/Idumea', 785–822, and I. Stern's article in this volume.

Map no. 2: Southern Judah and Neighbours, 525-332 BCE

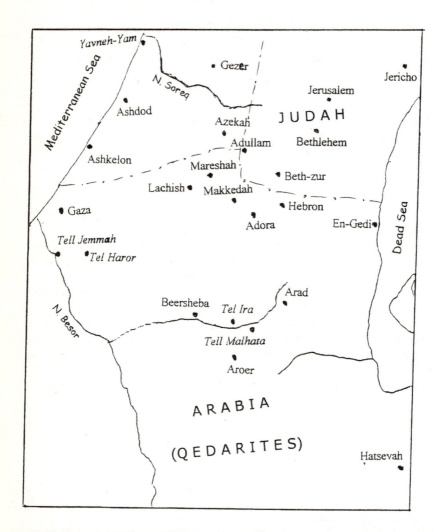

late sixth and fifth centuries. Lemaire takes the ostraca, the earliest of
which seem to date from about 363 BCE, during the reign of Artaxerxes
III,[59] to be evidence that an Idumean province, with its centre at
Makkedah, was in fact established during the first half of the fourth

---

59.   For which see Eph'al, 'The Origins of Idumaea', 78.

century.[60] Edelman has pointed to the successful rebellion by Egypt in 401 BCE as an event which could have prompted the Persians to make changes.[61] We, however, would point out once more that there seems to have been neither motive nor evidence of the establishment of such a province. Artaxerxes III had no reason to take this increasingly important area away from his Arab allies. Such a province is not mentioned in any of our sources for the period, literary or epigraphic. We know of no stamps or coins issued by such a province, at a time when they were being issued by everyone else. As Eph'al and Naveh have pointed out, 'our ostraca do not contain any administrative or professional titles, and indicate nothing about state or regional administration.'[62] The only reasonable conclusion is that despite the demographic and economic changes in the area, the Persians saw no reason to change its administrative status.

All that changed, however, in 333 BCE, when Alexander, coming down the coast towards Egypt, demanded the surrender of Gaza. The city was ruled at the time by one Batis, presumably an Arab, who insisted on asserting his loyalty to the Persian king Darius III. As a result, Alexander besieged the city for two months, flattened it to the ground, and dragged Batis around the city while tied to his chariot.[63] Gaza lost its status as the major port of the southern coast and the Qedarites lost their control of the trade routes. This is reflected in the total cessation of use of the 'Philisto-Arabian' coins after 332.[64] In the years immediately following the death of Alexander, the area was contested by Alexander's heirs, Ptolemy (later Ptolemy I Soter, king of Egypt) and Antigonus Monophthalmos. In 312, Ptolemy, aided by Seleucus, defeated Antigonus at 'Old Gaza' and continued up the coast as far as Sidon (Diodorus xix 80–86). He then retreated back to Egypt, razing the coastal cities, including Gaza, on the way (ibid. 94). Ashkelon, having been spared by Alexander, was burned to the ground around 300 BCE, apparently by Ptolemy.[65] Following this, Antigonus mounted an expedition to the land of the 'Arabs who are called Nabataeans'. These, according to Diodorus (xix 94–95), were traders in spices who brought them down to the sea shore to sell.

---

60. Lemaire, *Nouvelles Inscriptions Araméennes d'Idumée au Musée d'Israël*, 148; see also J. Sapin, 'La frontière Judéo-iduméenne au IVe s. avant J.-C.', *Transeuphratène* 27 (2004), 109–54.

61. D. Edelman, *The Origins of the 'Second' Temple: Persian Imperial Policy and the Rebuilding of Jerusalem* (London: Equinox, 2005), pp. 271–75.

62. Eph'al and Naveh, *Aramaic Ostraca of the Fourth Century BC from Idumaea*, 15.

63. Diodorus xvii 48; Arrian, *Anabasis*, ii 25–26; Quintius Curtius iv 6; Strabo, 16.2.30, says that 'the city was razed to the ground by Alexander and remains uninhabited'; cf. also A. M. Devine, 'Diodorus' Account of the Battle of Gaza', *Acta Classica* 27 (1984), pp. 31–40.

64. Mildenberg, 'On Fractional Silver Issues in Palestine', 96.

65. Stager, *Ashkelon Discovered: From Canaanites and Philistines to Romans and Moslems*, 24.

The new rulers of the area made several changes in its administration. Since the Qedarites had disappeared from the area, the southern hills and the Shephelah were now organized as an '*eparchy*' or '*hyparchy*' (different sources use different terms). As recognized by Eph'al, the new district was now named after its main inhabitants.[66] In 312, Antigonus' general Athenaeus set out 'from the *eparchy* of Idumea' on his failed campaign against the Nabateans (Diodorus xix 95). The new order was in place: the Qedarites had been replaced by the Nabateans, and the province of Idumea had been born.

Map no. 3: Southern Judah and Neighbours, 312 BCE

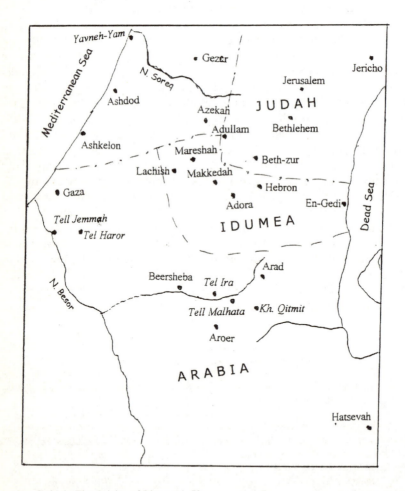

---

66.   Eph'al, 'The Origins of Idumaea', 79.

Index of References

INDEX OF AUTHORS